THE PLAIN AND NOBLE GARB OF TRUTH

THE PLAIN AND NOBLE GARB OF TRUTH

Nationalism & Impartiality in American Historical Writing, 1784–1860

EILEEN KA-MAY CHENG

THE UNIVERSITY OF GEORGIA PRESS

Athens and London

© 2008 by The University of Georgia Press
Athens, Georgia 30602
All rights reserved
Set in Minion by Graphic Composition, Inc.
Printed and bound by Thomson-Shore
The paper in this book meets the guidelines for
permanence and durability of the Committee on
Production Guidelines for Book Longevity of the
Council on Library Resources.

Printed in the United States of America
12 11 10 09 08 C 5 4 3 2 1

Library of Congress Cataloging-in-Publication Data
Cheng, Eileen K.
The plain and noble garb of truth : nationalism and impartiality in
American historical writing, 1784–1860 / Eileen Ka-May Cheng.
p.   cm.
Includes bibliographical references and index.
ISBN-13: 978-0-8203-3073-0 (hardcover : alk. paper)
ISBN-10: 0-8203-3073-6 (hardcover : alk. paper)
1. Historiography—United States—History—18th century.
2. Historiography—United States—History—19th century.
3. Historiography—Social aspects—United States—History.
4. United States—Historiography.
5. Nationalism—United States—History—18th century.
6. Nationalism—United States—History—19th century.
7. Fairness—History—18th century.
8. Fairness—History—19th century.
9. American literature—1783–1850—History and criticism.
10. American literature—19th century—History and criticism.   I. Title.
E175.C485   2008
973—dc22   2008010715

British Library Cataloging-in-Publication Data available

CONTENTS

ACKNOWLEDGMENTS

This book began as a dissertation at Yale University, and I would like to first acknowledge my debt to my adviser, David Brion Davis. Through his comments, his courses, and his own work, he has stimulated and challenged me intellectually, while his consistent enthusiasm for the dissertation encouraged me throughout the process of writing it. I was indeed very fortunate to have a committee that was both supportive and demanding, and I would like to express my appreciation to both John Demos and Frank Turner for all their helpful advice and suggestions. Other members of the faculty who provided helpful comments and advice on portions of the dissertation were Doron Ben-Atar and Paul Rahe. Among my graduate student colleagues, I would like to thank George Haddad, in particular, for reading lengthy portions of the dissertation and for our many stimulating conversations on history and memory, and Bob Bonner for reading and commenting on a chapter of the dissertation. I am also grateful to Gwen Kay for her constant willingness to listen to and share concerns about the dissertation and graduate school in general.

The faculty writing group at Sarah Lawrence College has provided a stimulating and supportive environment for revising the dissertation into a book, and the suggestions and criticisms made by members of the group were instrumental to the process of revision. I would like to express my appreciation to the members of the group who read and commented on drafts of various and, in some cases, all the chapters of the book: Neil Arditi, Mary Dillard, Melissa Frazier, Jennifer Jipson, Elizabeth Johnston, Ellen Neskar, Chi Ogunyemi, Sayuri Oyama, Mary Porter, Karen Rader, Rose Rejouis, Sandra Robinson, Lyde Sizer, Matilde Zimmermann, and Elke Zuern.

Derek Krissoff at the University of Georgia Press was enthusiastic about the project from the start, and I could not have asked for a more responsive and encouraging editor. I would also like to thank both the readers for the manuscript—Peter Hoffer and the anonymous reader—for their very detailed and constructive suggestions and comments.

I am grateful to the staffs at the Sterling Memorial and Beinecke Libraries of Yale University, the Massachusetts Historical Society, the Houghton Library at Harvard University, the New Hampshire Historical Society, the American

Antiquarian Society, the Hanover College Library, and the Esther Raushenbush Library at Sarah Lawrence College for aiding me in my research, and I thank Houghton Library, the Massachusetts Historical Society, and the New Hampshire Historical Society for permission to quote from their manuscript collections. A fellowship from the Massachusetts Historical Society provided me with financial support to do research in its collections, and I am also grateful to the society for the collegial atmosphere it offered to its research fellows, which made the process of doing research there truly a pleasure. Financial support for this project has also been provided by an Andrew W. Mellon Dissertation Fellowship, a University Fellowship from Yale, a Simpson Grant from Sarah Lawrence College, and a Faculty Research Grant from Hanover College. An earlier version of chapter 5 appeared as the article "American Historical Writers and the Loyalists, 1788–1856: Dissent, Consensus, and American Nationality," in the *Journal of the Early Republic* 23 (Winter 2003): 491–519, and I am grateful to the editors of the *Journal of the Early Republic* for allowing me to reproduce portions of the article for the book.

Finally, I would like to thank my family, whose support helped make this book possible.

Introduction

In a survey of historiography on the American Revolution published in 1912, the historian Sydney George Fisher offered a scathing indictment of his early national predecessors, which laid the basis for the prevailing view of American historical writing from that period. The very title of his paper, "The Legendary and Myth-Making Process in Histories of the American Revolution," suggested the general thrust of his critique. In his view, the Revolutionary generation of historians and their antebellum successors had drastically oversimplified the Revolution.[1] By glorifying the revolutionaries as uniformly heroic figures, these historians, according to Fisher, demonstrated their uncritical standards of scholarship and their lack of impartiality. Fisher ultimately attributed such deficiencies to nationalist imperatives, arguing that this one-sided interpretation of the Revolution grew naturally out of a desire to instill a sense of unity in the new nation. As Fisher explained, in their desire "to unite our people and build up a nation," early national historians "strove to give dignity and respect to everything; to make no damaging admissions, to let not the smallest fact creep out, that might be taken advantage of." Consequently, "they described a Revolution that never happened and never could happen. . . . All spontaneous, all united; merciful noble, perfect; all virtue and grand ideas on one side, all vice, wickedness, effeteness and degeneration on the other."[2] Ironically for someone attempting to demystify the Revolution, Fisher was engaged in some mythmaking of his own, for his argument for the superficiality of American historical understanding in the early national period was itself largely a myth.[3]

The myth that Fisher helped construct has proved remarkably persistent, as modern scholars have for the most part accepted and perpetuated his view of early national American historiography. For this reason, although the relationship between history and national identity in this period has long fascinated scholars, few of them have taken early national historiography seriously or given this topic sustained attention.[4] And so if modern scholars writing on the importance of history to national identity in this period have shown how nationalism generated an interest in history, they have also, like Fisher, emphasized how it limited the substance and depth of that historical consciousness.[5] In the conventional narrative of American historiography, antebellum historians were, if anything, more filiopietistic than their Revolutionary predecessors, as the influence of an increasingly chauvinistic brand of nationalism on them was compounded by a Romantic conception of history that gave primacy to drama and literary artistry over accuracy and impartiality. Only with the professionalization of history in the late nineteenth century, according to this narrative, did American historians start to develop a more complex understanding of the nation's past, turning from the view of history as a literary art to the view of history as a science defined by a commitment to the Rankean ideal of objective truth and embracing the methods of critical scholarship associated with that ideal. In this way, by contrasting the filiopietism and partiality of early national historians to the more objective outlook of Fisher's generation, Fisher's mythical view of early national historiography reflected and legitimized the development of history into a professional discipline that required specialized training and knowledge.[6]

American historical thought in the early nineteenth century was, however, more complex and sophisticated than modern scholars have acknowledged, for a small but significant group of historical writers had, by the 1820s, begun to develop many of the doctrines and concerns that characterize "modern" historical thought. Specifically, these historians played an important role in the development of history as an autonomous discipline defined by a commitment to the ideal of impartial truth.[7] Antebellum historians revealed their commitment to this ideal in both the approach and the content of their works, adopting the standards and methods of critical scholarship and actually seeking to revise orthodox patriotic accounts of American history. Accordingly, for example, they emphasized the importance of citation and primary sources; only through a systematic and critical analysis of original documents, they believed, could the historian achieve impartial truth. And, in their interpretations of American history, some of them offered surprisingly critical and balanced accounts of the American Revolution when they challenged patriotic myths that glorified the Revolution as a struggle against tyranny by acknowledging the perspectives of loyalists and Native Americans who opposed the Revolution. Admittedly, these historical writers were by no means representative of antebellum American historical thought, and many historians in this period were as simplistic in their view of history as modern scholars have claimed. Yet if those who offered a more complex view of history were not typical, they did constitute a significant and influential segment of the political and intellectual elite, and they represented an important strand in antebellum thought.

Conventional portrayals of antebellum American historical writing as superficial and unsophisticated are partly an outgrowth of what Peter Novick calls a "great man theory of historiography." Modern scholars have concentrated primarily on George Bancroft and a few prominent figures, and they have often taken Bancroft's fervently nationalistic interpretation of American history to be representative of historical thought in his time. Yet in doing so, these scholars have neglected the many other historians who wrote in this period.[8] I seek to remedy this neglect by including not only well-known historians like William Prescott and Bancroft but also their lesser-known counterparts like Jared Sparks and Lorenzo Sabine. Although I focus on the political and intellectual elite, I define the term *historian* broadly to include intellectuals and politicians not ordinarily classified as historians, such as Francis Bowen and Charles Francis Adams, who wrote extensively about history. At a time when history had not become a fully professionalized discipline and was still considered the province of gentlemen amateurs, the distinction between these writers and "historians" like Bancroft was not clear-cut.[9] In fact, these historians and writers formed a scholarly community of sorts. They exchanged ideas and information through their personal correspondence, in addition to reviewing and using one another's works for their own research. Besides narrative histories, these historians published biographies, periodical essays, historical novels, and collections of primary documents. While many of these historical writers came from the close-knit circle of politicians and intellectuals who dominated Boston's political and cultural life during the early nineteenth century, historians from other regions of the country, such as William Gilmore Simms and William Leete Stone, were also part of this scholarly community.

Ironically, then, in criticizing their predecessors for being simplistic and ahistorical, modern scholars have revealed the ahistorical character of their own approach to historiography. They have been ahistorical not only in their "great man" theory of historiography but also in their unwillingness to subject the history of their own discipline to the same kind of scrutiny as other historical topics. Thus even though modern scholars have sharply questioned the interpretations of American history advanced by the scientific historians of Fisher's generation, they have proved far more reluctant to interrogate that generation's characterization of American historiography by looking at early national historians for themselves. Indeed, modern scholars still specifically cite Fisher's article as a valuable source on early nineteenth-century historiography.[10] On a more fundamental level, modern historians have been remarkably reluctant to see the discipline of history as itself a product of history. Or, as Ellen Fitzpatrick has put it in her recent study of twentieth-century American historiography, "historians themselves seem drawn to ahistorical narratives of their own history."[11]

Hence when historians have written about the history of their own discipline, they have, for the most part, subscribed to what Peter Novick has characterized as a "Whig" interpretation of historiography that portrays the development of historical writing as a linear process of improvement, culminating with the present. Consequently, most surveys of American historiography have been structured around a celebratory narrative that traces the progress of historical writing from the backward and simplistic works of early American historians to the more objective and sophisticated scholarship of modern historians.[12] Indeed, much of the best work on historiography, such as David Levin's *History as Romantic Art* or Philip Gould's *Covenant and Republic*, has come from either literary scholars or scholars from an interdisciplinary background in American studies/civilization. Although recent work on historiography such as Novick's and Fitzpatrick's has revealed a greater willingness by historians to historicize the writing of history, the view of historiography as a field that is somehow different from "real" history still persists, showing the continued unwillingness to take historiography seriously as a form of original scholarship.[13] As Mark Salber Phillips has noted, if the writing of history is likened to fishing and scholars interested in historiography are those who choose to watch the fishing rather than fish themselves, "[p]rofessional historians generally see themselves as skillful fisherman [*sic*], and though they certainly have no objection to swapping a few good stories now and again, they are sometimes puzzled by colleagues who actually seem more interested in watching than fishing."[14]

To take Phillips's analogy one step further, my study is premised on the assumption that to understand the process of fishing it is necessary to analyze the "fishermen" on their own terms. In order to achieve this goal and avoid a "Whig" interpretation of historiography, I simultaneously take early national historians seriously as historians and look at them as products of their historical context. Accordingly, even as I demonstrate how early nineteenth-century historians anticipated the "modern" doctrine of objectivity in many ways, at the same time I show how this seemingly modern concern with impartiality was very much the product of its time. Ultimately, through such an analysis, I hope not only to revise the conventional narrative of American historiography, which associates the emergence of the ideal of objective truth in America with the professionalization of history during the late nineteenth century, but also to challenge the deeper assumptions about historiography that have perpetuated Fisher's myth.

Historians have been so reluctant to take historiography seriously ultimately because of its implications for objective truth. Specifically, the disregard for historiography is partly a function of the distinction between primary and secondary sources that has been a defining feature of the discipline. Because of this distinction, one historian quoted by Phillips could speak of historiography "as something we do when we can't get to the archives."[15] Historians have disparaged historiography in this way because, according to the Rankean ideal of objectivity, the historian could achieve objective truth only by critically analyzing primary sources, which, as the raw material of history, embodied the actual reality of the past. Therefore, analyzing historical writing in the same way as other historical sources—as the product of certain historical circumstances and social purposes—would, for some historians, undermine the very idea of truth by blurring the line between primary and secondary sources, and thus between actual reality and historians' interpretations of that reality—a concern that has only been fueled by postmodern efforts to collapse this distinction by claiming that all history is historiography. If we can never access a reality beyond the interpretations of historians, as some postmodern theorists have claimed, then the study of the past can never be more than the study of historians' interpretations of the past. Historians concerned with upholding the belief in objective truth have therefore been wary of according historiography the same status as other historical subjects, lest they give credence to postmodern attacks on the idea of objective truth as an illusion masking the constructed character of all history.[16] In his influential and controversial analysis of the origins and development of the ideal of objectivity in the American historical profession, Novick has challenged the view of historiography "as something we do when we can't get to the archives" by subjecting the discipline to the same kind of analysis as other historical topics; yet at the same time he has perpetuated the assumption that such an analysis would endanger the belief in objectivity by giving the impression that, as Thomas Haskell puts it, his purpose is to "persuade readers that the ideal of objectivity is all washed up."[17]

While I depart from Novick's analysis in dating the origins of this ideal back to the 1820s rather than to the late nineteenth century, I follow Novick in emphasizing the social and political function of the ideal of impartial truth. Because my purpose is to look at the ideal of impartiality from a historical perspective, my analysis does not directly engage in current philosophical debates about the validity of objectivity as an ideal, but my findings do have implications for contemporary debates about objectivity in the historical profession.[18] When the lineage of this ideal is extended back to the early nineteenth century, predictions about its imminent demise—and with it, the demise of the historical profession—appear more improbable and premature.[19] As the varied and conflicting uses of impartial or objective truth by historians from the early nineteenth century down to the present demonstrate, the ideal of objectivity was a powerful and malleable doctrine that could be adapted to many different social contexts and functions, which suggests that historians will find ways of adapting this ideal yet again to the challenges that confront it today. Thus recognizing the social and political function of impartiality does not necessarily endanger a belief in truth or the integrity of the discipline.

Specifically, in their concern with impartiality, antebellum historians expressed anxieties about the emergence of Jacksonian democracy, the rise of capitalism, and sectional conflict. Most important, rather than obstructing the development of this ideal, nationalist imperatives paradoxically contributed to their desire for impartial truth. By asserting that their narratives represented impartial truth, they obscured the subjective and particularistic character of their nationalist claims and instead gave those claims a transcendent and universal quality. In this way, antebellum historical writers used the ideal of impartial truth to define and legitimize their conception of American identity. These historians in turn differed over how they defined American identity. By examining these conflicts, my work builds on and contributes to the recent body of scholarship on the constructed and contested character of American nationalism.[20] Yet, for all the differences between them, antebellum historians shared a firm belief in the ideology of American exceptionalism. Rather than seeing their commitment to impartiality and their belief in American exceptionalism as mutually exclusive, historians in this period actually used the ideal of impartiality to promote exceptionalist doctrines.

By showing how exceptionalist ideology thus contributed to the rise of the ideal of impartial truth, my work at once draws on and challenges Dorothy Ross's analysis of the relationship between American exceptionalism and American historical consciousness. Ross, like other scholars, has emphasized the ways in which the doctrine of American exceptionalism inhibited the development of American historical consciousness. In this view, exceptionalist ideology was inherently antihistorical, for it was based partly on the assumption that America was unique in its hostility to history and its desire to escape the past; hence American historians were "historians against history," as David Noble has termed it in the title of his study of American historiography. As a new nation, America was not only free from the burden of the past, according to exceptionalist ideology. Even more fundamental, America was supposed to be exempt from the normal processes of historical change, for it possessed a special destiny to spread liberty throughout the world. Through nature, America could carry out this destiny and avoid the corruption and decay that had destroyed other republics. With its vast expanse of land, America could, in the exceptionalist vision, escape time by expanding through space.[21]

Yet by emphasizing the backward and antihistorical character of antebellum American historical writing and portraying their predecessors as "historians against history," modern American historians have in some ways revealed themselves to be historians against historiography. Ironically, even as they have shown how exceptionalist ideology limited the development of American historical consciousness, modern scholars have themselves subscribed to a species of American exceptionalism, for their unwillingness to take antebellum American historians seriously as historians reflects more general assumptions about the particularly shallow and superficial character of American intellectual history. Steven Conn has recently commented on this perception, noting that "[a]n Italian colleague of mine chuckles at the very notion that there is any American intellectual history."[22] Or, as a Canadian graduate student once put it to me, "American intellectual history? Isn't that an oxymoron?" This characterization of American intellectual history is in turn rooted in exceptionalist assumptions about how America's isolation and uniqueness cut off American thinkers from European intellectual traditions and developments. While this meant that American ideas were, at best, derivative and watered-down versions of their European counterparts, American commentators have often celebrated this tendency as both a cause and an effect of the qualities that distinguish America from other nations—its pragmatic temper and its concern with experience over theory.[23]

Thus, by demonstrating that antebellum historians expressed a more profound and complex understanding of history than modern scholars have assumed, my work raises questions about two fundamental aspects of American exceptionalism—the perception of America as a nation whose absorption in the present and future inhibited a meaningful and genuine sense of history, and the belief in an American cultural lag. Rather than lagging behind their European counterparts in the development of a modern historical consciousness, as Ross has argued, these historians took part in a larger transatlantic culture as they appropriated European ideas for their own purposes and adapted those ideas to exceptionalist assumptions.[24] In this way, even while questioning whether America was exceptional in its relationship to the past, I demonstrate how the *belief* in America's exceptional character intersected with and contributed to the development of a modern historical consciousness during the early nineteenth century. In turn, by revealing how the seemingly simplistic and chauvinistic ideology of American exceptionalism could actually be a source of intellectual vitality and conflict for antebellum historians, I show that this ideology was itself more malleable and more complex than scholars have often assumed.[25]

But what exactly did antebellum historians mean by "impartial truth"? Novick has written that defining the ideal of historical objectivity is like "nailing jelly to a wall," and defining what these historians meant by impartiality is no less difficult.[26] Part of the difficulty of defining what impartiality meant to antebellum historians is the temptation to impose modern conceptions of impartiality on them. Although some of their interpretations could indeed be considered "impartial" by modern standards, at the same time antebellum historians often appeared by those very standards to be highly partial in their views on history. But rather than measuring antebellum historians according to modern conceptions of impartiality, I take their professions of impartiality seriously and seek to understand how even the most partial of these historians could genuinely consider themselves impartial, while at the same time interrogating those claims by demonstrating how even the most seemingly impartial of these historians used impartiality for partisan purposes. Although they repeatedly used the term *impartiality* to signify their commitment to truth and held up this ideal as the historian's highest imperative, antebellum historians themselves often did not clearly define this term, further complicating the process of defining what impartiality meant to them. Nor did they all agree in their understanding of impartiality, coming into sharp conflict with one another over how to define this ideal and how to put it into practice.

Such conflicts had earlier roots, for the ideal of impartiality was by no means new to the early nineteenth century. Long a standard injunction for historians that went back to the classical tradition of historiography, impartiality had become an increasingly contested ideal by the eighteenth century. Even as eighteenth-century British historians like David Hume, Edward Gibbon, and William Robertson placed greater emphasis on their commitment to impartiality, they differed from one another over the meaning of this ideal, variously associating it with disinterested judgment, a skeptical perspective, and a comprehensive and inclusive view. Revolutionary American historians shared in the concern with impartiality as they likewise made claims to this ideal.[27] Antebellum American historians thus drew partly from earlier historians in both their desire for and understanding of impartiality. Their very choice of the word *impartiality* rather than *objectivity*—a term that would not be generally accepted in its modern sense to mean an unbiased view of actual reality until the mid-nineteenth century—to signify truth revealed the continuities with earlier conceptions of truth.[28]

Specifically, antebellum historians followed the lead of their early modern English predecessors in using *impartiality* to denote the historian's judicial role. This understanding of the term had roots in seventeenth- and eighteenth-century English historical writing, as the frequent use of *impartial* as an epithet for historians in that period invoked the ideal of judicial impartiality so important to the legal system to liken the historian to a judge. This usage of the term *impartiality* continued to be common practice in antebellum American historical writing. Thus the 1828 edition of Webster's dictionary retained the traditional connotations of the term with disinterestedness and indifference (which was in turn defined to mean freedom from bias, or "[e]quipoise or neutrality of mind between different persons or things; a state in which the mind is not inclined to one side more than the other") and pointed to its judicial associations when it defined *impartial* as "[n]ot partial; not biased in favor of one party more than another; indifferent; unprejudiced; disinterested; as an impartial judge or arbitrator," or "[n]ot favoring one party more than another; equitable; just; as an impartial judgment or decision; an impartial opinion."[29]

For antebellum historians, then, the ideal of impartiality prescribed that, like a judge, the historian was supposed to hear both sides of a case. And like a judge, the historian was supposed to be unprejudiced in his assessment of historical testimony—but this understanding of the historian's role still presumed that there were "sides" in history and that the historian, in the end, was supposed to make a judgment about which side was "right." In emphasizing the need for such judgments, antebellum American historians revealed their attachment to a didactic understanding of history as "philosophy teaching by examples." This understanding of history assigned to the historian a moral function that required him to make judgments praising the virtuous and condemning the profligate, for only through such judgments could the historian provide his readers with moral examples to imitate or avoid.[30] And so, just as their eighteenth-century British predecessor David Hume had construed impartiality as independent judgment, detached from party bias, impartiality, for antebellum historians, did not mean that the historian was supposed to eschew judgment; rather, it meant that the historian was supposed to make what they believed were fair and disinterested moral judgments.[31]

At the same time, antebellum historians embraced another definition of impartiality that more closely resembled the scientific ideal of objectivity associated with Leopold von Ranke as they identified impartial truth with an accurate representation of facts, independent of the historian's perspective. Although this conception of impartiality did have earlier seventeenth- and eighteenth-century antecedents, it would not come to fruition until the nineteenth century, culminating with the development of the Rankean ideal of objectivity. Hence antebellum historians went further than their eighteenth-century British and Revolutionary predecessors in associating with impartiality many of the same characteristics as those associated with the Rankean ideal.[32] Equating impartiality with detachment and balance, they, like Ranke, believed that truth required the historian to present all the facts, uncolored by personal bias. And like Ranke, they believed that such an approach would lead to truth, for truth consisted of an objective reality independent of the viewer. In other words, they, like Ranke, believed, as Novick puts it, that truth was "found, not made."[33] This definition of impartiality suggested that it was not sufficient for the historian simply to be disinterested and nonpartisan in his judgments; rather, he had to efface his own perspective by eschewing such judgments altogether. While this conception of the historian's role seemed to conflict with their judicial understanding of impartiality, antebellum historians reconciled these different meanings of impartiality through their assumption that an unbiased account of facts would ultimately reveal larger moral truths to the historian, for those truths themselves constituted objective reality.[34]

In turn, as they joined their scientific ideal of impartial truth to a Romantic vision of history as literary art, antebellum historians departed from their eighteenth-century American and British predecessors in simultaneously expressing a stronger commitment to the idea of truth as the unbiased representation of factual reality and showing a greater recognition of the subjective element to historical truth. Hence for these historians, impartiality did not mean that the historian was supposed to free himself of all emotional involvement in his subject. On the contrary, for antebellum historians, by divesting himself of personal bias, the historian would be better able to enter empathically into the feelings and prejudices of his subjects. Such empathy was so important because true impartiality required the historian to tell history from the point of view of historical actors—but to do this, the historian had to possess a certain kind of imaginative sympathy that enabled him to transport both himself and his readers back into the past. And so antebellum historians could both recognize the subjective nature of historical interpretation and believe in a truth that transcended the individual's interpretation. In this way, antebellum historians brought together seemingly contradictory assumptions about the nature of historical truth—truth was for them at once a moral entity, the re-creation of objective reality, and the rendering of feeling and subjective experience. In other words, these historians viewed history as a science, a branch of philosophy, and a form of art. At the same time, antebellum historians revealed the tensions and conflicts in their understanding of truth, as they differed over the relationship between these different perspectives on truth and over how to reconcile them with one another. Thus, while the transformation of history into an autonomous discipline defined by a commitment to the ideal of impartial truth was by no means complete by the mid-nineteenth century, the roots of this transformation were in the antebellum period.

As part of my effort to avoid a teleological framework, I have structured my analysis thematically rather than as a chronological narrative. Although my analysis focuses on antebellum historians, I begin each chapter with a discussion of their Revolutionary predecessors. By looking at antebellum historians in comparison with their predecessors, I hope to better illuminate the transitional character of antebellum historiography and the influence of the Revolutionary historians on that transition. On the one hand, the nature of the change effected by antebellum historians becomes more apparent when their ideas are viewed in contrast to those of their predecessors. On the other hand, the similarities between the two generations of historians revealed the continuities in early national historiography and the influence of the Revolutionary historians on their successors. Rather than completely repudiating their predecessors, then, antebellum historians were in dialogue with them. And so, in order to keep that dialogue intact, I have chosen to examine the ideas of the Revolutionary historians and antebellum historians in conjunction with one another in each chapter. In turn, by portraying the relationship between the two generations as a dialogue, rather than as a linear progression, I also hope to do justice to the complexity of Revolutionary historical thought and avoid a "Whiggish" view of these historians as backward and outmoded by the more "modern" outlook of their antebellum successors. Moreover, by structuring my analysis thematically, I avoid the "great man" approach to historiography. Rather than devoting each chapter to a particular historian, I bring together different historians as part of a larger constellation of ideas about the theme under discussion. Hence certain individuals whose ideas relate to more than one theme appear in different chapters.

In chapter 1, I outline the larger political and cultural forces that contributed to the emergence of history as an autonomous discipline and its influence on those forces by looking broadly at the social and material basis for this development and by placing it in the context of European historiography. One of the most important such forces was the rise of the novel, as chapter 2 demonstrates, for the novel contributed to early national historians' conception of history as a discipline defined by its commitment to truth, as well as to their understanding of what constituted truth. Yet the more they affirmed their devotion to truth, the more contested its meaning was for them. Hence the conflicts and tensions in their understanding of impartial truth are especially evident in chapter 3, which examines how early national historians sought to live up to this ideal in their methodology. In their prescriptions for the importance of citation and primary sources, antebellum historians revealed how a scientific view of history derived from German critical scholarship converged with a Romantic conception of history as a form of art in their understanding of truth. Chapter 4 analyzes the social and political sources of disputes over the meaning of impartial truth by looking at the interpretations of American history advanced by early national historians. Even while these interpretations revealed sharp differences over what impartiality meant in practice, antebellum historians agreed in using impartiality to express and further their belief in American exceptionalism. Paradoxically, even as these historians used the ideal of impartiality for nationalist purposes, this ideal ended up further dividing them, as chapter 5 reveals most dramatically. The more they sought to demonstrate their impartiality by revising interpretations of loyalists and Native Americans in the Revolution, then, the more they revealed the partisan function of this ideal.

I conclude by discussing the legacy of antebellum historiography for modern-day historians. Ultimately, such an analysis demonstrates that modern historians have not advanced beyond their early nineteenth-century predecessors as much as they would like to think they have. If, on the one hand, modern historians have revealed the limits to their own historical consciousness and the ahistorical character of their understanding of their own discipline in their dismissal of antebellum historiography, on the other hand, early nineteenth-century historians anticipated many of the concerns of modern historians in the sophistication and complexity of their ideas about truth. Thus, far from being irrelevant or backward, the ideas of these historians are very much relevant for historians today.

CHAPTER ONE

"TO BECOME A HISTORIAN"

A Discipline and a Society in Transition

In a letter to Lorenzo Sabine written in 1845, Francis Bowen sharply attacked the historian George Bancroft, proclaiming, "Bancroft's history, seems to be indefinitely, postponed. So long as he finds anything to be done in politics, he will not trouble himself with literature. I despise his taste. To become a historian, one must sacrifice all other objects, and he deserves to fail who will not give half of his affections—the whole, rather,—to this task." In his assumption that to be a historian the individual had to "sacrifice all other objects," Bowen revealed that he was developing a sense of history as a specialized discipline that required the historian's undivided attention and energy. At the same time, as his criticism of Bancroft for departing from this ideal revealed, early nineteenth-century historians did not all embrace this definition of the historian's role, and even those who professed to, like Bowen himself, were actually quite ambivalent about the relationship between history and other fields. Bowen and his contemporaries were thus deeply divided both between and within themselves about the definition of history as a discipline.[1]

Although firmly committed to a belief in the moral and political function of history, early nineteenth-century American historians also, like Bowen, increasingly came to view history as an autonomous discipline defined by a set of standards and ideals that distinguished it from other fields of inquiry. And whereas in their view of history as a specialized discipline, Bowen and his colleagues posited a conception of history as a science, Bowen's criticism of Bancroft for sacrificing literature to politics, at the same time, pointed to their view of history as a form of literary art. The ambivalence of these historians about the status of history as an autonomous discipline reflected in part the tensions between and within different historiographical models. If, on the one hand, in using history for nationalist purposes, they followed the example of the Revolutionary historians, they were, on the other hand, influenced by European historiography in both their desire to separate history from other activities and their ambivalence about such a separation, for European historians were themselves torn about the relationship between history and other fields. Just as the nation was going through a series of political, social, and economic transitions during the early nineteenth century, then, the status of history as a discipline was very much in transition in this period. Indeed, these transformations were integrally related to one another, for, as antebellum historians at once aligned their own discipline with and set it apart from other fields, they expressed and negotiated their uncertainties about the democratization of politics and the commercialization of the literary marketplace. Thus, paradoxically, as early national historians used history to define the nation, they in turn redefined the nature of history itself, and, in using history for political purposes, they contributed to the separation of history from politics.

Revolutionary Origins and Influences

The works of the Revolutionary historians were one of the most important influences on antebellum historical writers, for antebellum historians both drew on the histories written by their predecessors and were reacting against them. Antebellum historians followed their predecessors in using history for nationalist purposes; the Revolutionary historians sought above all to define and unify the nation through their writing. Firmly committed to a belief in the moral function of history, the Revolutionary historians did not see any conflict between their political purposes and their work as historians because they did not consider history an autonomous discipline separate from their other social activities.

The Revolution was central to the Revolutionary historians' own identity as historians; most of them came of age during the Revolution, and they all began writing history only in its aftermath. These historians had, for the most part, supported the Revolution, and many of them had actively participated in it. Mercy Otis Warren, for example, had served as a propagandist for the Revolutionary cause, while David Ramsay had served as a member of the South Carolina legislature and as a delegate to Congress during the Revolution. In addition to Warren and Ramsay, this generation of historians included Edmund Randolph, John Lendrum, William Gordon, Jeremy Belknap, John Daly Burk, Hugh McCall, George Minot, Hugh Williamson, and John Marshall. While the backgrounds and concerns of these historians varied, they shared important traits and assumptions. Writing at a time when history was supposed to be the vocation of the gentleman amateur, the Revolutionary historians came predominantly from the elites. Although their occupations varied, many of these historians were either lawyers or ministers. The Revolutionary historians presented a socially conservative interpretation of the Revolution that reflected their status as members of the elite. Using the Revolution to promote order and deference, they portrayed the Revolution as an orderly and rational process and obscured the radical implications of this event.[2]

Their emphasis on the orderly character of the Revolution also reflected their nationalist purposes. Writing at a time when national bonds were still tenuous and uncertain, these historians sought to promote a greater sense of national unity in their works by downplaying the differences that divided Americans. Predominantly Federalist in their political allegiances, the Revolutionary historians also included staunch Republicans like Mercy Otis Warren and John Daly Burk. Although their histories at times served partisan purposes, the Revolutionary historians for the most part sought to transcend partisan bias in their histories. Likewise, while their histories reflected their sectional loyalties, national unity took precedence over sectional allegiances. With the exception of Warren's and Ramsay's histories of the Revolution, these historians usually did not write about the nation's history as a whole. Coming from different regions of the country, the Revolutionary historians revealed their own strong sense of regional and provincial identity in choosing to write primarily about their states and localities. Hence the first history published in the new nation was Jeremy Belknap's *History of New Hampshire* (1784–92), and historians from other parts of the country followed suit by publishing studies of individual states, such as Burk's *History of Virginia* (1804–16) or Hugh Williamson's *History of North Carolina* (1812). Yet these historians saw no conflict between their local loyalties and their nationalistic purposes. They portrayed their region as the nation in miniature and projected their regional values onto the nation as a whole.[3]

The Revolutionary historians saw nothing wrong with using history for nationalist purposes because, like their European counterparts, they were deeply committed to the prevailing belief that history was "philosophy teaching by examples." Rather than seeing history as an autonomous field of inquiry, the Revolutionary historians viewed history as a branch of philosophy, whose purpose was to provide readers with examples of virtue and vice to imitate or avoid. History by definition, then, was supposed to serve a social function. The moral function of history was all the more important to these historians because they shared with many of their fellow revolutionaries a commitment to classical republican ideals. In republican ideology, a healthy republic depended on virtue, for the preservation of liberty against the encroachments of power required citizens to sacrifice for the public good. Virtue was public, not private; republicanism in this way set a premium on public affairs, since citizens could realize its ideal of civic virtue only through political or military activity. Because of the importance of virtue to republican ideals, these historians saw no conflict between their political concerns and the writing of history. The Revolutionary historians viewed the writing of history as itself a revolutionary act; by providing their readers with moral examples to follow, they hoped to instill the kind of virtue necessary for the preservation of liberty.[4]

Yet as the heated scholarly debate over republicanism has demonstrated, classical republicanism was only one of the many different intellectual influences on the political thought of the Revolutionary generation. Equally important for the Revolutionary historians, the gradual development of a capitalist economy during the seventeenth and eighteenth centuries was accompanied by the emergence of a liberal ideal of the social order that privileged the individual and the private realm. Although capitalism had by no means fully developed in America by the time of the Revolution, Americans were increasingly selling goods for profit in a larger market, rather than simply producing goods for their own use or to trade on a local basis. In turn, Americans were no longer just buying necessities but instead were using their earnings to buy luxuries, contributing to the emergence of a commercial economy in which consumption, not survival, served as an incentive to labor. This transformation was part of a broader transatlantic development; England also made the transition to a market economy based on trade and consumption in this period. With this economic transformation came a gradual change in the way that Americans and their English counterparts viewed the social order. Rather than living in a world of scarcity where individuals competed for a limited quantity of resources, Anglo-Americans increasingly came to believe in the possibility of economic growth and unlimited prosperity. According to liberal theory, economic prosperity would result unintentionally from the interaction of individuals pursuing their own interests. Whereas republican theorists held that individuals were supposed to sacrifice their interests for the public good, liberal thinkers believed that the pursuit of individual interest would in the end further the public good by increasing prosperity and productivity for society as a whole.[5]

The Revolutionary historians revealed the influence of liberal capitalism on their own endeavors when they expressed their desire for popularity and profit. Jeremy Belknap, for example, wrote to Ebenezer Hazard about his hope that the third volume of his history would be profitable: "I hope for a fuller sale, as there will then be complete sets to be sold. It has been a laborious and expensive undertaking, and my profits are all *to come*, —what a blessing is *hope!*"[6] Yet, as the state of American publishing demonstrated, the nation had by no means completed the transition to a market economy in this period. Most of the Revolutionary historians combined history with other occupations not only because they conceived of history as the vocation of the gentleman amateur but also because the conditions for authorship that existed in this period made it materially impossible for them—and most other writers of this period—to view writing as a full-time profession.[7] It would have been difficult for them to earn a living through their writing because a mass market for literature had not yet developed. Printers in some cases would publish a book only if they could sell it to enough subscribers in advance. Publishing for a population that was scattered across a wide area, at a time when roads and facilities for transportation were still limited, printers often could distribute and market books only to local audiences. Without an international copyright law, American historians had to compete with pirated foreign writers in the domestic market, while their own works could be pirated in other countries.[8]

Hence the Revolutionary historians achieved only limited popular success with their histories. David Ramsay, for example, lost money on his *History of the Revolution of South Carolina*, which sold at most 825 copies; nor was his *History of the American Revolution* much more successful.[9] Because of the poor sales of the first volume of his history, Jeremy Belknap had to petition the New Hampshire legislature for financial support to help cover the printing expenses for his history.[10] Yet if the Revolutionary historians for the most part failed to achieve popular success, they did influence the next generation of American historians, who at once drew on the Revolutionary histories and sought to revise them in their own writing.[11]

Nationalism and History in a "Post-heroic" Age

Like their Revolutionary predecessors, antebellum historians believed firmly in the moral function of history and used history for nationalist purposes. Yet just as the nature of nationalism changed in this period, so too did the character of history as a discipline. Thus, in both their definitions of national identity and their definitions of history, antebellum historians at once rejected and embraced the past. If these historians were in many ways even more committed than their predecessors to the nationalist function of history, they at the same time, unlike their predecessors, increasingly came to view history as an autonomous discipline, separate from other areas of endeavor.[12] Although seemingly contradictory, these two conceptions of the historian's role coexisted uneasily with each other.

Born too late to participate directly in the Revolution, this generation of historians came of age after the War of 1812—a turning point in the consolidation of American nationalism. Even though the war itself had resulted in a stalemate, Americans viewed it as a "Second War for Independence"; just by holding their own against the British and proving to themselves that they could survive as an independent nation, they increased their sense of national self-confidence. Further adding to this sense of confidence was the widespread and mistaken belief that the peace treaty with Britain had resulted from Andrew Jackson's famous victory at New Orleans. As a result, by the 1820s, Americans expressed a more strident and fervent sense of nationalism that differed in both degree and character from the nationalism of the Revolutionary generation.[13] Hence, while antebellum Americans agreed with their predecessors on the nation's exceptional character, they differed over the nature and basis for American exceptionalism. Although, as Jack Greene has demonstrated, a sense of American distinctiveness had already begun to develop even before the nation had achieved independence, it was not until the Revolution that Americans began to interpret their distinctiveness as superiority, and even then, according to Greene, that sense of superiority remained largely implicit in their portrayal of America as a model for Europe.[14]

By the antebellum period, however, Americans had developed a more exclusionary and chauvinistic version of exceptionalist ideology, and the emergence of the concept of manifest destiny embodied this growing sense of national superiority. The idea of manifest destiny—a term first coined by the Democratic newspaper editor John O'Sullivan in 1845—took the exceptionalist belief in America's special mission and made its racial element more pronounced and explicit. According to this ideology, America was destined to take over the North American continent not only because of its mission to spread democratic principles of liberty and equality but also because of America's innate racial superiority as a white Anglo-Saxon nation. The belief in manifest destiny served to justify the expansionism of this period, during which the nation annexed a vast expanse of territory extending from Texas to California. In this version of exceptionalist ideology, expansion was necessary not only in order to spread American principles but also in order to hold off the natural processes of decay and corruption that had destroyed other republics. The availability of land in the United States would, in theory, make economic independence and self-sufficiency possible for all white male Americans, thus preserving the nation from the social stratification and inequality that characterized Europe and ensuring republican virtue. In addition to spreading the ideals that made America exceptional, then, expansion was necessary to maintain the basis for American distinctiveness.[15]

In their hope that by expanding across space they could stop or at least postpone the nation's development in time, Americans revealed the antihistorical character of exceptionalist ideology. In exceptionalist ideology, part of what made America distinctive was its freedom from and rejection of the past. As John Lothrop Motley—one of the leading Romantic historians of this era—explained, in contrast to other countries, the United States was a nation without a history: "Every thing here is fresh, and of yesterday. The Present stretches to the Pilgrims; for the life of a nation is not measured by years.... Our Past is alive and visible." And so, he concluded, "America has no Past, but she has a Future." According to Motley, not only was the United States defined by its freedom from history; its survival and ability to carry out its special mission depended on that freedom, for, as he reasoned, "Upon this absence of the Past, it seems to us that much of the security of our institutions depends."[16] Yet, paradoxically, rather than discouraging an interest in history, this sense of exceptionalism made it all the more incumbent on historians to provide an account of the nation's past that would articulate and explain what made the United States distinctive. Hence the number of historical works that were published in this period rose from 42 in the second decade of the nineteenth century to 158 in the 1830s, both reflecting and contributing to a more general rise of popular interest in history beginning in the 1820s.[17] These histories varied widely in both form and content. They included state and regional histories like John Gorham Palfrey's *History of New England* and William Stevens's *History of Georgia*, as well as histories of the entire nation like George Bancroft's and Richard Hildreth's. The histories written in this period also took the form of biography—both collective biographies like Benjamin Bussey Thatcher's *Indian Biography* and Lorenzo Sabine's biographical dictionary of the loyalists and biographies of individuals, such as Jared Sparks's *Writings of George Washington* and William Leete Stone's *Life of Joseph Brant*. While some of these historians wrote about other nations, as Prescott did in his *Conquest of Mexico* and his *Conquest of Peru*, the nationalist purposes of antebellum historians made U.S. history a natural subject of study for them, and much of their work centered on the United States.[18]

The American Revolution in particular both stimulated and served as a focal point for the growing interest in history, for, like the Revolutionary historians, antebellum historians made the Revolution central to their own identity as well as to the nation's identity. With the passing of the Revolutionary generation, as epitomized by the almost simultaneous deaths of John Adams and Thomas Jefferson on 4 July 1826, the desire to record and commemorate the events of the Revolution before the memory of these events had completely faded away became all the more urgent for Americans. The publication of memoirs by and about Revolutionary veterans, seeking to establish their claims for Revolutionary War pensions, both contributed to and reflected the growing popular fascination with the memory of the Revolution.[19] Although his own histories focused on Spain and its colonies, William H. Prescott expressed the desire to commemorate the achievements of the revolutionaries, along with a sense that the memory of these achievements was slipping away, as he responded to a query from Washington Irving in 1842 about a controversy over who had been the real commander at the Battle of Bunker Hill. As Prescott explained, his father felt "a natural and very honourable desire to vindicate the claims of his father to his just share in the glory of the day, a share of which he has been most strangely defrauded by some later historians who should have been better informed." In contrast to his own generation, Prescott continued, his father "had the advantage of receiving the whole narrative when a boy from his own father. Nothing is so difficult as to arrive at truth among the contradictory testimony and affidavits of superannuated old soldiers, with one foot, and more than half their wits—including memory—already in the grave."[20] Here, Prescott attributed inaccurate knowledge of the Revolution not just to the distortions of historians without any firsthand knowledge of the event but also to the failing memory of aging Revolutionary veterans. As much as he admired and wished to vindicate the memory of his Revolutionary ancestor, then, Prescott's description of these veterans as "superannuated old soldiers" with "more than half their wits" in the grave was hardly flattering.

In this mixture of celebration and disparagement, Prescott expressed the anxieties and ambivalence of Americans living in a "post-heroic" age. As members of what George Forgie has termed the "post-heroic generation," born too late to participate in the Revolution but still close enough to this event for it to be a living memory, antebellum Americans felt an even greater imperative to preserve the memory of the Revolution. While they desired to emulate the heroism of the revolutionaries, the very greatness of the Revolutionary achievement precluded the need for that kind of heroism. Thus the only way for post-heroic Americans to achieve fame was to preserve and remember the accomplishments of their Revolutionary ancestors. But because all they could do was preserve, not create, they could never equal the greatness of the revolutionaries. And so the dilemma for post-heroic Americans was how to create room for themselves to achieve the fame and greatness of the revolutionaries without betraying or endangering the legacy of the Revolution.[21] One way to resolve this dilemma was through the writing of history. If they could not match the achievements of the revolutionaries as historical actors, post-heroic Americans could match and indeed exceed the revolutionaries as historical writers—

hence Prescott's simultaneous admiration for the deeds of his Revolutionary ancestors and his aspersions on their memory.

Even while Americans used history to express and promote an intensified sense of nationalism, the writing of history became increasingly sectionalized in this period as New England historians came to dominate the field. Forty-eight percent of the historians writing in the period between 1800 and 1860 came from New England, and half of these historians were from Massachusetts.[22] At once fervent nationalists and deeply attached to their own region, these historians reconciled their sectional and national loyalties by defining the nation in terms of New England. Like their Revolutionary predecessors, then, they projected their own regional values onto the nation as a whole. Specifically, these historians offered a vision of America and its past that represented the interests of the New England elite, for most of them were part of what modern scholars have termed the "Brahmin" elite.[23] Although the term *Brahmin* was not actually used by Oliver Wendell Holmes to describe this group until 1860, modern scholars have often used it to refer to the circle of intellectuals and politicians who constituted Boston's antebellum elite.[24] In addition to well-known Romantic historians such as George Bancroft and William H. Prescott, historians who were part of this Brahmin circle included Jared Sparks, Francis Bowen, Charles Upham, George Edward Ellis, Charles Francis Adams, Edward Everett, Alexander H. Everett, W. B. O. Peabody, O. W. B. Peabody, William Ware, Henry Ware, Benjamin Bussey Thatcher, John Gorham Palfrey, John Lothrop Motley, Richard Frothingham, Lorenzo Sabine, and Richard Hildreth. Although the Brahmin elite included those born from an established patrician ancestry, the criteria for membership within this circle varied, and its boundaries were not clearly fixed. Brahmin status was also based on wealth, and the elite included those who had more recently achieved their status and prominence through success in commercial enterprises. Wealth and family background were integrally related to each other for Boston Brahmins, for, closely knit through intermarriage, the Brahmin elite used family ties to advance and solidify their economic ascendancy. It was thus possible to move up into this group either through commercial success or through marriage into it.[25]

Although partly a matter of wealth and birth, then, Brahmin status was also determined by an individual's relationship to high culture, which provided another avenue into the elite. Hence, whereas some of these historians such as Charles Francis Adams were born into prominent families, a surprising number of them came from less privileged backgrounds and achieved their position in the Brahmin elite through their intellectual achievements. The son of a minister, George Bancroft, for example, came from an educated, but not a wealthy, background, and, like John Gorham Palfrey, he studied at Exeter and Harvard as a charity student. Only with his marriage into the wealthy Dwight family in 1827 did Bancroft establish himself financially. Jared Sparks came from even humbler origins. Born illegitimate in 1789, Sparks was already supporting himself as a teacher and carpenter by 1808. After attending Exeter on a scholarship, Sparks went on to study at Harvard, where he had to make his own living by teaching school. Likewise, neither Francis Bowen nor Lorenzo Sabine came from wealthy backgrounds; Sabine had to make his own living when he was orphaned at the age of fifteen, while Bowen had to support himself in his studies at Exeter and Harvard.[26]

Sabine pointed to their shared humble origins as he expressed his gratitude for Sparks's kindness to him in a letter of 1848. Although he told Sparks, "You have now 'attained'" and "I am still an humble, almost unknown man," they had come from similar circumstances. For this reason, Sabine believed that Sparks could imagine his gratitude if Sparks remembered his own early struggles against poverty and the gratitude he must have felt for the aid he received. As Sabine told Sparks, "Yet, like yours, my faith in early life, was one of thorns. Indeed, until a very recent period, my life has been a constant struggle against things and events distasteful to me." Those struggles included orphanage, poverty, ignorance, "and always, the harrassing [sic] anxieties of mercantile employments—which my poverty compelled me to adopt, and which, I have never ceased to loathe."[27]

Educated largely at Harvard, these historians studied there when the university had become a bastion for Unitarianism. Harvard had been at the center of the emerging rift between liberal and orthodox clergy in Massachusetts with the bitter struggle over who would succeed David Tappan as Hollis Professor of Divinity there after his death in 1803. The election of Henry Ware—a Unitarian—to this important position in 1805 against the protests of orthodox clergy marked a decisive shift in power to the Unitarians, and the division between Unitarians and orthodox Congregationalists ultimately contributed to the disestablishment of the Congregational Church in 1833. Although this generation of historians included orthodox Congregational ministers like Abiel Holmes, most of them embraced Unitarianism, revealing the growing ascendancy of the Unitarians. Like their Revolutionary predecessors, many of these historians began their careers in the clergy, and Jared Sparks, Edward Everett, George Edward Ellis, W. B. O. Peabody, and John Gorham Palfrey, for example, were all ordained as Unitarian ministers. Repudiating the Calvinist emphasis on innate human sinfulness, Unitarians instead offered a more optimistic view of human nature. They emphasized the importance of ethics and moral behavior to salvation, a view that repudiated the Calvinist belief in predestination. Seeking to bring together reason and revelation, Unitarians believed that it was possible to prove the existence of God through a rational examination of nature. With its emphasis on reason, harmony, and self-control, Unitarianism reflected and furthered the Brahmin elite's desire for social order.[28]

Deeply interested in intellectual and cultural pursuits outside theology, Unitarian ministers in the Brahmin elite viewed themselves as priests of high culture—and high culture as itself a religion of sorts—and allied themselves with wealthy merchants in an effort to promote the development of literature and the arts. Indeed, culture came to take precedence over their clerical duties, and many of them ended up leaving the ministry altogether. Sparks, for example, served as a Unitarian minister until 1823, when he left the ministry to pursue his literary and historical interests as editor of the *North American Review*, and Everett and Palfrey abandoned the church for careers in politics and literature. As these historians thus channeled into history the kind of fervent devotion and zeal that had traditionally been the province of religion, they revealed their developing sense of history as a specialized vocation that required their unqualified attention. And in doing so, these historians pointed to how they at once departed from and were influenced by a religious framework in that conception of history. Yet if they demonstrated such a sense of vocation in their exhaustive historical research and the stern labor regimen they imposed upon themselves, their forays into politics and the diverse array of literary topics covered by their contributions to the *North American Review*—which ranged far beyond history—indicated the limits to their desire for specialization.[29]

History in Transition: The Influence of European Historiography

The dualities in antebellum conceptions of the historian's role in turn reflected the influence of British and continental European historiography. Just as they reconciled their sectional loyalties with their nationalism, antebellum historians at once expressed a more chauvinistic sense of nationalism than their Revolutionary predecessors and were even more deeply attuned to European intellectual developments.[30] They frequently cited British historians like David Hume and James Grahame in their own works, and many of the historical works reviewed in American periodicals were by either British or Continental historians. In addition to reading the works of these historians, antebellum American historians established direct personal connections with their counterparts across the Atlantic. Hence Sparks's correspondents included both British and French historians such as James Mackintosh, Lord Mahon, and François Guizot; Prescott corresponded with Henry Hallam and Augustin Thierry; and Edward Everett exchanged letters with Hallam, Thomas Macaulay, and Mahon. Bancroft met regularly with Mahon, Macaulay, and Hallam while serving as ambassador to England from 1846 to 1849, and he met Guizot, Adolphe Thiers, and François Mignet on his periodic trips to France during his ambassadorship. Such connections served an important practical function for Bancroft, Prescott, and Sparks, for their European contacts aided them in obtaining primary sources and access to archives, as Guizot and Mignet did for both Sparks and Bancroft in France and Pascual de Gayangos did for Prescott in England, France, and Spain.[31]

The direction of influence between Europe and the United States was not just one way, however, as a letter by the English historian Lord Mahon—best known for his attack on Jared Sparks's editing of George Washington's writings—revealed. In response to a letter from Bancroft on his history of England, Mahon expressed his hope that Bancroft would continue his history: "I am quite sure to derive instruction from your pages, since writing as you do mainly for one side of the Atlantic, as I do mainly for the other, it is natural & necessary that you should go into far greater fullness of detail. It is natural also that many transactions should strike us in not wholly the same light; at best, according to an excellent illustration which I remember Mr. Prescott applying to this very subject it must be like the same tapestry viewed on opposite sides."[32] Not only did Mahon here acknowledge the usefulness of Bancroft's history; his reference to Prescott's metaphor of a tapestry as a way of explaining their differences of interpretation also revealed the impact of Prescott's correspondence on him. The publication of European editions of American historical works both reflected and furthered European interest in American historical writing. Guizot translated Motley's *Rise of the Dutch Republic* into French, for example, while Sparks's *Writings of George Washington* appeared in French and German editions, and the European editions of Prescott's histories included an Italian translation of his history of Ferdinand and Isabella and a French translation of his *Conquest of Mexico*.[33]

As a result of these connections, American historical writing revealed important similarities to British and continental European historiography in this period. Most important, on both sides of the Atlantic, the status of history as an independent profession was in transition during the early nineteenth century. If historians had, by this point, begun to develop an understanding of their discipline as a distinct field of its own, which required specialized training and knowledge, they still embraced the traditional association of history with philosophy and politics. Until the eighteenth century, historians had accepted the long-standing division between historians and antiquaries, or *érudits* as they were sometimes known, and its assumption that history did not require any special training or even extensive research in the field. On the contrary, the most important qualification for a historian was experience in politics, while research in manuscripts or archaeological sources was considered the province of antiquaries. Not only was such research considered unnecessary for the historian, but the philosophes even condemned it as pedantic and esoteric, as Voltaire famously did in his maxim "Woe to details!" Although Renaissance historical writers had begun to recognize some affinity between history and erudition, Edward Gibbon has generally been considered the first historian to successfully bridge the broad perspective of philosophical history and its concern with larger moral truths with the scholarship and research of the *érudits*.[34]

Nor was there any institutional recognition of history as an academic discipline until the eighteenth century. Until this period, throughout most of Europe, history had been taught both at the university level and below as an ancillary subject, subordinate to philosophy and rhetoric. The decision to make history a separate subject in schools was both a sign and a cause of its development into an independent professional discipline. The separation itself signified the recognition of history as an autonomous field that required specialized training to teach.[35] On a more practical level, the establishment of history as a separate subject in schools and universities enabled historians to make a living by teaching their subject, and it provided them with the kind of training and knowledge necessary to differentiate history from other disciplines. German scholars took the lead in developing what would become one of the distinguishing features of history as a profession—its commitment to a critical analysis of primary sources. Until the 1760s in Germany, the study of history had been viewed as subsidiary to philosophy and theology, as it was in England and France. The appointment of Johann Christoph Gatterer to the chair of history at Göttingen in 1759 marked an important step in the transformation of history into a serious scholarly discipline. A center for the study of philology and statistics, Göttingen contributed to the development of history into a science by placing the discipline on an empirical basis and providing historians with the technical skills necessary to collect and analyze their empirical data. With their training in philology and statistics, and in what were considered the "auxiliary sciences" of paleography and numismatics, historians could bring together the scholarship of the *érudits* with the synthetic perspective of the philosophical historians. The historian Barthold Georg Niebuhr revealed the importance of philology to the development of German critical scholarship as he applied its methods of textual criticism to the study of Roman history.[36] Through a systematic and critical examination of classical texts, especially poetic sources, for inaccuracies and inconsistencies, Niebuhr believed that it was possible to piece together the fragments of early Roman history and construct a more complete and reliable version of this subject than existing accounts.[37]

Niebuhr in turn directly influenced the most important figure in the emergence of history as an autonomous discipline—Leopold von Ranke. Both in his definition of the purpose of history and in the methods he prescribed, Ranke sought to differentiate history from other areas of endeavor. Following the lead of the Göttingen school, Ranke defined history as a science whose goal was supposed to be the disinterested pursuit of objective truth. Rather than viewing history as a branch of philosophy whose function was to provide moral examples for society, then, Ranke believed that the historian could achieve truth only if it was divorced from any social purpose and if the historian avoided making any moral judgments of his own. In order to discover history "as it actually was," to use Ranke's famous phrase, the historian had to conduct archival research and critically analyze primary sources—a process that required specialized graduate training in the research seminars that Ranke pioneered. As a result of Ranke's emphasis on the need for this kind of training, the research seminar was established as part of the training for historians at all German-speaking universities by 1848.[38] Although the emergence of the Rankean scientific ideal of objectivity in the United States has conventionally been associated with the late nineteenth century, Ranke published his *Histories of the Latin and Germanic Nations*, in which he made his famous statement that the goal of the historian was to show "what actually happened" in the past, in 1824, and his two best-known works—his *History of the Popes* and his *German History in the Time of the Reformation*—were published in the 1830s and 1840s.[39]

Antebellum American historians were familiar with both Niebuhr's and Ranke's histories. Niebuhr, whose history of Rome went through at least three American editions, was one of the most popular German historians in the United States, and the reviews of his work by American periodicals revealed his influence on American historians. Although Ranke was not as popular or widely reviewed as Niebuhr, translations of his *History of the Reformation in Germany, Ecclesiastical and Political History of the Popes of Rome*, and *Civil Wars and Monarchy in France* were published in the United States in 1841, 1844, and 1853, respectively, and American historians did refer to his histories in their own works.[40] Even more important to the development of history as an independent discipline in the United States, antebellum New England intellectuals were directly exposed to the ideas and methods of the Göttingen school, for Bancroft, Edward Everett, George Ticknor, and Joseph Cogswell—the first Americans to do graduate work in Germany—all studied at Göttingen. As a result of their studies there, these intellectuals combined their fervent nationalism with a cosmopolitan appreciation for the value and superiority of European learning, and they sought to import what they had learned in Europe back to the United States. Bancroft, for instance, brought back the influence of both German idealism and German critical scholarship. Bancroft had studied under A. H. L. Heeren—one of the leading pioneers of German critical scholarship—while at Göttingen, and a few years after his return to America, he published American translations of Heeren's *Reflections on the Politics of Ancient Greece* (1824), *History of the States of Antiquity* (1828), and *History of the Political System of Europe* (1828–29).[41]

Yet the status of history as a discipline was in a transitional stage throughout much of Europe and the United States during the first half of the nineteenth century, for history did not become a fully professionalized discipline until after 1848 in Germany and after 1870 in the rest of western Europe and the United States. The model of professional history was thus slower to develop in England and France than in Germany—on both the institutional and the individual level—and American historians resembled and were influenced by their English and French counterparts in combining an emerging sense of history as an autonomous discipline with the traditional view of history as the vocation of gentlemen amateurs.[42] In England, if the establishment of the Regius chairs of modern history at Oxford and Cambridge in 1724 in theory marked the recognition of history as an autonomous discipline, in practice both chairs did little to further historical scholarship. Because modern history had not yet been included as part of the curriculum, these chairs essentially served as political sinecures, and it was not until well into the nineteenth century that historians with any real scholarly qualifications were appointed to these positions on a regular basis.[43] In France, while the establishment of the chair of history and morals at the Collège de France in 1775 elevated history from its status as an ancillary discipline to a primary one at the university level, the pairing of history with "morals" still aligned history with philosophy. And it was not until Napoleon's reign that history chairs were established on a regular basis as university positions; even then, as of 1865, there were only seventeen faculty positions in history on the university level in all of France, while history was not taught as its own subject at the secondary school level in France until 1818.[44]

And so, even as Ranke's work reflected and contributed to the emergence of history as an independent profession, many of the best-known and most highly regarded European historians of this period—including among them the most widely read in the United States—were still "amateurs" without special training, who combined history with other professions and continued to ally history with other fields, namely, politics and philosophy. Both Augustin Thierry and François Guizot, two of the leading French historians in their time, were active and influential figures in French politics—Thierry as a journalist and Guizot as a journalist and later as minister of education and prime minister. Even Jules Michelet, who, as a writer and teacher of history, first at the École Normale and eventually as professor of history and morals at the Collège de France, did make a career of history, did not conceive of his subject as a specialized academic discipline; on the contrary, viewing himself as a revolutionary poet and prophet, he sought through his historical writing to revive and carry on the spirit of the French Revolution among the people as a whole.[45] Although Guizot was the most influential and widely reviewed of these French historians in the United States (his *General History of Civilization in Europe* alone had gone through eight American editions by 1856), translations of at least some of Michelet's and Thierry's histories were published in the United States, and the reviews of and references to their writings by American historians revealed that these historians were certainly familiar with Michelet and Thierry.[46]

Even more widely read in the United States were the works of British historians, and few of these historians received any special training in their field or devoted themselves exclusively to history as a profession. Henry Hallam and John Lingard—both of whose works were published and reviewed in the United States—were concerned with scholarship, but they assigned a political function to their historical writing. Trained as a lawyer, Hallam used his histories to warn the English Whigs against the dangers of overly rapid reform; Lingard was a Catholic priest who sought to further his religious views by providing a counter to the anti-Catholic bias of his predecessors. Thomas Carlyle—one of the most influential and widely reviewed historians in the United States—wrote widely on politics, philosophy, and religion, as well as history, and showed little concern for research or scholarship in his historical works.[47] Macaulay, whose work was immensely popular not only in England but in the United States as well, served as a member of Parliament from 1832 to 1847 and helped design the penal code for India as a member of the Supreme Council of India from 1834 to 1838. Although Macaulay was one of the few historians in this period whose work was successful enough for him to support himself by writing history, his ambivalence about the relationship between history and his other activities illustrated especially clearly the transitional status of history as a discipline in this period. Deeply committed to the belief that history was a form of both philosophy and literature, Macaulay believed that his political activities had furthered his work as a historian and viewed his history as an instrument for achieving his political goals. At the same time, Macaulay was relieved when he lost his parliamentary seat in 1847, for only with his retirement from politics was he able to devote himself completely to his history. Thus, although in many ways the embodiment of the ideal of the gentleman amateur, Macaulay also found it difficult to reconcile his political activities with the demands of his work as a historian.[48] The American historian George Bancroft pointed to Macaulay's belief that history was a field that required his full-time attention as he explained Macaulay's rationale for retiring from politics in a letter to William Prescott: "Mr. Macaulay says, one man can do but one thing well at a time; and so gave up his post in the cabinet, and took to the Historic Muse. I am of his opinion, now in my approaching old age."[49]

As Bancroft's comment revealed, not only did American historians share the ambivalence of British and continental European historians about the status of history as an independent discipline; there was also a direct connection between these developments. Like their British and Continental counterparts, then, American historians at once began to develop the institutional apparatus for the development of history as an independent discipline and continued to blur the boundaries between history and other fields. The creation of institutions devoted to the preservation of history in this period both furthered the development of history as its own discipline and revealed the limits to this development in the United States. The Massachusetts Historical Society, founded in 1791, was the first historical society established in the United States, and by 1860, 111 historical societies had been established throughout the nation. Following the example of their European counterparts, these societies collected and preserved historical manuscripts and sought to encourage popular interest in history by publishing these documents in their proceedings.[50] Organized efforts to collect and preserve historical documents in Europe and America were interdependent, for many of the documents collected by American scholars and historical societies were located in European archives.[51] Even as the creation of these societies made possible the development of history as an autonomous field of study defined by the critical analysis of primary documents, their membership revealed that history continued to be viewed as the pursuit of gentlemen amateurs rather than as the domain of professionally trained scholars. Although some of their members were known as historians, men from many other occupations such as law, medicine, and the clergy also belonged to these historical societies.[52]

As in Europe, history was beginning to be recognized by Americans as a separate—and important—field of study on the elementary and secondary level in this period. By 1839, most of the elementary schools in Connecticut taught history as an independent subject, and the number of private high schools in New York that taught history as a separate subject rose from 33 percent in 1825 to 92 percent in 1860. On the public school level, Massachusetts, Vermont, New York, Virginia, and Rhode Island all established requirements for the teaching of history in tax-supported high schools during the 1820s.[53] At the university level, the establishment of the McLean chair of ancient and modern history at Harvard in 1839—the first professorship of nonecclesiastical history in the United States—both signified and contributed to the recognition of history as an autonomous discipline.[54]

At the same time, Harvard was relatively unusual among American universities in separating history from philosophy, and the activities of the historians who were offered the McLean chair revealed that even they did not clearly differentiate between history and other fields.[55] Although Francis Bowen, for example, was known primarily as a philosopher and served as the Alford Professor of Natural Religion, Moral Philosophy, and Civil Polity at Harvard for thirty-six years, he was offered the McLean professorship in 1853 because of his extensive work in history.[56] For both Bowen and those who offered him this position, then, philosophy and history were so closely related that they considered it natural for him to move between the two fields in this way. Conversely, although known as a historian, Jared Sparks was first offered the Alford Professorship before being appointed to the McLean chair in 1839.[57]

Internal Dynamics: The Development of a Scholarly Community

American historians also formed their own community within this transatlantic network of historians, and the connections that they established with one another both reflected and contributed to the transitional status of history as an independent discipline in the early nineteenth century. Sharing the same intellectual background and connected by both social interest and family ties, these historians formed a scholarly community of sorts, providing one another with intellectual and emotional support. They sent queries to one another, asking for and giving information and advice about their research. They often shared their ideas or writing with one another and expressed anxieties about their own work, receiving both encouragement and criticism in return. These historians were often quite frank in their criticisms, expressing friendly disagreement with their correspondents or sometimes making disparaging remarks about their colleagues.[58] The very existence of this community contributed to a nascent sense of identity among its members as historians with distinct concerns and expertise, which they could communicate only to other historians who shared the same background and experience. Even as that sense of shared identity unified these historians, they were at the same time divided by sectional and political rivalries. Most significant, they were divided both within themselves and with other members of this community about the relationship between history and other fields, revealing the limits to their view of history as an autonomous discipline.

As one of the leading historians in this period, George Bancroft played a central role in this network of historians. But Jared Sparks, even more than his now better-known colleague, served as the linchpin in this network, for, considered by his contemporaries as one of the nation's preeminent historians, Sparks corresponded with virtually all the leading historians of this period. He wrote to them for help with his historical research, and they in turn consulted with him for aid and advice about their own projects. These correspondents included not only other members of Sparks's Brahmin circle such as Bancroft and Francis Bowen but also historians from outside that circle such as William Stevens and Charles Campbell. And so Sparks's correspondence with these historians can illuminate particularly clearly the workings of this scholarly community.[59]

In one such exchange with Sparks, William H. Prescott simultaneously encouraged him in his plans to write a history of the American Revolution and belittled their colleague George Bancroft's abilities as a historian. While acknowledging that it was unlikely anyone could convince Bancroft to change his mind about writing a history of the Revolution, Prescott reassured Sparks that their plans and approach were different enough for Bancroft's work to pose no threat to the success of Sparks's history: "There is all the difference in your plans that there is between the histories of Mignet and Thiers. You are as little likely to interfere in your manner of treating the story. He is sketchy, episodical, given to building castles in the air; you are on terra firma, the basis of original documents, which he sets much less value on than either of us do, and will not take half the pains, nor spend half the money you have, in collecting them." Commiserating with Sparks in his anxiety about the potential competition from Bancroft's projected history, Prescott used his own experience to assure Sparks that his fears were groundless, for, as Prescott told Sparks, "the most popular writer in the country cut into my subject, and helped himself to two of the biggest and fattest slices in it, the Conquest of Granada and the Discovery of America. I was sorely troubled at the time, but I believe it was treated on so different a plan from mine as to prove no injury."[60]

These writers also provided and asked for more tangible forms of assistance from one another, aiding their colleagues in finding and accessing primary documents and commissioning books and reviews from one another or recommending one another's works in these reviews. While serving as the American minister to Spain, for example, Alexander H. Everett offered to help Sparks gain access to the archives in Madrid for his research on the American Revolution.[61] After expressing concern that his publisher, Little and Brown, was not doing enough to publicize his biography of his ancestor the loyalist Peter Van Schaack, Henry Van Schaack asked Jared Sparks to use his influence as editor of the *North American Review* to help him advertise the book in the Boston area. If Sparks could get his book reviewed in the newspapers and recommend his book to influential local figures, Van Schaack wrote, "I have no doubt it would lead to sales in most if not all cases, & the book being thus put in circulation in a few leading families would get into the hands of others, be made the subject of conversation, & I shall then have no fear for the result. . . . The only difficulty is to get it into the hands of *readers*."[62]

Although dominated by New England historians, this community of scholars was not confined to historians from that region, and it extended beyond the New England elite to include both southern historians like William Gilmore Simms and Robert Howison and historians from the middle Atlantic states such as William Leete Stone and William B. Reed. Mutual ambivalence characterized the relationship between New England historians and their counterparts from other regions. Those historians outside the New England elite sought at once to be accepted by this Brahmin circle and to challenge its cultural dominance. In seeking the advice and support of leading Brahmin historians like Sparks and Bancroft, they recognized the New England elite as historical authorities, whereas in writing about the history of their own region, they sought to put themselves and their region on the same footing as that of New England.[63] For example, in a letter telling Bancroft of his interest in the diplomatic history of the United States, the southern historian William Henry Trescot asked Bancroft if he could suggest any useful documentary sources on the subject, and the Pennsylvania lawyer and historian William B. Reed corresponded with Bancroft as he prepared memoirs of his Revolutionary ancestors Joseph and Esther Reed. As Reed told Bancroft in 1848, he particularly valued Bancroft's approval of his life of Joseph Reed, for, while the memoir had fared "tolerably well at home," it was "too fully of original matter to be very popular." Because Bancroft's judgment was so important to him, in 1850 Reed asked Bancroft to read in manuscript the memoir that he was preparing of Esther Reed.[64]

Southern historians were especially ambivalent about their relationship to their New England counterparts, as they at once sought entrée into New

England scholarly circles and established their own intellectual network. One of the leading southern historians of his time, William Gilmore Simms served as the linchpin in this southern network of historians through his work as a periodical editor and reviewer and his correspondence with other southern historians seeking his advice and aid for their research. Simms both acknowledged the influence of New England historical scholarship and expressed his resentment at that influence when he suggested in 1849 that Nathaniel Beverly Tucker write a review of Bancroft's history for the *Southern Quarterly Review*, "under the provocation of the fourth volume, which is announced with the usual Yankee flourishes." While Simms here recognized that Bancroft's work was significant enough to warrant a review, his use of words like "provocation" and "the usual Yankee flourishes" revealed his resentment at Bancroft's New England bias. Simms made this resentment even clearer when he listed among the working principles of the *Southern Quarterly Review* the belief "that Yankee Histories of the United States are generally fraudulent from Peter Parley to Geo. Bancroft."[65]

Yet even as he defined himself in opposition to New England historians like Bancroft, Simms revealed his sense of community with those same historians in his correspondence with them. Thus he exchanged historical advice and information not only with his fellow southern historians but also with historical writers from other regions including Bancroft himself. In sharp contrast to his earlier disparagement of the "Yankee" bias of Bancroft's history, Simms expressed in his letters to Bancroft his agreement with Bancroft's assessment of John Church Hamilton's *History of the Republic of the United States of America* (1857–64) and sent Bancroft a copy of a favorable review he had published of the seventh volume of Bancroft's history, which he hoped Bancroft would consider "a proof of my desire to be pleased & gratified."[66]

In turn, New England historians were equally ambivalent about their relationship to historians outside their regional circle. Prescott articulated the complex relationship between New England historians and the rest of the nation in a letter to George Bancroft when he contrasted the sense of community he felt with those of his own region to his alienation from other areas of the nation. After confiding his doubts about whether his *History of Ferdinand and Isabella* would sell, Prescott took up Bancroft's offer to publicize the history to editors in New York and the South. As Prescott told Bancroft, "It would be a word in season. Here I am well cared for, I come out under very friendly auspices. But at N.Y. Philadelphia & Washington, I am in a land of strangers."[67] Fearing that he would not receive the same support in "a land of strangers" as he would under the "friendly auspices" of his own region, Prescott defined his scholarly circle in sectional terms and limited it to New England. At the same time, however, Bancroft's offer to help Prescott publicize his history outside New England revealed that this scholarly community was not entirely sectional in character and that its members were connected to writers from other regions.

Accordingly, although New England historians revealed a sectional bias in their assessment of historians from other regions, they did recognize the works of those historians as serious pieces of scholarship by reviewing them in periodicals like the *North American Review*, as they did with the histories of Simms, Stone, Campbell, Reed, and William Stevens.[68] And while they did not develop the same kind of personal connections to historians from outside their region as they did with one another, they did exchange criticism as well as advice and encouragement with these historians. Both Sparks and Bancroft, for example, wrote to the Virginia historian Charles Campbell—Bancroft with a query about when Richard Bland's *Inquiry into the Rights of the British Colonies* was first published and Sparks with his appreciation for the value of the Bland papers published by Campbell. After expressing to the historian William Stevens (who, although born in Maine, had settled in Georgia in 1837) his approval of Stevens's plan to write a history of Georgia, Sparks offered him suggestions on how to approach the subject. Sparks advised, "I would not come down later than the adoption of the constitution of the United States, because after that time the history of the States is so much blended with that of the Union, that the interest of the former is greatly diminished." Sparks also recommended that Stevens confine himself to brief extracts from his primary sources, for, as he told Stevens, "[t]he art of a historian is shewn in nothing to more advantage than in condensation."[69] Yet even while his encouragement to Stevens illustrated the connections that linked historians from different regions, his advice that Stevens confine his work to the period before the adoption of the Constitution at the same time revealed his sectional—and national—bias, for his claim that after the ratification of the Constitution "the history of the States is so much blended with that of the Union" went directly counter to southern arguments for states' rights.[70]

Conversely, as Sparks at once praised the southern historian William Trescot's historical work and expressed disagreement with Trescot's political views, he demonstrated the extent to which a sense of shared identity as fellow historians transcended—and even muted—the political and sectional differences that divided them. Sparks spoke highly of Trescot's history of diplomacy in the Revolution in letters to both Edward Everett and Trescot himself, and he even expressed to Everett his approval of Trescot's appointment as the secretary to the American legation in London.[71] As he told Trescot of his study of diplomacy in the Revolution, "It was no easy task to unravel such a network of facts, and to draw out the substance of them, and compress it within so narrow a compass. This analysis you have executed, as I think, with good judgment and fidelity, and in such a manner as to present a clear, candid, and just view of the whole subject. . . . The fairness with which you have spoken of the motives and characters of the principal actors is worthy of much praise."[72] Yet although he admitted to Trescot that he had explained "the mysteries of the secession doctrines" "very ingeniously and forcibly," he made clear his opposition to these doctrines when he added, "But you must not consider me a convert. Some of your arguments are strong, yet I think not unanswerable; and I hope the time may soon come when no one even at the south will see good reason for putting those doctrines in practice."[73]

Nor were New England historians entirely unified or harmonious among themselves, and their relationships with one another were also characterized by a mixture of conflict and collegiality, as a letter from Francis Bowen to Lorenzo Sabine written in 1844 revealed. Bowen had contributed biographies to Jared Sparks's *Library of American Biography* largely because of his friendship with Sparks, and he told Sabine, "My contributions to the Lib. of Am. Biography were written only to please the editor, my oldest and best friend. So you have seen Brownson's outrageous attack on me. It has only excited shouts of laughter with me and my friends." Even as he expressed his affection for Sparks, Bowen bitterly attacked both Orestes Brownson and George Bancroft in this letter in response to what he perceived as their attacks on him.[74]

As he made clear, Bowen's hatred of Bancroft was both personal and political in character. Denouncing Bancroft as an unprincipled hypocrite, Bowen angrily declared, "I have never taken the slightest notice of him, and this cool contempt has at last galled him. As for this attack, just consider George Bancroft, not O. A. Brownson, as its author, and you have the truth. Brownson held the pen, Bancroft supplied the materials and the venom." As Bowen explained, Bancroft was so false that he could attack Bowen only through Brownson: "[Bancroft] dares not attack me openly, and even affects to be on good terms when we meet. But he can never forgive the hard hit I gave him in my article on the Rhode Island matter, where he appears, though not by name, as the 'street orator' who made that abominable speech in State St., and he will not lack other causes for spite in future, if my pen holds out for the execution of some future projects. I detest the man's politics, principles—or want of principle, and character." Probably one of the most conservative members of the already conservative Brahmin elite, Bowen would have found Bancroft's support for the Democrats especially abhorrent. Bancroft and Bowen took their political and personal differences into the historical domain, as Bowen revealed in his scathing account of what he believed was Bancroft's weak effort to criticize his biography of James Otis. This attack, he told Sabine, "only redounded to his own discredit," for "[t]he only charge he could substantiate against it was, that by a slip of the pen or the printer—I know not which—'Timothy' was printed for 'Jeremy' Gridley. This was small enough."[75]

History and the "Vortex" of Politics

As a leading figure in the Massachusetts Democratic Party, Bancroft was thus something of a political renegade among his fellow Brahmin historians, for, deeply uneasy about the democratization of politics in this period, Bowen and most of them embraced the Whig Party. As a result of their ambivalence about democratic politics, these historians were divided about the relationship between their work as historians and political activity, and these divisions in turn revealed the transitional status of history as a discipline in this period. Like their Revolutionary predecessors, these historians were, for the most part, originally Federalist in their political sympathies. Discredited as traitors and secessionists because of the Hartford Convention and their opposition to the War of 1812, the Federalists faded as a national political force after 1816, when they ran their last presidential candidate. As the Federalists declined in political influence, the rise of Jacksonian democracy in this period further marginalized the New England elites. Although, in the years immediately after the American Revolution, many states still restricted the vote to white men with property, by the 1820s most states had eliminated these property requirements and enacted universal white male suffrage. The establishment of universal white male suffrage reflected and furthered a more general process of democratization, which gave primacy to the "common man," rather than the elites, as the ultimate source of authority and legitimacy in politics. Hence achieving popular appeal became increasingly important for politicians in this period. Because of his own humble background and his success in mobilizing mass support, Andrew Jackson came to embody the ascendancy of the "common man" in politics with his election to the presidency in 1828.[76]

In response to this development, with the demise of the Federalists the New England elites turned first to the National Republicans and then to the Whig Party, which formed in the 1830s as the major opposition party to the Jacksonian Democrats. Appealing to tradition and history rather than a belief in abstract natural rights as the source of political legitimacy, Whigs were naturally predisposed by their political ideology to take an interest in the study of history.[77] Like the Federalists, Whigs sought to uphold tradition by embracing a hierarchical social order that emphasized deference to the elites. Still faithful to the republican ideal of virtue, Whigs believed that only the elites could live up to the ideal of the disinterested statesman, for, by virtue of their superior education and ability, the elites would know best what would serve the public good.[78] As much as they valued the authority of the past, however, the Whigs were not entirely backward-looking. While holding onto the republican ideal of the disinterested statesman, Whigs sought to bridge the old and the new by adapting that ideal to a capitalist society. Rather then viewing capitalism as opposed to the public good, they encouraged commercial and industrial development, and they reconciled republican ideals with capitalism by emphasizing the importance of self-control. Believing that self-control would further capitalist development by encouraging the individual to be industrious and frugal and at the same time would promote order and morality in society, Whigs reconciled their desire for moral and material progress.[79]

Likewise, the New England elites were not totally reactionary in their response to Jacksonian democracy; rather, they sought in different ways to at once resist and adapt to the democratization of politics in this period. Although they feared the rise of Jacksonian democracy as a threat to their own authority, they also recognized that they had to accommodate popular politics if they wished to maintain their influence over society. And so Jared Sparks could describe Jackson in scathing terms and still affirm a democratic faith in the people to the Marquis de Lafayette in 1834. Sparks declared of Jackson, "He governs a nation as he would fight wild Indians. It would be difficult to decide, whether his incompetency to do right, or his obstinacy in doing wrong, is the most conspicuous." Even as he denounced Jackson, Sparks ultimately affirmed his faith in popular government. For this reason, he could express hope that

> even under this heavy dispensation of Providence, we need not fear for the Republic. The wisdom of our fathers has established it on a foundation too strong to be overthrown, and the good sense of the people will preserve it against the artifices of faction, & the unprincipled aims of ambitious demagogues. A general suffrage & frequency of elections are attended with many evils, but they afford the only possible check to despotism. It is to be lamented, that weak or wicked men should ever be exalted to the head of a nation, but happy are the people who can change them at their will.

As much as he despised Jackson, Sparks was optimistic that the nation would survive Jackson's incompetency and lack of principle, for he believed that America's democratic system would serve as a check on Jackson's power by allowing the people to recognize their mistake in voting for him and enabling them to replace him once they did. For all his elitism, then, Sparks did not repudiate either ordinary people for electing Jackson or democracy altogether; on the contrary, Sparks here expressed his faith both in democracy as a system and in the "good sense" of the people to recognize true merit.[80]

More divided about the relationship between history and politics than was the case with the Revolutionary generation of historians, New England historians revealed their desire to at once resist and adapt to Jacksonian democracy in their ambivalence about this relationship. If at one extreme were historians who sought to accommodate popular politics by combining their historical activities with political careers, at the other extreme some of these historians reacted against the rise of Jacksonian democracy by trying to divorce history from politics. One of the best-known and most successful examples of the former was George Bancroft. Bancroft demonstrated that he saw no conflict between history and politics: he pursued a political career, running unsuccessfully for governor of Massachusetts in 1844 and serving as the collector of the port of Boston, secretary of the navy, and U.S. minister to Britain, while at the same time working on his history.[81] And though Bancroft may have been atypical in his party loyalties, he was not alone in combining historical pursuits with a political career. In a letter to Lorenzo Sabine, Charles Hazewell expressed his own belief in the compatibility of history and politics and the reasons for this belief as he cited examples of historians and writers who had succeeded in combining literature with politics. Proclaiming his hope that Sabine's election to Congress would not prevent him from continuing to write history, Hazewell wrote,

> I trust that your connection with politics is not to so operate as to keep you from historical writing. I have not unfrequently thought that a History of Massachusetts, down to 1789, would be a capital subject for a man with the requisite talent, knowledge, and leisure. Literary pursuits are not incompatible with politics, and often are great aids to the politician—at least in the democratic party, as witness Bancroft, Bryant, Hawthorne, and lots more who sit down to only the second part of the Barnecide's dinner.[82]

Rather than viewing literature and politics as mutually exclusive, Hazewell pointed to writers like Bancroft and Hawthorne as examples of how literature could actually further a writer's political aspirations.

Nor was the belief in the compatibility of history and politics confined to Democrats like Hazewell and Bancroft. Edward Everett's many political offices included terms as a congressional representative, governor of Massachusetts, and American minister to England, and William B. Reed served as Pennsylvania's attorney general and as a representative to the Pennsylvania state legislature. Charles Francis Adams and John Gorham Palfrey were leading figures among the Conscience Whigs, and both men held political office first as representatives to the Massachusetts state legislature and then to Congress. If Bowen's attack on Bancroft revealed how partisan politics could divide these historians, Hazewell's encouragement to Sabine at the same time demonstrated how their sense of shared identity as historians could cut across party lines, for Hazewell had actually been Sabine's Democratic opponent in the congressional election of 1852. Thus antebellum historians viewed history simultaneously as an extension of politics and as a realm that transcended politics, revealing the transitional status of history as an autonomous discipline.

At the other extreme from Bancroft, Prescott articulated the emerging sense of history as an autonomous discipline that was supposed to be separate from politics in his correspondence with Bancroft. A frequent refrain in Prescott's letters was his amazement at Bancroft's ability to combine a career in history with one in politics, for he saw the two as mutually exclusive. As he wrote of Bancroft to Edward Everett, "How a man can woo the fair Muse of history and the ugly strumpet of faction with the same breath, does indeed astonish me. But so it is."[83] Prescott set up an opposition between history and politics as he urged Bancroft in 1838 to abandon the "rough-&-tumble scramble" of politics, which was "altogether unfit for one who should go with a tranquil spirit to the contemplation of the great & the good of other times," for history—"the noblest, and certainly the most independent career offered to man."[84] Paradoxically, however, this definition of the historian's function itself reflected Prescott's political concerns. Realizing that the rise of popular politics had diminished the influence of the elites and pessimistic about their ability to prevail against the tide of democracy, Prescott responded by repudiating the political arena altogether. Bowen was even more explicit about how his misgivings about democracy had contributed to his withdrawal from politics when he told Lorenzo Sabine that "the radical tendencies of the times have so disgusted me, that I left politics before I entered (in Irish phrases), and now stand coolly aside, merely throwing in a word now and then, as on the Judiciary and the Rhode Island matter, where I thought great principles were at stake."[85]

Not only did these historians differ with one another over the relationship between historical writing and politics; individuals were often themselves inconsistent about this relationship, revealing even more clearly their ambivalence about the status of history as an independent discipline. And so, even while Prescott himself rejected politics as opposed to history and could not understand how Bancroft reconciled the two, his praise for Bancroft as a historian implicitly acknowledged that political activity did not always preclude historical scholarship. And, as Marshall Foletta has pointed out, for all his reproaches to Bancroft about his political activities, Prescott at times wondered whether his own choice of history as a career over politics had rendered him ineffectual and irrelevant to society.[86] Likewise, even while condemning Bancroft for refusing to devote himself entirely to history, Bowen himself wrote on political subjects when he believed that "great principles were at stake," as was the case with his article on the Dorr Rebellion. Indeed, his appointment to the McLean Professorship of History was denied because of the controversy over his political views—specifically, his condemnation of the Hungarian revolutionary Louis Kossuth and his support for the Compromise of 1850.[87] Conversely, although, like Bancroft, Edward Everett successfully joined history with politics as an active and influential figure both in Massachusetts politics and in Brahmin intellectual circles, he pointed to what he saw as the incompatibility of the two pursuits when he told Lord Mahon in 1845 how unusual Mahon was in his ability to combine a historical with a political career. Everett explained to Mahon, "As I advance in years I find the tranquillity of literary pursuits and academical life more congenial to my taste, than the political occupations in which I have been engaged for the last twenty years.—You are one of the happy few who are able to unite both pursuits; if I do not mistake your disposition, the time will come, when you will approve my preference."[88]

As their concerns about independence and faction revealed, these inconsistencies about the relationship between history and politics ultimately reflected the ambivalence of the New England elite about democratic politics. As much as they tried to adapt to the rise of democracy, the New England elites found it difficult to reconcile their commitment to deference and republican virtue with the kind of electioneering and partisanship necessary to succeed in democratic politics. In order to compete with the Democrats, the Whigs had to appeal to the people, but how could they do this without sacrificing their independence and status as disinterested statesmen concerned only with the public good? And, as the conflict between Whigs and Democrats intensified and the very idea of party conflict was increasingly accepted, how could they reconcile the discord and infighting of party politics, or, as Prescott put it, "the ugly strumpet of faction," with their vision of an organic social order knit together by hierarchy and a unitary conception of the public good?[89] Jared Sparks revealed his unease about partisan conflict as he explained to John Bowring in 1838 why he had turned down numerous invitations to run for Congress. As Sparks declared, "I have hitherto escaped the vortex of politics, although some temptations have been held out to draw me into it." He explained his decision to turn down an offer to run for Edward Everett's congressional seat when Everett became governor "on the ground of its being inconsistent with my pursuits, & with my future plans. In truth I have little taste for the strifes of a political career."[90] Not only did Sparks here see a political career as incompatible with his work as a historian. His references to the "vortex" of politics and the "strifes" of a political career suggest that he also repudiated the classical republican view of the political realm as an arena for the expression and cultivation of virtue. His use of these negative terms indicates his fear of this realm as a destructive and corrupting force that would only draw him into a world of conflict beyond his control.

Yet if, unlike Bancroft or Charles Francis Adams, Sparks saw a political career as incompatible with his work as a historian, this view did not mean that he divorced history from politics altogether. On the contrary, Sparks turned to literature as a vehicle for furthering his political goals. In using culture as a medium for politics, Sparks and many of his fellow Brahmin historians found a middle ground between Bowen's and Prescott's desire to separate history from politics and Bancroft's effort to merge the two realms. Not only could Brahmin historians in this way reconcile their commitment to history as a scholarly discipline with their desire to participate in public affairs. This view of culture also enabled Brahmin elites to reconcile the tensions between Jacksonian democracy and their deferential vision of politics, for they used culture as a means of both resisting and adapting the ideal of the disinterested statesman to a democratic political context. Through literature and cultural pursuits, the New England elites hoped to shore up their authority and regain the social influence that they had once possessed in politics. If it had now become increasingly difficult to express or promote virtue in the political arena, Sparks and his fellow Brahmins still believed that it was possible to instill virtue and morality through literature.[91]

One of the most important cultural organs intended for this purpose was the *North American Review*. Founded in 1815 by William Tudor as a successor to the *Monthly Anthology*, the *North American Review* served as the institutional basis for the scholarly community of Brahmin historians. In a letter to Jared Sparks, Tudor's successor as editor of the *North American Review*, Alexander H. Everett pointed to the importance of this periodical as a vehicle for influencing society. Everett urged Sparks to make the review his "first object," for, Everett believed, "[I]t is a work of national importance and a most effective instrument for all good purposes"; he added, "I doubt whether the president of the U.S. has a higher trust to be accountable for than the Editor of the N.A." In comparing the responsibility entrusted to Sparks as editor to that of the president, Everett suggested that Sparks, through his position as editor of the review, could have as much, if not more, influence over society as he could through politics.[92]

Nor was the belief in the political and moral function of culture confined to the New England elites. The southern historian and writer William Gilmore Simms expressed even more clearly the belief in the importance of literature as an agent of virtue when he wrote to his friend Nathaniel Tucker in 1849 about his hopes for the *Southern Quarterly Review*. As he told Tucker, his work as editor of the review was so important because "[i]n this present juncture of affairs in this country, with such a tangled web of federal politics,—and morality so equally loose and reckless among our politicians,—our recourse is really to the Southern *people*; and the more we enable them to receive the truth—the more we elevate their standards of intellect as well as politics—the greater the prospect for refuge and security in the day of our difficulty." Thus, by educating and instilling virtue in the people, Simms hoped that the *Southern Quarterly Review* could counteract and make up for the decline of virtue in formal politics.[93]

The Dissemination of Scholarly History: Other Genres of Historical Writing

Sparks's and Simms's positions as editors of these periodicals pointed to the central role that historians played as editors of and contributors to the literary periodicals of the period, and that role both reflected and furthered the stature and influence of antebellum historians as leading figures in the intellectual elite. In addition to Sparks, Alexander Everett, Francis Bowen, John Gorham Palfrey, and Edward Everett all edited the *North American Review*; George Edward Ellis edited the *Christian Examiner*, and Benjamin Blake Minor edited the *Southern Literary Messenger*. Among the many historians who contributed articles to these periodicals were well-known figures such as Bancroft and Prescott, as well as less prominent writers such as Charles Upham, Lorenzo Sabine, and William B. Reed. In turn, literary periodicals like the *North American Review* and the *Southern Quarterly Review* played an important role in disseminating the ideas of these historians to larger audiences. Thus, while by no means representative of historical thought in their time, the influence of these historians did extend beyond their own scholarly circle.

Respected as serious works of scholarship, their histories were cited in other historical works and reviewed in the major literary periodicals of that time. Although the *North American Review* was the best known of these journals, other periodicals reflected a variety of regional and denominational affiliations, revealing that the influence of the histories they reviewed was not confined to the Brahmin elite. In addition to the *Southern Quarterly Review*, for example, both the *Southern Literary Messenger* and *De Bow's Review* represented southern perspectives, while the middle states could claim the *New York Review* and the *American Quarterly Review* (published in Philadelphia). Representing opposing ends of the political spectrum were the *Democratic Review* and the *Whig Review*, and alternatives to the Unitarian orientation of the *Christian Examiner* included the *Princeton Review* (originally founded as a Presbyterian organ) and the *Methodist Quarterly Review*. The reviews in these periodicals were important not only as a measure of the reception for the works they assessed. These reviews were important in their own right as works of history, for critics alternated between giving lengthy extracts of the work under review and using the review simply as a vehicle to express their own views on history, with little reference to the work they were supposed to discuss. Admittedly, the circulation of these periodicals was relatively limited, and their readership most likely came predominantly from the educated elites. The circulation figure for the *Southern Quarterly Review* was 2,000 in 1846, and at its highest point before the Civil War, even the circulation of the more established and lasting *North American Review* reached only about 3,200 in 1830.[94]

Yet the changing character of the literary marketplace enabled these historians to reach far larger audiences than their Revolutionary predecessors did, and the influence of their histories was not confined to the intellectual elites. While history was still considered the avocation of gentlemen amateurs, the development of a mass market for literature in this period now made it possible for these historians to make a living from their writing—a transformation that both contributed to and limited the development of history into a professional discipline. Although Americans had already begun the shift to a capitalist economy during the eighteenth century, the market revolution did not fully take hold until the early nineteenth century. By the 1820s, the grasp of the emerging liberal capitalist economy extended to the book trade as technical advances in printing, aggressive marketing techniques, and improved facilities for distribution made it possible for publishers to print and sell books at a lower cost and in far larger quantities than before. This period saw the emergence of large publishing houses in urban centers like New York and Boston that centralized the production and distribution of books for a national market. As the supply of books increased, so too did the demand, for the rise in literacy rates dramatically enlarged the popular audience for books.[95]

Consequently, even those historians whose livelihood did not come from literary pursuits were concerned about sales for their books. Although from a wealthy Brahmin family, Prescott demonstrated that he was just as concerned with sales as Sparks—who did make a living from his writing—as he detailed his plans for marketing his history of Ferdinand and Isabella to George Bancroft in 1837. Recognizing that sales depended not just on the content of a work but also on its appearance, Prescott urged Bancroft, "[P]ray notice the physique of the book—which will help the sale, and is but due to them." Newspaper advertising, Prescott believed, would also contribute to sales, and he listed particular sections of his history that he believed "may attract the attention of common readers."[96]

As Prescott made clear in his reference to "common readers," early nineteenth-century historians were concerned with reaching more than just the intellectual elites. History was read by popular audiences in this period, and the line between popular and scholarly history was less sharply drawn than it is today. Hence, these historians desired to give their works popular appeal and to some extent succeeded in this goal. One of the most successful histories published in this period was Bancroft's history of the United States—the first volume alone had already gone through ten editions ten years after it was first published.[97] Sparks was equally successful, selling 7,000 sets of his multivolume edition of Washington's writings by 1852 and more than 600,000 copies of his books in his lifetime—numbers that dwarfed, for example, the sales of his Revolutionary predecessor David Ramsay's history.[98] Likewise, William Prescott's *Conquest of Mexico* sold at least 175,000 copies in the 1840s, enough to make it a "best seller" for that period according to the standards used by Frank Luther Mott. Although not successful enough to be considered best sellers by Mott's standards, William Gilmore Simms's *Life of Francis Marion* (1844) and Benjamin Bussey Thatcher's *Indian Biography* (1832) both sold well enough for them to be included on Mott's list of "better sellers," and indeed Thatcher's work was so successful that it went through fourteen editions by 1860.[99]

The historical orations given at Fourth of July celebrations and other commemorative occasions also enabled antebellum historians to reach popular audiences. Yet as they at once blurred the line between these popular forms of history and their scholarly writing and differentiated between the two genres, they revealed their ambivalence about the relationship between popular and scholarly history. Fourth of July celebrations had become, by this point, staples of American political culture. Such popular celebrations proliferated, with the bicentennial anniversaries of the founding of New England towns, special events such as Lafayette's visit to the United States, and the building of monuments such as the Bunker Hill monument all providing additional occasions for commemoration. By virtue of their status as part of the intellectual and political elite, and as recognized authorities on history, many of these historians, including Bancroft, Everett, Palfrey, and Charles Francis Adams, gave orations at these celebrations. Widely attended by people from across the social spectrum, these celebrations provided the elites with an important vehicle for popularizing their views on history as they used pageantry and ritual to dramatize the historical message of their orations, which they regarded as the culmination of the festival.[100]

In 1857, George Edward Ellis pointed to what he believed was the influence of these orations as a popular medium for history when he commented on how "those who do not read history are kept in constant remembrance of the renown of their ancestors" as a result of the proliferation of "[o]ur Plymouth Rock and Fourth of July orations, our town and church centennials, and our New England festivals." Consistent with their commemorative purposes, these orations centered on historical subjects that would inspire national and sectional pride—which for the New England elites meant the Puritans and the American Revolution—and they in many cases presented a more simplistic and filiopietistic view of American history than that presented by historians of this period in their written work.[101] The commemorative and popular character of these orations did not necessarily disqualify them from claims to scholarship, as Prescott revealed when he cited Ellis's Bunker Hill oration of 17 June 1841 as the "most satisfactory, authentic and in all respects probable account," whose accuracy derived "not merely from oral testimony but from a careful perusal of the different narratives" in the debate over who had commanded Revolutionary forces at Bunker Hill.[102]

Yet if Prescott did not discriminate here between popular orations and scholarly history, Ellis himself made such a distinction when he acquitted "our formal and elaborate histories" from responsibility for "our prevailing views and the reiteration of the glory of our Puritan fathers" and instead implicated Fourth of July and other commemorative orations in what he believed was the idealized view of the Puritans so widely held in his time. Ellis made clear his disapproval of such idealization and suggested that others shared that disapproval when he declared that "all men of sense" recognized the "stilted exaggeration" that characterized these orations.[103] In setting up an opposition between the popular view of the Puritans embodied by these orations and the more tempered view shared by "men of sense," Ellis suggested that by "men of sense" he really meant the intellectual elite— specifically the Brahmin elite. Ellis thus defined an elite understanding of history in opposition to that of Fourth of July and other commemorative orations. But why would he wish to differentiate the

Brahmin elite from such orations when it was those very "men of sense"—including himself—who were propagating the "stilted exaggeration" of these orations? In critiquing these orations, Ellis expressed elite historians' ambivalence about their relationship to the larger public. While they desired popularity, they were also uneasy about catering to public opinion. And so, if they recognized the importance of making history accessible to the people through their use of commemorative orations, they at the same time wished to show their independence from and superiority to the people by setting up an opposition between the popular version of history represented by these orations and the more impartial view of American history they presented in their written work.[104]

Antebellum historians made this ambivalence and its roots in the development of a mass market for literature even more evident in their attitude toward other popular genres of history. If the expansion of the market for literature furthered the separation of history into an independent discipline by making it financially possible for historians like Sparks to make a living from writing history, historians in this period were deeply ambivalent about writing for such a market, and their ambivalence in turn revealed that this development had mixed implications for the definition of history as an autonomous discipline. Although a mass market offered elite historians greater opportunities to sell and distribute their books, this marketplace also created new sources of competition, with the rise of "popular" genres of writing aimed specifically at mass audiences. Hence, even as they blurred the line between popular and scholarly histories by seeking popularity for themselves, these historians differentiated between their own works and what they considered more "popular" histories. Their ambivalence about the relationship between "popular" and "scholarly" history in turn reflected the transitional status of history as an autonomous discipline in this period. If, in their effort to differentiate their own works from popular history, they expressed an emerging sense of history as a specialized discipline that had to live up to higher standards of scholarship, their concern with making their works popular and accessible revealed the limits to their desire for specialization. These historians thus made a distinction between popular history and history that was popular. In a letter describing the popularity of Macaulay's history in the United States, Edward Everett illuminated the nature of this distinction when he told H. H. Milman, "When I mention these little incidents, as shewing 'the kind of Popularity' of Macaulay's book, I do not of course mean that it is confined to *this class* of readers; but to show you how completely it has taken hold of the entire public mind."[105] Although very popular, Macaulay's history was not a popular history in Everett's eyes, for Macaulay had not written his history solely and specifically for the masses. Ideally, then, for these historians, a true historian was supposed to achieve popular success without aiming his history only at ordinary readers.

Sparks's correspondence with Joel Tyler Headley—one of the most success-ful "popular" historians of this period—revealed the complex relationship be-tween popular and scholarly history in this period.[106] Headley was the author of an immensely popular series of military histories, and his books were re-viewed in most of the major literary periodicals, such as the *North American Review* and the *Methodist Quarterly Review*, revealing that the intellectual elites did to some extent take his histories seriously as works of historical scholarship. This assessment had some basis, for Headley did draw on serious historical works like Sparks's *Writings of Washington* for his own research and even wrote to Sparks asking for help with his research. And, as Headley pointed to the in-fluence of Sparks on his own work, he demonstrated how "popular" histories like his own enabled historians like Sparks to disseminate the results of their research to larger audiences. Specifically, Headley was struck by Sparks's char-acterization of Washington as a man of passion, and he wrote to Sparks asking for examples of Washington's passionate nature. Headley remarked to Sparks, "You say justly in your work that he was a 'man of strong passions' and I would be glad if you would give me some of the *strong* not to say *rough* xpressions [*sic*] he sometimes used especially in battle."[107]

Yet historians like Sparks would only go so far in accepting Headley's work. Although Sparks acknowledged the merits of Headley's study of Washington, he still differentiated between his own work and Headley's. In a letter to Head-ley, Sparks acknowledged that he disagreed with Headley on specific points but praised him for his "graphic sketches of characters and events." As a result, he believed that "[y]ou have caught the spirit of the times, and wrought it deeply into your pages" and that "many readers will be attracted to these volumes, who would hesitate at the threshold of a more formal history." Here, even while praising Headley for his success in making his work appealing to popular audi-ences, he differentiated between this kind of popular history and what he called "more formal history," by which he meant more scholarly works like his own.[108] In this way, Sparks defined scholarly history in opposition to popular history.

Headley's reviewers were even more mixed in their assessments of his work. Although he did receive favorable reviews, he was often criticized for being bombastic and overly militaristic, and the hostility to Headley revealed that his critics subscribed to Sparks's distinction between Headley's type of popu-lar history and more scholarly "formal" histories like Sparks's. In one of the most scathing attacks on Headley, a critic for the *Methodist Quarterly Review* in 1847 made this distinction in a far less temperate and diplomatic way than

Sparks did. Contrasting Headley to those writers whom he considered serious historians like Sparks, John Marshall, George Bancroft, and William Prescott, this critic believed that in Headley's histories, Clio had been "tricked out in the frippery garb of an Italian improvisatrice, she mouths and rants, and pours forth a voluble strain of incoherent words, and of extravagant, half-incubated thoughts." In particular, this reviewer believed that Headley's "partial observations upon men and events; his discoloring of facts, his stupid idolatry of that lurid glory which lights up the hero" disqualified him from being considered a true historian. The *Methodist Quarterly* reviewer attributed Headley's oversimplified and distorted view of history specifically to his desire for popularity. "Preferring the feverish, unreasoning, fitful, and clamorous clappings of the populace before that steady growth and accumulation of men's love, admiration, and gratitude, which makes its object the property of 'no age, but of all time,'" this critic explained, Headley "burns to achieve—not fame, but—popularity." For this reason, he associated Headley with "that numerous class in literature,—known by their spawn of books with flaunting yellow covers, startling titles, and contemptible woodcuts,—who are analogous to the demagogue in politics." In comparing Headley to the "demagogue in politics," the *Methodist Quarterly* reviewer revealed how elite anxieties about the rise of democracy contributed to their reservations about popular history.[109]

In characterizing Headley's histories as "tricked out in the frippery garb of an Italian improvisatrice," the *Methodist Quarterly* critic revealed the feminine associations of popular history and defined scholarly history as masculine by contrast. For this reason, although, as Nina Baym has demonstrated, women were writing history in many different forms during this period, established historians did not for the most part recognize their works as serious pieces of scholarship. One sign of women's exclusion from Brahmin scholarly circles was the paucity of reviews by or about women authors in the *North American Review*.[110] Only Elizabeth Ellet was able to achieve a somewhat marginal place in this scholarly circle through her three-volume history of women in the Revolution, published between 1848 and 1850, and her *Domestic History of the American Revolution*, published in 1850. While she did seek to live up to the scholarly standards of Sparks and his circle by basing her research on the critical analysis of primary sources, she also departed from those standards in her reliance on oral tradition and in her emphasis on "domestic" history. As he did with Headley, Sparks for this reason maintained a distinction between Ellet's work and "formal" histories such as his own. Even while praising Ellet for her "diligence in collecting facts, and skill and judgment in weaving them together," Sparks denied that Ellet's work could be considered a "formal" history when he told

her, "I have been much gratified with your narrative, clear in style and compriz-
ing a great many incidents, very interesting in themselves, but which have not
found a place in more formal histories."[111] For Sparks, Ellet's work was valuable
not because it could claim to be a "formal" history, but precisely because it had
filled a gap left by "more formal histories."

Ellet herself was uncertain about how to classify her history, and her re-
quests for Sparks's aid and approval revealed both her desire to be accepted
by Sparks as a fellow historian and her doubts about whether she was qualified as such. As Ellet told Sparks, "But I am dubious about the title. 'Domestic
Sketches of the Rev.' would convey the idea of detached sketches or anecdotes,
and leave one in doubt if they were fictitious or otherwise. 'Domestic History
of the Revol.' which my publishers urge—seems rather ambitious, but it best
represents what will be aimed at. Would you think such a title a justifiable one?
If so, I will adopt it." Although confident that her work should be considered
more than just sketches and that the word "history" most accurately represented
the kind of book she intended to write, Ellet was hesitant to claim the mantle
of "history" for herself without Sparks's approval. Yet even though Sparks implicitly denied her that approval in the distinction that he made between her
work and "more formal histories," Ellet in the end did decide to call her work a
"history."[112] Other female historical writers of this period did not achieve even
Ellet's limited acceptance by Sparks's scholarly circle, revealing the limits to this
scholarly community and the role of gender in defining it.

Antebellum historians made the masculine associations of scholarly history
even more clear in their ambivalence about the novel—another popular genre
that at once competed with scholarly history and enabled historians to disseminate their ideas. Their ambivalence about the novel was partly a function of
gender, for the novel was particularly important as a historical genre for women
and was, as a result, closely associated with women.[113] Although, for this reason, scholarly historians sought to differentiate themselves from historical
novelists, the similarities in their interpretations of American history and their
definitions of historical truth at the same time blurred the line between the two
genres. While the nature and direction of their influence on one another would
be difficult to determine, historians were certainly familiar with the historical
novels of writers like Catharine Sedgwick, James Fenimore Cooper, and Lydia
Maria Child, as their reviews of these works demonstrated.[114]

A letter from Sparks to Sedgwick written in 1833 revealed that novelists and
historians, at the very least, did not develop their ideas in isolation from each
other and that historians in some cases could have influenced the interpretations of novelists in this period. In response to a query from Sedgwick, Sparks

offered her advice about what sources she should use for her historical novel about New York during the Revolutionary era. In particular, he recommended that she devote her attention to the loyalists in New York, for, he believed, "[o]ne of the most striking features of the war, in New York, was the affair of the Tories. It probably affected the state of society more than any thing else." For this reason, Sparks felt that the subject demanded "a good deal of attention." In Sparks's view, the loyalists did not deserve the vilification they suffered both during and after the Revolution, and he noted to Sedgwick, "The tories were harshly treated; more so in my opinion, than their personal deserts required. They were mostly sincere in their opinions, & risked every thing in support of them. But it was a time in which no compromise could be made with an opinion, honest or not. The public cause demanded that such opinions should not be professed, & severities apparently cruel were the necessary consequence." While he recognized that such harsh treatment was necessary, he concluded sympathetically, "I have more charity for the Tories than most people; & would treat their names tenderly, where there is no wicked act, or malicious design connected with them."[115]

Sedgwick did, as Sparks recommended, devote considerable attention to the loyalists in her novel *The Linwoods*, published just two years after this letter was written, and the similarities between her interpretation of the loyalists and Sparks's assessment suggested that his letter did influence her. Not only did the novel characterize the Revolution as a civil war by showing how the conflict between the revolutionaries and the loyalists divided a single family. Through its depiction of the heroine Isabella's father, a loyalist, it also made some effort to portray the loyalists sympathetically—in much the same way as Sparks had urged—as sincere, but misguided, in their belief that American interests would be best served by remaining within the British empire. Even though, like Sparks, Sedgwick in the end vindicated the Revolution, she also acknowledged the costs that Revolutionary persecution of the loyalists exacted through her depiction of the sufferings of the Linwood family. And so, rather than departing from the patriotic and filiopietistic character of contemporary historiography as some scholars have argued, historical novelists like Nathaniel Hawthorne and Catharine Sedgwick actually mirrored historians of their time in their revision of patriotic myths about American history.[116]

If novels like Sedgwick's enabled historians to disseminate their views to a wider public audience, these historians also viewed such novels as a threat to their own influence and status as they competed with novels for readers. Thus, even as they sought to emulate the popularity of the novel, historians at the same time sought to differentiate their genre from the novel by virtue of their commitment to truth. Not only did the desire to distinguish the novel from history contribute to the emerging sense of history as a specialized discipline, then. The novel also played an important role in the development of one of the ideals that would define history as a discipline—the ideal of impartial truth—and the next chapter examines more closely how these historians at once defined historical truth in opposition to the novel and were influenced by the novel in their definitions of truth.

CHAPTER TWO

"Histories in Novels,"
"Novels in Histories"

Imagination, Fact, and the Moral Truths of History

In 1836, a reviewer for the second edition of James Thacher's *History of the Town of Plymouth*, published in 1835, praised it for its attention to the history of everyday life and advocated more local histories like Thacher's, for, he claimed, "[w]e need the retail of history, as well as the wholesale. . . . We need the little things which lead to the great things, and which follow from them." As a result, "[t]here would be no more complaint of the dullness and dryness of history." Enlivening history in this way was important specifically to counteract the influence of the novel. This critic reasoned, "The work of historical novels,—the most successful the world has seen, because the most true,—would be superseded by the historian's taking his own business into his own hands. We should have novels in histories, instead of histories in novels; and all, of course, not by the infusion of fiction or imagination, . . . but of truth."[1] In calling for more "novels in histories," the reviewer pointed to one of the central concerns facing historians of this period—the rise of the novel. Early national historians were writing at a time when the novel was emerging as a popular genre, and, like this reviewer, these historians repeatedly spoke of their work in terms of the novel. Like Thacher's reviewer, early national historians at once defined truth in opposition to the novel and were influenced by the novel in their understanding of truth as they sought to achieve the appeal of the novel without sacrificing what they believed made history distinctive—its adherence to truth.

Early national historians reconciled these two imperatives in different ways, for they differed over the meaning of truth itself. If, like Thacher's reviewer, the Revolutionary historians for the most part defined fiction and the imagination in opposition to historical truth, they were also unable to disavow the imagination altogether, since they recognized the appeal of fiction. Even more aware of this appeal, Romantic historians like Prescott sought to emulate the novel by expanding the contribution of the imagination to historical truth. Yet antebellum historians would only go so far in that expansion, as Thacher's reviewer revealed when he suggested another way for historians to co-opt the appeal of the novel—by broadening the historian's definition of fact to include what he called the "little things" and the "retail" of history—that is, the history of everyday social life, or what would now be termed "social history." And so, even as antebellum historians differentiated between history and the novel by emphasizing their concern with facts, their very definition of what constituted a historical fact reflected the influence of the novel. As discussions of the relationship between history and biography revealed, these divisions over the meaning of and boundaries to historical truth were ultimately rooted in differences over the moral component to truth. Although antebellum historians differed over the location of and basis for morality, their shared belief in the moral function of history enabled them to redefine truth in response to the novel and, at the same time, limited the extent of that redefinition. William Gilmore Simms revealed this most clearly, as he simultaneously went the furthest in expanding a role for the historical imagination and affirmed his commitment to the historian's moral purpose.

In their responses to the novel, antebellum historians were ultimately grappling with the implications of an expressive theory of art for historical truth. If, according to Romantic aesthetic theory, the artist was supposed to shape and illuminate reality by exercising the imagination, how could historians live up to this ideal without abandoning their desire to uncover what they believed was the actual reality of the past?[2] Although they reconciled this Romantic understanding of the imagination with their commitment to both factual truth and moral truth in different ways, antebellum historians were similar in bringing together two seemingly contradictory views of truth— a belief in the existence of a truth that was independent of the historian's interpretation and a belief that the historian played a role in creating and interpreting truth.

"By the help of imagination and conjecture"? Embellishment and Exemplary History

The Revolutionary historians revealed the roots of this duality in their ambivalence about the rise of the novel. Even as they sought to differentiate history from the novel, these historians also recognized a likeness between the two genres. Their ambivalence about the relationship between these genres was in turn rooted in their ambivalence about the relationship between the imagination and historical truth. The Revolutionary historians distrusted the imagination as opposed to factual truth; at the same time, however, in different ways they allowed a certain role for the imagination in historical understanding. Paradoxically, their appeals to the imagination were a product of the same forces that gave rise to their distrust of this quality. Their belief in the moral function of truth thus at once led them to blur the distinction between history and the novel and made it all the more important for them to distinguish between the two genres. Even as the Revolutionary historians used truth to differentiate between history and the novel, then, their definition of truth itself blurred the boundaries between the two genres. In the process, they both defined truth as an entity to be discovered by the historian and recognized that the historian played a role in interpreting truth.[3]

The Revolutionary historians shared in a more widespread ambivalence about the novel as Americans of the new republic simultaneously embraced and decried its emergence as a genre. English writers Daniel Defoe, Henry Fielding, and Samuel Richardson led the way in pioneering the development of the novel in the eighteenth century, and the popular success of their books encouraged the growth and expansion of the market for novels in both Britain and the new American nation. The importation and piracy of English novels made such works widely available to early national Americans, even as American writers—led by William Hill Brown, who published his *Power of Sympathy* in 1789—began producing novels of their own by the late eighteenth century. In turn, the growing availability of novels fueled popular enthusiasm for these works to an even greater extent. Like their English models, early American novels varied widely in subject matter, ranging from stories of female seduction like Susanna Rowson's *Charlotte Temple* to Gothic dramas like Charles Brockden Brown's *Wieland*. At the same time, the very popularity of novels provoked hostility to this genre from American periodical critics and commentators of the early republic, who feared that the allure of novels would draw popular attention away from more serious, edifying genres like history. John Adams expressed such fears when he lamented in 1813, "While thousands of frivolous novels are read with eagerness and got by heart the history of our own native country is not only neglected, but despised and abhorred." The popularity of the novel thus brought the relationship between history and fiction to the fore and directly confronted the Revolutionary historians with the problem of how to differentiate between the two.[4]

The definition of the novel itself as a genre was contested and uncertain, and the nature of this uncertainty revealed both another reason for the widespread distrust of the novel and the basis for the distinction that the Revolutionary historians made between history and fiction. Even as English novelists like Fielding and Richardson self-consciously differentiated their works from other forms of fiction, especially the romance, by claiming for the novel a greater sense of realism, the boundaries between romance and the novel were not clearly fixed. Following the lead of late seventeenth- and early eighteenth-century English writers, who had often used the terms *novel* and *romance* interchangeably or grouped them together in the same category, early national American critics and historical writers continued to conflate the two forms. Romance was itself a protean term that variously referred to specific fictional forms such as medieval chivalric tales or the seventeenth-century French heroic romance. What these forms shared was a concern with the heroic and ideal, and they centered on events that took place in distant and exotic settings. Consequently, the word was also used broadly as a term of disparagement to describe a false or fantastic account. Thus, if the generic confusion between the novel and romance was partly a product of their affinity as fictional prose forms, the blurring of the distinction between the two genres also implicitly denied the novel's claims to realism and revealed the persisting assumption that, as products of the imagination, all forms of fiction were by definition opposed to reality and truth.[5]

For American critics of fiction, then, the distinguishing feature of the novel and the source of their hostility to fiction in general was its imaginative character. Equating true reality with actual experience, they viewed the imagination as opposed to reality because it only comprehended possible experience, which, because it was beyond the realm of the actual, was for them in its very nature antithetical to truth. Therefore, they believed, imaginative works like novels were dangerous because, as depictions of possible experience, they would only confuse and mislead readers by giving them a false and distorted perception of reality, or "unreal and delusive pictures of life," as Samuel Miller put it in his *Brief Retrospect of the Eighteenth Century* (1803). These critics privileged history instead as the antithesis of and antidote to fiction; history was, for them, the record of actual occurrences, making it a genre founded in reality. Their assumption of the opposition between imagination and reality was thus premised on a sharp dichotomy between actual and possible experience that had in turn been established by the Scottish common sense philosophy of Thomas Reid and his followers, in particular William Hamilton and Dugald Stewart. Although these philosophers differed from one another, they tended to give primacy to actual experience, which they identified with reality itself, as part of their quest to affirm the validity of empirical knowledge—that is, the reality of objects of sensory perception outside the mind. Hence, for them, as a creation of the mind, the realm of possible experience, which included the imagination, could not claim to represent reality.[6]

The Revolutionary historians took this opposition between actual and possible experience into their view of the relationship between history and novel, privileging, like American critics of fiction, history on the basis of its grounding in truth. Like these critics, then, the Revolutionary historians believed that the distinguishing feature of the novel was its fictional character. Equating fiction with the imagination, these historians sought to differentiate history from the novel because they too associated truth and reality with actual experience and distrusted the imagination as a faculty that could only grasp possible experience. Believing that the imagination was therefore by definition opposed to truth, the historian Jeremy Belknap went the furthest in repudiating a role for the imagination in history. Belknap was one of the most highly regarded historians of the Revolutionary generation, and his *History of New Hampshire*, whose first volume was published in 1784, was the first major work of American history to appear in the new republic. Belknap did not reject the imagination altogether, as he revealed by writing *The Foresters* (1792), a fictional allegory of the history of the British colonies in America.[7] As Hayden White has pointed out, Enlightenment historians like Voltaire were not entirely opposed to the use of the imagination, "[b]ut they did tend to compartmentalize the psyche in such a way as to lead them to draw rigid distinctions between the imagination's area of legitimate expression on the one side and reason's proper domain on the other."[8] Likewise, Belknap saw nothing wrong with using the imagination to write about historical subjects, as long as the writer clearly labeled such a work as fiction and differentiated it from history.

Using the imagination to write history, however, was a different matter for Belknap. To do so would be to take the imagination beyond its "area of legitimate expression"—fiction—into a domain where reason was supposed to be paramount. Accordingly, Belknap prefaced his history with the disclaimer that "the critical reader will doubtless find some chasms, which, in such a work, it would be improper to fill by the help of imagination and conjecture."[9] Belknap rejected the imagination in history because he believed that only through reason could the historian achieve truth. In opposing the imagination to truth, Belknap suggested that historical truth involved an unembellished account of actual experience. Because such experience was external to the historian, the historian's role was to uncover and faithfully record that experience, rather than to dramatize or embellish it. At the same time, Belknap believed that historical truth entailed more than just a chronicle of facts. For this reason, he declared that his goal was "not barely to relate facts, but to delineate the characters, the passions, the interests and tempers of the persons who are the subjects of his narration, and to describe the most striking features of the times in which they lived." This statement suggested that truth required the historian to draw larger conclusions about the character of his individual subjects and their context—an objective that implied an active role for the historian in presenting and analyzing the facts. Belknap did not see any conflict between this view of the historian's role and his belief that the historian was supposed to uncover, not interpret, the truth; through the accumulation of individual anecdotes and experiences, he believed, the historian could illuminate "the most striking features of the times" without resorting to imagination or conjecture.[10]

Sharing Belknap's definition of historical truth as the faithful representation of actual reality, John Daly Burk differentiated between history and fiction even more explicitly. Born in Ireland, Burk emigrated in 1796 to America, where he embarked on an active literary career. Like Belknap, Burk himself wrote fiction about historical subjects, and he is in fact best known for his play *Bunker Hill*, first performed in 1797. Burk followed this work with his *History of Virginia*, whose first volume appeared in 1804. And like Belknap, Burk sought to confine the imagination to its own realm of fiction, since he believed that the kind of imagination required for fiction was opposed to historical truth. For this reason, a frequent refrain in Burk's history was his fear that readers would dismiss truthful accounts of historical incidents as "romance," which he equated with fiction. After relating the story of Pocahontas, for example, Burk was apprehensive that posterity would consider it "an interesting romance; perhaps recalling the palpable fictions of early travellers and navigators, they may suppose, that in those times, a portion of fiction was deemed essential to the embellishment of history." In his anxiety to prevent readers from reducing historical fact to the status of fiction, Burk revealed his belief that fiction and historical truth were opposed to each other. Burk saw these two genres as opposed because he associated fiction with "embellishment," and, like Belknap, he viewed historical truth as an unembellished account of events.[11]

Yet there was another element in Burk's understanding of historical truth, for he also embraced the moral conception of history so prevalent in the eighteenth century. Although the Revolutionary historians varied in their definitions of truth, they shared the didactic view of history that prevailed in the eighteenth century, encapsulated by Lord Bolingbroke's famous dictum that history was "philosophy teaching by examples." This exemplary theory assigned a moral function to history. The historian was supposed to inculcate virtue and morality in his readers by providing them with examples to imitate or avoid—a role that required the historian to make moral judgments about his subjects. As Mark Salber Phillips has pointed out, the view of history as instruction had long coexisted uneasily with the view of history as mimesis—that is, the belief that history was supposed to be a faithful record of what had happened in the past—for both these conceptions of history were part of the classical tradition of historiography. Although these two views of history were potentially contradictory, historians had found different ways of reconciling or obscuring the tensions between them.[12]

Burk revealed how he reconciled this exemplary theory of history with his desire for a faithful record of actual events as he explained the importance and utility of history. According to Burk, history was valuable because "[i]t is universally considered as a grand field of experience, where, as in philosophical experiments, principles and systems are tested by their processes and results; and it is in this species of composition, at once the simplest and most diversified, whilst it is obviously the most authentic, that we find so many sublime examples of virtue and intelligence." For this reason, "[i]t never can be a matter of indifference to a gallant and intelligent people, that there be a faithful record of their lives and manners. It is a debt which their ancestors have paid to them; it is a duty they owe to posterity: To *themselves*, it is an inexhaustible magazine of precepts and models for all human occasions." This statement suggested that "authentic" and "faithful" history was important not only for its own sake but also because the historian's ability to inculcate morality and virtue in his readers depended on it.[13]

For Burk, then, history was both philosophy and science. He even drew direct comparisons between history and science when he described history as a "grand field of experience" that could serve a function similar to that of "philosophical experiments." By philosophical experiments, Burk meant scientific experiments, for Enlightenment thinkers viewed science as a form of philosophy and used the term *natural philosophy* to speak of science. The actual experience of history would enable the historian to test larger moral principles, just as scientists used experiments to test their "principles and systems." Ultimately, according to Enlightenment thinkers, these experiments would reveal the natural laws that governed the universe, which could then be applied to understanding and improving human society. Hence the importance of accurate empirical data—only in this way could the scientist come to a true understanding of these natural laws. Likewise, Burk believed, the more accurate and complete the historical record, the more sound the moral lessons the historian could draw, for the historian could base his conclusions on a wider and more diverse body of evidence. By associating truth with fact, Burk defined truth as an external reality independent of the historian. The role of historians was to give meaning to that truth by drawing moral lessons from the facts of history, just as scientists gave meaning to their experimental results by coming up with natural laws that explained those results. Because these lessons were supposed to conform to universal moral verities, in drawing such conclusions, the historian was revealing moral truths, rather than presenting his own interpretation of truth. Burk thus did not see any conflict between such moral judgments and the historian's obligation to disinterested truth, for he defined historical truth itself in moral terms.[14]

The very assumptions that made the Revolutionary historians so concerned with truth at the same time allowed for certain kinds of conjecture in history—namely, the desire to develop a science of society and the closely related belief in a universal human nature. Even while disavowing the use of the imagination, Burk repeatedly found himself resorting to conjecture throughout his history of Virginia as the only remedy for the paucity of historical sources on his subject. In one such instance, Burk could only speculate on the reasons why Accomac County changed its allegiance during Bacon's Rebellion to support Governor William Berkeley. He surmised, "With the imperfect lights, which have survived, perhaps it is allowable to conjecture that their hopes were fed with promises of a favorable report of their loyalty to the king, and of the exertion of the governor's personal influence for either a total removal or a considerable abatement of the commercial restraints which had been complained of."[15] Burk did not see such conjectures as incompatible with his desire for a faithful and unembellished rendering of the past, for they differed in character and purpose from the kind of imagination associated with fiction. Although using the imagination to embellish and enliven a historical account would distort historical truth, the use of conjecture to explain human behavior would further truth by adding to the historian's understanding of the larger principles that governed human nature.

This understanding of the relationship between conjecture and truth was consistent with the assumptions of Scottish conjectural history. Conjectural history has been closely associated with the Scottish Enlightenment, for its leading practitioners included Scottish philosophers and historians like Adam Ferguson, William Robertson, and Adam Smith. While most of these historians would not themselves have used the term *conjectural* to speak of their work, the Scottish moral philosopher Dugald Stewart first used the term *conjectural history* to describe this school of historical writing. Scottish conjectural historians are best known for their four-stage theory of history, which sought to explain the rise of commercial society by dividing human development into a series of stages—the hunting, herding, agricultural, and commercial stages. The work of these historians came to be known as conjectural history because of their belief that the gaps in the historical record and the lack of historical documents for the earlier stages in their theory required them to conjecture about what had happened in those earlier stages.[16]

Believing that the purpose of history was to contribute to a science of society, these historians did not consider their conjectures a form of speculation because they based their conclusions on what they believed were larger universal truths about human nature. By using what they knew about human nature to explain human behavior in earlier periods of history, they could fill in the gaps in their factual knowledge about the past. In turn, by explaining human development in this way, these historians hoped to make knowledge about human nature and society more systematic and scientific. Such knowledge would serve a moral function, since it would teach readers how to be better citizens by establishing a better understanding of the basis for virtue. For conjectural historians, then, the historian was not just supposed to record what had happened in the past; in order to illuminate larger moral truths about human nature, the historian had to draw his own conclusions about the facts, requiring an act of interpretation by the historian.[17]

The historian and dramatist Mercy Otis Warren was both more critical of and more willing to emulate novels than was Burk or Belknap. In her criticism of novels, Warren revealed that she, like Burk, believed that history should convey moral truths and that, at the same time, historical truth required an exact account of actual events. Yet she went further than Burk did in allowing a role for imagination and embellishment in history, further complicating her definition of truth. Like Belknap and Burk, Warren was not entirely hostile to fiction and even wrote plays herself. She viewed novels, however, more critically than she viewed drama. In a letter to her niece Mary Warren urging the importance of female education, Warren warned her niece against dissipating time on "books that have not a tendency to instill lessons of virtue and science." Such lessons, she argued, "may be drawn from the various pictures of human life exhibited in the faithful pages of authentic history, which is now written in a style equally elegant to the many volumes of *romance*, which in the present age crowd upon the public." It was her hope that, once women adopted this program, "most novels will be excluded from the libraries of those ladies who fill up their time in a manner that evinces they have a proper estimate of its value."[18]

Warren here used the term *novel* loosely, equating it with romance. In urging her niece and other women to abandon reading novels in favor of history, Warren echoed other critics of the novel and repudiated novels as a useless form of diversion. Novels were frivolous, in her view, because they did not instill "lessons of virtue and science." Novels could not instill such lessons partly because of their subject matter, for many of them centered on the topics of seduction and romance—in other words, private rather than public affairs—which were considered trivial or even immoral. History, in contrast, Warren believed, was valuable precisely because it could impart such lessons. And unlike novels, according to Warren, history was "authentic"—that is, it was true. By truth, Warren meant an accurate representation of actual reality, as she revealed by using words like "authentic" and "faithful." Like Burk, Warren saw no conflict between her belief in the moral function of history and her desire for a faithful record of the past. On the contrary, she suggested, history possessed the ability to edify because, unlike novels, it was based on truth and reality.[19]

As she praised historians for achieving the same elegance of style as that found in novels, Warren complicated the relationship between history and the novel, for she acknowledged that, at least in terms of style, novels did possess some merit and were worthy of emulation by historians. Warren could recognize an affinity between these two genres because, in her view, embellishment—in the form of an elegant style—and historical truth were not mutually exclusive. Thus, according to Warren, it was possible for the historian to write in a style like that of the novel without making his or her work any less authentic or true. A faithful record of the past did not require the historian to limit him- or herself only to an unvarnished account of facts and events in history. Indeed, by writing in an "elegant" style, the historian would be better able to convey moral lessons to his or her readers, for this style would enable the historian to compete more successfully with the novelist for the attention of readers.[20]

Warren's willingness to allow for a certain degree of embellishment and imagination in her conception of truth reflected her concerns as a woman writing history. Warren herself pointed to the relationship between gender and genre in directing her comments about the novel to women. As she did so, Warren revealed one of the reasons for the widespread distrust of the novel—the belief in the feminine appeal of novels. Critics in Warren's time considered the novel frivolous partly because they identified the novel with women. Women were especially prominent in the rise of the novel, as both authors and readers. Two of the most popular American novelists in this period, Susanna Rowson and Hannah Foster, were women, and numerous other female novelists joined their fold. Although men did in fact read novels too, the popularity of novels among women readers reinforced the tendency to associate novels with the feminine sphere. Women found novels especially appealing because, unlike other genres, they often directly addressed women readers and spoke to women's concerns by centering on female characters and focusing on topics like seduction and romance.[21]

The characterization of novels as frivolous because of their association with women both reflected and reinforced a gender ideology that subordinated women to men and emphasized women's weakness and irrationality. In turn, by defining history in opposition to the novel, critics of the novel privileged history as a masculine genre that was more serious in character than were novels. Because history dealt with public affairs, then considered the province of men, only men could grasp or benefit from the moral lessons of history. And if reason was necessary to achieve truth, then truth was possible only for male historians and readers, for men were associated with reason and women with emotion. In this way, the opposition between history and the novel defined historical truth itself in masculine terms.[22]

Warren at once upheld the gender boundaries between history and novel and blurred those boundaries as she both reinforced and undermined the masculine associations of historical truth. In the preface to her history of the American Revolution, published in 1805, she admitted that "it is the more peculiar province of masculine strength, not only to repel the bold invader of the rights of his country and of mankind, but in the nervous style of manly eloquence, to describe the blood-stained field, and relate the story of slaughtered armies." Here, Warren reasoned that it fell to men to write about history, for they were the actors in the events that she considered the proper subject matter of history—war and political affairs. When she spoke of "manly eloquence," Warren suggested that the very ability to recount and describe these events was a male attribute. For this reason, Warren expressed great trepidation at the thought of writing a history herself and spoke of how "the trembling heart has recoiled at the magnitude of the undertaking." In emphasizing her "trembling heart," Warren reaffirmed the association between women and emotion that had traditionally disqualified women from writing about history.[23]

Yet in urging women to read history and in writing history herself, she subverted the masculine associations of historical truth and redefined the meaning of truth itself. As she did so, she associated one of the defining qualities of the novel—the imagination—with historical truth. Historical truth was, in Warren's view, not an inherently masculine attribute; she suggested that women too could access truth. For this reason, she could state, "The historian has never laid aside the tenderness of the sex or the friend; at the same time, she has endeavoured, on all occasions, that the strictest veracity should govern her heart, and the most exact impartiality be the guide of her pen." In claiming that she could maintain "veracity" and "impartiality" without putting aside the "tenderness of the sex," Warren suggested that she could achieve truth not despite but because of her gender.[24]

Warren could make this claim because, for her, impartiality did not mean total emotional detachment by the historian. On the contrary, to be impartial, the historian had to be able to sympathize with his or her subjects. Thus, after proclaiming that "truth has been the guide of my pen" and that she had not written to promote the interests of any group or party, Warren spoke of how "[t]he sympathizing heart has looked abroad and wept the many victims of affliction" who had endured the sufferings of war. Because women were supposed to possess a greater capacity for sympathy than men, Warren suggested that she could actually better achieve impartiality than a male historian could. In this way, Warren implied that the very quality that was supposed to prevent women from being impartial—their susceptibility to emotion—would actually further their ability to achieve impartiality. In associating sympathy with impartiality, she suggested that truth required more than just an accurate account of what had happened in the past; truth also involved the ability to imagine and convey the feelings of participants in these events.[25]

Hence, in direct contrast to Belknap, who had disavowed the help of the imagination, Warren invoked the imagination to convey the sufferings endured by the South during the Revolutionary War. Attempting to dramatize for her readers the horrors that this region had experienced, she declared,

> Imagination may easily paint the distresses, when surveying on the one side, a proud and potent army flushed with recent success, and irritated by opposition from an enemy they despised, both as Americans and as rebels; their spirit of revenge continually whetted by a body of refugees who followed them, embittered beyond description against their countrymen, and who were joined by a banditti who had no country, but the spot that yielded a temporary harvest to their rapacious hands: rapine and devastation had no check.

Here, by using the imagination to re-create the "distresses" created by unchecked "rapine and devastation," Warren revealed her own sympathy for those Americans who endured such "distresses," and she sought to make her readers sympathize with the victims of these horrors. And by appealing to the imagination, Warren blurred the distinction between history and the novel, for she called on the very quality that was supposed to differentiate the novel from history.[26]

Ultimately, as much as the Revolutionary historians sought to differentiate between history and novel, these two genres were more similar than they admitted; indeed, the very qualities that the Revolutionary historians used to distinguish history from the novel also characterized the novel. Specifically, while critics of the novel, like Warren, lamented the immoral and frivolous character of novels, novelists themselves claimed a didactic purpose for their works.[27] In a letter of 1808, the historian David Ramsay went the furthest in acknowledging the similarities between history and the novel when he observed, "Novel writers take fiction & make it a vehicle of their opinions on a variety of subjects. I take truth & the facts of history for the same purpose." In claiming that the historian used truth as a vehicle for his opinions, Ramsay recognized the subjective element to history; rather than just uncovering the truth, the historian shaped the truth for his own purposes. Yet even as he acknowledged the likeness between history and the novel, he differentiated between the two genres by emphasizing the basis of history in truth and fact. Thus, for Ramsay, the recognition that the historian used history to express his own opinions did not take away from his claims to truth, and he affirmed his faith in the existence of a truth that was independent of the historian's interpretation. In this way, he brought together two seemingly contradictory views of truth—truth, for him, was both made and found by the historian.[28]

Yet even in their claims to truth, novels were more similar to history than historians acknowledged. To confer legitimacy on their new genre, English and American novelists often described their works as histories and emphasized the factual basis for their novels. And, as Ian Watt has argued, a concern with particularity and reality distinguished novels from other fictional genres. These similarities suggest, then, that ultimately the reason that historians were so concerned about the novel—and considered the novel a greater danger than other forms of fiction—was not because of its differences from history but because of its very likeness to history. The narrative structure of the novel made it more similar to historical writing than other fictional genres like plays or poetry, thus creating the illusion that the novel represented a true account of real events. And as novelists trespassed on their domain, historians affirmed all the more strongly their own commitment to authentic truth. Thus, the Revolutionary historians sought to differentiate between history and the novel paradoxically because of the likeness between the two genres, and their commitment to truth was both a cause and an effect of their desire to set these two genres apart.[29]

"Imagination based on facts": Romantic History and Moral Judgment

Hence as the rise of the historical novel in the 1820s further blurred the boundaries between history and the novel, historical writers at once were more willing to recognize the affinity between these two genres and sought all the more to differentiate between them. The most influential figure in the emergence of the historical novel was Sir Walter Scott, and he established the defining model for this genre with the publication of *Waverly* in 1814. Scott followed *Waverly* with a whole series of novels that used Scottish history as the setting for his dramatic stories of adventure and romance. Tremendously popular in England and the United States, Scott's novels had an immense influence on both fictional and historical writing. Although his stories centered on fictional characters, he based his novels on serious historical research, drawing on documentary sources as well as popular folklore and traditions. Through this combination of the real and the imaginary, Scott achieved unparalleled success in bringing the past to life for his readers. As a result, his novels not only stimulated interest in history but transformed the nature of that interest. Historical novels proliferated in this period, inspired by Scott's example, and his novels served as a model for many of the leading American novelists in this period, including James Fenimore Cooper and Nathaniel Hawthorne.[30]

By bringing together history and the novel in this way, Scott's works conferred new prestige and legitimacy on the novel as a literary form, and early antipathy to this genre among cultural commentators gradually eroded in the early nineteenth century.[31] Scott's novels both fed and benefited from the emergence of a mass market for novels in the 1820s and 1830s, a development that also contributed to the growing legitimacy of the novel. In this period, the supply and demand for novels increased exponentially. Not only were more authors writing novels; the development of a mass market for literature also encouraged publishers to produce more copies of these works. These developments both fed and reflected the rapidly expanding popular appetite for novels. Even as the novel became increasingly popular and respectable, hostility to this genre and concerns about its insidious moral effects persisted. Instead of automatically rejecting the novel as a threat to their social and moral aims, however, social authorities attempted to co-opt its appeal for their own purposes.[32]

Antebellum historical writers revealed this ambivalence especially clearly. Responding to the growing popularity and respectability of the novel, they increasingly sought to emulate the novel in their historical works. At the same time, they were even more insistent than their Revolutionary predecessors about the distinctiveness and superiority of history as a genre founded in truth. While sharing their Revolutionary predecessors' commitment to truth, then, antebellum historians defined truth itself differently. If in their desire to emulate the novel they assigned a greater role for the imagination in illuminating historical truth, they differentiated history from the novel by affirming all the more strongly their understanding of impartial truth as the representation of an objective reality grounded in fact. William Hickling Prescott demonstrated most clearly how they reconciled these two imperatives by writing in a Romantic narrative style that viewed history as a form of literary art. Yet if Prescott and his adherents in this way brought together a belief in a truth that was independent of the historian's interpretation with a recognition of the subjective element to historical truth, his contemporaries were more divided about whether his use of the imagination could be reconciled with the historian's moral function. As Prescott's supporters and critics contended over whether Prescott's artistic approach threatened the historian's moral purpose, they revealed how their shared belief in the moral dimension to truth at once allowed an expanded role for the imagination in historical understanding and limited that role.

History was, for nineteenth-century historians, as David Levin has termed it, a form of Romantic art. The leading Romantic historians of this period—William Hickling Prescott, George Bancroft, John Lothrop Motley, and Francis Parkman—expressed their view of history as art by repeatedly using metaphors of painting and portraiture to describe their work. Although better known as a philosopher than as a Romantic historian, Francis Bowen summed up this artistic conception of history in a letter to John Gorham Palfrey when he asserted, "The little facts thus made known seem to me to be rather the materials for history, than history itself; they should be expanded into broad pictures, and worked up with high coloring. After all, imagination is as necessary for the historian as research; only it must be imagination based on facts." In urging the need for "broad pictures" and "high coloring" in history, Bowen likened history to art. And like art, history had to be dramatic and vivid—hence the need for "high coloring." For this reason, Bowen believed that facts were a necessary, but not a sufficient, basis for history. Rather than just cataloging endless facts and details, the historian's goal was to enable readers to visualize the past as they would a painting. The historian could do this only by using the imagination to describe and connect those facts into a coherent and vivid narrative.[33]

Bowen derived his view of the imagination from Romantic aesthetics. The imagination was central to Romantic aesthetic theory, for the Romantic artist was, to use M. H. Abrams's famous distinction, not a mirror but a lamp. Abrams used this distinction to describe the shift from a mimetic to an expressive theory of art that characterized Romantic thought. In neoclassical aesthetics, the artist was supposed to be a mirror, whose goal was to reflect eternal and unchanging truths. In contrast, according to Romantic aesthetic theory, the artist was a lamp who actively shaped perceptions of reality through the use of his own imagination. Rather than simply reflecting the outer world, the artist would actually transform what he perceived by projecting his own vitality and passion into his perception of the world. And so, whereas in neoclassical aesthetics the artist was supposed to capture external truths, in Romantic aesthetics, the artist's goal was to be true to his own inner experience and feelings. This view of the imagination thus made the individual's experience of events more important to truth than the events themselves. But if the imagination played an active role in shaping truth, this could lead to the conclusion that truth was largely subjective, a conclusion that threatened the defining characteristic of historical truth—its claims to represent actual reality. Hence, Bowen was careful to qualify his claims for the imagination by declaring that the historian's imagination had to be based on fact. For Romantic historians who viewed history as a form of art, then, the dilemma was how to allow a role for the imagination without abandoning their belief that truth entailed the re-creation of the objective reality of the past.[34]

As one of the most successful and influential Romantic historians, William Hickling Prescott demonstrated especially clearly how they reconciled these two imperatives. Born into a wealthy Boston family, Prescott took up literary pursuits soon after his graduation from Harvard, and he wrote extensively on both literary and historical subjects for periodicals like the *North American Review*.[35] He published the first of his histories, the *History of the Reign of Ferdinand and Isabella*, in 1837. This history immediately achieved critical and popular acclaim, and Prescott's reputation would only grow with his subsequent books—the *History of the Conquest of Mexico* and the *History of the Conquest of Peru*. Romantic historians like Prescott applied an expressive theory of art to history, extending to their historical subjects the Romantic emphasis on inner experience over action. To convey the truth of an event, the historian could not just relate what had happened in the past; he had to re-create his subjects' experience of that event and enable readers to relive that experience. In other words, rather than a "narrative of action," as Mark Phillips puts it, historical truth entailed a "rendering of experience."[36] The historian's role, then, was to use the imagination to enter into the feelings of his subjects and present their experiences in a way that was vivid to readers, not to project his own feelings and perspective into his account of those experiences. In this way, Prescott and other Romantic historians could prescribe an active role for the historian's imagination while maintaining a belief in a historical truth that was independent of the historian's perspective.

Unlike Belknap, rather than viewing a dramatic and graphic style of description as "embellishment" that distorted the truth of the past, Prescott and other Romantic historians believed that such a style was necessary to achieve their goal of vividly re-creating internal experience. Thus, repeatedly throughout his *History of the Conquest of Mexico*, Prescott wrote in a style that would enable the reader to see the events he described through the eyes of the Spanish conquerors. In this way he sought to re-create the sense of foreboding and uncertainty that Spanish soldiers felt just before the "noche triste"—according to Prescott, the greatest Spanish defeat in the New World:

> The night was cloudy, and a drizzling rain, which fell without intermission, added to the obscurity. The great square before the palace was deserted, as, indeed, it had been since the fall of Montezuma. Steadily, and as noiselessly as possible, the Spaniards held their way along the great street of Tlacopan, which so lately had resounded to the tumult of battle. All was now hushed in silence; and they were only reminded of the past by the occasional presence of some solitary corpse, or a dark heap of the slain, which too plainly told where the strife had been hottest. As they passed along the lanes and alleys which opened into the great street, or looked down the canals, whose polished surface gleamed with a sort of ebon lustre through the obscurity of night, they easily fancied that they discerned the shadowy forms of their foe lurking in ambush, and ready to spring on them.[37]

In associating truth with the imaginative re-creation of personal experience, Romantic historians were responding not only to Romantic aesthetics but also to the rise of the novel. Hence they looked most often to a novelist—Sir Walter Scott—for inspiration. They modeled their works on his historical novels, which they believed had realized most successfully their aspirations to make history come alive for the reader.[38] Even as they were influenced by the novel in their conception of truth, they at the same time defined truth in opposition to the novel. And so, despite their admiration for historical novelists like Scott, they continued to differentiate history from the novel. As they did so, they placed strict limits on the contribution of the imagination to historical truth. Prescott illuminated the nature of these limits as he at once likened his work to and distinguished it from fiction. While discussing the subject matter for his history of the conquest of Mexico, published in 1843, he enthused, "The story is so full of marvels, perilous adventures, curious manners, scenery etc. that it is more like a romance than a history, and yet every page is substantiated by abundance of original testimony." What made this topic so compelling for Prescott was that it possessed the fascination and excitement of "romance," but unlike romance, it was grounded in truth.[39]

Equating "romance" with fiction, Prescott revealed what he meant by truth as he elaborated on what differentiated his work from romance. Although his subject "has the air of romance rather than of sober history," Prescott emphasized, "I have conscientiously endeavored to distinguish fact from fiction, and to establish the narrative on as broad a basis as possible of contemporary evidence."[40] Unlike fiction, according to Prescott, history was based on fact. In turn, he associated fact with "original testimony" and "contemporary evidence," meaning the testimony of primary sources. In this emphasis on fact, Prescott revealed that Romantic historians would only go so far in their use of the imagination. Through the imagination, the historian could enhance and illuminate the reality of the past by making it more dramatic and vivid, but he did not actually play any role in creating that reality. Indeed, when he likened his history to "romance" by pointing to the "marvels" and "perilous adventures" it contained, Prescott suggested that the drama and vitality of his history came as much from the inherent character of his subject as from his presentation of the material, further limiting the contribution of the imagination to historical truth.

Prescott's reviewers made these limits even clearer in the distinction they made between history and the novel. While they praised Prescott's histories for their likeness to novels, Prescott's reviewers continued to differentiate between these two genres, basing this distinction on historical adherence to the truth. In 1843, William Howard Gardiner predicted that Prescott's *History of the Conquest of Mexico* would be even more popular than his first book, "not because it is more meritorious (for what do *the people* know about that?)—but because the subject and the manner of treating it make an excellent substitute for one of Scott's best historical novels. It's as good as fiction—which ought to be highly gratifying to the compiler of facts."[41] In describing the historian as a "compiler of facts," Gardiner suggested the limits to the historian's role in interpreting truth. Not only was the historian's imagination confined by fact, but even his role in analyzing and describing those facts was limited. Although Gardiner's reference to Prescott's "manner of treating" his subject implied that Prescott had achieved the appeal of Scott's novels through his style of presentation, Gardiner's use of the term "compiler" suggested that Prescott had achieved this goal not through his own creative interpretation and description but through the gathering and accumulation of facts.

Likewise, in another assessment of Prescott's *Conquest of Mexico* for the *North American Review*, George Stillman Hillard commended his picturesque portrayal of the Mexicans, which "enable the writer to throw the charm of fiction over his pages, while adhering scrupulously to the unvarnished truth."[42] For Hillard, even while Prescott's history possessed the "charm of fiction," it differed from fiction in its devotion to the "unvarnished truth." In using the phrase "unvarnished truth," Hillard revealed his belief in a truth that was independent of the historian's own perspective and unembellished by the historian. For Hillard, as for Gardiner, the historian could use the imagination to make history more charming and picturesque—and more like novels—without himself shaping the nature of truth.

In another review of Prescott's works published in 1848, E. P. Whipple revealed most clearly how Romantic historians brought together a belief in a truth that was independent of the historian's interpretation with a recognition of the subjective element to historical truth. Like Hillard and Gardiner, he praised Prescott's achievement in imparting the dramatic interest of novels to his narrative without abandoning the historian's quest for truth: "Mr. Prescott understands what has made historical novels so much more readable than histories, and he has succeeded in making history as fascinating as romance. In accomplishing this it was not necessary that he should introduce anything fictitious." On the contrary, for Whipple, fidelity to the truth, effectively presented, would actually be more compelling than fiction, and "[t]he nearer his narrative approached the vital truth of the matter, the more complete would be the interest it would awaken."[43] But what, exactly, did Whipple mean by the "vital truth of the matter"? To achieve truth, Whipple believed, the historian could not allow his own personal feelings or perspective to influence his account of an event. Instead, he had to depict his subjects on their own terms. Because he believed that Prescott had achieved this goal, Whipple praised Prescott's work for "its singular objectiveness." As a result of Prescott's ability "to consider his subject as everything, and himself as nothing," "[o]bjects stand out on his page in clear light, undiscolored by the hues of his own passions, unmixed with any peculiarities of his own character."[44] As his use of the term "objectiveness" revealed, Whipple's conception of truth presumed that the historian could divest himself of personal bias and separate himself from his presentation of his subject.

But, for Whipple, to be free from bias did not necessarily mean to be without emotion—it only meant to be without emotional involvement of a certain kind. Whipple described the kind of emotional involvement that he believed was necessary for historical truth as he mocked the tendency of historians to dispense explicit moral judgments throughout their works. Believing that such judgments would have little effect on the reader, Whipple argued that although "it is not necessary that he [the historian] should set certain commonplaces at stated distances in his narrative, declaring how naughty it is for men to cut each other's throats and blow out each other's brains . . . it is important that, in representing a battle, he should make us vitally feel the sufferings it occasions, and the demoniacal passions it unleashes." In urging the need to make the reader "vitally feel" the sufferings and passions of historical actors, Whipple revealed his belief that truth required the reader to feel a sense of emotional identification with historical subjects; the reader had to be able to imagine and experience for himself the emotions of historical actors.[45]

This definition of truth in turn required a certain kind of emotional involvement by the historian; only through his own sympathetic understanding for his subject could he elicit the same sentiments from his reader. Whipple made this assumption clear when he attributed the "peculiar charm and interest" of Prescott's histories to his "power of pictorial representation and imaginative insight," combined with his "large share of sensibility." As Whipple explained, "By the readiness with which he himself sympathizes with his incidents and characters, he awakens the sympathies of the reader." For Whipple, then, even as the historian was supposed to divest himself of the prejudices of his own time, he had to enter into the prejudices and emotions of his subjects. In emphasizing the need for sympathy and "sensibility" from the historian, Whipple associated truth with the subjective realm of feeling and emotion. In this way, Whipple at once made truth independent of the historian's perspective and recognized that truth required an act of imaginative interpretation by the historian, for the historian could enter that realm only by exercising the imagination.[46]

Yet if Whipple departed from the Revolutionary historians in his emphasis on the importance of the imagination to truth, he revealed the limits to that departure as he, like them, affirmed a staunch belief in the moral function of history. Whipple saw no conflict between these imperatives, for, he believed, the more vivid and real the historian's account of the past, the more effective it would be in conveying moral lessons to the reader. Reasoning that the historian did not have to spell out the lessons of his story by periodically issuing moral pronouncements for the reader, Whipple proclaimed that Prescott "produces morality of effect by truth of representation. This is as much better than moralizing, as the perfume which escapes from a rose is better than rose water. If the historian has the heart and brain to grasp the truth, he may safely leave the rest to the reader's moral instincts." In arguing that "truth of representation" would naturally lead the reader to draw the correct moral lessons, Whipple, like his Revolutionary predecessors, identified the moral truths of history with the actual truth of the past, though he differed from them over what "truth of representation" entailed.[47]

Prescott himself agreed with Whipple in seeing no conflict between a moral conception of truth and his belief that truth required the imaginative re-creation of experience. He made explicit his own commitment to an exemplary theory of history when he praised the Abbé Mably for "his notion of the necessity of giving an interest as well as utility to History by letting events tend to some obvious point or moral."[48] In claiming that this didactic approach would impart "interest as well as utility" to his work, Prescott suggested that the historian's moral function would actually further his artistic purposes by adding to the dramatic value of his history. Accordingly, Prescott injected such judgments throughout his history, as when he pronounced his verdict on the actions of

the Spanish conquerors of Mexico. Prescott declared, "We shall, perhaps, pronounce more impartially on the conduct of the Conquerors, if we compare it
with that of our own contemporaries under somewhat similar circumstances."
Prescott explained that such a comparison "should render us more lenient in
our judgments of the past, showing, as they do, that man in a state of excitement, savage or civilised, is much the same in every age." Prescott drew from
this example the lesson that "even among the most polished people" it was incumbent on the government to "submit to every sacrifice, save that of honor,
before authorizing an appeal to arms" in order to avoid the "*inevitable* evils
of war."[49]

As his use of the word "impartially" demonstrated, Prescott did not see
any conflict between such judgments and his desire for impartial truth. He revealed more clearly what he meant by impartiality as he elaborated on the nature of the judgments the historian was supposed to make. Disclaiming any
desire to excuse the "cruel deeds" committed by the Spanish against the Mexicans, Prescott qualified his condemnation by declaring, "But, to judge them
fairly, we must not do it by the lights of our own age. We must carry ourselves
back to theirs, and take the point of view afforded by the civilisation of their
time. Thus only can we arrive at impartial criticism in reviewing the generations that are past." Like Whipple, Prescott believed that, to be impartial, the
historian had to divest himself of the prejudices of his own time and understand the past from the point of view of historical actors. Impartiality thus required an act of imagination by the historian; only in this way could historians "carry ourselves back" to the time of their subjects. By taking the context
and circumstances of his subjects into account, Prescott believed, the historian
would arrive at a more balanced judgment of their actions, for this kind of
understanding would enable the historian to temper his condemnation of their
moral failings. Thus, for Prescott, to be impartial was to judge fairly, not to
eschew judgment completely.[50]

As he made this understanding of impartiality explicit, Prescott revealed
the duality in his conception of truth. Summing up his assessment of the Spanish conquerors of Mexico, Prescott proclaimed that in his efforts to be impartial, "on the one hand, I have not hesitated to expose in their strongest colors
the excesses of the Conquerors; on the other, I have given them the benefit of
such mitigating reflections as might be suggested by the circumstances and the
period in which they lived." Such an impartial assessment would lead to truth,
for, as Prescott explained, "I have endeavored not only to present a picture true
in itself, but to place it in its proper light, and to put the spectator in a proper
point of view for seeing it to the best advantage. I have endeavored . . . to sur-

round him with the spirit of the times, and, in a word, to make him, if I may so express myself, a contemporary of the sixteenth century."[51] Prescott's desire to "present a picture true in itself" implied the existence of a truth that was independent of the historian's perspective; his goal was to articulate a vision of the past that was inherently true. While the historian did not create truth, Prescott's desire to place truth "in its proper light" suggested that there could be different perspectives on the truth and that the historian could illuminate truth through his interpretation of the facts. And for Prescott, the historian's role in illuminating truth was to enable his readers to understand historical actors on their own terms. In this way, Prescott could at once believe in a truth that was independent of the historian's interpretation and maintain that the historian played a role in shaping perspectives on the truth.

Yet this understanding of impartiality also provoked sharp criticism from contemporaries who believed that it threatened a moral conception of truth. If, for both Whipple and Prescott, the historian could understand his subjects on their own terms without undermining his moral function, Prescott's critics argued that these two imperatives were mutually exclusive. As they did so, they demonstrated especially clearly how a moral definition of truth at once limited and contributed to a willingness to admit a role for the imagination in historical understanding. A writer for the *Democratic Review* criticized Prescott's *Conquest of Mexico* on this basis in 1844. Condemning Prescott for divesting himself of his nineteenth-century perspective and trying to understand sixteenth-century actors on their own terms, this critic complained, "[I]n discussing these deeds of the sixteenth century, he [Prescott] might have endeavored to see and analyze them all by the aid of the increased knowledge of the nineteenth, instead of studiously excluding it."[52] According to this writer, the problem with viewing history in this way was that it represented an abandonment of the historian's responsibility to judge historical actors and provide posterity with moral examples to imitate or avoid, for the historian could make such judgments only if he held his subjects up to the superior moral standards of his own time. As this critic explained, "The historian is, or should be, the genius of retribution; but when he refuses to discriminate; when he abdicates a part of his own wisdom and virtue, to bring himself down to the level of his subjects; he may heighten the interest of his characters and incidents, but he abdicates at the same time a portion of his usefulness and a portion of his power."[53]

For this critic, then, by bringing himself "down to the level of his subjects," Prescott had chosen to enliven and dramatize history for his readers at the expense of his role as a moral arbiter. When he attributed Prescott's failure to fulfill the historian's moral function to an "artistic point of view," this critic pointed to the tensions between Prescott's view of history as literary art—with its emphasis on the importance of imagination to truth—and a didactic view of history that defined truth in moral terms and revealed how resistance to the primacy that Prescott gave to the imagination derived from that moral definition of truth.[54]

Writing in 1849 for the *Massachusetts Quarterly Review*, Theodore Parker condemned Prescott even more harshly for abdicating the historian's moral purpose. Yet if he, like the critic for the *Democratic Review*, believed that Prescott had betrayed this office by refusing to judge historical actors according to contemporary moral standards, he still reconciled in his own way an expressive theory of art that gave primacy to the historian's imagination with a belief in the moral function of history. Firmly maintaining a didactic understanding of history as "philosophy teaching by examples," Parker declared, "In telling what has been, the Historian is also to tell what ought to be, for he is to pass judgment on events." If the historian made such judgments, "History . . . becomes Philosophy teaching by experience," as "it tells the lessons of the Past for the warning of the Present and the edification of the Future." According to Parker, in making such judgments, the historian necessarily had to intrude his individual perspective into his work. Parker therefore proclaimed, "Now the subjective character of an Historian continually appears, colors his narrative, and affects the judgment he passes on men and things."[55] In Parker's view, however, Prescott had failed to impress his own character onto his work, for he had refrained from making these kinds of judgments. Like Whipple, Parker believed that Prescott had withdrawn himself from the text. Yet Parker differed from Whipple in seeing this trait as a defect rather than a cause for praise. Prescott's refusal to judge his subjects was, for Parker, the main problem with his history. Ending his review with a scathing indictment of Prescott, he concluded, "The book lacks Philosophy to a degree exceeding belief." Although "[h]e narrates events in their order of time, with considerable skill," Prescott "tells the fact for the fact's sake."[56]

In contrast to Whipple, Parker did not believe that the moral lessons of history would be automatically revealed by the historian as he conveyed and recreated the actual experiences of the past. Rather, these moral lessons required the historian to intervene and interpret the facts for the reader. Yet in arguing that the historian's "subjective character" would shape the nature of these lessons, Parker suggested that individuals would differ over the lessons they drew from the facts, for each would project his own "philosophical, political, moral, and religious creed" into those lessons. Thus, Parker went further than

Prescott in extending an expressive theory of art to history. Whereas Prescott and Whipple argued that the historian was supposed to use the imagination to illuminate the perspective of his subjects, not express his own point of view, for Parker, the historian, like the artist, was a lamp who could shed light on the past by projecting his own perspective and character directly into his work.[57]

In recognizing the subjective character of the historian's moral judgments, Parker was not promoting moral relativism. Parker made this clear as he elaborated on the basis for the historian's moral judgments. While "[i]t is the duty of an Historian to measure men by the general standard of their times," Parker asserted, "it is also the Historian's duty to criticize that spirit, and when a superior man rises, he must not be judged merely by the low standard of his age, but the absolute standard of all ages."[58] According to Parker, the nobler the character of the historian, the closer he would come to grasping the higher moral truths that governed humanity, for "[a] man cannot comprehend what wholly transcends himself." In this way, Parker reconciled his appreciation for the subjective character of moral judgment with a belief in the existence of eternal and transcendent moral truths. But in making moral judgment a function of the historian's character, Parker pointed to the tensions between the view of history as mimesis and the view of history as instruction, for unlike both Prescott and his Revolutionary predecessors, Parker separated the moral lessons of history from the actual truth of the past.[59]

"The gossip of history": Domestic History, Gender, and the Meaning of Fact

For Parker, another problem with Prescott's history was that "there are no pictures from the lives of the humble." Parker saw this quality as a deficiency because "[a] few facts from the every-day life of the merchant, the slave, the peasant, the mechanic, are often worth more, as signs of the times, than a chapter which relates the intrigues of a courtier, though these are not to be overlooked."[60] While Parker's concern with the history of ordinary people was partly a reflection of his own social activism and his sympathy for the disfranchised, this concern was also part of a more general trend as historians during the 1830s and 1840s urged more attention to the history of ordinary social life—what modern historians would call "social history," or, as contemporaries termed it, "domestic history."[61]

Challenging the traditional assumption that only public events were significant enough to count as historical facts, advocates of "domestic history" broadened their definition of facts to include the private realm of everyday life. By defining facts in this way, historians could emulate the novel without sacrificing the quality that made history distinctive—its concern with fact. And so, even as historians defined truth in opposition to the novel, their very definition of what constituted a historical fact reflected the influence of the novel.[62] Yet, if in their demands for social history, historians were simply taking a scientific desire for factual accuracy to its logical conclusion, their concern with factual accuracy also limited their ability to realize these demands. And while these historians departed from an exclusively masculine definition of truth in their desire to broaden the scope of history, the feminine associations of domestic history prevented them from acting on this desire. The disparity between the theory and practice of social history thus revealed the tensions in their view of truth. Elizabeth Ellet resolved these tensions in her effort to carry out prescriptions for domestic history. As she did so, she reconciled in her own way the belief that truth entailed a re-creation of the objective reality of the past with an appreciation for the importance of subjective feeling and perception to truth.[63]

The desire to broaden the scope of history went back to the eighteenth century, when Enlightenment thinkers began to question the traditional political emphasis of historical writing. Following the lead of David Hume and Voltaire's *Essai sur les moeurs*, British historians by the second half of the eighteenth century increasingly expressed the need to expand the scope of history to include the history of social life and "manners," or what would now be classified as social and cultural history—the arts, commerce, and everyday life. British historians in this period by no means abandoned political history, but they sought to place political history in a larger context and to explore the interconnections between politics and other aspects of society—including what had traditionally been considered the private domain. Thus, even while the Revolutionary historians still focused on political topics in their histories, they, like their British contemporaries, recognized the intersection between public and private as they relocated virtue in the institutions of everyday life, such as commerce, religion, and the family.[64]

The challenge to the primacy of political history was therefore part of a larger redefinition of virtue that took its inspiration from Scottish Enlightenment thought. The traditional emphasis on political history was partly a function of classical republican ideology, which located the exercise and realization of virtue in the public arena of government and military pursuits. Yet, as Nicholas Phillipson has argued, Scottish Enlightenment thinkers had, in different ways, begun to question this definition of virtue, turning instead to the institutions of civil society, which lay outside the formal political arena—commerce, literature and the arts, and social clubs—as arenas for the exercise of virtue. In this way, Scottish moral thinkers contributed to the redefinition of virtue as a private rather than a public quality. With its emphasis on the individual's private rights and interests, the rise of liberal capitalism in this period further abetted this redefinition. In turn, as virtue increasingly became associated with the private rather than the public realm, so too did the locus of historical inquiry.[65]

The desire to recover the history of everyday social life and manners deepened, as the Romantic fascination with national character and the *Volksgeist*, or spirit of the people, made popular folklore and traditions all the more important as sources for understanding the spirit of the people. Here again Scott played a key role, demonstrating how the novel contributed to the growing interest in the history of manners and everyday life. Not only did his use of folk ballads and legends contribute to the Romantic interest in popular folklore; in using these sources to illuminate the history of Scottish manners and customs, he both reflected and contributed directly to the concern with this realm of the past.[66] As a genre that was associated with the private sphere, the novel seemed especially suited to an investigation of everyday domestic life. Thus novelists not only claimed for themselves a special ability to illuminate domestic manners and customs but also suggested that this ability enabled them to provide a truer picture of the past than that presented by historians who focused on the public sphere. For this reason, writing in 1822, the novelist James Fenimore Cooper could agree with his predecessor Henry Fielding's classification of himself as one of those "true historians" whose goal was "to give us just notions of what manner of men the ancient Greeks were, in their domestic affections, and retired deportment." In sum, as Cooper quoted Fielding, "'Those dignified authors who produce what are called true histories, are indeed writers of fictions, while I am a true historian, a describer of society as it exists, and of men as they are.'"[67]

Historians at once embraced and challenged this view of history, as the English historian Thomas Macaulay—one of the most prominent and successful practitioners of social history—demonstrated. In the renowned third chapter of his *History of England*, Macaulay fulfilled demands for a more comprehensive history of society by re-creating English social conditions in 1685. This work achieved instant popular acclaim in America with its publication there in 1849.[68] In their assessments of Macaulay's history, American reviewers shared in his concern with social history, singling out his attention to domestic and private life for special praise. In one such review, southern critic John Reuben Thompson in 1849 commended Macaulay's work as a much-needed corrective to the political focus of most historical writing. Unlike other historians,

Macaulay "desires to know how they [the people] lived . . . what degree of mental or moral culture they enjoyed . . . what was the fare, the drink and the amusements of the day . . . and a thousand other things, all relating to the domestic life of his ancestors."[69]

In his concern with social history, Macaulay was responding directly to the popularity of the novel. Even while he agreed with novelists on the importance of studying the history of domestic life, he denied that novelists possessed a monopoly on this realm. On the contrary, by writing social history, he sought to co-opt the appeal of the novel for history. Urging the addition of everyday, domestic details to the political subjects found in traditional histories, Macaulay declared that in this way, "[t]he perfect historian . . . gives to truth those attractions which have been usurped by fiction."[70] American historical writers shared Macaulay's belief that social history would enable the historian to reclaim for history one of the features that made fiction so attractive. A reviewer for the *American Literary Magazine* in 1849 praised Macaulay's comprehensive account of everyday customs and details for this very reason. According to this reviewer, Macaulay had transformed "the confused mass of information concerning the manners and customs of the past," into "minute and graphic views, gracefully grouped, of the fashions, the literature, the localities, the costume, the religion and the civilization of the eras of which he is the chronicler." In the process, Macaulay "takes back from fiction the minuteness, which makes fiction most attractive."[71] For this reviewer, Macaulay's attention to manners and customs had enabled him to achieve the kind of particularity and detail that made fiction so appealing to readers.

Because such particularity was based on fact, the historian would actually further his quest for truth by imitating the novel in this way. The interest in social history not only reflected the influence of the novel, then, but also followed from the belief in the importance of fact to historical truth. If history was supposed to be a record of fact, then the broader the historian's definition of fact and the more facts he included, the more true his history would be. In a review of James Thacher's history of Plymouth, Benjamin Bussey Thatcher used just this reasoning to explain why Thacher's emphasis on the details of everyday life was so valuable. Thatcher's decision to write about an ordinary individual in *Traits of the Tea Party* (1835)—his memoir of the shoemaker George Robert Twelves Hewes and the work for which he is best known today—revealed his interest in the history of everyday life. Thatcher also challenged the tendency to focus on great men in his other literary ventures, which included a collective biography of North American Indians as well as a memoir of Phillis Wheatley. Thatcher was an active philanthropist and social reformer, and thus his interest in this facet of the past was consistent with his contemporary social concerns.[72]

Praising Thacher's attention to the trivia of ordinary life, Thatcher declared of such details, "All this, indeed, may be the gossip of history. Yet who would be willing to part with it? Who does not see that it pours a flood of light on the character of men, and on the condition of the times? Who does not perceive, that it is the multitude of trifles, like these, which make up the life of the volume?" For Thatcher, the more such details, "the better," for he considered these details historical facts, and only through the accumulation of facts would the historian achieve truth.[73]

Thatcher revealed the importance of fact to his conception of truth when he declared, "The art of inventing facts is an accomplishment as little to be desired, with the historian, as the art of suppressing them. . . . We do not want showmen in history, but workmen. We do not want effects, but facts. We want no machinery, nor theory, but the truth." Here Thatcher differentiated between truth and theory, revealing his belief in the existence of a truth independent of the historian's interpretation. And in arguing that the historian was supposed to be a workman rather than a showman who used facts to create certain effects for his audience, he suggested that all the historian needed to do to convey the truth was to collect these facts for the reader; because the facts would speak for themselves, the historian did not have to interpret or dramatize his facts as a showman would.[74]

In his belief that historical truth was based on a record of fact, he embraced the scientific conception of history associated with Leopold von Ranke, who believed that only through a "strict presentation of facts" could the historian determine the truth of the past. Thatcher made his scientific understanding of truth even clearer when he declared that "the character which has been the vitality of all the Pilgrim institutions . . . might then be subjected to a scrutiny almost as rigid as a chemical analysis." Echoing Ranke's famous injunction to discover history "as it actually was," Thatcher claimed that this kind of scientific scrutiny would enable the historian to "see men and things,—worth seeing,—as they were, and are." In this shared emphasis on recovering what really happened in the past, Thatcher, like Ranke, suggested that truth meant an accurate representation of objective reality, and he expressed his faith that the historian could reconstruct that reality without allowing his own biases to influence his interpretation of the truth. At the same time, by claiming that more attention to this realm would add to the "interest" and "life" of history, Thatcher expressed his commitment to a Romantic conception of history that sought to re-create the experience of the past for readers. Through social history, then, Thatcher brought together two different approaches to historical truth—a Rankean view of history as science and the Romantic view of history as literary art.[75]

These two conceptions of history came together even more clearly for the *American Quarterly* reviewer who urged more "novels in histories" like Thacher's history of Plymouth. Like Thatcher, this reviewer saw the historian as a scientist, whose role was to collect as many facts as he could, not to interpret or draw larger conclusions from those facts. For this reason he believed that the "the charm of history" "is to be furnished with the facts, not with a collection or a selection of them, according to the taste, and still less according to the theory of the compiler; but with all of them."[76] The more complete the record of fact, the closer the historian would come to truth. And like Thatcher, this writer believed that truth meant knowing "men and things as they were, and are." Yet, as his use of the word "charm" revealed, this reviewer did not see any conflict between this scientific conception of truth and his desire to enliven history for readers. On the contrary, by defining historical facts to include everyday life, this reviewer sought to emulate the appeal of novels. Through the details of everyday life, the historian could make history alive and vivid in the way that imagination did for fiction. As the reviewer put it, "We could '*live o'er*' the scene and 'be what we behold.'" Such details thus served as a substitute for the imagination, allowing the historian to achieve the vitality of the novel—specifically, its ability to re-create its subjects' experience of events—without sacrificing a commitment to factual truth. Sharing Thatcher's belief that history was both science and art, this reviewer suggested that truth required not just factual accuracy but also a vivid re-creation of the past.[77]

But how was the historian to uncover these details and put these prescriptions into practice? Reviewers for Thacher's history pointed to one of the means by which historians put prescriptions for this type of history into practice—local history. Thacher's was just the most prominent of the many local and town histories that proliferated beginning in the 1820s. These works included William Lincoln's *History of Worcester* (1837), Lemuel Shattuck's *History of Concord* (1835), Erastus Worthington's *History of Dedham* (1827), and John Watson's *Annals of Philadelphia* (1830), to name just a few.[78] Historians made only a limited attempt to enact their prescriptions for a history of social and domestic life, however, and they continued to emphasize political and military events when venturing beyond local topics.

While a Rankean ideal of historical truth contributed to the interest in social history by emphasizing the importance of fact, this ideal at the same time discouraged historians from acting on this interest. Peter Burke has argued that Ranke's scientific conception of history marginalized social history and restored the ascendancy of political history until the twentieth century. Ranke contributed to the prestige of political history by giving primacy to this subject in his own work. On a more fundamental level, the scientific methodology he promoted made the eighteenth-century concern with the history of manners appear unsystematic and unscientific, as these accounts were often impressionistic or speculative in character.[79] Not only did Ranke associate historical truth with facts; he also established more rigorous standards for authenticating historical facts. For Ranke, facts had to be substantiated by the evidence of primary sources, and only through a critical and systematic analysis of these sources could the historian determine what really happened in the past. Hence Ranke emphasized the importance of archival research. Although the desire for a critical analysis of primary sources was not inherently opposed to the study of social history, the limited sources on social history that were available at this time made it difficult for historians to write a work of social history that lived up to these standards.[80] And so, committed to an ideal of truth that made primary sources essential, historians for the most part continued to focus on political and military topics. The disparity between the theory and practice of social history thus revealed the tensions created by Ranke's scientific ideal of historical truth—between the concern with fact and the belief that primary sources determined what was a fact.

In one of the few systematic and comprehensive attempts to write "domestic history," Elizabeth Ellet revealed the dilemma this scientific conception of truth presented for social historians, and she provided her own solution to that dilemma. Ellet was a prolific author who wrote on a wide variety of topics, ranging from American history to original poetry and literary criticism. Her first major historical work was *Women of the American Revolution* (1848–50), a three-volume collective biography of women during the Revolution that ventured into social history by examining the lives of ordinary women. Her *Domestic History of the American Revolution* followed in 1850. This work represented an even more ambitious and self-conscious attempt by Ellet to re-create the history of social life during the Revolution. Ellet made this clear in the preface to the history, declaring that her goal was "to exhibit the spirit and character of the Revolutionary period; to portray, as far as possible in so brief a record, the social and domestic condition of the times, and the state of feeling among the people."[81]

Ellet structured her history in accordance with this goal. She not only depicted ordinary life during the Revolution; she also sought to integrate this subject into the conventional narrative of political and military events. After opening her history with a summary of the political developments preceding the rift between Britain and the American colonies, Ellet shifted her attention to the state of colonial society and devoted her fourth chapter to describing social life in this period. The rest of her history followed a similar pattern, alternating between discussions of conventional subjects like battles and military strategy and accounts of the domestic side to these events, which described the social experiences of different groups during the war, ranging from women camp followers to American military prisoners.[82]

Ellet sought to achieve her goal of re-creating the "social and domestic condition of the times" by using individual experiences to exemplify broader social trends. As she explained, "Wherever account is given of individual experience, it is for the purpose of showing what *many* did or suffered."[83] Women, in particular, were important to Ellet's analysis. Because she believed that social character depended largely on the influence of women, she repeatedly used comments and observations by women of the time to illuminate general social conditions. In a typical example, Ellet quoted extensively from the journal of an anonymous New Jersey woman in order to convey the brutality of British military campaigns in that state, explaining that this extract "shows something of the condition of that part of the country."[84]

Like other proponents of domestic history, Ellet was reacting to the popularity of fiction—especially that of historical novels—by broadening history in this way. And like those who advocated domestic history, she sought through social history to emulate the popularity and dramatic effect of the historical novel while maintaining history's distinctive claims to truth. Exclaiming over "the effect of a historical romance in impressing events on the memory," Ellet urged, "[H]ow much greater should be the advantage derived from domestic pictures drawn from *actual life* over those which are at best but admirable imitations!" Unlike novels, domestic history, because it depicted "actual life," was based on truth. And because it was true, domestic history would enable the historian not just to equal but to surpass historical romance in its effect on the reader. Ellet thus defined historical truth in opposition to the novel. She expressed her hostility to novels when she declared her "just aversion" to "the romancing trash under which, at the present day, the simple and picturesque—because simple—realities of our American story seem in danger of being buried." For Ellet, the problem with novels was not only that they threatened to divert popular attention from history; on a more fundamental level, she associated novels with "fanciful embellishment"—a quality that she emphatically disavowed in her history.[85]

In her hostility to "embellishment," Ellet shared Ranke's view that truth required only a simple account of the facts. Ellet made this view of truth clear in the preface to *Women of the American Revolution*. After pointing to the scarcity of sources on women's history, she was careful to emphasize that "the deficiency of material has in no case been supplied by fanciful embellishment." Instead, her history represented "a simple and homely narrative of real occurrences."[86] And like Ranke, Ellet emphasized the importance of primary sources in determining truth. For this reason, in both *Domestic History* and *Women of the American Revolution*, she repeatedly distinguished between what she called "tradition" and "authentic" history. Accordingly, she declared proudly of the *Domestic History*, "Not only has no aid of fiction been employed, but no traditional matter has been introduced, unless sustained by indisputable authority."[87] By "tradition" Ellet meant popular legends. She believed that, unless "tradition" was supported by "indisputable authority," it could not provide the historian with access to authentic truth, for this kind of knowledge was too apt to be distorted by the bias or ignorance of those individuals who passed down such traditions. In contrast, according to Ellet, because firsthand sources would provide the most reliable and accurate accounts of what had actually happened in the past, the evidence of primary sources constituted "indisputable authority" for the truth. As she explained in *Women of the American Revolution*, "Whatever has not been preserved by contemporaneous written testimony, or derived at an early period from immediate actors in the scenes, is liable to the suspicion of being distorted or discolored by the imperfect knowledge, the prejudices, or the fancy of its narrators."[88]

But even as Ellet emphasized her commitment to critical standards of scholarship and to a scientific conception of truth, she departed from those standards by looking beyond written records for her sources. Along with primary documents and secondary works on the Revolution, she turned to the descendants of women who had participated in the Revolution and used their reminiscences of their Revolutionary ancestors as sources for her research in *Women of the American Revolution*. While printed sources could provide her with information about women's actions, memory could tell her how women felt about such actions. Through memory, then, Ellet could access the private emotional world of women. She believed that memory could contribute to historical truth in this way because of her assumption that the emotional attachment of their descendants gave them insight into her subjects' characters; thus she identified feeling with truth. As Scott Casper puts it, Ellet "asserted the factuality of feeling: not only the significance of Revolutionary women's 'home-sentiment' but also the reliability of familial attachment as an historical source."[89]

Feeling was important to Ellet in another way—only by looking at their "state of feeling" could the historian understand the "spirit" of the people. In her *Domestic History*, Ellet revealed her interest in the "spirit" of the people when she justified her decision to pass over minor military details, "which form the bulk of almost every history of the war," by asserting that "a really better idea of the Revolution may be obtained from anecdotes that exhibit the spirit which was abroad among all classes, and which prompted to action, than from the most accurate transcript of the manoeuvres by which different battles were lost and won, and the most precise statement of the number engaged, or of killed and wounded on either side." Not only did Ellet question the exclusive value of military history as a subject for historical study; her language here also suggested that precision and factual accuracy alone did not determine historical truth. No matter how "accurate" or "precise" the historian's account of military events, for Ellet, the historian could better convey the truth about the Revolution by examining the more intangible domain of spirit and feeling. Ellet thus extended the Romantic emphasis on experience and feeling over action beyond the individual to society as a whole and brought together in her own way Romantic and scientific conceptions of historical truth. Although her concern with revealing "actual life" and "real occurrences" suggested that the historian would achieve truth by uncovering the objective reality of the past, Ellet at the same time recognized the subjective element to truth in her appeal to sentiment and feeling.[90]

Such an approach was necessary not just to compensate for the scarcity of sources on her subject; it also served a social function, for, by taking this approach, Ellet sought to legitimize her status as a woman writing history at a time when the ideology of domesticity excluded women from the public world of historical scholarship. History was public in two senses—with the act of publishing a historical work, the historian entered the public arena, and the subject matter of history had traditionally focused on public affairs. Domestic ideology divided the world into two sharply differentiated realms—the public and the private—and assigned different roles for women and men based on beliefs about natural gender differences. If men were by nature rational, women were emotional. According to the canons of domesticity, the private realm was a refuge from the competition and selfishness that characterized the public arena. Men were best qualified to reign over the public arena, whereas women's special piety, purity, submissiveness, and domesticity fitted them for the private sphere of the home. By glorifying the private sphere as a specifically feminine preserve, the cult of domesticity simultaneously empowered women and legitimated their exclusion from the polity.[91]

Ellet revealed the double-edged character of domestic ideology in her approach to history. Because domestic ideology associated women with emotion, Ellet, like Warren, suggested that, as a woman, she was especially well equipped to access this realm in her history. In this way, she used domestic ideology to challenge women's exclusion from the public arena of historical writing. Likewise, by focusing on the private realm of everyday life, Ellet both challenged and upheld the assumptions of domesticity. As she did so, she illuminated another reason for the reluctance of historians to actually write social history—their ambivalence about the relationship between gender and historical truth. In arguing that historical truth had to include domestic history, historical writers threatened to feminize truth itself. The very terms that historical writers used to speak of social history, such as "domestic history" or the "gossip of history," pointed to the feminine associations of this kind of history. These associations in turn reflected the assumptions of domestic ideology, which identified the private realm with women. Because of these associations, however, male historians were reluctant to enact their prescriptions for more social history, since they still defined historical truth in masculine terms. In writing domestic history, then, Ellet at once challenged this masculine definition of truth and reinforced the feminine associations of domestic history. If the private realm was the feminine sphere, then it followed that women would be especially well suited to writing a history of private life. In this way, even as Ellet emphasized the importance of domestic history, she contributed to its marginalization by male historians.[92]

Yet if Ellet in some ways upheld the division of history into separate realms for men and women, she at the same time blurred the boundaries between masculine and feminine in her definition of historical truth. By emphasizing her commitment to a scientific ideal of truth that gave primacy to factual accuracy, she sought to demonstrate that her work possessed the same authority as that of male historians who embraced that ideal. In doing so, Ellet undermined the masculine associations of this ideal and suggested that women too could access historical truth. In turn, by asserting that true history had to take into account what was conventionally considered the feminine world of emotion and private life, she implied that this world was not solely the domain of women. Thus, as she sought to integrate political with social history, and the female world of sentiment with the male world of critical scholarship, she redefined truth itself as both masculine and feminine.[93]

"Entertainment with instruction": Biography and the "Dignity of History"

As much as they insisted on the need for more domestic history, most of Ellet's contemporaries continued to write about the history of public affairs. In doing so, they upheld the traditional belief in the "dignity of history"; this doctrine differentiated between history and biography and identified the private sphere with biography. And so, in their discussions of the relationship between history and biography, antebellum historical writers revealed yet another reason for their reluctance to write about private life—their continued attachment to classical republican assumptions about the primacy of public virtue, which persisted and coexisted uneasily with the liberal conception of virtue as a private quality. Ultimately, then, in their debates about the scope of historical inquiry, these historians were also contending over the nature of the historian's moral function. Even though all these historians agreed on the moral dimension to truth, they revealed in their ambivalence about the locus and meaning of virtue tensions and conflicts over who was supposed to benefit from the historian's moral lessons and over how to convey those lessons. Jared Sparks illuminated the nature of these tensions in his concern that historians would limit the audience for their moral lessons by privileging the public sphere as their proper domain. As he sought, through biography, to balance the "dignity" of the public sphere with popularity, Sparks revealed both the extent of his willingness to redefine truth in response to the novel and the limits to that redefinition. If Sparks defined truth in opposition to the novel by making truth an account of fact, unembellished by the historian, he at the same time sought to achieve the popularity of the novel by giving the historian an active role in presenting and interpreting truth.

In focusing on the public arena, antebellum historical writers adhered to traditional generic distinctions between biography and history and to the closely related belief in the "dignity of history." The traditional hierarchy of genres assigned to history and biography distinct, but related, functions. In this hierarchy, the province of biography was the private realm, whereas the domain of history was the public. Because of the primacy traditionally accorded to the public arena, history was considered a higher genre than biography. The concept that encapsulated this view of history was the belief in the "dignity of history." According to this doctrine, because history was supposed to possess a certain gravity and decorum, only public events were serious and important enough to be worthy of the historian's attention. Therefore, for the historian to delve into the world of private life would not befit the "dignity of history." This characterization of history was predicated on the belief in the moral purpose of history and on classical republican assumptions about the primacy of civic virtue. If the purpose of history was to instill morality and virtue, and if the highest form of virtue was the citizen's willingness to sacrifice for the public good, then the best way to convey lessons of public virtue was by focusing on the history of public affairs.[94]

This view of history was hierarchical and exclusionary in its social implications, for republican ideology excluded from the public realm all who lacked the independence necessary for virtue. Thus, by restricting the subject matter of history to the public realm, the belief in the dignity of history excluded all who could not participate in that realm, both as readers and as subjects. If history was supposed to convey moral lessons, and if the dignity of history prescribed that such lessons were to be drawn from the public actions of great political and military leaders, then the only people who could benefit from these lessons or act upon them were those who possessed a status comparable to that of the historian's subjects.[95]

Recognizing that the exalted character of history would make it difficult for most people to identify with the events it described, the British biographer Samuel Johnson urged the value of biography as a remedy for this problem. One of the most influential contributors to the theory and practice of biography in the eighteenth century, Johnson upheld and reaffirmed the distinction between history and biography by defining biography as a chronicle of the individual subject's private life. According to Johnson, "the business of the biographer is often to pass slightly over those performances and incidents, which produce vulgar greatness, to lead the thoughts into domestick privacies, and display the minute details of daily life, where exterior appendages are cast aside, and men excel each other only by prudence and virtue." For Johnson, because biography was supposed to focus on everyday private life, the lessons it could offer were more relevant and interesting to ordinary people than the lessons offered by history. In his claims for the value of studying private life, Johnson thus questioned the belief in the dignity of history and the assumption that the public orientation of history made it superior to biography. Rather than dignity, history, in its emphasis on "the motions of armies, and the schemes of conspirators" distant from the experience of most people, more often constituted the study of "vulgar greatness." In this way, Johnson's theory of biography contributed at once to the interest in the history of private life and to the continuing exclusion of this subject from most histories.[96]

Mason Locke Weems, one of the most popular American biographers in the early nineteenth century, was even more explicit about how a concern with private life would enhance the popular appeal of biography as he adapted Johnson's theory to an American context. As Weems explained why he had decided to focus on Washington's private virtues in his immensely popular biography of George Washington, first published in 1800, he reasoned, like Johnson, that ordinary people who would never have the chance to perform heroic deeds of leadership or military valor would find Washington's private character far more relevant to their own lives than his public character. Whereas, according to Weems, Washington's public actions were of little concern to children because few of them would achieve Washington's prominent public position, they would aspire to and identify with Washington's private virtues because "[i]n these, every youth is interested, because in these every youth may become a Washington—a Washington in piety and patriotism,—in industry and honour—and consequently a Washington, in what alone deserves the name, SELF ESTEEM AND UNIVERSAL RESPECT."[97]

Appealing to ordinary people was all the more imperative with the advent of "Jacksonian democracy" and the rise of a mass market for literature. Elites were deeply ambivalent about the growing importance of popular appeal in both literature and politics. They feared this development as a threat to their own authority, but they also recognized the need to accommodate the rise of democracy. If political power rested increasingly with the "common man," then a healthy republic depended on the virtue of ordinary people. But in order to instill virtue in the people, the historian and the biographer not only had to make their moral lessons accessible to ordinary people; they also had to compete successfully against the allure of novels by making their works equally entertaining.[98] American biographers to some extent succeeded in this goal, as the popularity of biography grew exponentially in America during the 1830s to a point that made one critic in 1830 term this trend "Biographical Mania." The products of this "mania" varied widely in form and content. They ranged from studies of single individuals, such as William Wirt's biography of Patrick Henry, to collective biographies like John Sanderson's multivolume work on the signers of the Declaration of Independence. If at one extreme stood semifictitious works like Weems's life of Washington, at the other were historical biographies, such as William Tudor's biography of James Otis and George Tucker's study of Thomas Jefferson, which possessed genuine pretensions to scholarship.[99]

Yet both critics of biography and biographers themselves were deeply ambivalent about the association between biography and the private sphere, and their ambivalence about this association explained why historians at once expressed such an interest in the domestic sphere and were so reluctant to act on that interest. As antebellum American critics differentiated between biography and history and argued for the value of biography as a genre affiliated with the private sphere, they revealed the growing importance of the private realm as a historical subject. The author of a review essay on American biography, published in 1827 for the *American Quarterly Review*, made just such a distinction between biography and history as he quoted from the English writer John Dryden and cited Dryden's view of biography as a form particularly suited to represent the trivial details of private life. The *American Quarterly* critic embraced the distinction that Dryden made between the private character of biography and the public orientation of history as he endorsed "the justness of the foregoing discrimination." The problem with modern biographers, however, was their inability to abide by Dryden's distinction, and the *American Quarterly* reviewer lamented the tendency of biographers to focus on public events at the expense of private life. Rather than restricting himself to the "public affairs of nations, only as they relate to his hero," the modern biographer "embraces almost every contemporary public concern, event, and character, of chief importance." In doing so, this critic suggested, biographers departed from their proper sphere and trespassed into the realm of history—the public arena. As a result, the biographer "rarely leads you into the private lodgings of the hero— never places before you the poor reasonable animal, as naked as nature made him; but represents him uniformly as a demi-god."[100]

In his complaint that biographers had included too much history at the expense of the individual subject, this reviewer expressed a refrain common in early nineteenth-century American biographical reviews. Like this critic, reviewers in this period repeatedly criticized biographies for neglecting the private domain and for paying too much attention to the public realm of history. In an 1832 review of Jared Sparks's biography of Gouverneur Morris, Oliver William B. Peabody lamented the widespread tendency of biographers to disregard private life: "There is no sin which more easily besets the biographer of public men, than a reluctance to admit the fact, that they ever had any private life; yet we know not that the dignity of a statesman would be impaired by such an admission, or that the parlor and the fire-side are much less interesting, than the cabinet or the legislative hall."[101] Upholding the distinction between the public realm of history and the private realm of biography, Peabody endorsed the English historian and biographer James Mackintosh's contention that "the biographer should introduce historical detail no farther, than the clearness and accuracy of his narrative require; and that the historian, on the other hand, should be careful to avoid all private particulars, which cannot be regarded as essential," as a "judicious one."[102]

Such complaints revealed that these critics shared Johnson's belief in the importance of studying private life. However, the distinction they made between biography and history still defined the private sphere as the realm of the biographer, not the historian, thus reinforcing the belief that the private sphere was below the dignity of history. And in pointing to the widespread unwillingness of biographers to actually write about private life, these complaints revealed that biographers themselves were ambivalent about the relationship between biography and the private sphere. Like historians, most biographers in this period concentrated on the public character and actions of individuals. Neither Tudor nor Austin, for example, delved at all into the private lives of Otis and Gerry, respectively, for their biographies of these figures. The disparity between the theory and practice of biography in this period thus revealed the ambivalence of American historical writers about the locus and meaning of virtue. If, in their criticisms of biography for focusing too much on public events, reviewers suggested that the most effective way to instill virtue was by turning to the private sphere, biographers, in resisting these strictures, revealed the persistence of the classical republican ideal of civic virtue and the difficulty of separating between private and public. And if even biographers, whose domain was supposed to be the private sphere, were unwilling to confine themselves to this realm, then it was all the more understandable why historians would be reluctant to depart from their traditional domain of public affairs and write about domestic history.[103]

Yet, as Jared Sparks, like Johnson and Weems, realized, by confining themselves to the public arena, both biographers and historians would find it more difficult to make their moral lessons relevant and interesting to ordinary people. Now best known for bowdlerizing George Washington's writings, Sparks was, during his lifetime, a well-respected historian of the American colonial and Revolutionary era and one of the leading biographers in this period. In addition to Washington's papers, Sparks edited the correspondence of other Revolutionary figures and wrote biographies to accompany these editions. Sparks also edited the *Library of American Biography*, a series of popular biographies about prominent figures in American history published during the 1830s and 1840s. Rather than turning to the private sphere as Weems and Johnson urged, Sparks sought to reconcile his desire for popular appeal with his belief in the primacy of the public sphere by collapsing the distinction between history and biography and embracing biography as a substitute for, not a supplement to, history. Through biography, Sparks believed, it was possible for the historian to achieve the appeal of novels without sacrificing the dignity of history or his commitment to truth. But in order to reconcile these imperatives, the historian had to take an active role in representing his subject. And so, even as Sparks's emphasis on the public sphere signified his commitment to a Rankean ideal of truth as an objective record of fact, he departed from that ideal as he acknowledged the historian's role in interpreting truth.[104]

Challenging the traditional distinction between biography and history, which privileged history over biography, Sparks argued for the value of biography as "only another form of history."[105] In his notes for a series of lectures on the study of history, Sparks elaborated on why he identified history with biography: "Biography tells the story of an individual; history is concerned with the affairs of men in society. History is the biography of a community of men taken as one body."[106] In his claim that history "is the biography of a community of men," Sparks echoed Thomas Carlyle's famous declaration that "[h]istory is the essence of innumerable biographies."[107] Even as historical writers continued to differentiate between history and biography, then, Sparks revealed the existence of a countercurrent that blurred the boundaries between these two genres.

Although he challenged the traditional distinction between history and biography, Sparks still believed firmly in the dignity of history. And so, in keeping with this doctrine, he believed that the proper sphere of history was public affairs. But because he viewed biography as another form of history, Sparks extended this belief to his biographical subjects, focusing on public, not private, life in his biographies. For Sparks, the dignity of history not only required the historian to confine himself to the public arena; it also meant that he had to protect the dignity of his subjects. These two concerns were closely related to each other, for the historian could best achieve the latter by avoiding personal matters that could take away from the dignity of his subjects. Yet not only did Sparks abstain from discussing private life; he also played a more active role in protecting Washington's dignity. Engaging in a practice that was controversial even in his own time, Sparks changed or omitted passages in Washington's letters to preserve his dignity. In addition to correcting grammatical errors, he altered slang expressions used by Washington—changing, for instance, "Old Put" to "General Putnam" and "but a flea-bite at present" to "totally inadequate to our demands at this time"—to make Washington seem more dignified.[108]

In 1851, the British historian Lord Mahon provoked a heated controversy over these editorial practices with a scathing attack on Sparks in the appendix to his *History of England*, accusing Sparks of "tampering with the truth of history."[109] Yet Sparks was no less committed to historical truth than Mahon was. If, in changing Washington's language, Sparks departed from the Rankean ideal of truth as an unvarnished account of fact based on documentary evidence, he at the same time revealed his commitment to this Rankean ideal as he explained why he had focused on the public arena in his biographies. Sparks believed that, as a form of history, biography had to adhere to the truth. And for him truth was based on the evidence of primary documents. Sparks paid little attention to the private life of his subjects because he believed that the scarcity of documents about the private life of individuals made it impossible for the historian to recover the truth about this subject. Sparks warned against writing biographies of ordinary individuals for the same reason. As he explained in his 1818 review of William Wirt's biography of Patrick Henry, when writing about an ordinary person, the biographer "is obliged to resort to his invention for incidents, and to his fancy for embellishments" because "his materials are few." Because for Sparks "invention" and "embellishment" were by definition opposed to historical truth, only by studying the public lives of prominent individuals could the historian achieve truth.[110]

Thus Sparks saw no conflict between his belief in the dignity of history and his commitment to a scientific conception of truth as unembellished fact, for both concerns contributed to his preoccupation with the public arena. In explaining why there were so few personal anecdotes in his biography of Washington, he declared, "I have seen many particulars of this description which I knew not to be true, and others which I did not believe." Sparks decided not to include such anecdotes because he did not want to relate "any fact for which I was not convinced there was credible authority." Sparks made it clear that his goal was to achieve both truth and dignity in taking this approach: "If this forbearance has been practised at the expense of the reader's entertainment, he must submit to the sacrifice as due to truth and the dignity of the subject." At the same time, this statement revealed the tensions that Sparks's desire for truth and dignity created for another goal—that of entertaining the reader. As Sparks here recognized, including more personal anecdotes would have made his work more entertaining to his audiences.[111]

Sparks did not believe that entertainment was inherently opposed to truth. On the contrary, he envisioned his *Library of American Biography* as a work that would be distinct from fiction in its adherence to truth while possessing the same ability to entertain and engage the reader. In the preface to *Library of American Biography*, he made these objectives clear when he declared that biography "admits of no embellishments, that would give it the air of fiction; and yet its office is but half done, unless it mingles entertainment with instruction."[112] Sparks here defined historical truth in opposition to fiction, for he viewed truth as a record of unembellished fact, and he associated fiction with "embellishment." At the same time, in his desire to make his work as entertaining as fiction, he redefined the historian's purpose in terms of fiction. As he revealed in his injunction to mingle "entertainment with instruction," entertainment was not just an end in itself; rather, it was inextricable from the historian's responsibility to offer the people moral guidance. Like other historians and biographers of his time, then, Sparks believed firmly in the moral function of truth. He therefore expressed agreement with "an old definition of history, that it is 'Philosophy teaching by example,'" reasoning that "[e]xperience is the great teacher of wisdom, and the best guide of conduct."[113]

As Sparks recognized, however, achieving this goal depended on the historian's ability to reach popular audiences. At a time when the commercialization of literature made popular appeal increasingly important, and when history had to compete with the novel for popular attention, Sparks realized that the historian could succeed in his purpose only by broadening the appeal of history and making it as engaging as novels. While the subject matter of his biographies reflected his belief in the dignity of history, Sparks modified this doctrine for a democratic context by challenging the assumption that only the elites could benefit from the lessons of history. Like Johnson, Sparks viewed biography as a genre that could convey moral lessons to a wider audience than that reached by traditional historical narratives. But unlike Johnson, Sparks did not believe that it was necessary to write about private life to make these lessons accessible to the people. Through literary artistry, not through private life, could the historian achieve popular appeal. In this way, Sparks believed, the historian could fulfill his moral purpose without sacrificing his commitment to factual truth. In 1832, as he described his plans for the *Library of American Biography* to George Bancroft, Sparks made his desire to balance factual truth with popular appeal explicit: "It is intended that much care shall be given to the literary execution, as well as the accuracy of facts, so that the work will have both authority, and attraction for readers."[114]

Although Sparks disavowed any role for embellishment in his biographies, he did believe in the importance of literary artistry, or "literary execution," as he called it, for only in this way could the historian make his work attractive to readers. If he viewed "embellishment" as opposed to truth, he did not see any conflict between "literary execution" and "accuracy of facts." For Sparks, then, history could not stand on its dignity alone; the historian had to play an active role in making its lessons accessible to readers. Writing in 1839, Sparks revealed how such a role would enhance the popular appeal of history in a reply to Alexander Slidell Mackenzie's query about how to approach his biography of Paul Jones. After distinguishing between different kinds of biography, Sparks recommended that Mackenzie write a personal narrative, "in which the individual is always kept before the reader, and the incidents are made to follow each other in consecutive order." According to Sparks, of the different types of biography, personal narrative "is the most difficult to execute, because it requires a clear and spirited style, discrimination in selecting facts, and judgment in arranging them so as to preserve just proportions."[115]

In his emphasis on the historian's "discrimination" and "judgment" in selecting and arranging facts, Sparks assigned to the historian an active role in interpreting historical facts. Such an approach would make his work easier to

follow and therefore more appealing to readers, as Sparks made clear when
he explained why Mackenzie should keep his extracts from Jones's letters to a
minimum: "You will be more successful by condensing the facts they contain
in your own language," Sparks wrote, for doing so would enable Mackenzie to
"hold your thread unbroken, and the reader will follow you with more ease
and pleasure." According to Sparks, the historian could put the facts in his own
language without distorting historical truth, for he embraced two seemingly
contradictory conceptions of truth—in his emphasis on factual accuracy, he
suggested that truth was supposed to be an account of objective facts that existed independent of the historian's interpretation; at the same time, he believed
that the historian was supposed to play an active role in interpreting truth for
the reader.[116]

Sparks brought together these two views of the historian's relationship to
truth as he summed up his ideal of a biography that was at once truthful, entertaining, and instructive in a letter to John Armstrong written in 1834. As Sparks
told Armstrong, he wished to avoid the two extremes "of writing biography;
long and short, dry and dull, by compiling letters & enumerating dates, or by
being imaginative & amusing at the expense of accuracy." Instead, Sparks's goal
was "that there shall be a strict regard to facts, but at the same time that the matter shall pass through the writer's mind and receive the impress of his thoughts."
Here, Sparks expressed his belief that a successful biography could and should
reflect the perspective of its author while remaining true to the objective reality
of the past. For him, if the historian balanced both these imperatives, the result
would be "to make a book that will be read, & contribute something to the
reader's improvement."[117]

"It is the artist only who is the true historian":
Imagination and Moral Truth

The southern writer William Gilmore Simms at once diverged from and conformed to his contemporaries' understanding of historical truth as he brought
together and went beyond all these different responses to the novel. Best known
as a novelist and as an exponent of southern sectional interests, Simms was also
a sophisticated historian who practiced and wrote about many different genres
of historical writing. He published a biography of Francis Marion, a history
of South Carolina, and numerous historical novels about the Revolution, in
addition to commenting on Romantic history and social history in the many
historical essays and reviews that he contributed to journals like the *Southern*

Literary Messenger and the *Southern Quarterly Review*.[118] While Simms shared Ellet's interest in social history and Prescott's desire to bring the past to life, he assigned a greater role to the imagination in achieving these goals than Ellet or Prescott did. Whereas other historians of his time—even those most committed to enlarging the contribution of the imagination to historical truth—were careful to ground their use of the imagination in fact, Simms privileged imagination over fact as a basis for truth when he likened the novelist to the historian. Yet even as he differed from his contemporaries in blurring the boundaries between history and the novel and in privileging the novelist's ability to access historical truth, he shared their belief in the moral character of truth. Paradoxically, Simms could challenge their belief in the factual basis for historical truth because of this shared commitment to the moral function of history. But even he could not entirely abandon the concern with fact, and in his novels he sought to reconcile in his own way his belief that the historian played a role in creating truth with a desire to recover the objective reality of the past.

In a favorable review of Ellet's history of women in the Revolution for the *Southern Quarterly Review*, Simms revealed his belief in the importance of domestic history as he applauded Ellet for her vivid reconstruction of southern society during the Revolution. Because social character was shaped largely in the household, he reasoned, a history of the domestic realm was necessary for understanding a nation's formative influences. Locating virtue in the private realm of the home, Simms proclaimed, "It is the family fireside—the source of all the virtues—that the lawgiver must first learn to protect and make grateful to the affections of those who seek warmth upon its hearthstones. Hence spring all the virtues and securities of a nation. . . . The household, in fact, is not only the source but the true guardian of the nation." Therefore, Simms concluded, "these domestic histories are really so many keys and clues to the history of the nation." He made explicit the feminine associations of domestic history when he argued that women were the best sources and chroniclers of this kind of history. Drawing on the assumptions of domestic ideology for his argument, Simms reasoned that "[i]t is the domestic histories which the mother finds it most easy to remember, and which she loves most to repeat."[119] Here, then, like Ellet, Simms at once marginalized domestic history by associating it with the feminine realm and recognized the interdependence between the private sphere of the home and the public realm of the "lawgiver."

Although Simms was more critical of Prescott's approach to history, he actually agreed with Prescott on both the artistic and moral character of history; he criticized Prescott because—contrary to Prescott's own understanding of his purposes—he believed that Prescott had emphasized the artistic element of history at the expense of its moral dimension. In an 1848 review of Prescott's *Conquest of Peru*, Simms divided historians into two main categories, the philosophical and the "simply narrative." Classifying Prescott among the latter, he could give only qualified praise to Prescott's history. Simms admired Prescott's artistic skill as a narrator but, like Parker, ultimately criticized his refusal to make the broader ethical judgments that characterized philosophical historians. In contrast to Prescott, the philosophical historian was "a philosopher, who chooses to take history for his subject of analysis, rather than morality or art,— and embodies these, as topics, to which his theme, is rendered tributary." Both required the exercise of the imagination, but in different ways. Philosophical historians like François Guizot and Jules Michelet, no less than their narrative counterparts, "employ the imagination, but it is in diving through the obscure, rather than in embodying the picturesque. Where the artistical narrator colors highly, they conjecture boldly." Thus, Simms suggested, whereas narrative historians like Prescott used the imagination to make their descriptions more vivid and picturesque, philosophical historians used the imagination to extract deeper moral truths by connecting and filling in the gaps left by the historical record. All the narrative historian did was to dramatize what was already known by telling a story; in contrast, the philosophical historian analyzed history for larger principles, making him more of an "essayist" than a "narrator." For this reason, although not indifferent to fact, the philosophical historian labors "not so much after details as principles" and "disdains minutiae in his search after generalities, and is better prepared with a speculation than a fact."[120]

Simms did not see philosophical and narrative history as mutually exclusive. On the contrary, for him, the historian would ideally unite both these approaches, and "[t]he record, thus appealing to superior faculties than those either of logic or conscientiousness, enables the historian to arrive at a three-fold triumph, when he crowns his story with a moral, in which truth prevails in the embrace of the beautiful." In suggesting that truth would prevail "in the embrace of the beautiful," Simms echoed the poet John Keats's famous pronouncement that "truth is beauty" and "beauty is truth." The "artistical" historian, according to Simms, would aid the philosophical historian in conveying the moral truths of history by using the imagination to make these truths more beautiful. Because Simms believed that the reader's aesthetic appreciation for beauty came from a faculty "superior" to "logic or conscientiousness," moral truth, when conveyed in this way, would have more of an effect on the reader than would an appeal to reason or abstract principle. Rather than seeing any conflict between imagination and morality, Simms believed that both were necessary for historical truth.[121]

While, like Prescott, Simms incorporated both imagination and morality into his definition of truth, he went much further than Prescott in expanding the role of the imagination in historical understanding; hence, he differed from Prescott and other historians of his time in his view of the relationship between history and what he called "romance." By romance, Simms meant historical novels like his own and Scott's. Unlike other historians of his time, who used the terms *novel* and *romance* interchangeably, Simms clearly differentiated between the novel and the romance in the advertisement to his novel *The Yemassee*, describing the romance as a "loftier" form than the novel, one that represented an "amalgam" of the novel and the poem. In contrast to the "domestic" novels of Richardson and Fielding, which were "confined to the felicitous narration of common and daily occurring events," the romance for Simms "seeks for its adventures among the wild and wonderful," giving it the sense of dramatic unity and excitement that characterized ancient epics. The subject matter of romance, centered as it was on the exotic and the extraordinary, according to Simms, thus gave it a heroic grandeur that distinguished it from the novel. The very distinction Simms made between romance and the novel revealed that he held historical novels (or what he would term romances) in higher esteem than did other historians of his time. And so, whereas his contemporaries differentiated between history and the novel by emphasizing the historian's commitment to fact, Simms blurred the boundaries between these two genres by emphasizing the contribution of the imagination to historical understanding.[122]

In an essay entitled "History for the Purposes of Art," published in 1845, Simms declared boldly that "it is the artist only who is the true historian," for the artist alone possessed the imagination to give coherence and life to otherwise disjointed and scattered historical materials. The artistic imagination was especially indispensable for bridging the many gaps in the historical record. Simms reasoned,

> For what is the philosophy of history but a happy conjecturing, of what might have been from the imperfect skeleton of what we know. The long analysis of probabilities keenly pursued through buried fragments and dissolving dust, is the toil of an active imagination, informed by experience, obeying certain known laws of study, and recognizing, as guiding rules, certain general standards of examination.[123]

Simms's contention that the artist could achieve a closer communion with the past than could the historian challenged the very basis for the historian's claim to superiority—the unique ability of history to reconstruct truth. Simms, unlike his contemporaries, did not believe that the historian possessed a monopoly on historical truth, for he differed from his contemporaries in his understanding of truth itself. For Simms, in contrast to Thatcher, historical truth was not just a matter of collecting facts because the historian's knowledge of these facts would always be imperfect and incomplete. Hence, according to Simms, all the historian could do was to take these limited facts—"the imperfect skeleton of what we know"—and use them to conjecture about "what might have been," a process that required "an active imagination." And because of the limits to the historian's factual knowledge, Simms could, in his description of history as the "long analysis of probabilities," conclude that it was impossible for the historian to achieve certain truth about what actually happened in the past.

Indeed, by equating the artist with the historian, Simms came close to arguing that history was itself a form of fiction, consisting of creative conjecture by the historian. He himself suggested how easily history could merge into fiction when he concluded tentatively "[t]hat much of most histories is built upon conjecture—that this conjecture, assuming bolder privileges, becomes romance—that all ages and nations have possessed this romance—that many ages and nations are now known only by its vitative agency."[124] As his reference to romance suggested, although Simms used the term artist broadly, he was particularly concerned with the romancer or novelist. He believed that the "privileges of the prose romancer" were "very superior" to those of other artists, for "his privileges combine, in turn, those of all the rest." Because history was largely based on conjecture, the line between history and "romance" was only a matter of degree. And because all it took for history to become romance was for conjecture to assume "bolder privileges," romance was all that many nations knew of their history. But if history was ultimately a form of romance, as Simms implied, then that could lead to the conclusion that it was impossible for the historian to access the real truth about the past or that there was no such thing as objective historical truth at all. Simms thus expressed a relativistic and subjective view of truth that sharply challenged his contemporaries' belief in an "authentic" truth that could be discerned and verified by the accumulation of facts.[125]

Paradoxically, however, Simms grounded this view of truth in conventional assumptions about the historian's moral function. As his discussion of "philosophical historians" indicated, he shared his contemporaries' view of history as a source of moral lessons. Nor was he any less committed than his contemporaries to the concept of absolute truth. What made possible Simms's permissive attitude toward conjecture and historical fact was his emphasis on the ethical content of truth. Specific historical facts and details were immaterial to him as long as the historian fulfilled his primary role of conveying these higher moral truths to the people. As he proclaimed, "We care not so much for the intrinsic truth of history, as for the great moral truths, which, drawn from such sources, induce excellence in the student." Identifying such facts with the "intrinsic truth of history," Simms distinguished between this type of truth and moral truth. Accuracy in history was unimportant because "[t]hat moral truth, educed by thought from conjecture, is one wholly independent of details." The historian would grasp these moral truths not by collecting facts but through conjecture.[126]

Recognizing the dangerous implications of Simms's argument for their understanding of truth, contemporary reviewers sharply attacked his essay. Because they identified fact with truth, they interpreted Simms's disregard for factual accuracy as a denial that the historian should or could aim to uncover the truth. Writing for the *North American Review* in 1846, Cornelius Conway Felton condemned Simms for privileging fiction over fact and for abandoning the historian's obligation to retrieve the truth. Felton derided Simms's "mania for fiction" as "a pernicious sentimentality, as much at war with genuine art as with the cause of truth." He challenged Simms's assertions of the "preeminence of art over history, of fiction over fact, of invention over truth," for, he believed, "[t]he truth of history is quite as interesting, and often more picturesque, than any romance that can be substituted for it."[127] In an even more severe assessment for the *Southern Literary Messenger*, George Atkinson Ward argued that Simms did not deserve the title "historian" at all because Simms's indifference to facts and details amounted to a repudiation of the essence of history itself—its foundation in factual truth. He jeered, "With us 'names and dates' are something in history, and they will continue to be so until the 'Yemassee' and 'Guy Rivers' become more authentic than the 'Conquest of Mexico,' and until the name of W. Gilmore Simms, as an historian, outshines that of William Prescott."[128] In their emphasis on fact, these reviewers revealed their belief in the existence of an objective truth that could be determined and verified by the historian.

Ward's article in turn provoked a staunch defense of Simms by William T. Sherman in a review for the *Southern Literary Messenger* in 1847. Sherman was no less committed than Simms's critics to the desire for objective historical truth; he differed, however, in seeing no contradiction between this ideal and Simms's assertion of the kinship between history and fiction. Accordingly, Sherman anxiously sought to refute Ward's charges that Simms favored a relativistic and subjective view of the past. Arguing that Ward had misinterpreted Simms and taken his statements out of context, Sherman assured readers that "[t]he purpose of the essay is nowhere to assail or to disparage history. The true is the absolute, and so acknowledged by the writer." He explained that Simms advocated resort to the imagination only in those cases where historical knowledge was lacking, and he "nowhere claims the right to pervert or to overthrow chronicles—claims nothing more than to provide where they fail." In Sherman's view, then, Simms was not trying to question the belief in an absolute truth or the assumption that this truth was based on fact; the imagination was supposed to supplement fact, not take its place.[129]

Simms confirmed this reading of his argument as he retreated from its more subversive implications in response to Ward's attack. In 1847, commenting on the controversy his essay had provoked, Simms clarified his position, emphasizing: "I am speaking in the character of the artist especially & not of the historian— . . . I am not disparaging the history which is known, but [am] suggesting the free use which the imaginative mind may make of that which is unknown, fragmentary & in ruins—the *debris* of history, and not the perfect fabric."[130] Not only did Simms limit the use of the imagination to the "debris" of history, that is, to areas where the facts were unknown; in differentiating between the "character of the artist" and the historian, he suggested that even these limited claims for the imagination applied only to artists. In doing so, he sharply diminished the role of the imagination in the historian's enterprise.

Simms had in fact been ambiguous and inconsistent on this point in the text of his essay. In contrast to the far-reaching character of his opening claims about the identity between the artist and the historian, the second part of his essay placed limits on the role of the imagination. Rather than equating history with romance, he distinguished between the historian's domain and the realm of the romancer and stressed that the "privileges of the romancer only begin where those of the historian cease." Simms restricted the romancer to obscure and undocumented periods of history, in which the danger of violating factual truth was minimal. He argued that "[a] certain degree of obscurity, then, must hang over the realm of the romancer" because the "events of history and of time, which he employs, must be such as will admit of the full exercise of the great characteristic of genius—imagination." Here, Simms at once privileged the imagination and associated it with the "realm of the romancer," not that of the historian. Simms continued, "He must be free to conceive and to invent—to create and to endow;—without any dread of crossing the confines of ordinary truth, and of such history as may be found in undisputed records." As his references to "ordinary truth" and "undisputed records" suggest, Simms did believe in the existence of an objective reality that could be accessed by the historian. The artist had to direct his imagination to areas where this kind of knowledge was lacking, for he could fully exercise his imaginative genius only if he was free from the restrictions imposed by actual reality. Not only did Simms relegate imagination and fact to separate realms; in pointing to how factual knowledge could inhibit the imagination, he suggested that the imagination and factual truth were in some sense opposed to each other.[131]

Simms's ambivalence about the importance of factual accuracy to historical truth and its relationship to the imagination was even more evident in his historical novels, especially his trilogy about the Revolution in South Carolina. He published the first novel in this series, *The Partisan*, in 1835. Simms followed this work the next year with *Mellichampe* and concluded the trilogy with *Katharine Walton* in 1851. He repeatedly stressed the fidelity of these novels to truth and their value as faithful representations of South Carolina's history. In using a work of fiction to represent the truth, Simms demonstrated and put into practice his belief in the ability of the imagination to illuminate truth. At the same time, his emphasis on the factual basis for these works demonstrated a persisting concern with historical accuracy and precision, a concern seemingly at odds with his strictures about the irrelevance of these attributes.[132]

Typical in this regard were Simms's claims about the historical veracity of *Mellichampe*, the second novel in this series. He was careful to emphasize that this work "is imbued with the facts, and, I believe, so far as I myself may be admitted as a judge, it portrays truly the condition of the time. The events made use of are all historical; and scarcely a page of the work . . . is wanting in the evidence which must support the assertion." For Simms, this evidence took two forms. "[T]he unquestionable records of history"—published histories and documentary sources—validated the status of his claims as fact. Equally important, "in the regard of the novelist," were "the scarcely less credible testimonies of that venerable and moss-mantled Druid, Tradition." Here, like Ellet, Simms emphasized the importance of both written documents and oral tradition in authenticating fact. But unlike Ellet, Simms suggested that his status as a novelist allowed him to draw on tradition without violating accepted standards of historical truth.[133] Simms found tradition especially useful as a source for social history. For this reason, he claimed for his novels a special ability to illuminate the "social aspects" of history, as he did in *Katharine Walton*. One of this work's merits, according to Simms, was its historically faithful portrayal of society in Revolutionary Charleston, for the "descriptions of life, manners, customs, movements, the social aspects in general, have all been drawn from sources as unquestionable as abundant. . . . The anecdotes, the very repartees, though never before in print, are gathered from tradition and authority."[134]

By using his novels to illuminate the history of social life, Simms offered his own solution to the scarcity of documentary sources on this subject—through the imagination, the historian could fill in the gaps left by the documentary record. And so, unlike Ellet and other proponents of domestic history, who saw the details of social life as a substitute for the imagination, Simms believed that the need to recover such details made the imagination all the more important. In the preface to *The Partisan*, he pointed to the role of the imagination in reconstructing this aspect of the past when he declared that imagination "only ventures to embody and model those features of the Past, which the sober History has left indistinct." For Simms, social history was just such an area left indistinct by conventional history, which was "too apt to overlook the best essentials of society" "in order to dilate on great events." As a result of this tendency, "a single favourite overtops all the rest . . . absorbing within himself all the consideration which a more veracious and philosophical mode of writing would distribute over states and communities, and the humblest walks of life." In contrast, he suggested, his novels represented a "more veracious" form of historical writing than conventional history because, as a novelist, he was free to use imagination and tradition to reconstruct the "essentials of society." By arguing that the novelist could, through the imagination, contribute not just to moral truth but also to truth in the sense of actual social experience, Simms reconciled an expressive theory of art—which privileged the role of the imagination in illuminating reality—with his belief in the existence of an objective reality independent of the observer.[135]

As Simms demonstrated, defining the relationship between history and the novel was much more than a question of form. In their debates about this relationship, historians were ultimately arguing over the meaning of truth itself. For historians in this period, there were three main components to historical truth: fact, imagination, and morality. But historians differed over the meaning of these attributes and over the relationship between them. While they disagreed over the relationship between the imagination and historical truth and over what constituted a historical fact, they agreed on the moral function of history. Paradoxically, this shared belief was at the root of their conflicts over historical truth, for they disagreed over how to realize the historian's moral purpose. If Romantic historians like Prescott saw no conflict between the imagination and the historian's moral function, his critics believed that privileging the imagination in this way undermined the historian's moral purpose. If advocates of social history sought to emulate the novel by redefining historical facts, most historians resisted these demands to broaden the scope of history because of their implications for definitions of morality, as Sparks demonstrated most clearly. At the same time, because of his commitment to the moral function of history, Sparks redefined the dignity of history to give the historian an active role in broadening the appeal of history. Simms went even further than Sparks in making truth a function of the historian's perspective as he challenged the distinction between history and fiction altogether. Yet he could embrace this seemingly radically subjective understanding of truth because he shared Sparks's belief in the moral character of truth.

Even as they differentiated between history and the novel, early nineteenth-century historians had to take into account the qualities associated with the novel—its use of imagination, its concern with the private sphere, and its popular appeal—as they struggled over the meaning of historical truth. The novel had other implications for their ideas about truth, for yet another distinguishing feature of the novel was the rejection of tradition and the embrace of newness, as revealed by the use of the very term *novel* to describe this genre. Defining the novel in terms of newness, the novelist William Hill Brown demanded in 1807, "What is a novel without novelty?"[136] The novel thus confronted historians with another challenge—how to achieve novelty and innovation without sacrificing their commitment to impartial truth—and the next chapter considers how they responded to this challenge.

CHAPTER THREE

"TO EXPRESS OLD THINGS IN A NEW WAY"

Originality and Impartiality in American Historical Methodology

Responding in 1836 to a proposal by Stephen Williams to write a biography of his father, John Williams, for the *Library of American Biography*, Jared Sparks informed Williams,

> The object is a strict *personal narrative*. . . . It should be written with spirit, and in a style that will attract readers. To this end, extracts should be avoided (or sparingly used) and every thing that will give it the appearance of a compilation, or a dry summary from books. In short, the whole matter should pass through the writer's mind, and be wrought into original composition. It will thus have a freshness, and an air of novelty, that are required by the present popular taste, which is not easily captivated by antiquity in its homely garb.

Sparks pointed to the growing concern with originality and uniqueness in the early nineteenth century as he emphasized the need for "novelty" and "freshness" in his advice to Williams. Sparks derived his desire for originality from an expressive theory of art, for his definition of originality presumed that the historian was an active agent of perception, rather than simply a mirror of external reality. He revealed this assumption when he declared that "original composition" required that "the whole matter should pass through the writer's mind." For Sparks, the historian would achieve uniqueness by playing an active role in interpreting his sources and imposing his own perspective onto his subject. At the same time, in his injunction to Williams that "[s]trict accuracy should be observed in stating historical facts," he expressed his desire for truth and revealed his assumption that truth required the historian to be faithful to factual reality. Sparks thus pointed to the dilemma that faced historians in his time—how to be original without sacrificing the belief that truth was based on the re-creation of the objective reality of the past. He also provided part of their solution to this dilemma as he urged Williams to include "full and exact" references and reminded him that "wherever quotations are made in the text, they should be carefully marked," for Sparks's contemporaries used citation to reconcile these two goals.[1]

As Sparks revealed in his concern with citation, early national historians were more sophisticated in their methodology than modern scholars have often assumed. Conventional accounts of American historiography have emphasized the undeveloped and unscientific state of historical methodology in this time, arguing that early national historians routinely plagiarized from other works and rarely employed footnotes. Contrary to this view, although plagiarism was a common practice for the Revolutionary historians, their successors of the early nineteenth century developed increasingly rigorous standards for citation that stigmatized plagiarism. This development went hand in hand with the growing importance of primary sources to historians in this period. Through footnotes, the historian would not only acknowledge his sources; he could also demonstrate that he had based his research on primary documents.[2] Sharing Sparks's desire for both originality and impartial truth, early nineteenth-century historians put such a premium on citation and primary sources ultimately as a way to signify their commitment to these ideals.[3]

Even as early nineteenth-century historical writers anticipated modern historians in their desire for originality and impartiality, their understanding of what these ideals entailed was very much a product of their own intellectual and cultural context. Specifically, in his belief that originality would enhance the popular appeal of his work, Sparks revealed how concerns about writing for a capitalist marketplace intersected with Romantic aesthetic theory to put a premium on originality for early nineteenth-century historians. If aesthetic and material considerations came together in precepts for originality, the view of history as art and the view of history as science converged in the desire for impartiality as historians of this period adhered to both the Romantic exaltation of subjective experience and the ideals of German critical scholarship in identifying truth with the use of footnotes and primary sources.[4]

Although they agreed on the importance of citation and primary sources as instruments for mediating between these imperatives, early nineteenth-century historians turned to different historical genres—ranging from chronological annals and documentary collections to Romantic narrative histories—to implement these dictates. Their differences over choice of genre in turn revealed the contested and complex meanings of originality and impartiality for historians in this period. Not only did early nineteenth-century historians disagree over how to put these ideals into practice; they also differed over the very meaning of these ideals and their relationship to each other. Even as impartiality and originality converged in demands for footnotes and primary documents, there were also tensions between these two ideals, for, as Sparks revealed, they signified different views of the relationship between the historian and truth. If the ideal of impartiality implied that truth was an entity independent of the historian, the concern with originality suggested that the historian actively shaped historical truth and that truth varied according to each individual's perspective. Rather than being mutually exclusive, however, these two conceptions of the historian's role were integrally related to each other for historians in the early nineteenth century.

"For the establishment of their verity": Plagiarism, Originality, and the Meaning of Authorship and Truth in Revolutionary Historical Writing

The Revolutionary historians varied widely in their approach to citation, and their attitudes toward plagiarism were more diverse and complex than modern scholars have acknowledged. Although many of these historians did plagiarize by copying from other sources without citation or attribution, some of them began to recognize plagiarism as an offense and provided footnotes that cited their sources. In their inconsistency on the issues of plagiarism and citation, the Revolutionary historians revealed the contested meaning of authorship in this period and their ambivalence about the historian's authorial role. If, in their acceptance of plagiarism, they subscribed to a view of the author as a compiler of the words and ideas of other writers, their repudiation of this practice signified the emergence of an ideal of originality that privileged the author's individual perspective. This ambivalence was most evident in John Marshall, who revealed how his understanding of impartial truth at once contributed to and limited both his commitment to citation and his conception of originality.

According to modern canons of scholarship, plagiarism occurs when a writer takes material from another author and passes this material off as his or her own creation. Plagiarism can involve simply the theft of ideas and arguments from another writer, as well as the specific words and language used by that writer. The conventional view of plagiarism as a transhistorical standard that could be used to assess the legitimacy and value of a literary work was predicated on the ideal of the autonomous author—that is, on the notion of the author as the individual creator of a text. Yet as modern scholars have begun to complicate this conception of the author, pointing to the cultural processes involved in literary production and characterizing the very idea of authorship as the product of certain historical conditions, they have also begun to historicize the concept of plagiarism. If the idea of the author was a historical construct, then so too was the belief that an individual who copied from other writers could not be considered a "true" author. Derived from the word *plagiary*, which had traditionally been used to mean a kidnapper, the term *plagiarism* was not used to denote literary or artistic theft until the seventeenth century. While plagiarism had become an increasingly prevalent concern by the mid-eighteenth century, it was still a hotly contested issue. Not only did writers disagree over what constituted plagiarism; the very concept of plagiarism as a literary offense had not yet fully taken hold in this period.[5]

The Revolutionary historians reflected these conflicts over the idea and meaning of plagiarism in the their inconsistent approach to citation. Plagiarism in the modern sense was commonplace among these historians, and it took many forms. Sometimes these historians plagiarized by paraphrasing or summarizing another source without acknowledging that source. Sometimes they plagiarized even more directly, copying long extracts almost verbatim without using footnotes or quotation marks to distinguish these appropriations from their own writing. William Gordon plagiarized in this way from the *Annual Register*, an English Whig journal that chronicled yearly British political and diplomatic developments. In the preface to his history of the Revolution, published in 1788, Gordon did make a general acknowledgment of his debt to the *Annual Register*. Beyond that, however, he rarely indicated specifically where he had used other sources or identified those sources in the body of the text. He openly admitted to extracting from the *Annual Register* without specific attribution, revealing that such plagiarism was a conventional and sanctioned practice. He declared, "That Register and other publications have been of service to the compiler of the present work, who has frequently quoted from them, without varying the language, except for method and conciseness."[6] Following his lead, other historians of this generation plagiarized directly from the *Annual Register*, from Gordon himself, or from one another. Even David Ramsay, one of the most important and highly regarded historians of this era, copied from Alexander Hewat's history of South Carolina for his history of that state and from Gordon and the *Annual Register* for his history of the Revolution. For example, in his account of the mutiny by Pennsylvania soldiers in 1781, he copied almost word for word from Gordon's history.[7]

As they engaged in this practice, the Revolutionary historians conformed to traditional assumptions about the historian's role and about authorship in general. Beginning with the ancients, it had been standard practice for historians to assemble their own works by appropriating and combining extracts from other histories, generally without citation or even quotation. Such an approach was also part of a larger matrix of beliefs about the nature of authorship, which placed little premium on originality in the modern sense of innovation and singularity. The roles of author and editor had traditionally been almost indistinguishable from each other; the author's function was not to create a new and unique work of his own but to integrate and diffuse the words and ideas of his predecessors. This conception of authorship was consistent with the neoclassical view of the artist as a mirror, whose purpose was to reflect the external world and conform to universal standards and ideals, not serve as a vehicle for creative individual expression. This definition of authorship thus made it possible for the Revolutionary historians to copy from other writers without viewing such appropriations as plagiarism.[8]

Because he embraced this traditional view of authorship, the historian John Lendrum saw nothing wrong with copying from other writers in this way. In the preface to his history of the Revolution, published in 1795, he explained his approach to sources by stating that for his discussion of the colonial period "the authorities are quoted." In the rest of the work, however, "it was thought unnecessary to swell it with quotations." Instead, "[t]he compiler has endeavoured to unite brevity with perspicacity; and has accordingly abridged the matter from his authorities, as he judged necessary." As the term "compiler" revealed, Lendrum subscribed to an editorial conception of authorship. His goal as a historian was to collect and bring together information from other sources, not originate his own ideas or interpretation of those sources. This definition of the historian's role in turn allowed Lendrum to appropriate the language and interpretations of other writers without scruple. For this reason, he could conclude by admitting, "He has likewise frequently used the words as well as the ideas of the writers, without particularly apprizing the reader of it." Yet Lendrum was not entirely consistent in his treatment of citation. Although he frequently copied without attribution and openly confessed to doing so, he also sporadically provided footnotes throughout his history. Likewise, at least some of Lendrum's contemporaries demonstrated a limited regard for citation. Mercy Otis Warren, for example, occasionally footnoted her sources in her history of the Revolution, and Jeremy Belknap supplied citations on a regular basis throughout his history of New Hampshire.[9]

Indeed, although not a standard practice among eighteenth-century historians, footnotes were far from unknown to them. Writing contemporaneously with the Revolutionary historians was one of the best-known practitioners of the art of the footnote—Edward Gibbon. The forerunners to Gibbon in this practice traced back at least to the seventeenth century, when Pierre Bayle set an influential precedent with the meticulous and exhaustive footnotes of his *Historical and Critical Dictionary*. The Revolutionary historians' regard for citation gained added urgency from the broader cultural campaign against plagiarism that took hold during the second half of the eighteenth century. Footnoting sources increasingly became an imperative as accusations of plagiarism proliferated to become a widespread cultural preoccupation in this period. Paul Revere and Thomas Jefferson were just two of the most notable figures implicated in such charges when critics questioned the originality of Revere's engraving of the Boston Massacre and Jefferson's authorship of the Declaration of Independence.[10]

The crusade against plagiarism was a symptom of changing attitudes toward originality, which began to develop its modern meaning during the eighteenth century. The term *original* had traditionally possessed a retrospective meaning, derived from its root word, *origin*, and referred to the earliest stage or source of a subsequent development. By the eighteenth century, *original* acquired an additional meaning as something new and innovative. In an important sign of this shift, Edward Young's *Conjectures on Original Composition*, published in 1759, used the word *original* in this new sense as Young argued for the value of originality over imitation. In Young's oft-quoted words: "[A]n *Original* . . . rises spontaneously from the vital root of *Genius*; it *grows*, it is not *made*: *Imitations* are often a sort of *Manufacture*, wrought up by those *Mechanics*, *Art*, and *Labour*, out of pre-existent materials not their own." The emergence of the term *originality* as an expression of praise embodied the growing premium on uniqueness and novelty, which in turn entailed a transformed definition of the author's function. No longer was it sufficient for the author to collate and assemble the ideas of others; he had to create something new and singular, making plagiarism a doubly ignominious offense. In copying from other writers, the plagiarizer not only diminished and violated the individuality of their works; he also displayed his own lack of originality.[11]

And so, new and old conceptions of originality and authorship coexisted uneasily with each other in this period, often coming together even in the same individual, as the eminent jurist and historian John Marshall demonstrated. Although best known for his constitutional decisions as chief justice of the Supreme Court, Marshall also wrote a five-volume biography of George Washington, the first volume published in 1804 and the last in 1807. Although he had "compiled" his work primarily from Washington's correspondence, Marshall admitted that Washington's correspondence did not provide information about all the facts related to Washington's life. He confessed frankly in the preface to this work, "Such facts have been taken from the histories of the day, and the authority relied on for the establishment of their verity has been cited. Various publications have, for this purpose, been occasionally resorted to, and are quoted for all those facts which are detailed in part on their authority." Marshall continued, "Their very language has sometimes been employed without distinguishing the passages, especially when intermingled with others, by marks of quotation; but, in such instances, the book is cited in the margin." Marshall was hopeful "that his public declaration will rescue him from the imputation of receiving aids he is unwilling to acknowledge, or of wishing, by a concealed plagiarism, to usher to the world as his own, the labours of others."[12]

As this statement demonstrated, Marshall did not condone plagiarism. In his desire to preempt accusations of plagiarism, he displayed a limited concern with individuality and originality. When he expressed his regret at "the impossibility of giving to the public, in the first part of this work, many facts not already in their possession," he revealed his own desire for originality and uniqueness. Because other writers had studied the Revolutionary War so thoroughly, Marshall admitted that on this subject, "the author can promise not much that is new. He can only engage for the correctness with which facts are stated." As much as he would have liked to have presented something new, for Marshall, fidelity to known facts was more important than originality. In his emphasis on factual "correctness," Marshall suggested that historical truth was based on the accumulation of facts. The idea that the historian could achieve originality through his interpretation of the facts was inconceivable to Marshall, for he assumed that truth was an objective entity independent of the historian's interpretation. In this way, his understanding of truth limited the scope of his desire for uniqueness and individuality.[13]

Marshall made the limits to his concern with originality even clearer by continuing to practice what would now be considered plagiarism and openly admitting to this practice. He could both plagiarize and deny that he was guilty of this practice because his definition of plagiarism differed from that of modern scholars. Copying the words of others did not in itself constitute plagiarism for Marshall. In his willingness to use the language of other historians, without distinguishing their language from his own, he subscribed to the traditional conception of the author as a compiler of other historians' words, rather than a purely innovative creator of his own ideas. In his view, such an approach would be illegitimate only if the historian concealed his reliance on other writers. Thus for Marshall plagiarism was an offense more because it involved deception than because it violated the individuality of other authors.[14]

Ultimately, then, Marshall's understanding of plagiarism and his approach to citation were rooted in his desire for impartial truth and his assumption that truth was a matter of recovering the factual reality of the past. Even though he did not use quotation marks to indicate where he was using the language of other writers, he was careful to emphasize that he did cite the books from which he took these passages. In making this distinction, Marshall implied that the authors of these works deserved acknowledgment for the content rather than the form of what they wrote. Because he assumed there was nothing unique about the language they used, there was no need for him to distinguish their language from his own. This assumption revealed Marshall's attachment to a mimetic rather than an expressive theory of art in which the language of the artist expressed and reflected his unique perspective. Marshall viewed the historian as a mirror, whose goal was to reflect the external reality of the past. Since he believed that the historian could achieve this goal by gathering facts from other sources, what was important for Marshall was the facts these works had provided, not how they were presented. In this way, Marshall suggested, truth was based on the accumulation of fact, and this imperative took precedence over originality. And by citing the works from which he had taken these facts, he hoped to verify and strengthen his claims to truth, for he viewed these works as authority "for the establishment of their verity." Thus, Marshall's desire for truth both limited and contributed to his willingness to acknowledge other authors.[15]

"The men are visible in their work": Gender, Impartiality, and the Limits of Originality

For the Revolutionary historians, then, originality and impartiality at once coexisted and conflicted with each other, as Hannah Adams demonstrated even more clearly in her heated dispute with Jedidiah Morse and Elijah Parish over their use of her *Summary History of New England*, published in 1799. This was a conflict not only over who was guilty of plagiarism but also over what plagiarism meant in practice. In her understanding of what constituted plagiarism, Adams revealed both her desire for originality and the limits to that desire. Although Adams privileged the historian's individual perspective in her concern with originality, she would only go so far in expressing that perspective, for only by effacing her identity as an individual could she justify her intrusion into the male domain of history and further her claims to truth. And so, if Adams's definition of truth, like Marshall's, limited her conception of originality, she differed from Marshall in her concern with the gender connotations of truth.

Adams's plans for an abridgment of her *Summary History* precipitated her involved and heated dispute with her fellow historians Morse and Parish.

This dispute became so heated in part because both sides shared the same concerns—namely, both sides objected strongly to plagiarism, believing that this practice violated their own claims to originality. Adams took strong exception to the abridged history of New England that Morse and Parish published in 1804, considering it a potential rival to her own projected abridgment. In Adams's view, Morse and Parish had willfully encroached on her prior claim to publication and diminished the value of her work. In consequence, she believed, the sales of her own abridgment, published the following year, had suffered materially from the competition with their work. As this controversy escalated, the charges against Morse and Parish spiraled to include plagiarism—specifically, that they had used Adams's writings without proper acknowledgment. Although Adams denied making this accusation, she endorsed its substance and found herself unable to "absolve him [Morse] from blame in regard to the use he made of my published work, taken in connection with the manner in which he mentions it in the Preface to his History."[16]

In turn, such insinuations incensed Parish. He responded angrily to a letter from Adams, "Excuse me, Madam, you do not, you can not, mean to insinuate that I have copied yours [work]." He went on to rebut these charges by observing, "I well recollect writing your name as an authority, sometimes when the thing taken was an extract you had made from another: and it would perhaps have been more exact to have inserted another name: but this I did, to show my respect for you, and to keep your book in view." Parish's response implied that Adams, if anyone, had been the one guilty of copying and plagiarizing from others. As this indignant refutation and the allegations themselves revealed, contestants on both sides alike disapproved of plagiarism.[17]

There were indeed some grounds for Parish's accusation. After listing the histories she had examined for her *Summary History of New England*, Adams openly admitted to copying from them when she declared, "In abridging the works of those excellent authors, she is sensible of her inability to do them justice, and has sometimes made use of their own words."[18] In failing to identify these passages with quotation marks, Adams had in fact committed what would now be considered plagiarism. At the same time, Adams revealed her genuine commitment to citation in identifying her sources in brief, but consistent, footnotes throughout her *Summary History* and her later abridgment of this work. Her understanding of what constituted plagiarism thus differed from modern definitions of this concept. For Adams, like Marshall, as long as she acknowledged the sources of her information, there was no need to differentiate their specific words from her own. And so, in her hostility to plagiarism, Adams subscribed to a modern conception of authorship that gave primacy to originality and uniqueness and displayed some sense of ownership in her work as her individual creation. But in her definition of plagiarism, she revealed that she would only go so far in viewing historical writing as an expression of the author's individuality.

Thus Adams still adhered to a traditional view of the author as editor when she used the term "abridging" to describe her work as a historian. She did not consider it plagiarism to merge the language of others with her own because her goal was not to create a work entirely anew. Referring to herself as a "compiler," like Lendrum, she sought to condense and synthesize the words of other writers. Yet if Adams embraced a traditional understanding of the historian's role, she used this view of her role for subversive purposes. Specifically, she adopted this conception of authorship partly because of her concerns as a woman writing history at a time when conventional gender assumptions excluded women from this realm. History was considered the province of men, for women, as beings governed by the passions, were supposed to lack the rational capacity necessary for this kind of intellectual enterprise. Adams at once upheld and subverted these assumptions as she appealed to prevailing beliefs about female inferiority to defend against charges of plagiarism and used a traditional conception of authorship to counter doubts about whether she was qualified to write history.[19]

As she went on to explain why she had copied more extensively from other writers in her account of the Revolutionary War, Adams apologized that "her ignorance of military terms has rendered it necessary to transcribe more literally from the words of the authors" in this section "than in the other parts of the history. But though a female cannot be supposed to be accurate in describing, and must shrink with horror in relating the calamities of war, yet she may be allowed to *feel a lively interest in the great cause, for which the sword was drawn in America.*" As a woman, whose delicate nature and unfamiliarity with the male realm of war made it impossible for her to comprehend the horrors of battle, Adams reasoned, she could not be expected to accurately describe the Revolutionary War on her own. For this reason, she felt justified in copying from other authors for those sections of her work; in her view, such an approach would ensure a more accurate account of this event. Like Marshall, then, Adams believed that it was acceptable and even necessary to copy from other historians if doing so would contribute to truth. But unlike for Marshall, concerns about truth and gender intersected for Adams, as she also defended her appropriation of other works by appealing to conventional assumptions about women's fragility and weakness. In this way, she simultaneously defined historical truth as a male preserve and suggested that it was possible for a woman to access the truth by copying from male authors.[20]

Adams demonstrated even more clearly how she used a traditional conception of authorship to legitimize her claims to truth as she concluded with an
even more self-deprecating apology for her history. She acknowledged, "The
compiler is apprized of the numerous defects of the work, and sensible it will
not bear the test of criticism," and she expressed the hope that her readers
would be generous to "the assiduous, though, perhaps, unsuccessful efforts of
a female pen." But even while expressing doubts about the merits of her work,
Adams sought to give authority and legitimacy to her history by portraying
herself as a "compiler." Her history was not just a single woman's rendering of
past events; rather, as a compilation, it represented the accumulated wisdom of
other authors. And, as she made clear by listing the particular historians she had
used—Jeremy Belknap, Benjamin Trumbull, David Ramsay, William Gordon,
George Minot, Samuel Williams, James Sullivan, and Jedidiah Morse—she was
drawing specifically on the wisdom of male historians. Indeed, for Adams, considering "her inability to do them justice," the intellectual superiority of these
male authors at times made it necessary for her to copy their language, for only
by doing so could she successfully convey their insights. Here, then, even as she
deferred to the assumption of female weakness and inferiority, Adams validated
her credentials as a historian in defiance of traditional prohibitions on female
authorship. In this way, she at once accepted and subverted the designation of
history as the province of men.[21]

An 1805 review of Morse's history in the *Monthly Anthology* directly connected Adams's editorial conception of authorship to the desire for truth as it
emphasized the importance of impartiality. Taking Adams's side in this controversy, the reviewer criticized Morse for failing to acknowledge his debt to her
Summary History. In making this criticism, the reviewer demonstrated some
regard for originality, for he recognized Adams's history as her individual creation. In doing so, this reviewer, like Adams, subscribed to an ideal of authorship that privileged the historian's individual perspective. At the same time,
however, he firmly avowed his commitment to an ideal of impartiality that
required the historian to obscure that perspective as he criticized Morse's history for its failure to be impartial. Whereas Adams's history was "a clear and
unbiassed narration of facts," declared this critic, Morse's work was "tinctured
with the spirit of bigotry." While, as this critic concluded, "[t]he judicious and
impartial author of the Abridgement conceals herself; in the Compendious
History the men are visible in their work." For the reviewer, then, Adams was
more impartial because she, unlike Morse, had effaced her authorial presence
in the text. In this way, even while the *Monthly Anthology* critic united a desire

for impartiality and originality, he revealed the tensions between these ideals, for he associated impartiality with a conception of the historian's role that went directly counter to the dictates of originality.[22]

"Every historian should have his own character": Annals, Accuracy, and Impartiality

Thus, although both Marshall and Adams showed some concern with originality, their understanding of impartial truth limited the extent and nature of that concern. By the early nineteenth century, however, originality had become an increasingly important ideal for American historians.[23] Yet these historians did not embrace originality at the expense of impartial truth. On the contrary, as originality became more of a concern for them, so too did impartiality. The annalistic histories published by Abiel Holmes and John Leeds Bozman revealed the integral relationship between these two ideals for historians in the early nineteenth century. As a genre whose purpose was to provide a chronological account of events without explaining or giving coherence to those events, annals seemed to embody the concept of the historian as an impartial chronicler of facts by completely effacing the historian's perspective.[24] While nothing seemed more contrary to these chronological accounts than a concern with the historian's individual expression, Holmes and Bozman viewed historical truth as a function of individual perspective to a greater extent than their Revolutionary predecessors did. Holmes reconciled these two seemingly contradictory visions of the historian's role through citation, using footnotes to at once express and suppress the historian's individual perspective. In the end, rather than undermining their commitment to impartiality, Holmes's and Bozman's recognition of the subjective element to historical understanding actually reinforced and furthered their belief in the existence and attainability of objective truth. As Holmes and Bozman revealed, then, early nineteenth-century historians could bring together impartiality and originality because they defined impartial truth itself differently than did their Revolutionary predecessors to allow for a greater degree of subjectivity.

Plagiarism became an increasingly touchy subject for historians writing in the 1820s; they used accusations of plagiarism to criticize their rivals, turning such charges into a common form of imputation. For example, these historians sought to differentiate themselves and demonstrate their own concern with citation by accusing their Revolutionary predecessors of plagiarism. Simply in the need to differentiate themselves from their predecessors, these historians revealed their desire to be unique and original. If the Revolutionary historians were not as indifferent to footnotes as their successors claimed, historians of the 1820s were overall more exacting and self-conscious about their use of citation, as Abiel Holmes demonstrated. Holmes made the first major attempt at a comprehensive history of the United States with his *Annals of America*. A Congregational minister from New England born in 1763, just as the Revolutionary crisis was beginning, Holmes published the first edition of the *Annals* in 1805 and the second in 1829. In his *Annals*, not only did he provide far more detailed and extensive references than his Revolutionary predecessors did; he also used footnotes in different ways. Whereas the Revolutionary historians at most offered a brief reference identifying their sources, Holmes used his footnotes to assess as well as to cite his sources.[25]

Holmes was himself conscious of this difference, as he made clear in an 1818 review of David Ramsay's *History of the United States*. Taking Ramsay to task for the deficiency of his citations, Holmes revealed why he was so concerned about footnotes. He criticized Ramsay for not citing his authorities, for "such an omission, especially where large and numerous paragraphs are literally copied from preceding writers, we cannot but think exceptionable." Holmes wished that Ramsay had "more uniformly taken the materials, and wrought them up with his own skilful hand." For Holmes, Ramsay's failure to do so detracted from the coherence and originality of his work, and Holmes concluded by "discountenancing a method of compiling history, which tends to cramp genius, to prevent originality of composition, to make, in short, mere copyists, instead of such historians as have rendered Greece and Rome immortal." Here, Holmes made citation a direct function of originality. By "originality" Holmes meant uniqueness and individuality, as he revealed in his injunction that "[e]very historian should have his own character, and preserve it." Unlike his predecessors, then, Holmes saw authorship as an act of individual creation, not just compilation. It was therefore incumbent on the historian to avoid composing a work that was derivative in character or, at the very least, to acknowledge and identify the particular contributions of other historians through footnotes. In doing so, the historian recognized the originality of those historians. And by distinguishing their ideas from his own, he highlighted the original aspects of his work. For Holmes, originality was a matter not just of content but also of form. Unlike Adams or Marshall, Holmes believed that it was necessary for the historian to develop a distinctive style and language that expressed what was unique about his own character—hence his concern with "originality of composition."[26]

At the same time, Holmes's use of footnotes revealed a duality in his conception of the historian's function. His emphasis on originality implied a direct interpretive role for the historian whereby a historical work would reveal his perspective as an individual. And in his footnotes, Holmes did play that kind of role. In these notes he offered interpretive comments, assessing the reliability of particular sources or making judgments about subjects discussed in the text. One such footnote gave Holmes's appraisal of the Spanish conquest of Mexico. In his view, "Nothing was wanted but a good cause, to render this conquest one of the most illustrious achievements recorded in ancient or modern history. But, while we admire the action, as great, we condemn it, as criminal," for "[t]he victors, in one year of merciless massacre, sacrificed more human victims to avarice and ambition, than the Indians, during the existence of their empire, devoted to their gods." Through such judgments, Holmes injected his own perspective into his work. Yet this kind of authorial intervention was largely absent from the body of his history; he rarely intruded his own point of view in any explicit way on the text of the *Annals*. For all his emphasis on "originality of composition," Holmes showed little of this quality in his own writing, presenting his subject in a straightforward but nondescriptive style. The result was a dry, chronological narrative that made little attempt to explain or assess the events it related. This approach presumed that the historian's role was to efface his authorial presence and give the reader an unmediated and unembellished account of what happened in the past. Holmes thus embraced two seemingly opposed conceptions of the historian's function—he at once privileged the historian's individual perspective and marginalized it.[27]

Holmes's unwillingness to interpose himself into the text signified his attachment to another ideal—the desire for impartiality. Holmes associated impartiality with factual accuracy, as he revealed while pointing out the obstacles to this goal. Admitting that even the most conscientious historian could inadvertently distort the truth, he remarked pessimistically, "Professions of impartiality are of little significance. Although not conscious of having recorded one fact, without such evidence as was satisfactory to my own mind, or of having suppressed one, which appeared to come within the limits of my design; yet I do not flatter myself with the hope of exemption from error." Holmes's definition of impartiality prescribed detachment and neutrality for the historian, turning him into a disinterested chronicler of events—hence his reluctance to express his own opinions and judgments in the text. Only by presenting all the facts, uncolored by personal bias, could the historian achieve truth. In his emphasis on fact and his concern with "error," Holmes defined truth to mean the re-creation of an objective reality, separate from the historian's interpretation. The more the historian conformed to that reality, the closer to truth he would come. Rather than aiding him in this endeavor, the historian's individual perspective could get in the way of truth by causing him to unconsciously suppress facts or to include erroneous information.[28]

While questioning the historian's ability to fully realize this goal, Holmes did not despair of achieving truth. If complete impartiality was impossible, the historian could at least minimize the obstacles to truth, and Holmes used citation for this purpose. Through his footnotes, he created a double narrative that segregated his factual statements from his interpretive comments. In this double narrative, he could express his individual perspective while insulating his text from the distorting influence of that perspective by effacing his authorial presence in the text and allowing his personality to reveal itself only in the footnotes. In this way, Holmes could remain true to his desire for originality without undermining his commitment to impartiality.[29]

Holmes's use of citation reflected and furthered his attachment to impartiality in more than one way. His footnotes formed part of another double narrative in which the text constituted the end product of his research while the references described how he arrived at this outcome. And so Holmes used his footnotes to detail his sources and research experiences, involving the reader in his investigations and reasoning as a historian.[30] As they demonstrated how Holmes had reached his conclusions, footnotes in turn allowed readers to make their own assessment of the truthfulness and impartiality of his account. Holmes revealed his assumption that readers would wish to test and question the historian's claims for themselves when he explained why he had included so many citations in his *Annals*. He admitted that "[t]he numerous references may have the appearance of superfluity, perhaps of ostentation." "The reason for inserting so many authorities was," he explained, to allow the reader who wanted additional information to consult "the more copious histories for himself."[31] In the process, Holmes offset any inadvertent distortions caused by his own bias by enabling readers to detect and expose such deficiencies for themselves. Thus Holmes's skepticism about the possibility of impartiality did not mean that he abandoned a belief in the existence and attainability of historical truth. On the contrary, this skepticism reflected and reinforced his desire to solidify the basis for truth, for, as Holmes realized, the historian had to identify the obstacles to truth before he could overcome them. And the more aware he was of these obstacles, the more he would try to minimize the sources of error.[32]

The preoccupation with footnotes was not confined to Holmes. Although from a markedly different background than Holmes, John Leeds Bozman employed footnotes in a similar way for his history of Maryland. In the process, he both illuminated the tensions between originality and impartiality and demonstrated how he reconciled these two ideals. A Maryland lawyer of loyalist sympathies during the Revolution, Bozman began work on the first volume of his history of Maryland in 1805 and published it in 1811. He died before he could complete a continuation of this work, but his nephew arranged for the publication of the incomplete manuscript in 1837. As was the case with Holmes's *Annals*, Bozman attached extensive footnotes to a text that was essentially a factual, annalistic account. In addition to citing his sources, these notes provided commentary by Bozman on these sources and topics mentioned in the text. Like Holmes, Bozman contrasted his own diligence about citation with his predecessors' disregard for this practice. Appropriately, Bozman made this point in a footnote, which criticized the Revolutionary historian Hugh Williamson for failing to cite the sources for his *History of North Carolina*: "Although this historian is judicious enough in his remarks, yet, agreeably to the fashion of many American historians, he never deigns to cite any authorities for the facts set forth by him."[33] For Bozman, then, footnotes verified the truthfulness of a historical account by identifying the sources for the historian's claims to fact.

It was all the more important for the historian to specify his sources or "authorities," for Bozman shared Holmes's doubts about the individual historian's ability to achieve impartiality. As he went into why this was so difficult, he spelled out what he meant by impartiality and truth. According to Bozman, truth depended largely on the individual's perspective, and "the same facts may present themselves to different writers in different points of view. One may state some circumstances attending a transaction, which throw much light on it, while others may omit the same, considering them as immaterial to the purpose." For Bozman, then, no matter how much the historian tried to be accurate, his own individual perspective would shape his selection and presentation of historical facts. Even without intending to distort, the historian might inadvertently leave out information that another writer considered essential. In this explanation of the obstacles to impartiality, Bozman revealed the tensions between this ideal and the desire for originality. The defining characteristic of originality—individuality—was the very quality that made complete impartiality impossible. And in this emphasis on the role of individual perspective, Bozman recognized that truth was partly a matter of interpretation. But he would only go so far in recognizing the subjective character of truth, and like Holmes, he firmly rejected the relativistic implications of this belief—if truth varied according to the interpreter, it was possible to conclude that no one could access truth or that there was no such thing as truth at all.[34]

Rather than leading him to draw this conclusion, Bozman's doubts about

impartiality simply strengthened his commitment to establishing a more secure basis for truth. Footnotes could help the historian in this goal by providing readers with the sources for the historian's facts. Like Holmes, Bozman
suggested that such references made each historian's selection or omission of
particular details less of a threat to truth, for readers could go directly to the
historian's original sources and determine for themselves which circumstances
were "immaterial" to and which would "throw much light" on a particular
event. Thus Bozman in the end firmly maintained his belief in the existence
and attainability of a truth that transcended the historian's subjective view of
the facts. He reconciled this belief with his understanding of how truth varied
according to the individual's point of view by concluding that examining a "variety of historians, therefore, contributes much to the preservation of historical
truth." For Bozman, if each historian's version of the truth was subject to his
individual point of view, only by comparing and bringing together the different
perspectives of these historians was it possible to piece together the truth about
the past.[35]

The Historian's "Peculiar Turn of Thinking": Romantic History and the Literary Marketplace

Although nothing could be more different from the annalistic works published
by Holmes and Bozman than William Hickling Prescott's Romantic narratives,
Prescott shared their antipathy toward plagiarism, and his footnotes were as
extensive and detailed as theirs.[36] As with Holmes and Bozman, Prescott's regard for citation signified a concern with originality. Deriving his conception of
originality from Romantic aesthetic ideals, Prescott attached such importance
to footnotes not despite but because of his Romantic perspective. At the same
time, originality was for Prescott also a function of material concerns about
writing for a liberal capitalist marketplace. As he articulated these concerns,
he made the tensions between originality and impartiality explicit. As Prescott
recognized, if the ideal of originality presumed that each individual would and
should express a unique perspective, then no individual could claim to present
a truth that transcended that perspective. Rather than abandoning a belief in
the existence and attainability of such a truth, Prescott attached all the more
importance to footnotes as a remedy for this problem. Thus Prescott reconciled
in his own way two seemingly contradictory assumptions about the historian's
relationship to truth; even as he recognized that individuals would vary in their
interpretations of the truth, he firmly maintained his faith in a truth independent of the historian's interpretation.

Prescott was an eloquent and staunch proponent of citation in both theory and practice; all his histories consistently provided detailed and lengthy footnotes that acknowledged and assessed his sources. To do otherwise, according to Prescott, would constitute plagiarism. He made this assumption explicit while commenting on his history of Ferdinand and Isabella. As proof of his hostility to plagiarism, Prescott singled out his footnotes, asserting, "I believe the notes, to the last chapter especially, will show I have not been a plagiarist here."[37] Like Holmes's and Bozman's, Prescott's antipathy to plagiarism was part of a broader preoccupation with originality. Prescott revealed his devotion to this ideal in the strictures he placed on himself while working on his *History of the Conquest of Mexico*. He warned himself, "Don't look into Irving for style; nor into Irving, nor Robertson, for events &c till I have written on them; else danger of *imitation:—a sure blow to my reputation*."[38] He reasoned, "The best, undoubtedly, for every writer, is the form of expression best suited to his peculiar turn of thinking," for "[o]riginality—the originality of nature—compensates for a thousand minor blemishes."[39] Here, Prescott made originality partly a question of style. For him, unlike for his Revolutionary predecessors, it was important to write in a distinctive style because the historian's "form of expression" should ideally reflect his "peculiar turn of thinking." Prescott thus believed that an original style was important not just for its own sake; on a more fundamental level, he believed that each writer possessed a unique point of view, and that the goal of the historian should be to express that point of view through his style.[40]

In his concern with expressing the historian's "peculiar turn of thinking," Prescott embraced an expressive theory of art, demonstrating how Romantic aesthetics contributed to his desire for originality. Just as this theory made art the expression of the artist's own imagination, Prescott viewed historical writing as a form of individual expression. And, like Romantic theorists, Prescott believed that originality was the result of a natural and spontaneous process that came from within the writer. Neoclassical aesthetic theory had emphasized the importance of studying and following external models to artistic creation, for it viewed art as a craft that required cultivation and learning. As Romantic artists embraced the idea of natural genius, they repudiated imitation and learning more generally as a source of artistic creation. Because artistic invention was for the natural genius an organic process that was involuntary and untutored, following external rules or models would only inhibit the artist's creativity. Arguing that such rules would curb the writer's originality, Prescott appealed to this conception of natural genius when he declared, "The best rule is, to dispense with nearly all rules, except those of grammar, and to consult the natural bent of one's own genius."[41]

The Romantic ideal of the author or artist as original genius was in turn partly the product of the material conditions for authorship in the late eighteenth and early nineteenth centuries. German Romantic writers took up this ideal in the latter part of the eighteenth century as part of their effort to promote the development of writing as a profession in a society that had only begun the transition to a commercialized market for literature defined by the view of a literary text as a commodity and of the author as the owner of the text.[42] While the emergence of a middle-class audience had expanded the market for books enough to create the hope that authors could make a living from their writing, German writers were unable to reap the benefits of the expanding market for their works without a copyright law to protect their rights to ownership in and profits from their writing. Premised on a traditional view of writing as a medium for expressing preexisting ideas that belonged to the larger public rather than to the author who articulated those ideas, the absence of a copyright law not only allowed publishers to enjoy whatever profits a book made at the expense of the author. It also made publishers more unwilling to publish the works of serious writers at all, as the widespread reprinting or what would now be termed piracy of popular books cut into the profits that publishers had once used to offset the costs of publishing serious books that were unlikely to be profitable.[43]

As German Romantic writers embarked on a campaign to enact copyright laws that would protect them both from piracy of their own works and from competition with the pirated works of more popular writers, they turned to the idea of the author as original genius in order to demonstrate how it was possible for them to claim property in something as intangible as writing or thought at a time when the very concept of intellectual property was not fully established. While, as the philosopher Johann Fichte acknowledged, the purchaser of a book owned the physical object of the book and readers shared with the author ownership of the content of the ideas in it to the extent that they comprehended those ideas, the author retained exclusive ownership over the *way* those ideas were expressed, for that form was unique to him. German Romantic writers thus claimed property in their writing as, in Martha Woodmansee's words, a "verbal embodiment or imprint of that [the author's] intellect at work."[44] To the extent that a book represented the unique expression of an author's style and mode of thinking, then, the author could claim property in that book.

Likewise, when Prescott argued that the historian's style should reflect his "peculiar turn of thinking," he asserted the basis for his claims to individual property in his writing at a time when those claims were still contested.[45] Prescott's concern with originality in this way at once reflected the development of a commercialized market for literature in the United States during the 1820s and 1830s and served as an instrument for combating the obstacles to that development. Although by the time Prescott published his histories conditions for professional authorship in the United States were more favorable than they were for earlier German Romantic writers, it was still difficult for American authors to make a living from their writing, for the commercialization of literature was by no means complete in the 1840s. While, for example, the passage of a domestic copyright law in 1790 laid the basis for the professionalization of authorship by recognizing the author's rights to property in his own work, thereby making it possible for the author to profit from his writing, the absence of an international copyright law revealed the resistance to the view of literature as a privately owned market commodity. Despite an extended campaign from 1837 to 1854 by American and British authors for an international copyright law, Congress repeatedly rejected bills and petitions for such a law until 1891.[46] If supporters of international copyright privileged the status of the individual author as the producer and owner of a text, opponents of international copyright embraced a "republican definition of authorship" that gave primacy to the public interest in making foreign texts as widely available as possible through cheap pirated reprints over the individual rights of foreign authors to property in their own work.[47] The resistance to international copyright was thus premised on an understanding of authorship that marginalized the individual author from the production of a text and decentralized textual production and ownership by locating these attributes in the work of reprinting and dissemination.[48]

Yet if the failure to pass an international copyright agreement revealed the limits to the commercialization of literature in the early nineteenth century, the demand for such an agreement illustrated the extent to which literary texts had come to be viewed as the property of the author and the growing importance of market considerations about profit and popularity to literary endeavor, as the professionalization of literature made it increasingly necessary for authors to take such considerations into account in order to make a living from their writing. The absence of an international copyright law in the United States impaired the ability of American writers to profit from their work by enabling foreign publishers to legally pirate their books without paying them royalties, while at the same time putting American authors at a disadvantage in the domestic market as they competed against cheaper pirated editions of books by European writers.[49] Very much concerned with securing his legal claims to individual property in his writing against such encroachments, Prescott therefore had tangible reason for espousing an understanding of authorship as the expression of individual genius that would legitimize those claims. Careful to take all the formal steps necessary to obtain domestic copyright protection for his published work in the United States, he also went to considerable lengths to find ways of circumventing the lack of copyright protection for American authors in England, trying, for example, to arrange the timing of the publication of his works in England and the United States so that he could claim English copyright under the provision of English law that American works could obtain such protection if they were published in England before or simultaneously with their appearance in the United States (a principle that would be overturned by the House of Lords in 1854). Accordingly, although not as outspoken or active in the movement for international copyright as its leading proponents, Prescott did express support for an international copyright law, which he believed "would be of worth to the sort of books of historical research which I am employed on."[50]

Prescott's desire to establish his property in his work was part of his more general interest in the commercial aspects of authorship. Prescott revealed the growing concern of American authors with profits and popularity as he devoted considerable attention to the financial details of his publishing arrangements and played an active role in the marketing and promotion of his books.[51] American authors' concern with profit was not just a product of the professionalization of authorship but was also spurred by the market revolution of the early nineteenth century, for a defining feature of the market revolution was the development of a capitalist economy based on the sale of goods for individual profit in an impersonal market. Not only did American authors adhere to the assumptions of market capitalism in their desire for profit, but the social and economic changes associated with the market revolution also helped make it possible for authors to actually make money from their writing. If the growth of urban centers such as New York or Philadelphia during the early nineteenth century centralized the production of books through large publishing houses located in these cities, the improved transportation facilities that came with the market revolution made it possible to distribute those books over wider distances to reach a national market. As technological advancements in the manufacture of books, together with increased literacy, helped enlarge and stabilize the market for books by expanding both the supply and demand for books and making them cheaper to produce, the publishing business—and with it, the profession of authorship—became more securely established by the 1840s. Yet as the publishing industry consolidated control over the financing and production of books, it became all the more necessary for authors to show some concern with the popular appeal of their works, for publishers were unwilling to print books without some prospect of popular success.[52]

Consequently, even Prescott—who was independently wealthy and did not depend on his writing for his livelihood—recognized the importance of popular appeal in an exchange with fellow historian George Bancroft. As he did so, he demonstrated how the competition for readers in a commercial marketplace contributed to the desire for originality. On learning that Bancroft and Jared Sparks were both planning to publish works on the Revolution, Prescott wrote each of them to preempt anxieties that this overlap in subject matter would detract from the success of either work. In a letter of 1847, Prescott reassured Bancroft by observing, "Between writers so different as you and he there can be no collision, hardly competition. Working over the same soil will produce two crops so different that one cannot interfere with the demand for the other, and probably will augment it by stimulating the literary appetite." Such fears of duplication illustrated how the primacy given to uniqueness and originality increased a sense of rivalry among historians. Prescott's reference to "demand" and "literary appetite" suggested that the competition to achieve uniqueness was not just an aesthetic concern; it also stemmed from a desire for popular appeal. In a competitive marketplace driven by popular taste, individuality was all the more necessary as a way to engage the interest of popular audiences. Thus, for Prescott, originality was so important because it would serve not only to legitimize the historian's claims to profit and property in his work but also to increase those profits by making his writing more appealing to readers.[53]

In Prescott's view, there was little danger that Bancroft and Sparks would duplicate each other even though they were writing on the same topic because each of them would approach the material so differently. If, as Prescott believed, the writer was supposed to express his own "peculiar turn of thinking" in his work, then it followed that different individuals would interpret the same events differently. But if that was the case, then how were readers supposed to distinguish between these different interpretations and settle on what was truth? This problem made citation all the more important for Prescott. Priding himself on his own scrupulous attention to citation, he explained to Bancroft why he was so careful about footnotes: "One merit I may certainly claim; that by ample citation and references, and by critical biographical notices of my authorities as Postscripts . . . I have enabled every reader to estimate the nature and value of the evidence for himself."[54] Here, Prescott revealed his expectation that readers would wish to assess the historian's claims for themselves. Like Holmes, Prescott did not believe that the reader would accept the authority of the historian as sufficient in itself. Prescott, however, attributed to the reader an even greater willingness to challenge and question the historian and was more explicit about how readers would use footnotes to do this.

In a review of Bancroft's *History of the United States*, published in 1841 for the *North American Review*, Prescott elaborated on why it was important for

the historian to provide citations: "[W]e want to see the grounds of his conclusions, the scaffolding by which he has raised his structure; to estimate the true
value of his authorities; to know something of their characters, positions in
society, and the probable influences to which they were exposed. Where there
is contradiction, we want to see it stated; the *pros* and the *cons*, and the grounds
for rejecting this, and admitting that." In sum, "[w]e want to have a reason for
our faith. Otherwise, we are merely led blindfold." No matter how reliable and
skillful the historian, "we like to use our own eyesight too, to observe somewhat
for ourselves, and to know, if possible, why he has taken this particular road,
in preference to that which his predecessors have travelled." For this reason,
Prescott regretted that Bancroft had not provided more extensive footnotes in
his history.[55] Recognizing that an individual's character and social background
would shape his account of an event, Prescott believed that footnotes could
help the reader assess the "true value" of the historian's sources by providing
the reader with information about these influences. Through footnotes, the
historian could divulge the conflicts between his sources and explain why he
had favored one source over another. In this way, footnotes would enable the
reader to discern not only the biases in the historian's sources but also the way
in which the historian's individual perspective shaped his interpretation of
those sources.

In turn, by providing this kind of information, Prescott believed, footnotes
would aid in the quest for truth, as he demonstrated in the footnotes to his
own work. In both his *History of the Conquest of Mexico*, and his *History of the
Conquest of Peru*, not only did he provide footnotes on most pages of his text;
these footnotes were also so detailed and extensive that they sometimes took
up more of the page than his text. Living up to his own prescriptions to provide
his readers with information that would help them assess the "true value of his
authorities," he often included in his citations biographical information about
the authors of his sources, background on the context and circumstances in
which these sources were written, and the nature of the sources that these writers themselves had used. Prescott periodically appended notes at the close of a
chapter specifically for this purpose, using them to give a detailed assessment of
the major sources he had used for that chapter. In one such note for his *History
of the Conquest of Mexico*, after identifying Juan de Torquemada and the Abbé
Clavigero as the two major sources for his second chapter, Prescott informed
the reader that "[t]he former, a Provincial of the Franciscan order, came to the
New World about the middle of the sixteenth century. As the generation of the
Conquerors had not then passed away, he had ample opportunities of gathering the particulars of their enterprise from their own lips." Although Prescott

admitted that Torquemada's work displayed the "bigotry" of his religious back-ground, overall, he believed, "the student, aware of his author's infirmities, will find few better guides than Torquemada in tracing the stream of historic truth up to the fountain head; such is his manifest integrity, and so great were his facilities for information on the most curious points of Mexican antiquity."[56]

After providing similar information about Clavigero's background, Prescott concluded, "[B]ut the later and more cultivated period, in which he wrote, is vis-ible in the superior address with which he has managed his complicated subject." Although his desire to "vindicate his countrymen from what he conceived to be the misrepresentations of Robertson, Raynal, and De Pau ... might naturally suggest unfavorable ideas of his impartiality," Prescott decided, "on the whole, he seems to have conducted the discussion with good faith; and, if he has been led by national zeal to overcharge the picture with brilliant colors, he will be found much more temperate, on this score, than those who preceded him, while he has applied sound principles of criticism, of which they were incapable."[57]

As these assessments revealed, Prescott could question the impartiality of individual writers while at the same time maintaining his belief in the ideal of impartial truth. Though recognizing that both Torquemada's and Clavigero's ac-counts were biased in some way, he still believed that they had contributed to the quest for truth. As he suggested when he argued that the historian, "aware of his author's infirmities," would have difficulty finding a better source for "his-toric truth" than Torquemada's work, he believed that it was possible to discern truth if the historian recognized and identified the biases in his sources. By revealing these biases, footnotes would thus help readers of his work to distin-guish truth.[58]

And so Prescott's understanding of the obstacles to truth and his commit-ment to this ideal were integrally related to each other, as he made explicit when he explained why no two individuals would interpret events in the same way, no matter how committed they were to truth. He reasoned, "The points of view, under which a thing may be contemplated, are as diversified as the mind itself. The most honest inquirers after truth rarely come to precisely the same results, such is the influence of education, prejudice, principle."[59] Here, Prescott pointed to the difficulties that his conception of originality created for the ideal of truth. If his conception of originality presumed that each individual possessed a unique way of thinking, then each individual would have different perceptions of the truth, for the individual could never escape the influence of his own biases. As Prescott recognized, the subjective nature of individual perception thus made total impartiality impossible for the individual historian, for, according to the ideal of impartiality, the historian was supposed to be a dispassionate and unbiased chronicler of events whose goal was to uncover the objective reality of the past.

But rather than abandoning this ideal, Prescott affirmed his belief in the attainability and existence of a truth that transcended these different points of view. He reconciled this faith with his recognition of the subjective element in historical interpretation by concluding, "Truth, indeed, is single, but opinions are infinitely various; and it is only by comparing these opinions together, that we can hope to ascertain what is truth." For Prescott, the historian did not create truth through his interpretation. Rather, his interpretation represented just one of many different opinions of the truth. Like Bozman, Prescott suggested that if, limited by his own point of view, no one historian could claim a monopoly on truth, it was possible to achieve truth by bringing together the perspectives of many different writers. In this way, Prescott implied, the more aware the historian was of the subjective element to historical interpretation, the better equipped he would be to achieve truth, for it was less likely that he would be misled by the bias of any one individual's point of view.[60]

"The plain and noble garb of truth": Footnotes and "Sceptical Criticism"

As Prescott's emphasis on interrogating the historian's sources revealed, the critical methods of scholarship associated with Ranke's scientific conception of history emerged at the same time as Romantic history. And, as Prescott demonstrated, far from being opposed, these two approaches to history were integrally related to each other. Not only did they converge in the same individual; they also both contributed to the growing concern with citation. Prescott's contemporaries of the 1830s and 1840s made the connection between this critical tendency and demands for citation even clearer as they turned footnotes into a sign of and means to impartiality and accuracy. Recognizing, like Prescott, the many obstacles to truth, these historians demonstrated in their own way how doubts about truth actually fueled a desire to put truth on a more secure basis. In equating truth with accuracy, however, these historians defined truth differently than Prescott did, for they viewed truth as an objective account of fact, uncolored by the historian's imagination or interpretation. Paradoxically, even as they gave primacy to detachment and neutrality in their definition of truth, they revealed the social function of impartiality all the more clearly in using this ideal for nationalist purposes.

Many of Prescott's contemporaries of the 1830s and 1840s shared his concern with citation, to the point where they used footnotes as a standard of assessment in determining the value and credibility of a historical text. Accordingly, one reviewer praised Robert Howison's *History of Virginia*, published in 1846, for its use of references in particular. He commended Howison for the "extensive, laborious, and competent research" present throughout the work. As testimony to Howison's scrupulous research, "[t]he margin is studded with notes of reference and citation; sometimes, even to excess. . . . Yet we consider the abundance of historical authority as a principal excellence of the book."[61] As this review indicated, the interest in citation was not just theoretical; historians themselves embraced and put these prescriptions into practice. Throughout his work, Howison, a lawyer and Presbyterian clergyman from Virginia, was diligent about providing footnotes that specified his sources and stated his own opinions about them. William Stevens, one of the founders of the Georgia Historical Society, who published the first volume of his *History of Georgia* in 1847, displayed a similar regard for citation. Although his references were shorter and less regular than Howison's, he was reasonably conscientious about footnoting his sources in the first volume of his history. He made clear the importance of this practice to his own standards of scholarship as he commented on his predecessors' deficiencies. The history of Georgia written by Hugh McCall was inadequate, in Stevens's view, because it was "mostly made up from Hewitt and other authors, from whom he has borrowed ten, twenty, and thirty pages at a time, without the slightest acknowledgment." As a result, although it was a valuable work, "many of his statements are not trust-worthy."[62]

Stevens viewed footnotes as a sign of truthfulness and accuracy, as he revealed when he criticized McCall's work as untrustworthy. In 1848, a reviewer for Charles Campbell's history of Virginia elaborated on why historians associated footnotes so closely with these qualities. This reviewer praised Campbell's detailed references as part of a more general tendency to examine history critically: "These things savour of exactness, and happily characterize the best histories in our day. Sceptical criticism, in regard to traditionary narrative, has reached such a height, that the greatest masters in this kind are coming more and more to resort to the simple mode of verifying their statements. We therefore find no fault with the author for giving us chapter and verse, even for seemingly unimportant statements."[63] This type of critical approach, or, as Campbell's reviewer termed it, "sceptical criticism," required the historian to question and challenge previous historical accounts. Only in this way would the historian rid his narrative of their distortions and establish his own accuracy. Footnotes that specified the historian's sources demonstrated his commitment to such an approach, for they attested that the historian had investigated and verified his claims, rather than simply repeating the statements of other writers. And by providing his references, the historian would allow others to check on his veracity in the same way.[64]

In turn, as emblems of accuracy, footnotes enhanced the credibility of the historian's claims to truth and demonstrated his fidelity to this ideal. Howison singled out his footnotes for just this reason. Attributing his painstaking research to his desire for truth, he proclaimed in his preface, "Convinced that *truth* should be the first object of the historian, he has laboured with earnestness in examining, sifting, and comparing the evidence . . . upon which he has relied." In support of this assertion, Howison pointed to his footnotes, declaring that "[e]very material statement of fact has been verified by a reference to the original authority, in order to guide those who may wish to test the accuracy of the work."[65] Thus, for Howison, truth was based on factual accuracy, and factual accuracy was in turn based on the evidence of primary sources—or, to use Howison's term, "original authority."

In their calls for "sceptical criticism" and their insistence on accuracy, antebellum historians embraced the scientific ideals of critical scholarship most closely identified with Leopold von Ranke. Critical methods of scholarship did not originate with Ranke, for Renaissance scholars had already begun to develop the techniques of source criticism associated with the Rankean ideal, and historians of the Göttingen school played an important role in establishing the basis for critical scholarship and a more "scientific" approach to history during the second half of the eighteenth century as they used their training in philology and statistics, and in what were considered the "auxiliary sciences" of paleography and numismatics, to analyze historical data. As the most influential exponent of this approach, however, Ranke has come to embody the ideal of critical scholarship. According to the Rankean ideal, the historian could achieve factual accuracy only through a systematic and critical analysis of primary sources. Not only did Ranke believe, like Howison, that the evidence of primary sources was necessary to verify the historian's claims to fact; the historian also had to determine the reliability of these sources by weighing them against one another for inaccuracies and inconsistencies as Howison did. Factual accuracy was so important to Howison and other antebellum proponents of "sceptical criticism" because, like Ranke, they viewed historical truth as an unvarnished record of fact. Thus, like Ranke, these historians suggested that the historian would achieve truth by divesting himself of bias and letting the facts speak for themselves—in other words, by being impartial.[66]

Francis Markoe made these assumptions about truth explicit, and revealed how they fueled hostility to plagiarism, in an 1835 article for the *American Quar-*

terly Review. Markoe opened his essay on Peter Force's *Documentary History of the American Revolution* (later published as the *American Archives*) with a famous story in which Sir Walter Raleigh burned the history he was writing after finding it impossible to locate two witnesses who could agree in their account of a disturbance he saw from his prison window. Using this story to illustrate the uncertainty of history, Markoe recognized how the subjective character of individual perspective made it difficult to ascertain truth. Even more important, Markoe condemned plagiarism as an obstacle to historical truth, for he attributed what he believed was the endemic inaccuracy of existing history to this practice. He used historical accounts of the Tea Act crisis to illustrate this problem. After noting that many of these accounts had simply copied from other works, he pointed to the inaccuracies that had resulted from such plagiarism. Markoe demonstrated how these errors derived originally from mistakes committed by William Gordon and the *Annual Register*, which other historians proceeded to copy, thereby perpetuating and turning them into commonly held "facts." For Markoe, this example provided a case study in the general tendency for authors "to follow implicitly, and without investigation, what they find in preceding writers." As a result, "[m]ost books, indeed, are mere repetitions, and where the originals and models are in error, it follows, as a necessary consequence, that every new book serves only to multiply and perpetuate errors."[67]

Yet such skepticism about the accuracy of existing historical accounts did not lead Markoe to renounce the possibility of truthful history altogether. Just because prior historians had failed in this endeavor did not mean that accurate history was itself impossible, for, he believed, America possessed "all, or nearly all . . . the materials necessary . . . to place its history upon an immoveable basis, and to make it, what all history ought to be, a record of facts, beyond cavil or doubt—a simple relation of what has actually occurred, clothed in the plain and noble garb of truth." Here Markoe affirmed his belief in the existence of truth and explained what he meant by this ideal. Truth, for him, consisted of a chronicle of facts—all the historian had to do was to present and recover those facts. In his definition of truth as a "simple relation of what has actually occurred," Markoe sounded much like Ranke when he declared that the historian's goal was to discover "what actually happened" in the past. And so, like Ranke, Markoe believed that the historian could recover the objective reality of the past without allowing his own prejudices or biases to influence his account of the truth.[68]

For Markoe, citation alone would not rectify the mistakes of past historians because, like Ranke, he believed that original documents were necessary to achieve truth. America was exceptional in this respect because of its unique abundance of such documents. As Markoe explained, "We have no 'dark ages,' no mythology, no time beyond which the memory of man doth not run. The whole story includes a period of authentic history, and falls within the sphere of sober truth." With his claim that, unlike other nations, America had no "dark ages," Markoe expressed a common refrain that had been previously articulated by the loyalist historian George Chalmers and continued to be reiterated by early national historical writers and orators who repeatedly proclaimed that America's recent origins made its past uniquely transparent and intelligible. Yet American writers and critics were deeply ambivalent about this trait. Even as they glorified America's newness, they worried that America would, as a result, lack the materials necessary to develop any real sense of cultural nationalism. As a nation without a distant and mysterious past, these commentators feared, America could not use tradition and myth as a basis for national unity. Equally important, they feared, because historical romance was based on such myths, America could not develop a national literature that would express its own identity and demonstrate its cultural greatness. By celebrating this quality, Markoe turned what seemed to be a deficiency into an advantage and a sign of national greatness.[69] More than that, in his assertion that the availability of primary documents gave America a unique ability to achieve truth, Markoe used a Rankean conception of truth to promote a belief in American exceptionalism. In this way, Markoe's commitment to an ideal of truth that emphasized the historian's detachment and impartiality paradoxically served political purposes.

"A piece of figured tapestry": Documents as Romantic Art

Adopting another hallmark of modern critical scholarship, many of Markoe's contemporaries lived up to his prescriptions about the importance of original documents. Not only did they use primary sources for their research. They also made primary documents the basis for a whole genre of historical writing as documentary collections made up largely of primary sources became increasingly popular in this period. And like Markoe, these historical writers attached such importance to primary sources because of their desire for truth. But, as they revealed in their use of documents, they defined truth differently than Markoe did. If Markoe's regard for primary documents conformed to Ranke's scientific ideal of truth, these historians demonstrated how Romantic ideals also contributed to the emphasis on original documents. Truth for them did not just consist of a record of facts; it also required emotional engagement and imagination. Yet these writers would only go so far in expanding the historian's interpretive role. If they viewed the historian as more than just a dispassionate chronicler of facts, they at the same time did not wish to reduce truth to purely a matter of interpretation. Through documents, these historians sought to reconcile their awareness of the subjective element to historical understanding with their vision of a truth that represented an objective reality independent of the historian's interpretation. As they did so, they at once revealed and resolved the tensions between impartiality and originality.[70]

The numerous documentary collections published in this period took the interest in primary sources to its furthest extreme. These collections consisted of primary sources assembled with little analysis or direct interpretation by the historian, apart from brief prefatory comments and notes by the editor. The most notable of these documentary collections included Hezekiah Niles's *Principles and Acts of the Revolution*, published in 1822; Jonathan Elliot's *Debates, Resolutions, and Other Proceedings in Convention on the Adoption of the Federal Constitution*, published between 1827 and 1830; and Peter Force's *American Archives*, published between 1837 and 1853. Another such work was Alexander Young's *Chronicles of the Pilgrim Fathers*, a collection of primary sources on the Pilgrims, published in 1841. In a review of this work, William Brigham recommended Young's documentary approach as the best method of attaining historical truth. Brigham praised Young's book because, unlike most other recent histories, "[i]t is not a compilation, nor does it give the inferences or views of its learned editor." In contrast, "the modern histories of our country" are "perfectly inadequate" "to express the real truths of our early history," for "[m]ost of them are mere compilations, or partake of the bias and coloring of the author's mind." As a result, "we read them rather to learn what are the conclusions of the author, than the real truths which history teaches."[71]

As he explained what distinguished Young's work, Brigham defined the historian's relationship to truth. Brigham admired Young's book because Young had freed his text from the biases that distorted most other historical works by allowing the documents to speak for themselves. In Brigham's view, then, the historian obstructed truth when he allowed his personal perspective to intrude on his work. This assessment presumed a belief in the existence of some kind of objective truth independent of the historian's interpretation—hence the distinction that Brigham made between the author's conclusions and the "real truths" of history. And for Brigham, the "true path of history" was "to describe facts, and to discuss philosophical theories, or to deduce certain effects from causes with which none other can see any connexion."[72]

Yet, as this injunction revealed, if Brigham required detachment from the historian, this did not mean that the historian was supposed to efface himself altogether from the text. Believing that historical truth entailed more than just a collection of facts and details about the past, he still assigned to the historian an active interpretive role in recovering and presenting those truths. For this reason, Brigham also disparaged "compilation" as antithetical to truth. He used "compilation" as a derogatory term, in direct contrast to his Revolutionary predecessors, who had no qualms about describing themselves as compilers. Whereas the term *compiler* had once denoted the author of a work, Brigham used this word in its modern sense, defining compilation in opposition to original authorship—a difference that revealed how the very idea of authorship had changed since the eighteenth century. Through his approach to primary documents, according to Brigham, Young avoided two equally undesirable extremes—he eschewed the derivative character of compilations without injecting his individual biases into his account. Brigham believed that Young had achieved this balance through his "copious notes and numerous references." Revealing the editor's "great skill" and "historical knowledge," these notes were "necessary to a full explanation, and a proper understanding of the text, and tend to give unity" to the different sections of the work.[73]

But if truth was not just a chronicle of facts, what, then, did constitute truth? And why did these historical writers believe that primary documents provided the surest means of achieving that truth? In an 1847 review of Robert Howison's *History of Virginia* for the *Southern Literary Messenger*, John Moncure Daniel offered one answer to these questions as he argued for the superiority of primary sources over compilations. Like Brigham, Daniel believed that historians could not recover historical truth from compilations. Daniel was even more scathing than Brigham in his denunciation of compilation, reasoning that someone with firsthand knowledge of an event "will narrate it with a larger number of attendant circumstances, with greater *specialty*, and consequently, with greater vividness than he who has to tell it second-hand," for a narrator whose knowledge of events was based on secondhand accounts, rather than direct experience, "first revolves them in his own mind, strips them of that circumstantial minuteness, and gives a general, lengthy outline." In turn, "[h]e who comes after him, and compiles from compilers, of course has still less specialty of fact." He concluded, "Thus history resembles a piece of figured tapestry, and compilers the moths. One moth eats up half the limbs of a man—another goes to work on what the first has left; and the next generation of moths leaves nothing but a nose and a body."[74]

Using the term "compiler" in opposition to "original writers," Daniel characterized virtually all secondary historical accounts as compilations, for by "original writers," Daniel meant authors of primary sources. For Daniel, the problem with compilation was that it interfered with the historian's ability to revitalize history for his readers. Only contemporaries who had experienced firsthand the events they described could provide the kind of detail and specificity necessary to bring these events to life. More distant from their subject, writers of secondary accounts could not access or appreciate such particulars in the same way. Compilers of secondary sources would further strip the vitality from historical accounts as they progressively condensed their sources and trimmed away any remaining details. And so, while Daniel shared Markoe's concern with truth—and Markoe's belief that primary documents would further this goal—he defined this ideal in a different way. Factual accuracy and impartiality alone were not sufficient to achieve truth; the historian would achieve truth only by making the past come to life for the reader. Facts and details were important not in themselves but because they provided the historian with the means of doing this. Hence Daniel compared history to a "figured tapestry," whereas Markoe spoke of the "plain and noble garb" of truth. In contrast to Markoe, whose language stripped truth of any embellishment, turning it into a record of bare fact, Daniel's image of history as "figured tapestry" suggested that there was an artistic and creative dimension to historical truth.

Daniel made his belief in the artistic dimension to history clear when he singled out Shakespeare as "the greatest" of those authors "who have made compilations of historical facts, who are valuable because of the great insight they have thus been able to give into human character." At the same time, in classifying not only historians like George Bancroft and John Daly Burk as "compilers" but even the plays of Shakespeare as "compilations," Daniel placed strict limits on the historian's creative and interpretive role. No matter how vivid or insightful, writers of secondary accounts could be considered only "compilers," not "authors," because they were simply re-creating what had happened in the past, not creating something new of their own.[75]

As Charles Upham explained why primary sources were so important to this artistic conception of historical truth, he expressed a complex understanding of the historian's role. Through documents, he sought to reconcile two seemingly contradictory doctrines—in his emphasis on the artistic and creative character of history, he recognized the interpretive and subjective dimension of history while at the same time denying that historical truth was subject to interpretation. Best known for his account of the Salem witchcraft trials, published in 1831, Upham also wrote extensively on other subjects in American history. Like Brigham and Daniel, Upham advocated the use of primary sources as an antidote to the bias and distortion that he associated with secondhand accounts. For this reason, he claimed that the abundance of such sources on the Revolution furnished its historians with a uniquely impartial view of the past. Echoing Markoe on America's superior ability to achieve historical truth, he declared, "[I]t is the peculiar charm of the history of the American Revolution" that "[i]t will not be a narrative related by another, but a story told by the actors themselves, passing, as it were, in very life across the stage." In contrast, "[h]istory in reference to most other epochs is a decoction of the lees of events and characters, selected by the arbitrary, prejudiced, and necessarily limited judgments of writers distant from the scene and the period, and boiled down into a reduced and confused compound."[76]

In his condemnation of the "arbitrary" and "prejudiced" character of most secondary sources, he suggested that truth required impartiality and detachment from the historian. But these qualities, while necessary, were not sufficient to achieve truth. Like Daniel, Upham predicated truth on the revival of the experience and feeling of the past—his goal was to take readers back in time and enable them to relive the past for themselves. And like Daniel, Upham argued that this goal made primary documents all the more necessary. Upham made this clear when he discussed the approach he took to his biography of Sir Henry Vane, published in 1844 as part of Jared Sparks's *Library of American Biography* series. For this biography, Upham put his own prescriptions about the importance of primary documents into practice. Reasoning that the best way to close the gap between past and present was to expose the reader to the words and language of that time, he included lengthy extracts from Vane's writings. As Upham explained to Sparks, "In writing the life of a man who was himself an author, I am quite sure that it is best to make him speak for himself as far as may be, from stage to stage—particularly if there is any thing in his style that is peculiar to his age and representative of its characteristics." Through such passages, the reader "passes beyond the biographer, and becomes personally acquainted, as it were, with the subject of the story, and, in fact, transported to the age in which he lived."[77]

This perspective was consistent with the Romantic vision of the historian as an artist whose purpose was to make the past come to life for the reader. And like Prescott, Upham emphasized the importance of style; however, whereas for Prescott style was an expression of the historian's "peculiar turn of thinking," for Upham, style was important because it would reflect what was unique about his subject's time. Upham's view of history as a form of art was even more evident when he stated that his goal in including so many extracts from Vane's writings was "to present living pictures as it were of his successive stages in life, showing them to the reader as painted, at the time, by the original himself."[78] In embracing this artistic conception of history, Upham turned historical understanding into an active interpretive enterprise. It took imagination and emotional involvement to make history vivid in this way. Yet if Upham did not believe it was enough to let the facts speak for themselves, he did not prescribe direct authorial intervention from the historian either. On the contrary, he, like Markoe, directed that the historian efface his authorial presence. Only by letting Vane speak for himself could the historian achieve the artistic goal of taking the reader back into the past. In this way, for Upham, the artist and his work were one and the same. Upham thus expressed a paradoxical understanding of the historian's role—the historian could best fulfill his interpretive function by withdrawing his authorial presence from the text. As Upham himself put it, "Of course, I could not, make any thing of Vane unless I recovered him from the neglect and abuse of the historians—By adducing his own writings and speeches I have made him *recover himself*."[79]

Such an approach would not only promote truth; it would also impart originality to Upham's biography. Ironically, modern scholars have often disparaged this type of documentary history as the very kind of derivative and uncritical compilations that antebellum historians condemned. Yet contrary to this view, Upham singled out originality as one of the primary merits of his book, directly attributing this quality to his use of primary sources. He felt fortunate in his choice of subject matter, for Vane was "a character, the history of whom will be invested with the charms of perfect *novelty* to the reader—His merit and actions are almost wholly unknown."[80] His biography was unique, Upham believed, not just because of its subject matter but also because of his inclusion of previously unknown writings by Vane. So here, for Upham, originality was a question of content; the historian could achieve uniqueness simply by introducing readers to previously unknown information and sources. And in making originality a matter of content rather than interpretation, Upham reconciled this ideal with his desire for impartial truth, for this conception of originality did not require the historian to express his own perspective. Not only did both these goals make primary sources an imperative; on a more fundamental level, even as he achieved uniqueness by recovering hitherto neglected subjects and sources, Upham would contribute to truth by filling in gaps in the historical record.

Upham took this documentary approach even further in his *Life of George Washington*, published in 1852. As he did so, however, he complicated his definition of originality and revealed the tensions between this goal and his desire for truth. For this work, Upham expanded his use of documentary extracts to put together what he termed an "autobiography" of Washington. This biography related Washington's life primarily through selections from Washington's own writings, connected by occasional analytical comments from Upham. Even more forcefully than in his work on Vane, Upham urged this method as the most effective and illuminating form of biography, for he believed that "[t]he excellence of Biography consists, in keeping the author out of sight, and concentrating uninterrupted attention upon the subject." Yet in doing so, he recognized, he diminished his own originality as an author. For this reason, he made the disclaimer that his biography "can lay claim, only in a limited degree, to the character of an original work. The writer feels, that in the manner of its construction, he has done nothing to promote his own reputation as an author."[81]

Here, then, for Upham, truth came at the cost of originality. While his use of documents would best capture Washington's life and character for the reader, it also diminished his own authorial role. And in presuming that originality required him to express his own perspective as an author, he suggested that originality was more than a matter of content. To be original, the historian also had to present a distinctive interpretation and point of view. In seeing a conflict between truth and originality in this sense, Upham restricted the historian's role in interpreting truth. Although his conception of history as a form of art implied some kind of creative role for the historian, he still believed that truth was something to be discovered, not made. The art of the historian consisted not of creating his own truth but of recovering a truth that existed independent of him. Hence, it was impossible for the historian to be original when the subject matter was familiar and well known, as was the case with Washington. All the historian could do was to correct the distortions and omissions of others; if he tried to impose his own perspective on the text, he would himself run the risk of distorting truth. For all his emphasis on the artistic and subjective dimension of historical understanding, Upham in this way firmly rejected the belief that truth was just a matter of individual interpretation.

"A passive spectator of events": Documents, Deception, and the Domestic Sphere

In his emphasis on revitalizing the past, Upham associated emotion with truth. Charles Francis Adams went even further in equating truth with feeling as he gave primacy to private over public documents as the basis for historical truth. In doing so, he brought together the methods of critical scholarship with both Romantic ideals and prescriptions for the value of social history. At the same time, in his explanation for why private letters were more truthful than public documents, Adams adhered to the assumptions of sentimental culture and expressed broader cultural uncertainties about deception and the relationship between public and private character in an increasingly impersonal market society. He ultimately sought to resolve these uncertainties by identifying truth with the qualities that defined women—disinterestedness and sentiment. As he did so, Adams reconciled his belief in the importance of subjective feeling to truth with his desire for an objective account of the past by feminizing truth itself.[82]

Adams was deeply interested in history and wrote extensively on the subject. He demonstrated his appreciation for documentary sources in his most important and best-known historical publication—his multivolume edition of his grandfather John Adams's writings, published between 1850 and 1856. Before publishing this work, Adams revealed his particular interest in private letters by editing collections of both John Adams's and Abigail Adams's personal correspondence. In Adams's view, personal letters like those of Abigail Adams were valuable because they alone could illuminate the private realm of feeling and sentiment. Accordingly, he prefaced this collection by distinguishing "between the materials for a history of action and those for one of feeling." As sources for a history of feeling, Abigail Adams's letters, Adams believed, filled an important gap in the historical record. In his desire for such a history, Adams expressed the Romantic concern with recapturing inward experience and feeling. For Adams, it was not enough just to describe the actions of historical actors; like Romantic thinkers, he also wished to recover the individual's experience of an action. He elaborated on why he believed that a history of feeling was so important when he differentiated "between the action of men aiming at distinction among their fellow-beings, and the private, familiar sentiments, that run into the texture of the social system, without remark or the hope of observation."[83] For Adams, only by understanding the "private, familiar sentiments" could the historian discern the underlying social forces that influenced everyday life. In his concern with "the texture of the social system," Adams joined in the widespread interest in social history. And by advocating the study of women's private letters, he offered his own remedy for the scarcity of documentary sources on domestic history. If Adams's contemporaries for the most part avoided writing social history because they could not reconcile this interest with a critical ideal of scholarship that emphasized the importance of primary documents to truth, for Adams, women's private letters would enable historians to engage in social history without abandoning their commitment to this ideal.

In direct opposition to what was starting to become by 1840 an important strain in American biographical criticism, which claimed that the sanctity of the private sphere and of private documents made them inappropriate subjects for biography, Adams believed that truth required the historian to gain access to the domain of the private and familiar. Not only would the historian achieve a more complete picture of the past. On a more fundamental level, for Adams there was a qualitative difference between public and private utterances that made private letters more reliable as a source of truth. Public documents were in his view untrustworthy because of their disingenuous character—hence his belief that historians had distorted the Revolution by disregarding the private realm in favor of public documents and actions. Because "[o]ur history is for the most part wrapped up in the forms of office," he asserted, the "great men of the Revolution, in the eyes of posterity, are many of them like heroes of a mythological age." Adams reasoned, "They are seen, for the most part, when conscious that they are acting upon a theatre, where individual sentiment must be sometimes disguised, and often sacrificed, for the public good." However, since "[s]tatesmen and generals rarely say all they think or feel," "in the papers which come from them, they are made to assume a uniform of grave hue, which, though it doubtless exalts the opinion entertained of their perfections, somewhat diminishes the interest with which later generations study their character." According to Adams, because historical actors often felt compelled to suppress or disguise their views while in the public eye, the tendency to focus on their public activities had resulted in an idealized and inaccurate portrait of the revolutionaries, again in contrast to American biographical critics, who condemned such idealization as a by-product of the biographer's failure to respect the sanctity of the private sphere.[84]

Here, then, as he recognized how conscious deception by historical actors could distort truth, Adams displayed the kind of skeptical criticism of historical sources advocated by Markoe and other historians of his time. But in attributing such deception to the revolutionaries' concern for the public good, he revealed the limits to his critical perspective. While questioning the idealization of the revolutionaries as mythical heroes, Adams did not wish to repudiate their heroic status altogether. By turning their use of deception into a sign of their disinterestedness and concern for the public good, Adams reconciled his admiration for the revolutionaries with his skepticism about the truthfulness of their public statements, and thus in his own way he brought together a nationalist outlook with a critical ideal of scholarship. In the process, however, Adams revealed his ambivalence about whether to place the locus of morality in the public or the private sphere. In emphasizing the revolutionaries' concern with the public good, Adams both demonstrated their commitment to classical republican ideals and gave primacy to the public arena as the site of virtue. But in arguing that truth could be found only in the private utterances of historical actors, Adams adhered to Samuel Johnson's theory of biography, which privileged the private realm as the true index to individual character and morality.[85]

Adams's concern with the disparity between private sentiment and public professions and his effort to explain that disparity in terms of deception also had roots in the eighteenth-century Anglo-American cultural preoccupation with deception. The fear of deception had become especially prevalent among Anglo-Americans of this period, as they attributed to duplicity what appeared to be the growing disparity between professions and actions, and between intent and results, of an increasingly impersonal and interdependent social order. This sense of disparity was in turn partly the product of an emerging liberal capitalist economy, for the discrepancy between cause and effect, and between reality and appearances, seemed to widen with the development of a system of market relations that dissolved the moral correspondence between intent and result by characterizing public prosperity as the unintended consequence of the pursuit of private interest.[86]

Deception became an all the more pressing problem for antebellum Americans as the the impersonal market relations of a capitalist economy and the growth of cities created an anonymous "world of strangers" unlike the more personal face-to-face society of the colonial era. In a world of strangers, surface appearances became increasingly important, for appearance was often all an individual had to go on in assessing personal character. Yet this emphasis on appearance created the danger that the unscrupulous could manipulate the perceptions of others by simply putting on a facade of virtue, resulting in a disjunction between inner character and outward appearance. This sense of disjunction was so pervasive that Adams projected it onto the revolutionaries when he described them as "conscious that they were acting upon a theatre"; the need to maintain surface appearances and make a good impression was so powerful in Adams's view that it required even the revolutionaries—who were in his mind as far from being unscrupulous hypocrites as it was possible to be—to play a role that did not reflect their real character and beliefs.[87]

Middle-class Americans of the early nineteenth century responded to these fears about hypocrisy and deceptive appearances by developing a cult of sincerity that provided exhaustive guidelines for how to both demonstrate one's own sincerity and determine the sincerity of others. It was possible to ascertain the sincerity of social actors only by entering the private arena, for it was here that individuals could safely express their true sentiments, without fear that they would be seduced or taken advantage of by duplicitous strangers. And according to the cult of sincerity, individuals could show their sincerity by displaying their inner feelings, for sincerity was a function of emotion or "sensibility"—the more emotionally responsive the individual, the more sincere and transparent his or her character. The rise of a sentimental culture that privileged emotional sensitivity and the sincere expression of inner feeling as the yardstick to character was in this way a product of anxieties about how to define and determine social identity in a world in which social relations had become increasingly complicated and impersonal.[88]

As he explained why private letters would provide the historian with greater access to truth than public documents would, Adams used language that was strikingly similar to that associated with the cult of sincerity, for he likewise associated sincerity and truth with the expression of inner feeling and located these qualities in the private arena. These similarities suggest that the same cultural anxieties about social identity in a world of strangers that gave rise to the cult of sincerity also contributed to both Adams's view of deception as an obstacle to historical truth and his belief that private documents were the solution to this problem. Just as antebellum advice manuals identified the private sphere of the home as the only safe arena for the transparent display of character prescribed by the cult of sincerity, Adams advocated the study of private documents because only there could be seen "the confidential whisper to a friend, never meant to reach the ear of the multitude, the secret wishes, not to be blazoned forth to catch applause, . . . that most betray the springs of action" and offered the best "guides to character."[89] Because they allowed the historian to probe beneath public appearances into this realm of unguarded private expression, Adams believed that private letters would provide a truer understanding of human character than would public documents.

And like the cult of sincerity, Adams ultimately viewed women as the guarantors of truth and sincerity in the historical realm. According to the cult of sincerity, women were both inherently more sincere by virtue of their emotional nature and freer to be sincere without fear that this quality would make them vulnerable to the duplicity of strangers, confined as they were to the safety of the private realm. Likewise, Adams defined sincerity as a feminine trait when he claimed that private correspondence by women possessed exceptional claims to veracity by virtue of their uniquely disinterested role in society. For women confined to the domestic realm, "[t]here is not so much room for the doctrines of expediency, and the promptings of private interest, to compromise the force of public example." During upheavals like the Revolution, "the sacrifice of feelings made by the female sex is unmixed with a hope of worldly compensation," for women had "no ambition to gratify, no fame to be gained by the simply negative virtue of privations suffered in silence." In sum, "[t]he lot of woman, in times of trouble, is to be a passive spectator of events, which she can scarcely hope to make subservient to her own fame, or to control." Consequently, Adams implied, excluded from the competitive arena of public affairs, and without any motive for deception, women were most likely to articulate their true feelings in their letters. Hence, Adams concluded, "If it were possible to get at the expression of feelings by women in the heart of a community, at a moment of extraordinary trial, recorded in a shape evidently designed to be secret and confidential, this would seem to present the surest and most unfailing index to its general character."[90]

Rather than associating truth with the masculine realm, then, Adams defined truth in feminine terms. In this definition of historical truth, Adams drew on the assumptions of nineteenth-century domestic ideology, revealing the double-edged implications of this ideology for women's relationship to history. Even as he divested women of agency in historical events, he assigned to them a crucial role in the recording of those events. Precisely because they were not the subjects of history, they could be more objective and disinterested about the past. All the traits that disqualified women from taking an active role in historical events—their supposed purity and selflessness—made them ideal chroniclers of the past.[91] And because Adams identified truth with sentiment and feeling, he believed that women could best represent truth, for, according to domestic ideology, women were naturally more emotional than men. For Adams, then, truth required both detachment and a capacity for emotion—two qualities that women combined. But just as the feminine associations of domestic history prevented most historians from actually writing social history, despite all their injunctions to the contrary, Adams made only a limited effort to put his precepts for the value of women's private letters into practice, confining his own research in such sources to those of his own grandmother.

"American history has never been written with *criticism Kritik*": George Bancroft as Critical Historian

Often viewed as the quintessential Romantic historian of this era, George Bancroft was representative of antebellum historical thought, but not in the way that modern scholars have assumed. Rather than embodying a commitment to an artistic view of history that was both unscientific and uncritical in its methodology, Bancroft demonstrated how aesthetic and economic imperatives converged with a scientific ideal of critical scholarship in his concern with originality and impartiality as he, like his contemporaries, sought to reconcile these ideals through his use of footnotes and primary documents.[92] In the process,

however, he made the contested meaning of originality—and its complex relationship to impartiality—especially apparent. If, on the one hand, Bancroft was
even more avid than Prescott about expressing his hostility to plagiarism and
the economic basis for that hostility, he was, on the other hand, more inconsistent about citation in practice than Prescott was. Ultimately, the inconsistencies
in Bancroft's understanding of plagiarism signified his ambivalence about the
historian's interpretive role, as he at once privileged and limited the expression
of the historian's individual perspective. In doing so, Bancroft brought together
the different conceptions of authorship signaled by the commercialization of
literature and the resistance to that development, and he revealed how his commitment to the German ideal of "historical skepticism" both furthered his desire for originality and restricted the exercise of that desire. If, in his ambition to
be unique, Bancroft gave the historian an active role in interpreting his sources,
he would only go so far in that role, for his ideal of critical history assumed that
truth was an entity independent of the historian's interpretation.

In 1834, Bancroft published the first volume of his *History of the United
States*. As the most comprehensive and ambitious account of American history
to that point, Bancroft's work immediately achieved a commanding influence
over nineteenth-century American historical writing. Although notorious for
his devoutly filiopietistic interpretation of American history, Bancroft was a
more sophisticated historian than many scholars have acknowledged. In both
its sources and interpretation, his *History* combined a deep sense of nationalism with a cosmopolitan perspective, and his extensive research included
both colonial and European archival sources. Heeding the growing demand
for citation, Bancroft supplied footnotes throughout most of his *History*. The
consistency of his notes varied from volume to volume, and his treatment of
quotations was admittedly suspect. Bancroft often combined different quotes,
or interpolated his own language into them, without indicating or distinguishing his modifications to the original quotation. Such changes often made these
quotes agree more closely with his own arguments and style and grew out of his
desire to give meaning and coherence to his narrative. Yet Bancroft was, overall, far more scrupulous about citation than his predecessors were. For most of
the first six volumes in the *History*, he provided regular, though not extensive,
footnotes. These notes generally contained a brief citation of his source, occasionally supplemented by commentary of his own.[93]

Bancroft expressed his commitment to citation and his antipathy to plagiarism in an angry letter of 1845 accusing the historian Henry Brown of plagiarizing from his work. Although Brown had used Bancroft's history to write his
own *History of Illinois*, published in 1844, he offered little acknowledgment of
his sources other than a handful of rudimentary footnotes scattered through-

out the text, which themselves only listed the author's last name, without page numbers or, for the most part, even titles of the works he cited. Brown did acknowledge Bancroft in a few such footnotes, marking his citations with asterisks followed by "Bancroft" at the bottom of the page, along with two quotations for which he cited Bancroft as his source in the body of the text. Yet, as Brown himself recognized when he apologized in his preface that "he has not more frequently given credit; and on some occasions, done better justice to those from whose works he has so liberally extracted," such citations did not indicate the full extent of his indebtedness to other historians.[94] In contrast to his Revolutionary predecessors, Bancroft did not consider this kind of general disclaimer a legitimate substitute for more specific references, as he made clear when he sharply rebuked Brown for "the manner in which you have appropriated my labors without acknowledgment. Such conduct is not usual and is not considered right among men of letters. You take to yourself statements of history which it cost me weeks and months of labor to collect and make; and borrowing facts, reflections and almost language, you leave the public to read it as your own." He continued angrily, "It is no excuse for this, that the quotations are not literal. The few changes do not alter the character of your unacknowledged pages. I think your preface contains no sufficient apology for what you have done."[95]

Although, as Bancroft admitted, Brown had made some changes in wording, these changes had not fundamentally altered the language or content of the sections he had appropriated from Bancroft. Bancroft was so outraged by Brown's use of his work not just because it took away from his originality but also because he believed that it violated his property rights. In this condemnation of plagiarism, Bancroft appealed to a doctrine of intellectual property rights derived from John Locke. According to Locke, an individual established his right to private property through labor. In emphasizing the labor that went into the material plagiarized by Brown, and claiming ownership of it on that basis, Bancroft applied a Lockean conception of individual property to the intellectual realm. Through this rationale, Bancroft revealed how the Romantic regard for originality converged with the assumptions of Lockean liberalism to put a premium on citation. The individualistic orientation of Lockean theory reinforced a notion of originality that privileged uniqueness and innovation and a definition of authorship predicated on these qualities. In turn, the Lockean emphasis on the sanctity of private property rights contributed to the growing conviction that an author, as the originator of his own language and ideas, possessed exclusive ownership of them. Consequently, plagiarism increasingly came into disrepute as both a form of theft and a betrayal of the ideal of author as individual creator, making citation all the more imperative for historians.[96]

Paradoxically, Bancroft was at once more explicit than Prescott about the

view of literature as a form of individual property underlying the Romantic
ideal of originality and more ambivalent about this conception of authorship. If
Bancroft's claims to property in his writing adhered to the definition of authorship implicated in the commercialization and professionalization of literature,
his ambivalence about the idea of writing as a form of individual property and
expression was consonant with the opposition to this conception of authorship
embodied by what Meredith McGill terms the "culture of reprinting."[97] Hence
Bancroft seemed contradictory in his attitude toward plagiarism, as he brought
together these contending definitions of authorship in his use and citation of
sources. And so, even as Bancroft embraced a Lockean understanding of authorship in claiming property in his own writing, he did not extend that same
understanding to the works of other historians. Consequently, prior to his attack on Brown for plagiarizing from his history, Bancroft had himself been the
target of accusations of plagiarism, and indeed these accusations could have
contributed to his attack on Brown by making him more touchy and defensive
on the subject of plagiarism—after all, what better way to prove his own hostility to and, by extension, innocence of plagiarism than by implicating someone
else in the practice?

   Bancroft's own friend William Prescott had criticized him for his failure to
provide more extensive citations in his history.[98] Even more serious, Bancroft was
the target of charges that he had plagiarized from the loyalist historian George
Chalmers. Denying such charges yet engaging in what would now be deemed
plagiarism, Bancroft revealed especially clearly the conflicted and ambiguous
meaning of plagiarism and originality in this period. Bancroft expressed his
hostility to plagiarism as he indignantly repudiated these accusations in 1844,
deriding them as "a tissue of falsehoods from beginning to end. I gave it no attention, as bearing its own ear-marks of falsehood and folly." Bancroft was so
outraged by this accusation because it impugned his claims to originality. It was
ludicrous to believe he would have forfeited his individuality as an author by
copying from Chalmers, for, as he demanded angrily, "who would suppose that
I would break the unity and consistency of my own style and narrative by patch-
ing upon it the language and doctrines of an English tory respecting our American revolution? The suggestion is ridiculous."[99] In characterizing plagiarism as
a violation of the "unity" of his own style, Bancroft, like Prescott, embraced a
Romantic understanding of originality that defined this ideal in terms of the
uniqueness and coherence of an author's individual form of expression. Bancroft's refutation doubly stigmatized plagiarism as an aesthetic offense against
this ideal and a political offense against the nation, for plagiarizing from a loyalist would also in his view betray his efforts to vindicate the Revolution.

Notwithstanding Bancroft's indignant denials, there was some basis for this accusation, for Bancroft had committed what would be considered plagiarism today. He had, in fact, relied heavily on Chalmers's *Political Annals*, and his language often closely replicated Chalmers's. Bancroft was not simply being self-serving or hypocritical in the disparity between his rhetoric and actions. He saw no conflict between his condemnation of plagiarism and his use of Chalmers because he defined plagiarism differently than modern scholars do. As his use of Chalmers demonstrated, his seeming inconsistency about plagiarism ultimately reflected his ambivalence about the historian's interpretive role. Unlike his Revolutionary predecessors, rather than simply copying long extracts verbatim, Bancroft consciously paraphrased and reinterpreted Chalmers's statements for his own purposes. He repeatedly appropriated segments of Chalmers's narrative but used these selections to draw conclusions that were completely opposite to those of Chalmers. Bancroft reinterpreted Chalmers in just this way for his account of Culpeper's Rebellion of 1677. Chalmers offered a highly critical rendering of the revolt, believing that it exemplified the colonists' rebellious and anarchic tendencies. After describing how the rebels overthrew and seized control of the government so that "they, for years, exercised all the authority of an independent state," Chalmers concluded, "And thus the people are made the constant bubbles of their own credulity and of others crimes: We may deplore their miseries, though it seems to little purpose, what cannot possibly be in the future prevented! When Eastchurch at length arrived, to whose commission or conduct there could be no objection, the insurgents derided his authority and denied him obedience."[100]

Although Bancroft to some extent followed Chalmers in the structure and language of his account of Culpeper's Rebellion, he adapted Chalmers's version for his own purposes by making certain omissions and additions that portrayed the rebels much more favorably than had Chalmers. Specifically, Bancroft eliminated Chalmers's disparaging reference to the people as "the constant bubbles of their own credulity and of others crimes." Instead, Bancroft added phrases of his own that emphasized the people's respect for order, in contrast to Chalmers's interpretation of the revolt as an expression of popular anarchy. For example, Bancroft described the revolt as "a deliberate rising of the people" in which they soon "recovered from anarchy, tranquilly organized a government, and established courts of justice." For Bancroft, this rebellion foreshadowed the Revolution, as he made clear when he spoke of how the rebels "formed conclusions as just as those which a century later pervaded the country." In his view, the rebels displayed the same devotion to order and liberty that would characterize the revolutionaries. Therefore, in defending these rebels against

Chalmers's accusations, Bancroft was, by extension, vindicating the revolution-aries as well. Bancroft thus reinterpreted Chalmers to serve the nationalist pur-pose of glorifying and defending the Revolution.[101]

In doing so, Bancroft differentiated his work from that of Chalmers, thereby enabling him to see it as original. Bancroft was himself conscious of how his interpretation differed from that of Chalmers, using his footnotes to underline the contrast between them. While Bancroft actually cited Hugh Williamson—who had himself plagiarized from Chalmers for his *History of North Carolina* (1812)—in the footnote to this passage, he criticized Williamson for being too influenced "by the judgments of royalists" like Chalmers who had condemned the rebellion, and he directly attacked Chalmers's trustworthiness as a source, noting that his "coloring is always wrong; the facts usually perverted," in two footnotes later in his discussion of Culpeper's revolt.[102] For Bancroft, then, originality was less a question of the particular words the historian used than of the larger framework or "coloring" that gave coherence to those words. Because he had offered a perspective that was fundamentally different from Chalmers's, he did not consider his use of Chalmers's text plagiarism, even though he had borrowed some of Chalmers's words and language. Conversely, even though Brown had changed some of the wording of his extracts from Bancroft, Ban-croft still accused Brown of plagiarism because those changes had not affected the meaning of his ideas. And so, in his use of Chalmers, Bancroft revealed both the extent and limits to his view of historical writing as a form of individual expression. Although Bancroft expressed his own perspective in his reinterpre-tation of Chalmers, at the same time, his willingness to appropriate Chalmers's language demonstrated that his desire to express his own point of view did not extend to using completely different words.[103]

This duality in Bancroft's treatment of Chalmers was consistent with the complex understanding of authorship that characterized what McGill describes as the "culture of reprinting" so central to the literary culture of the 1830s and 1840s. Bancroft's plagiarism of Chalmers's language was a practice akin to the widespread American reprinting of foreign texts made possible by the absence of an international copyright law in that both represented a form of unauthor-ized copying from other writers. Both practices were in turn premised on shared assumptions about the limits on authorship as a vehicle for individual expres-sion. Yet if American reprinters did not give the same primacy to originality as Romantic theory did, neither did they view their own reproductions as en-tirely derivative. American reprinters, thus, did make some effort to distinguish their reproductions of foreign texts from the original versions by adapting and reframing those texts to serve nationalist purposes, just as Bancroft appropri-ated and revised Chalmers to further nationalist objectives.[104] In this way, the effort to be original—by imposing their own framework on the sources they appropriated—served a nationalist function for both Bancroft and American reprinters.

At the same time, Bancroft revealed the importance of German critical scholarship to both his desire for originality and his belief in the limits to the historian's interpretive role as he explained how his methodology would enable him to realize this ideal. Firmly committed to "the principles of historical scepticism, and, not allowing myself to grow weary in comparing witnesses or consulting codes of laws," Bancroft proclaimed in the preface to his history, "I have endeavored to impart originality to my narrative, by deriving it entirely from writings and sources, which were the contemporaries of the events that are described." As his reference to "historical scepticism" revealed, Bancroft believed that the historian had to take a critical and questioning view of his sources; he could not just accept their assertions at face value. This was why examining primary sources was so important. Only by comparing these sources to one another and to secondary accounts could the historian test and verify the claims of historical actors as well as those of other historians.[105] Like Upham, Bancroft suggested that his use of primary sources would confer originality on his work by providing the reader with new information and facts on American history. But in this definition of originality, Bancroft suggested that originality was more a matter of content than of the historian's interpretation. In this way, he could make his work unique without turning it into an expression of his individual perspective.

This understanding of the historian's role was partly the product of Bancroft's affinity for German historiography, for Bancroft subscribed to German critical ideals of scholarship in his quest for "historical scepticism." Exposed to German thought and scholarship during his studies in Göttingen, Bancroft developed a lifelong interest in and appreciation for German culture and philosophy. While his Romantic proclivities had roots in German idealism, Bancroft also owed a debt to the critical tradition of German historiography. He was first introduced to this tradition while studying for his doctorate at the University of Göttingen, which had become a center for the development of a more critical and scientific approach to history during the second half of the eighteenth century. One of Bancroft's teachers at Göttingen was A. H. L. Heeren, who was an instrumental figure in pioneering this approach. Bancroft expressed his admiration for Heeren by publishing translations of Heeren's historical works on ancient Greece and Europe, in 1824 and 1829, respectively. In particular, Bancroft valued Heeren's accuracy, employment of original documents, and impartiality, suggesting Heeren's influence on his own commitment to these ideals. When Bancroft declared that "American history has never been written with *criti-*

cism Kritik," his use of the German term *Kritik* pointed directly to the German sources of his engagement in the methods and practices of critical scholarship. In this statement, Bancroft also indicated another way that his devotion to such methods would further his quest for originality. Because such an approach was unprecedented in American historiography, Bancroft suggested that he would confer uniqueness and originality on his work simply by engaging in a critical analysis of his sources.[106]

And so, for Bancroft, footnotes would establish his originality not only by showing that he had not copied from other historians but also by revealing that he had adopted a new and unprecedented methodology in American historical writing, for he sought to demonstrate how he had lived up to German critical ideals through the sources he cited and his commentary on those sources. Although, as his footnotes revealed, Bancroft relied primarily on published sources for his first three volumes, those sources included both the works of other historians like Holmes and Jeremy Belknap and primary sources like William Hening's statutes of Virginia and John Winthrop's journal. And when he did use primary sources, he often made a special point of telling the reader in a footnote, as he did when he stated, "I have followed the contemporaries of the events which I describe." Among the primary sources he listed in one footnote were the Massachusetts colony records, Edward Johnson's *Wonder-Working Providence*, and John Winthrop's correspondence. As his history progressed, not only did Bancroft rely more heavily on primary sources for his analysis; these primary sources also increasingly consisted of unpublished manuscripts and archival material.[107]

In addition to citing these sources, Bancroft used his footnotes to engage in exactly the kind of systematic and critical analysis of sources that he prescribed. Although his footnotes often provided only a brief citation of his sources, they also periodically compared these sources with one another. In many cases, Bancroft would simply tell the reader to "compare" the different sources he cited, without making explicit his own views on which source he found more reliable, as he did when he wrote in one footnote, "Compare Hillard's Life of Smith, in Sparks's American Biography."[108] At other times, however, he would offer a fuller assessment of his sources, not only stating which he found more reliable but also explaining the basis for his assessment. In one such footnote to his discussion of Ferdinand de Soto's exploration of Mississippi, Bancroft declared,

> On Soto's expedition, by far the best account is that of the Portuguese Eye-witness, first published in 1557, and by Hakluyt, in English, in 1609. . . . This narrative is remarkably good, and contains internal evidence of its credibility. Nuttall

erroneously attributes it to Vega. In the work of Vega, numbers and distances are magnified; and every thing embellished with great boldness. His history is not without its value, but must be consulted with extreme caution. Herrera . . . is not an original authority.[109]

Ultimately, by demonstrating his attachment to "historical scepticism," footnotes would attest to the impartiality of his account, for, like his contemporaries, Bancroft believed that a critical approach to sources would contribute to impartial truth. Because of this assumption, he could claim for himself, "Now I should want leave without respect of persons to speak the truth, to quote the passages which are wrong, to set down the evidence of the error."[110] But in this definition of impartial truth, Bancroft pointed to the limits he imposed on the historian's interpretive role and the influence of German critical ideals on those limits. For Bancroft, such a critical approach would promote truth by enabling the historian to eradicate error and inaccuracy. In setting up an opposition between truth and "error," Bancroft expressed a scientific definition of truth as the accurate representation of objective reality. This definition of truth turned disagreements into a conflict between truth and error rather than a conflict between different interpretations of the same event. And so, Bancroft suggested, the historian's goal was to discover truth, not create or interpret it, thus limiting the extent to which the historian could express his individual perspective in his work.

Bancroft made this assumption even clearer as he elaborated on what he meant by historical impartiality. Affirming the vital importance of impartiality, he declared, "The historian, not less than philosophers and naturalists, must bring to his pursuit the freedom of an unbiassed mind; in his case the submission of reason to prejudice would have a deeper criminality; for he cannot neglect to be impartial without at once falsifying nature and denying providence." In this proclamation, even as Bancroft expressed his firm commitment to impartiality, he complicated the meaning of this ideal. In his emphasis on the "unbiassed mind," he embraced a scientific ideal of truth that required detachment from the historian. Yet in arguing that it would be criminal, and indeed irreligious, for the historian to do otherwise, he revealed at the same time a moral component to his conception of truth. Bancroft brought together these two conceptions of truth as he likened the historian to both philosophers and naturalists. Historical truth, for Bancroft, was not just a matter of fact; it consisted of moral verities established by providence. For Bancroft, these moral verities did not reflect the historian's own personal perspective but represented objective truths external to the historian. For this reason, he saw no conflict between his emphasis on moral judgment and his desire for impartiality. On the contrary, only by being impartial could the historian recover those deeper truths.[111]

All these historians shared a belief in the importance of citation and primary sources, but they varied over why these practices were important and over how to use them. As they did so, they revealed more fundamental differences over the nature of historical truth. If for Markoe truth was supposed to be an unvarnished account of fact, for Upham truth involved an imaginative re-creation of the past. If for Charles Francis Adams truth was based on the expression of inner feeling, for Holmes truth required the historian to suppress his personal feelings. These different conceptions of truth were not mutually exclusive, and historians brought them together in different ways. Despite the differences between them, then, these historians all in their own way sought to reconcile their recognition of how truth varied according to individual perspective with their belief in a truth that existed independent of that perspective. Indeed, these two assumptions were integrally related to each other, as doubts about the possibility of impartial truth actually fueled efforts to establish a more secure foundation for truth. Thus, even though impartiality and originality implied conflicting views of the historian's role, these two ideals developed in close conjunction with each other, converging in demands for footnotes and primary sources.

In this way, the development of a more systematic and rigorous approach to sources and citation brought together seemingly contradictory tendencies. As antebellum historians used footnotes to demonstrate their originality, they at once claimed ownership of their writing as property and conceived of it as a transcendent aesthetic creation.[112] In turn, the importance of citation as an emblem of both originality and critical accuracy demonstrated that historians in this period did not consider the Romantic view of history as literary art and a scientific approach to history mutually exclusive. And while these tendencies grew partly out of European intellectual and aesthetic developments, they also served nationalist ends, for the emphasis on the value of primary sources enabled American historians to claim that the nation's abundance of such documents gave the United States an exceptional capacity to achieve historical truth. The next chapter looks more closely at the nationalist function of impartiality by examining how early nineteenth-century historians at once sought to live up to this ideal and affirmed their commitment to American exceptionalist ideology in their interpretations of the nation's history.

CHAPTER FOUR

PURITANISM, SLAVERY, AND THE AMERICAN REVOLUTION

American Exceptionalism and Impartiality

Writing in 1858 to the historian John Gorham Palfrey, Francis Bowen criticized Palfrey for idealizing the Puritans in his *History of New England*. As he explained to Palfrey,

> [Y]our tone in reference to the Puritan fathers seems too uniformly apologetic and laudatory. I admire them as much as you do; but to make others share your admiration, you must *appear*, as well as *be*, impartial. As it is, you will be charged with defending them through thick and thin. After all, they were mortal men; they made blunders, they shared the errors of their times. Better even to go out of your way to acknowledge thus much, than to excite surprise and distrust by what may appear to be excessive laudation.

In criticizing Palfrey for his "apologetic and laudatory" portrayal of the Puritans, Bowen sounded much like modern scholars, who have characterized antebellum interpretations of American history as filiopietistic and uncritically patriotic. Yet if Palfrey's view of the Puritans conformed to conventional characterizations of American historiography, Bowen's criticism of Palfrey demonstrated that antebellum historiography was more complex—and more concerned with impartiality—than modern scholars have assumed.[1]

As Bowen made clear, he did not admire the Puritans any less than Palfrey did. Bowen recognized, however, that Palfrey would be more successful in promoting admiration for the Puritans if he was more impartial. Although Bowen was more conscious and explicit than most of his contemporaries were about the social ramifications of historical interpretation, this did not mean that he was being disingenuous in his call for impartiality. On the contrary, that consciousness made him all the more aware of the need for Palfrey to actually live up to his professions of impartiality, which, for Bowen, meant a balanced perspective that recognized the Puritans' faults as well as their virtues. In

Bowen's view, "excessive laudation" would simply undermine the credibility of Palfrey's claims about the Puritans, making his readers question whether any of his statements could be trusted. Conversely, Bowen believed, an acknowledgment of the Puritans' faults would make Palfrey's defense of the Puritans all the more compelling, for, rather than appearing to be an expression of his own partiality, his praise for the Puritans would take on the aura and authority of impartial truth. In this way, Bowen suggested, impartiality would actually further Palfrey's nationalist and sectional desire to glorify the Puritans. Yet Palfrey was no less committed to the ideal of impartiality than was Bowen; he differed from Bowen, however, in his assumption that his celebratory view of the Puritans represented impartial truth. And so, if for Bowen "impartiality" could serve partial purposes, Palfrey believed that his seemingly partial view of the Puritans would actually further the cause of "impartial" truth. Rather than a conflict between impartial and partial history, then, the disagreement between Palfrey and Bowen was one between two different conceptions of impartiality, revealing the contested character of impartiality in this period.

Thus, although early nineteenth-century historians agreed on the importance of impartiality, they, like Palfrey and Bowen, differed over what this ideal meant and over how to put it into practice. Hence, these historians varied widely in their interpretations of American history. At one extreme was George Bancroft's celebratory interpretation of American history. Like Palfrey, Bancroft saw himself as impartial or "objective" in his laudatory account of American history as the progress of democracy, and he in different ways reconciled his commitment to impartiality with his nationalist purposes. While influential, Bancroft's interpretation of American history was by no means uncontested, and his contemporaries sharply challenged both his portrayal of the Puritans and his explanation for the Revolution, maintaining, like Bowen, that impartial truth required a more critical view of the nation's founders. And, like Bowen, believing that such a critical perspective would, in the end, enhance, not detract from, the reputation of their subjects, these historians reconciled their desire for impartiality with their nationalist purposes. Ultimately, then, for all their differences with Bancroft and with one another, these historians shared a deep commitment to the ideology of American exceptionalism and used the ideal of impartiality to further that commitment.

Yet if their attachment to exceptionalist ideology revealed a supreme self-confidence about the nation's special destiny, the conflicts and tensions in their understanding of impartiality at the same time reflected deeper divisions between and within antebellum historians over the rise of democracy and the problem of slavery.[2] Richard Hildreth illuminated the nature of these divisions and the uses of impartiality as a vehicle for combating slavery in both the content of and response to his history. Hildreth was thus actually more similar to his contemporaries than modern scholars have recognized in both his commitment to impartiality and in using that ideal for political purposes. Where Hildreth differed from other historians of his time was in his rejection of exceptionalist ideology, and the critical response to his history at once revealed this difference and demonstrated how his contemporaries reconciled impartiality with the belief in American exceptionalism.

America's Uncertain Destiny: Revolutionary Historiography and the Roots of Exceptionalist Ideology

The ideology of American exceptionalism had a long lineage, dating from the sixteenth century. As Jack Greene has demonstrated, the image of America as a unique and exceptional place had begun to develop even before the United States had become an independent nation. According to Greene, exceptionalist ideology rested on two premises—first, the belief that America was unique, and second, the belief that such uniqueness made America superior to other nations. While commentators on America had long emphasized its distinctiveness from Europe, they did not equate American distinctiveness with superiority until the Revolution. The Revolutionary historians played an important role in articulating the basis for this sense of superiority as they asserted their belief in the nation's special destiny. At the same time, uncertain about whether that destiny was inevitable, these historians left room for contingency and human agency in their interpretations of the Revolution. And so, while chauvinistic in their celebration of American distinctiveness, the Revolutionary historians revealed the limits to that chauvinism and the open and fluid character of their exceptionalism in their ambivalence about whether the nation's destiny was preordained.[3]

In their assumption that providence had assigned to America a special role in the advancement of liberty, the Revolutionary historians embraced a key component of exceptionalist ideology and revealed the influence of Protestant millennial thought on that ideology. This sense of providential destiny drew from Protestant millennialism the idea that history was progressing toward a divinely ordained end, adapting the millennial vision of a chosen people whose purpose was to act as God's instrument of human regeneration to the belief in America's special mission to spread republican ideals. Jedidiah Morse articulated the belief in the nation's providential destiny while praising the early New

England settlers as a remarkable people, "of a character peculiarly adapted to those important designs in Providence, which they were to fulfil. They were destined to plant and subdue a wilderness, filled with savage and ferocious enemies; to lay the foundation of a great empire." While the belief in the nation's special destiny had roots in the Puritan colonists' vision of their society as a city upon a hill, this belief also served nationalist purposes for the Revolutionary historians. Writing at a time when the bonds uniting the newly formed nation were still tenuous and uncertain, these historians hoped to shore up national bonds by claiming for the United States a special destiny as a republican nation. Such a view would promote national unity, they hoped, by enhancing a sense of national greatness and by giving a basis for national identity to a nation that lacked the usual bonds of nationhood.[4]

Yet, as Morse revealed in privileging New England's role as an agent of American destiny, there was also a sectional element to this sense of nationalism. Hence, while the Revolutionary historians agreed that liberty was deeply rooted in the nation's history, they located the origins of this ideal in different regions. If for New England historians like Morse liberty had originated with the Puritan colonists, historians from outside New England emphasized the role of their respective regions in the advancement of liberty. The Virginia historian John Daly Burk, for example, gave primacy to his own state's role in this process in his account of how the arrival of Lord Delaware's expedition in 1610 saved Jamestown from abandonment. This expedition was so important because it "carried with it the altars and the destinies of liberty: The germ of human happiness is on board," and "the wretched colonists carry with them the sacred fire, which shall bless their posterity, and animate the world."[5]

Although they differed over where liberty had originated in America, simply in their concern with locating the colonial origins of liberty, the Revolutionary historians were similar in advancing a teleological view of American history that reflected and furthered the exceptionalist belief in American destiny. Hence, rather than analyzing the colonial past on its own terms, they viewed it primarily as a precursor to the Revolution, which had for them in turn effected the achievement of liberty in America.[6] Interpreting the Revolution as a struggle for abstract principle, the Revolutionary historians made liberty both a cause and an effect of the Revolution. As the historian John Lendrum summed up in 1795, "It was a love of liberty and a quick sense of injury which led the Americans to rise in arms against the mother country."[7] Specifically, in their view, Americans opposed British policies like the Stamp Act out of the belief that Parliament could not tax them unless they were represented, for they viewed this right as essential to liberty. In her history of New England, published in

1799, Hannah Adams argued that colonial opposition to parliamentary taxation was widespread because "it was a prevailing sentiment through the colonies, that taxation and representation were inseparable, and that they could be neither free nor happy, if their property could be taken from them, without their consent."[8]

While believing in a sense of American destiny, the Revolutionary historians also left room for contingency and human agency in their accounts of the Revolution, reconciling these potentially contradictory assumptions in different ways. And so, though they agreed with Morse that America's special destiny had been divinely ordained, they differed over the exact role that providence had played in effecting this purpose. Even those historians most insistent about their belief in providential design did not structure their narratives around this belief. Referring only intermittently to providence in their histories, they limited providence to an auxiliary role, as David Ramsay did in his explanation for the rift that developed between Britain and the American colonies. He commented, "It is probable that neither party, in the beginning, intended to go thus far, but by the inscrutable operations of providence, each was permitted to adopt such measures as not only rent the empire, but involved them both, with their own consent, in all the calamities of a long and bloody war." Here, while Ramsay ascribed the Revolution to the "inscrutable operations of providence," providence played a passive, supporting role; it "permitted" the escalation of hostilities between Britain and the colonies but did not actively steer events toward a certain goal. In this way, Ramsay at once made the Revolution part of providential design and allotted a role for human agency in effecting that design.[9]

Likewise, in his analysis of the secular causes that had brought about the Revolution, Ramsay at once adhered to a teleological framework and allowed for human agency within that framework. Like his contemporaries, Ramsay rooted the Revolution in events well before the taxation disputes of the 1760s, ultimately attributing the Revolution to the love of liberty and the spirit of independence that the colonists had implanted in and developed from the earliest settlements. For Ramsay, the colonial devotion to liberty originated with the timing and character of the earliest settlers. Because colonial settlement began just as the English struggle against the Stuart monarchs was approaching its zenith, the colonists who came to America were those who were "most hostile to the claims of prerogative." As a result, "[t]he English Colonists were from their first settlement in America, devoted to liberty, on English ideas, and English principles."[10] Along with distance, geography, social conditions, and the political arrangements of the colonies, the religion of the colonists played a decisive role in reinforcing these principles, according to Ramsay. Primarily Protestants, adherents to a faith that "is founded on a strong claim to natural liberty, and the right of private judgement," the Puritan settlers of New England, in particular, were "hostile to all interference of authority, in matters of opinion, and predisposed to a jealousy for civil liberty."[11] Ramsay's account was teleological in viewing the colonial past as a prelude to the Revolution and explaining colonial history in terms of this result. By interpreting American history in linear terms and portraying the Revolution as the culmination of the colonial past, Ramsay reflected and furthered the exceptionalist view of the Revolution as the realization of American destiny.

At the same time, Ramsay made it clear that there was nothing inevitable about the fulfillment of this destiny, for he emphasized that the events he described were simply preconditions, not determinants, of independence. Together, Ramsay concluded, these forces "produced a warm love for liberty, a high sense of the rights of human nature, and a predilection for independence."[12] As a result, on the eve of the Revolutionary crisis, matters stood thus for the colonists: "Foreseeing their future importance, from the rapid increase of their numbers, and extension of their commerce, and being extremely jealous of their rights, they readily admitted, and with pleasure indulged, ideas and sentiments which were favourable to independence." By using such words as "predilection" and "favourable," which suggested that colonial developments were conducive to, but did not necessitate, independence, Ramsay left room for human agency and contingency in his account of the Revolution.[13]

Viewing their work as extensions of their Revolutionary activism, the Revolutionary historians assigned such importance to the writing of history precisely because of their belief in human agency. Specifically, the Revolutionary historians wrote partly in response to the political partisanship of this period and what appeared to be a growing absorption in material gain, which they believed went directly counter to the republican ideals of virtue and self-sacrifice that had effected the Revolution. In writing history for this purpose, the Revolutionary historians revealed that as much as they affirmed a belief in America's special destiny, that destiny was by no means fixed or inevitable for them. And so, desiring to combat what he saw as the present-day lapse from the principles of the Revolution, Ramsay sought to revive the spirit of the revolutionaries by holding them up as exemplars of republican virtue for present-day Americans to emulate. Through such exhortations, Ramsay hoped to avert the fate of earlier republics and prevent America from falling into the same cycle of corruption and decay that had destroyed other republican societies. Thus, Ramsay's exemplary theory of history both was premised on the belief in human agency and sought to further that belief. Just as the revolutionaries had effected the Revolution by their own efforts, Ramsay implied, so too were present-day

Americans responsible for their own future. And because it was still very much in doubt whether Americans would heed these exhortations to virtue, the Revolutionary historians could not be complacent or certain about their vision of America as a chosen nation.[14]

"If there is democracy in the history it is not subjective, but objective as they say here": George Bancroft as Impartial Historian

And so, while the Revolutionary historians helped lay the basis for American exceptionalist ideology, their antebellum successors developed a more chauvinistic and complacent version of that ideology, for they were more confident about America's special destiny than their predecessors were. Paradoxically, even as antebellum historians embraced a more chauvinistic form of nationalism than that of their Revolutionary predecessors, they expressed a stronger commitment to impartiality. These two tendencies came together in George Bancroft, one of the best-known and most influential historians of the early nineteenth century. After publishing the first volume of his history of the United States in 1834 to wide popular and critical acclaim, he followed with nine other volumes published at irregular intervals, with the last volume appearing in 1874.

What made Bancroft so successful and important, according to modern scholars, was his ability to articulate and crystallize the exceptionalist assumptions embraced by his contemporaries. For modern scholars, Bancroft's formulation of the exceptionalist narrative possessed such power because of its mythic quality—that is, its ability to give American history higher meaning by combining the sacred with the secular. In their emphasis on the chauvinistic and biased character of Bancroft's mythic perspective, modern scholars have paid less attention to another characteristic of Bancroft's history—its concern with impartiality. As partial as his celebratory view of American history appeared to be, Bancroft expressed a genuine commitment to the ideal of impartial truth. Rather than viewing his nationalist purposes and his desire for impartiality as mutually exclusive, he believed that these two goals were integrally related to each other, and he used his conception of impartiality in different ways to reinforce exceptionalist assumptions. Ultimately, then, what made Bancroft's account of American history—and his vision of American exceptionalism—so compelling was not just its mythic quality but its claims to impartial truth, for by making his account appear to be impartial, he conferred on myth the mantle and legitimacy of objective reality.[15]

Although his *History of the United States* covered the entire span of Ameri-

can history up through the Constitution, Bancroft, like his Revolutionary predecessors, made the Revolution the focus of this work. In both its content and
structure, however, Bancroft was more unequivocal than the Revolutionary historians in his portrayal of the Revolution as the inevitable culmination of the
nation's destiny. Consequently, the teleological element present in the Revolutionary histories was even more pronounced in Bancroft's account, as Bancroft
turned it into the unifying principle of his narrative. Hence he interpreted the
colonial past, and indeed, all of human history, as precursors leading inexorably
up to the Revolution. As he summed up, "prepared by glorious forerunners,"
the Revolution "grew naturally and necessarily out of the series of past events
by the formative principle of a living belief." Believing that the Revolution was
inevitable because it had been decreed by "the grand design of Providence," Bancroft explained, the revolutionaries "fulfilled their duty not from the accidental
impulse of the moment; their action was the slowly ripened fruit of Providence
and of time. The light that led them on, was combined of rays from the whole
history of the race." Here, then, Bancroft articulated and gave historical legitimacy to two of the central assumptions of American exceptionalism—the belief
that America's historical development fulfilled a divine purpose, and the belief
that the Revolution represented a turning point in human history.[16] The Revolution was, for Bancroft, such a turning point because it had brought about the
realization of America's destiny to advance the cause of liberty. Arguing that the
Revolution was "an inevitable result of a living affection for freedom," Bancroft
sought to create a sense of inevitability by structuring his analysis around the
development of liberty in America. He took a long view of this process, dating
the origins of liberty in America back to the Reformation, for he believed that
the Reformation "was the common people awakening to freedom of mind."[17]
Thus he provided in the first three volumes of this work a detailed analysis of
how liberty had gradually taken root in the American colonies.

    This account of the origins of liberty served political and social purposes.
An ardent Jacksonian, Bancroft gave historical legitimacy to the democratic
principles he espoused by tracing their descent back to the Reformation and
down through the Revolution. The famous charge that every volume of his
history "voted for Jackson" epitomized the partisan character of his work.[18]
Yet if his Jacksonian sympathies made him a political outcast among his fellow
Boston Brahmins, he was by no means the radical insurgent they labeled him.
Indeed, for Bancroft, America was exceptional not just by virtue of the democratic principles it embodied but also by virtue of its ability to effect democracy
without radical social upheaval.[19] Therefore, even while celebrating the Revolution as a turning point in history, Bancroft emphasized its un-Revolutionary

character. Rather than bringing about a dramatic transformation in the social order, the Revolution had simply brought to fruition ideals and practices
that had been deeply rooted in the colonies from the start. Bancroft explained
that, in contrast to the violence and bitterness of European revolutions, the
American revolutionaries did not feel the need to completely overturn existing
political institutions because of "[t]heir large inheritance of English liberties."
"[H]appily the scaffold was not wet with the blood of their statesmen," for, according to Bancroft, "there was no root of a desperate hatred of England, such
as the Netherlands kept up for centuries against Spain," making "the transition
of the colonies into self-existent commonwealths" "free from vindictive bitterness, and attended by no violent or wide departure from the past." As this statement made clear, although sympathetic to popular interests, Bancroft shared
his Whig opponents' desire to maintain social order. He sought to improve the
lot of the working classes through moderate reform, not radical social change.
Accordingly, by making democracy the fruit of gradual historical development,
Bancroft discountenanced attempts to effect democratic principles through radical social upheaval.[20]

If for Bancroft the Revolution did not bring about a complete rupture with
the past, neither did the revolutionaries cling blindly to tradition. As Bancroft
put it,

> America neither separated abruptly from the past, nor adhered to its decaying
> forms. The principles that gave life to the new institutions pervaded history like a
> prophecy. They did not compel a sudden change of social or of internal political
> relations; but they were as a light shining more and more brightly into the darkness.
> In a country which enjoyed freedom of conscience, of inquiry, of speech, of the
> press, and of government, the universal intuition of truth promised a never-ending
> career of progress and reform.[21]

Although the principles of the Revolution did not require a dramatic change in
the nation's social or political system, the vitality of the principles themselves
made them a source of continual renovation and reform for Bancroft. Hence,
with the fulfillment of these principles during the Revolution, America had embarked on a path of "never-ending" progress. For Bancroft, the nation could
remain unchanged even as it was defined by a state of continual revolution, for
that revolution was itself defined by continuity.[22] In his belief that the nation
could remain indefinitely in a state of revolution without undergoing fundamental change, Bancroft summed up the exceptionalist vision of America as a
nation that was not only unique in its commitment to liberty but also exempt
from the normal processes of historical change and decay. Insulated by dis-

tance and by its closeness to nature from the conflicts that had stratified and corrupted European society, Americans could, for Bancroft, preserve in nature a state of timeless harmony and equality. [23] Viewing American history as a process of "'realization' rather than change," as Dorothy Ross puts it, Bancroft thus saw America as unique by virtue of its ability to escape from history without breaking from the past. [24]

For all the apparent partiality of his depiction of America as a chosen nation, Bancroft saw his work as impartial, and indeed, his commitment to impartiality was integrally related to his belief in American exceptionalism. When Ranke noted of his history in 1867 that it was "written from the democratic point of view," Bancroft responded by declaring, "[I]f there is democracy in the history it is not subjective, but objective as they say here." While this exchange has been taken to signify the contrast between Bancroft's Romantic idealism and Ranke's scientific approach, the two historians were more alike than many scholars have recognized, and Bancroft had in fact studied with Ranke. The similarities between them suggested that both Bancroft's belief in a divine purpose to history and his ability to reconcile that belief with a desire for impartiality were not exclusively American in origin. [25] Contrary to his reputation, Ranke did not define objectivity to mean the sheer accumulation of facts devoid of larger philosophical generalizations. The conventional perception of Ranke as an empiricist who rejected any speculation into higher causes was based on a misunderstanding of Ranke by American historians at the turn of the twentieth century. Rather than rejecting German philosophical idealism, Ranke was deeply influenced by this tradition, and, like these philosophers, he embraced a pantheistic view that all of history represented the expression of God's will. Sounding much like Bancroft in his emphasis on a divine plan for human history, Ranke proclaimed, "God dwells, lives, and can be known in all of history." Consequently, Ranke believed, "Every deed attests to Him, every moment preaches His name, but most of all, it seems to me, the connectedness of history in the large." [26]

In his famous injunction to study the past "wie es eigentlich gewesen [as it actually was]," the word *eigentlich* has conventionally been translated to mean "actually." However, the meaning of *eigentlich* was ambiguous in the nineteenth century, for it could also mean "essentially." This translation suggests that Ranke's goal was not just to present the facts of history but to uncover the spiritual essences behind those facts. [27] Ranke made his concern with the spiritual dimension to history clear when he declared, "No one could be more convinced than I that historical research requires the strictest method: criticism of the authors, the banning of all fable, the extraction of the pure facts. But I am also convinced that this fact has a spiritual content." [28] As he at once affirmed his commitment to an ideal of objectivity that made history an account of empirically proven facts and his belief in an overarching spiritual force to history, Ranke reconciled a secular mode of explanation with his firm conviction of providential design.[29]

If Ranke was more of a philosophical idealist than his American admirers recognized, then Bancroft was more committed to impartiality than his detractors have acknowledged, and like Ranke, he saw no conflict between his claims to impartiality and his providential perspective, for he believed that an impartial view of American history would reveal the unfolding of providential design. Thus he could assert that a history written from a democratic point of view was objective because of his assumption that democracy was part of that design.[30] If an impartial history revealed for Bancroft the advance of democracy, democracy would in turn, he believed, promote impartiality. Bancroft drew a direct connection between democracy and impartiality as he praised Jeremy Belknap for his ability "to exhibit the faults of our ancestors without impairing admiration for their virtues." As this statement revealed, impartiality for Bancroft entailed a fair and balanced view of the past that recognized both the flaws and virtues of the historian's subjects. He suggested that there was something peculiarly American about impartiality itself when he described Belknap's "tone of feeling" as "truly American; national, yet candid." For Bancroft, Belknap's ability to balance reverence for his subjects with a critical perspective reflected the "new spirit in literature, which naturally grew out of our revolution." Attributing Belknap's openness about the faults of his ancestors to "the liberal purposes of free inquiry," Bancroft suggested that the Revolution had made such openness possible by establishing the principles of freedom of thought and speech in America. Hence Bancroft could not think of any European history that was superior to Belknap's. Thus, he implied, not only was America exceptional in its commitment to liberty; this principle, in turn, had given America an exceptional ability to achieve impartiality. In this way, Bancroft's definition of impartiality itself served nationalist purposes.[31]

For Bancroft, impartiality in this sense was so important because "[i]ndiscriminate praise neither paints to the life, nor teaches by example, nor advances social science; history is no mosaic of funeral eulogies and family epitaphs, nor can the hand of truth sketch character without shadows as well as light. The crimes and the follies which stand in the line of causes of revolution, or modify the development of a state, or color the morals of an age, must be brought up for judgment." Here, Bancroft embraced three different conceptions of historical truth—history as art, as philosophy, and as science. In his view, a balanced view of the past was necessary for truth in all three senses. A historian who uncritically glorified his subjects would not be able to bring history to life for

his readers. Nor would he able to provide moral lessons for his readers to follow, for without an understanding of the "crimes and follies" that his subjects
had committed, the historian would not have a basis to make proper moral
judgments. In turn, unless he took such "crimes and follies" into account, the
historian would not be able to contribute to a science of society by discern-
ing the universal moral laws that governed human behavior. At the same time,
Bancroft admitted and praised what he believed was the historian's natural
tendency to focus on the noble side of history. As he explained, the historian
"contemplates more willingly those inspirations of the beautiful and the good,
which lift the soul above the interests of the moment, demonstrate our affinity with something higher than ourselves, point the way to principles that are
eternal, and constitute the vital element of progress." While it was important
to acknowledge "shadows, as well as light," only by focusing on the "beautiful
and the good" would the historian access the higher principles that for Bancroft
constituted truth in the ultimate sense.[32]

Hence, despite his injunctions to impartiality, Bancroft imparted a celebratory quality to his history as he emphasized the "beautiful and good" in the
American past. This tendency was most evident in his portrayal of the New England Puritans, who were central to his account of the development of democracy in America. Living up to his own injunction that impartiality required the
historian to acknowledge "shadows, as well as light," in his historical subjects,
Bancroft recognized and condemned Puritan intolerance of religious dissenters. At the same time, however, he revealed his desire to focus on the "beautiful
and the good" as he minimized the extent of Puritan intolerance and attributed
this policy to the need for self-defense against dissenters who threatened the security and stability of the colony. Denying that intolerance was intrinsic to Puritan ideals, Bancroft characterized Puritan persecution of dissenters as "tran-
sient" and incidental. As he explained, "The people did not attempt to convert
others, but to protect themselves; they never punished opinion as such; they
never attempted to torture or terrify men into orthodoxy."[33] Bancroft revealed
his penchant for the "beautiful and the good" most clearly by emphasizing the
democratic character of Puritanism. Puritanism was, according to Bancroft,
"religion struggling for the People," for it made "not the Christian clergy, but
the Christian people, the interpreter of the divine will." As such, its destined
purpose was to implant "the undying principles of democratic liberty" on "the
old European system of a feudal aristocracy and popular servitude."[34] Through
this paean to Puritanism, Bancroft sought to access and reveal what he believed
were eternal principles—the undying truth of democracy. At the same time,
this portrayal of the Puritans reflected Bancroft's own sectional loyalties, for,

by locating the roots of democracy in New England, he asserted the primacy of his own region in American development and defined the nation in terms of New England.[35]

Although Bancroft was often criticized by both his contemporaries and modern scholars for his partiality to New England, his intention was to present what he saw as an impartial account of the nation's origins that recognized how each region of the country had contributed to the progress of liberty. Such an account was for Bancroft "impartial" in that it did not favor one region of the country over another. And so, recognizing that Puritanism was just one of the many strands that contributed to American independence, Bancroft gave credit to victims of Puritan persecution like Roger Williams and to William Penn and the settlers of Virginia for instituting the principles of liberty in their respective regions. By giving each section a role in the advance of democracy, Bancroft sought to promote national unity, and the development of union in America was, along with the liberty, the other major theme of his work. But even as Bancroft hoped that his impartiality toward different regions of the country would further nationalist purposes, his history ironically had the opposite effect, for his critics saw his work as a sectional vehicle that promoted the interests of New England at the expense of other regions of the country.[36]

Yet if Bancroft's efforts to be impartial backfired for these critics, at least some of his contemporaries believed that he had succeeded in this goal. In a letter of 1852 thanking Bancroft for sending him the first two volumes of his history, the English historian Lord Mahon praised Bancroft's history specifically for its lack of sectional bias. For Mahon, Bancroft had been "so fair and so equable" in his treatment of "the several American states" that he believed it would be difficult to determine "to which of them in birth and affection you personally belong." Averring that "[t]he same spirit of candour and upright dealing accompanies you to England," Mahon declared that while he did not always agree with Bancroft, he did not believe "that any national bias has rendered you unduly harsh or acrimonious towards our leading statesmen of the time."[37]

For Mahon, what made Bancroft's history so praiseworthy was that it had succeeded in transcending not only sectional bias but also national bias against England. Bancroft had in fact provided a cosmopolitan perspective on American history by devoting much of his analysis to European developments. He was so concerned with the international context for American history because impartiality for him meant a broad view of history that recognized the connections between American developments and the rest of world. Jared Sparks had, Bancroft believed, demonstrated just this kind of broad perspective in his edition of George Washington's writings. Sounding much like Ranke in his assumption that truth required the historian to free himself of bias, Bancroft declared that what made Sparks so exceptional as a historian was that his mind "seems to know no bias. He pursues the truth, and is enamoured of inquiry." As testament to Sparks's "reverence for historic truth," Bancroft singled out Sparks's recognition that the history of the Revolution and of Washington's life "could not be derived from American sources alone; and with a wide grasp, which proves his mind to be enlarged not less than accurate, he has sought materials in England and on the continent of Europe." For Bancroft, then, to be impartial was more than a matter of avoiding bias or prejudice; to be impartial was also to be unparochial, for only through such a broad perspective could the historian uncover historical truth.[38]

Bancroft believed that his history had achieved impartiality in both these senses. But how did he reconcile his claims to impartiality with the exceptionalist bias of his history and its assumption of American superiority? In equating impartiality with an unparochial perspective, Bancroft actually reinforced exceptionalist assumptions, for his cosmopolitan recognition of the influence of other nations on American development both reflected and furthered his teleological view of American history as the fulfillment of a divine plan. Specifically, in his quest to show how all of human history had inevitably been tending toward the realization of liberty in America, Bancroft could recognize how seemingly distant—and often adverse—European events had contributed to this development. Thus, locating the causes of the American Revolution as much in English as in colonial developments, Bancroft's volumes on the American Revolution were as much a history of English politics during the period as they were of the American colonies.[39]

More difficult to reconcile with Bancroft's claims to present an unbiased account of English history was the actual content of his interpretation, for while he recognized the importance of English historical developments to the colonies, his depiction of English society was far from flattering, and his analysis unabashedly favored the Americans over the English. In fact, Bancroft's very claims to impartiality revealed his partiality toward America, as he claimed superiority to the British on this basis. In contrast to the "deferentially forbearing" tone of American writers who "brought to their task no prejudices against England," Bancroft remarked, "experience has shown that it [impartiality] is practiced with most difficulty by those of the parent land" because the sense of pride and superiority that characterized British colonial policy had not only infused all the documents from the Revolutionary era but had also persisted to the present, so "that even now it sometimes hangs as a heavy bias on the judgment even of Englishmen professing liberal opinions."[40]

With all the apparent bias of his declamations against the defects of English society, Bancroft's claims to impartiality were not just empty professions. English writers like Mahon could, like Bancroft himself, believe that Bancroft had not been "unduly harsh" toward England, for, although critical of English society, Bancroft did not simplistically vilify the English, and he offered a complex analysis of the forces that shaped British colonial policy. Hence, in an 1852 letter commenting on the fourth volume of Bancroft's history, another of Bancroft's English correspondents, John Kenrick, did not dismiss Bancroft's claims to impartiality, even while recognizing that Bancroft was "an enthusiastic admirer" of his own country "and her institutions," for, as Kenrick remarked, "I have not observed that this admiration has led you to do any injustice to other countries," and "[i]ndeed I think on the whole George III fares better in your hands than in those of Lord Albemarle."[41] In turn, such praise for Bancroft's impartiality would have given him all the more reason for believing that he had lived up to this ideal.

Bancroft revealed this sense of complexity in his analysis of the Glorious Revolution as a turning point in the progress of liberty, which he argued laid the basis for the misguided colonial policy that precipitated the American Revolution. In Bancroft's account, the Glorious Revolution was an "aristocratic revolution" that had saved Britain and its colonies from monarchical tyranny only to subject them to the tyranny of Parliament by putting into place a Whig aristocracy concerned only with defending its own interests and privileges. Consequently, by the eighteenth century, the Whig aristocracy had outlived its effectiveness and began to show signs of debility.[42] According to Bancroft, this sense of impending collapse brought about Britain's ill-fated policy toward the colonies during the pre-Revolutionary crisis. Depicting England as a society in transition, Bancroft attributed the impolitic and inconsistent measures pursued by the British to the tensions and instability created by these changes. As he explained, "The imbecility which marked the conduct of British affairs in America, showed itself still more decidedly in the cabinet, which . . . was crumbling in pieces from the sense of its real weakness, and the weariness of the people of England at the unmixed government of the aristocracy."[43]

Bancroft elaborated on how the aristocracy's perception of its own weakness gave rise to the short-sighted and self-destructive policies that drove the colonies to independence. As part of a desperate and futile reaction against its imminent demise, the Whig aristocracy grasped at every momentary advantage, no matter what the long-term consequences. The result was that "America was the theme in all companies, yet was discussed according to its bearings on personal ambition; justice and prudence were lost sight of in unreflecting zeal for a momentary victory."[44] Instead of blaming particular individuals, then, for the oppressive policies of the British, Bancroft recognized the long-term structural and systemic causes behind these policies and interpreted British actions as the natural result of a deeper malaise—the decline of the Whig aristocracy. Bancroft could see himself as impartial in this explanation for British policy, for his emphasis on structural causes enabled him to criticize British actions without vilifying particular individuals. Yet in attributing British policy to deeply rooted structural causes, rather than to individuals, he made the American Revolution seem all the more inevitable. In this way, he reconciled his desire for impartiality with the exceptionalist belief in the inevitability of the Revolution.

While Bancroft's forceful judgments of historical actors were certainly partial, his emphasis on the role of unintended consequences in history enabled him—and others—to see these assessments as impartial. Recognizing the complex and paradoxical nature of historical causation, Bancroft demonstrated how historical change often came about as the unintended consequence of human actions as he repeatedly pointed to the ways in which the opponents of liberty had unintentionally furthered the advance of that ideal. Although, for example, he believed that nothing could have been further from the intentions of the Stuarts—despotic tyrants in his eyes—than the advancement of liberty in America, he described how they had unwittingly furthered the progress of this ideal. As "the crimes of the dynasty banished to our country men of learning, virtue, and fortitude," Bancroft explained, "[t]hus did despotism render benefits to freedom."[45] For this reason, he could exclaim, "So singular are the ways of Providence! The prosperity of our country grew out of the very vices of its sovereigns; and the bigotry of the Duke of York in England was the shield of religious tolerance in Pennsylvania."[46]

In his analysis of how the opponents of liberty had contributed to the ideals they abhorred, Bancroft repudiated a heroic view of history that attributed liberty to the conscious intent of great individuals. Instead, by portraying liberty as the unintended result of human actions, Bancroft at once recognized the limits to what even the most fervent proponents of liberty had achieved and gave their opponents credit for contributing to progress. Bancroft could thus view his assessment of both groups as balanced and impartial in its refusal to interpret progress as simply the result of good overcoming evil. And, as he revealed in attributing the irony of these unintended consequences to "the ways of Providence," Bancroft's sense of impartiality followed directly from his exceptionalist framework, for he developed this complex view of historical causation not despite but because of his providential understanding of history—

a key element of exceptionalist ideology. Because he viewed all historical oc-currences as part of a divine plan, he was attentive to the ways in which even seemingly adverse developments contributed to the realization of this plan.[47]

Bancroft's effort to be impartial by acknowledging the role of unintended consequences in history also reflected the influence of German idealism. Ban-croft first developed his admiration for German idealist philosophers during his studies at Göttingen, and he shared their desire for a "universal history" that would show how all of human history was part of a larger scheme of de-velopment. As one of the leading exponents of German idealism, Immanuel Kant, in particular, influenced Bancroft's understanding of historical causation. Bancroft took from Kant's idealist philosophy not only his view of history as the unfolding of divine purpose but also his understanding of the ironies of histori-cal development. Arguing that divine purpose came about often despite human intentions, Kant explained how individuals pursuing their own interests unin-tentionally contributed to the realization of a higher purpose: each individual "follows his own purpose, often in opposition to others," all the while further-ing some "unknown goal . . . even if they would set little store by it if they did know it." Like Bancroft's, then, Kant's appreciation for the role of unintended consequences in history was predicated on a teleological perspective, and the similarity between them pointed to Kant's influence on Bancroft's theory of causation. Thus, rather than encouraging a naively romantic view of causation that focused on the spiritual to the exclusion of more worldly or ignoble mo-tives, German idealist philosophy actually contributed to Bancroft's complex understanding of how historical change occurred not just despite but as a result of human deficiencies. In this way, for all his emphasis on the "beautiful and the good," it was possible for Bancroft to believe that he had lived up to his dictates requiring the impartial historian to acknowledge "shadows, as well as light," as he recognized how the baser side of human nature had also played a role in the historical process.[48]

"Religion struggling for the people"?
Reassessing the Puritans

Although influential, Bancroft's interpretation of American history was also hotly contested by historians in his time. One of the most controversial aspects of his history was his portrayal of the Puritans, as historians sharply questioned his celebratory view of the Puritans as exponents of liberty and democracy. These historians in turn differed among themselves in their reassessment of the

Puritans, for, although they all sought to live up to the ideal of impartiality in this reassessment, they disagreed with Bancroft and one another over what this ideal entailed and used it for different social purposes. Through their reassessment of the Puritans, these historians were variously responding to sectional tensions, sectarian rivalries, and social anxieties about democracy. Most important, as he used his critical perspective on the Puritans both to uphold the established social order and to affirm his belief in America's exceptional character, John Lothrop Motley demonstrated how the ideal of impartiality could further exceptionalist ideology.

As literary scholars have demonstrated, historical novelists played an important role in developing a more critical view of the Puritans during this period. The best-known challenge to Bancroft's heroic portrayal of the Puritans came from Nathaniel Hawthorne. Although literary critics have differed over the depth of Hawthorne's historical understanding and the extent to which he repudiated patriotic views of the Puritans, they have pointed to his recognition of their shortcomings as an important feature of his writing. Although deeply fascinated by the Puritans, Hawthorne at the same time made their intolerance and bigotry a central theme in his short stories and novels. Nor was Hawthorne alone in his desire to revise conventional views of the Puritans: novelists like Lydia Maria Child and Catharine Sedgwick criticized the Puritans for both their fanaticism and their treatment of Native Americans in their historical novels.[49]

Yet, rather than being a complete revision of contemporary historiography, the critical view of the Puritans advanced by these novelists was shared by other historians of the period. While these "revisionist" historians all portrayed themselves as impartial in their refusal to idealize the Puritans, the extent and character of their reassessments varied, revealing that they disagreed over how to put the ideal of impartiality into practice.[50] Thus, although these historians agreed that impartiality meant a more balanced view of the Puritans, they differed over what a more balanced view entailed. Did it mean acknowledging both the flaws and virtues of the Puritans? Or were Puritan failings so great that balance involved a recital of all their crimes and brutality? In a relatively measured appraisal, a critic writing for *DeBow's Review* in 1853 sought to correct the "fashion in high quarters to extol the Puritan character to the skies" without denying the achievements of the Puritans. Complaining that "history has been unduly partial" to the Puritans in giving them credit for the doctrine of religious toleration, this reviewer noted that, on the contrary, "[t]he Puritan character was deeply tinged with bigotry and intolerance." For this reason, he concluded, "Our country owes them much, but it does not owe them the doctrine of religious toleration."[51]

As the reviewer revealed, historians from outside New England wishing to challenge that region's preeminence in the writing of American history took the lead in reassessing the Puritans as they sought to demonstrate the contribution of their own region to the development of American liberty. Hence southern historians variously sought to counter the idealization of the Puritans by turning to the Cavalier myth or by giving alternative explanations for the origins of liberty in America. In one such alternative, the *DeBow's* critic sought to bring together the Cavalier myth with a recognition of the Puritan contribution to liberty by arguing that "[t]hree great elements enter into the character of the American people, derived from the colonization of three distinct classes of society"—"the Puritan, the Quaker, and the Cavalier." Rather than attributing the development of liberty to any one region of the country, then, this reviewer, like Bancroft, argued that each of the three major regions had contributed in its own way to this process.[52]

But more than sectionalism was at work in Puritan revisionism, for New England historians also questioned the tendency to glorify the Puritans. One of the most scathing indictments of the Puritans came from Boston lawyer Peter Oliver, whose attack on the Puritans reflected his religious sympathies as a staunch Anglican. Far more critical of the Puritans than the *DeBow's* critic was, Oliver castigated the Puritans as intolerant murderers and traitors, "hostile to the principles of liberty," and in his *Puritan Commonwealth*, published in 1856, Oliver provided a comprehensive and detailed chronicle of what he considered their tyranny and treachery.[53] Portraying the Puritans as hypocrites concerned only with their own power and self-interest, Oliver was especially cutting in his condemnation of their brutality toward the Indians, which he believed went directly counter to their professed desire to convert the Indians to Christianity. For the Puritans, he proclaimed, "To slaughter an Indian was a painful religious exercise, as much as to spend a day in bodily abstinence. For this reason, the Puritan soldiers were pitiless. The negation of works in their religion also cooperated to promote injustice in their policy; and where violence was not a Puritan rite, it was but too often a right of Puritanism." The result was, according to Oliver, that the Puritans "in the short space of fifty years swept from New England one hundred thousand human beings."[54]

Nor was a reassessment of the Puritans confined to historians on the margins of the predominantly Unitarian Brahmin elite, for Bancroft's fellow Brahmins also questioned the tendency to idealize the Puritans. Less hostile to the Puritans than Oliver was, these historians offered a more tempered critique than Oliver's. Impartiality served a different kind of religious function for Brahmin historians, as a balanced view of the Puritans that recognized both their flaws and their virtues enabled these historians to reconcile their reverence for

their Puritan ancestors with their own departure from Congregationalist orthodoxy. Hence, in an 1857 review of Oliver's history, even while historian and
Unitarian minister George Edward Ellis acknowledged that the "extravagant
praise which has been so lavishly bestowed on the Puritans, as holding opinions
and advancing principles utterly inconsistent with their most cherished convic-
tions as well as with their limitations of view and their prejudices" had deserv-
edly "provoked rebuke," he criticized Oliver for going to the opposite extreme
in his "excessively severe disquisition upon their policy."[55]

Like Ellis, John Lothrop Motley sought to avoid both the "[i]ndiscriminate
and fulsome eulogy" and the "virulent abuse" that had been inflicted on the
Puritans, believing that an impartial view of the Puritans meant acknowledging both their achievements and their flaws. This understanding of impartiality served a political function for Motley, as he used his reassessment of
the Puritans to express his anxieties about democracy. Along with Bancroft,
Prescott, and Francis Parkman, Motley has long been considered one of America's leading Romantic historians. Part of the same Boston Brahmin circle as
these other historians, Motley, like them, viewed history as a form of Romantic
art. Even before publishing his most famous work—the history of the Dutch
Republic—in 1856, Motley had already begun to write on historical subjects.
Deeply interested in the Puritans, he preceded his history with *Merry-Mount*
(1849), a novel about colonial Massachusetts. Reproaching both apologists and
critics of the Puritans for going to extremes, he aimed at a more impartial view
of the Puritans in an 1849 essay for the *North American Review*. Acknowledging that they possessed "indomitable courage, patience, fortitude, self-denial,
generosity, extreme purity of morals, piety, energy and singleness of purpose
almost superhuman," Motley also recognized that "their vices were few but formidable, for they were intolerance, cruelty, tyranny, and bigotry."[56]

For Motley, these defects made Bancroft's interpretation of the Puritans
untenable, and he directly attacked Bancroft and his followers for portraying
the Puritans as the conscious progenitors of democracy in America. Motley
freely admitted that liberty and democracy had resulted from Puritan colonization. He conceded, "Democracy was, no doubt, the result of the settlement of
America in the seventeenth century, and the principles of New England colonization had much to do with preparing such a result." He was careful to add,
however, that this result did not come about through the conscious design of
the Puritans. Attributing this "vast democracy" to "the unconscious work" of
the Puritans, Motley claimed that the "unintentional result" of their sufferings
for the sake of the "idea of a pure church" was "the establishment of the great
American democracy."[57] Indeed, he argued, the Puritans "had no notion of es-

tablishing a democracy," for their goals were entirely religious in character. As he explained, "The movement hither was purely a theological movement," and "we believe they would be as much puzzled to understand American liberty as American slavery, and would believe themselves to be about as much the founders of the one as of the other."[58] He emphasized that "as loyal subjects of a monarchy," the Puritans "never thought of establishing the majesty of the people, and it was a long time after they were in their graves before the majesty of the people established itself."[59] If anything, according to Motley, the Puritans embraced many ideals and practices hostile to democracy, for "[r]eligiously, socially, politically, the early government of Massachusetts was a severe, in many respects a tyrannical system."[60] And so, while Motley shared Bancroft's appreciation for the role of unintended consequences in history, he appropriated this insight for his own purposes, turning it against Bancroft's characterization of the Puritans as exponents of democracy.

Yet, for all his skepticism about Bancroft's heroic view of the Puritans, Motley was no less nationalistic than Bancroft, and like Bancroft, he fervently embraced a belief in America's destiny as an exceptional nation. Hence Motley opened his essay with an unequivocal affirmation of the nation's mission to expand across the continent. Comparing the western settlers of his own time to the seventeenth-century English colonists, Motley declared that these settlers "fulfil the mission which has been impressed upon the country . . . to carry the Anglo-American standard towards the setting sun." He did not see any conflict between his critical view of the Puritans and his nationalistic desire to celebrate America's special mission. On the contrary, Motley used his reassessment of the Puritans to reaffirm this belief, for, in his view, the fact that democracy had developed in America despite Puritan hostility to liberty and equality was all the more proof that it was America's destiny to spread democratic principles.[61]

Motley made his commitment to exceptionalist ideology even clearer as he used his reassessment of the Puritans to comment on Europe's prospects for democracy in the present. Like most of his fellow Boston Brahmins, Motley embraced Whig politics, and like them, he embraced an organic vision of social order that made progress the fruit of a gradual process of evolution. Believing that without a respect for order and control—both over oneself and others—society was prone to dissolve into licentious anarchy, Whigs gave primacy to tradition and experience as sources of social cohesion. Rooted as they were in the particular circumstances of a society, tradition and experience, according to Whig ideology, would serve as more powerful and secure social bonds than would appeals to abstract theory or principle. Whigs thus feared sudden or revolutionary change as a both a cause and an effect of the dissolution of social order.

Motley pointed to the connection between such fears and his reassessment of the Puritans as he explained why contemporary political developments gave new urgency to an understanding of the Puritans. According to Motley, the "events of the last few years in Europe" have given to "the granite character of New England" "a fresh importance."[62] Specifically, he had in mind the revolutions of 1848, which had taken place just the year before.

Although initially many Americans—including at least some Whigs—welcomed the French Revolution of 1848 as an extension of the democratic ideals instituted by their own revolution, they became increasingly critical of the Revolution of 1848 as demands for social and economic reform and the violence of the June days gave the Revolution a more radical cast. The election of Louis Bonaparte to the presidency simply confirmed American fears that the democratic excesses and extremism of the Revolution of 1848 would only end in tyranny. The outcome of the French Revolution of 1848, together with the failure of other revolutionary movements in Europe, made Americans increasingly doubtful about whether their system of democracy could ever be exported to Europe and fueled Whig fears of the dangers of revolutionary upheaval. Motley expressed such doubts and made clear his own hostility to the extremism associated with the revolutions of 1848 when he pointed out that, in contrast to Europe, Americans possessed the "inestimable advantage" that "[o]ne can be a republican, a democrat, without being a radical." He elaborated, "A *radical*, one who would *uproot*, is a man whose trade is dangerous to society."[63] Whereas the lack of preexisting obstacles had allowed democracy to emerge in America without destructive social upheaval, democracy could establish itself in Europe only by overturning existing institutions. For this reason, Motley was uncertain about whether democracy would succeed in Europe, and he confessed his doubts about whether the American example of democracy "is, upon the whole, good for Europe."[64]

Motley's refusal to identify the Puritans with democracy reflected these doubts. By denying that the Puritans had intended the emergence of democracy in America, he put into question the prospects of European revolutionaries who consciously aimed to establish democracy in the present. Their efforts were fruitless, he implied, for democracy had resulted unintentionally from a long course of evolution, not from revolutionary intentions and designs. More than that, Motley suggested, America was unique in its ability to realize this ideal, for only America possessed the social conditions that made such a gradual evolution possible. Thus, by portraying democracy as the unintended result of Puritan actions, Motley could both express misgivings about the democratic upheavals that were occurring in Europe and affirm a sense of nationalistic pride in America's democratic heritage. As he did so, he demonstrated in his own way how a commitment to impartiality could promote a belief in American exceptionalism; even as he recognized the Puritans' limits, he used that recognition to demonstrate and celebrate America's distinctiveness from Europe.[65]

Revisionist History and Its Limits: The Puritans, Slavery, and the Revolution

Yet historians of this period would only go so far in reassessing the Puritans. While they were willing to admit Puritan intolerance of religious dissenters, and even Puritan brutality toward Native Americans, they were far more unwilling to admit Puritan complicity in slavery, and this unwillingness revealed that they defined both impartiality and the nation in racially exclusionary terms. Not only did they interpret impartial truth to mean the exclusion of slavery from New England's history; they actively furthered this exclusion through their definition of impartial truth—in both the methodology and the content of their interpretations. And so, although these historians differed from Bancroft and one another in their understanding of what an impartial account of American history entailed, they, like Bancroft, used that understanding to advance both sectional and national purposes.

As Joanne Pope Melish has demonstrated, wishing to erase the presence of slavery from their region—in both the past and the present—antebellum white New Englanders for the most part either refused to acknowledge the existence of slavery in the New England colonies at all or minimized its role in their region's history. By denying the role of slavery in their own region's history, New Englanders in turn defined the nation as historically white, and both enslaved and free blacks as aliens in that nation, for they defined the nation in their own image. And by setting up a contrast between the slaveholding South and a historically free New England, white New Englanders could claim superiority to the South as the antithesis of everything the nation represented. Even abolitionists for the most part obscured the role of slavery in New England's history, for only by dissociating the Puritans from slavery could they claim the mantle of the Puritans for their own cause and portray themselves as heirs to the Puritans' moral fervor.[66]

Hence New England historians, regardless of their stance on slavery, for the most part avoided mentioning slavery at all in their historical writing. When Motley, for example, declared that the Puritans "would be as much puzzled to understand American liberty as American slavery, and would believe themselves to be about as much the founders of the one as of the other," he not only denied the existence of slavery in New England but suggested that the institution was so alien to the Puritans that it would have been utterly incomprehensible to them.[67] Although Oliver was more willing than Motley to recognize Puritan complicity in slavery, he still only made passing references to the presence of slavery in Puritan society. When he noted, for example, that with the arrival of the royal governor Sir Edmund Andros in 1686 "Quakers began to take courage, and slaves even felt that they were under the protection of the law," he was less concerned with commenting on the Puritans' involvement in slavery than with showing how much more humane and free royal government was for even the most oppressed inhabitants of Massachusetts Bay. Or when he did comment on Puritan complicity in slavery, he focused on Puritan enslavement of Native Americans rather than on slaves of African descent, and he cited such enslavement as simply another example of Puritan selfishness and brutality toward Native Americans.[68]

Even as Bancroft devoted more attention to the issue of slavery than did most of his New England colleagues, allotting a chapter of the first volume of his history specifically to the subject, he sought in his own way to minimize the influence of slavery in New England's history. Thus, for example, when he acknowledged the presence of slavery in New England, he did so only to obscure its significance, as he did when he spoke of the centrality of slavery in Newport as an exception to the peripheral role that slavery played in the rest of the New England colonies. As he declared of New England society on the eve of the Revolution, "Of slavery there was not enough to affect the character of the people," except in Newport, which "was conspicuous for engaging in the slave-trade, and where, in two or three towns, negroes composed even a third of the inhabitants."[69] Hence, Bancroft described "the relationship of master and slave" as "essentially a southern institution" and focused on its role in the southern colonies throughout his critical analysis of the inhumane and undemocratic character of slavery.[70] While recognizing that "it could not be truly said that all the colonies had been always without blame" in perpetuating the slave trade, or that "it had been exclusively the guilt of the king of Great Britain," Bancroft ultimately absolved both New England and the rest of the nation from responsibility for slavery and placed the onus for the institution on Britain. Thus repeatedly commenting on how Britain had blocked the colonists' efforts to ban the slave trade, he attributed the presence of the "one sixth part" of the nation's population who were "descendants of Africans" to the "eagerness" of English slave traders to sell slaves to the American colonies, "encouraged by English legislation, fostered by royal favor, and enforced for a century by every successive ministry of England."[71]

Even more of an apologist for the Puritans than Bancroft was in his history, John Gorham Palfrey demonstrated how impartiality could be used to marginalize slavery from New England's history. Like Bancroft, Palfrey was a member of the Boston Brahmin elite, and his activities included both literature and politics. Serving as editor for the *North American Review* from 1835 to 1842, Palfrey turned to politics in 1841, when he was elected to the Massachusetts state legislature. Unlike Bancroft, however, Palfrey embraced Whig politics. Himself the son of a slaveholder, Palfrey became increasingly active in opposing slavery as this issue became more central in national politics. After freeing the slaves he inherited from his father, he joined the Conscience Whigs when they formed in 1846. With his defeat as a Free Soil candidate for Congress in 1850, Palfrey turned from politics to the writing of history, publishing the first volume of his *History of New England* in 1858 and completing the five-volume work in 1890. As Francis Bowen's criticism of Palfrey's "excessive laudation" revealed, this work was unabashedly favorable to the Puritans, portraying them as rational and sober statesmen whose goal was to establish an independent state based on republican principles of liberty. Palfrey was quite open about his admiration for the Puritans, confessing in his preface that it would have been dishonest of him to "conceal" his "veneration for the founders of New England." At the same time, Palfrey did not believe that such admiration took away from his claims to truth, for he did not think that he had shown any "undue bias" in favor of the Puritans.[72] For all its biases, Palfrey's history was a serious work of scholarship based on extensive research in both secondary and primary sources, including archival sources in England. Through such research, Palfrey hoped to avoid "one-sided representations by constant reference to the views entertained by writers of various affinities, political and religious."[73] While recognizing the biases of his sources, he sought to overcome such biases by examining different and opposing points of view. Thus he could claim that he had sought to be "veracious and just" throughout his history.[74]

Expressing his hope that "extreme diligence in the authentication of facts" characterized his history, Palfrey provided such "authentication" by quoting extensively from primary sources and citing his sources in footnotes. In his assumption that truth was based on an unbiased accumulation of fact, and in his belief that the historian had to verify facts through citation and critical analysis of primary sources, he subscribed to a Rankean ideal of truth. Palfrey himself pointed to his generous use of extracts from his primary sources as a distinguishing feature of his history. His use of extracts was so extensive that he admitted it would be understandable if others thought him "to have indulged myself too freely in the interweaving of quotations."[75]

Paradoxically, the very features of Palfrey's history that demonstrated his commitment to unbiased truth served an important political function, for, through his use of footnotes and primary sources, Palfrey glossed over the role of slavery in New England's history. A fervent antislavery reformer, Palfrey at the same time shared the racial biases of most of his white contemporaries and embraced a racially exclusive vision of New England—and, by extension, American—identity as an Anglo-Saxon nation. For this reason, he could declare proudly that because of the Puritan origins of most of its population, "the people of New England are a singularly unmixed race. There is probably not a county in England occupied by a population of purer English blood than theirs."[76] Accordingly, desiring to exclude blacks, whether slave or free, from New England's past, Palfrey made only occasional and brief references to slavery in his lengthy five-volume history. When he did mention slavery, he often did so in footnotes. By marginalizing slavery from the text of his history, he could acknowledge the existence of slavery in New England while at the same time portraying slavery as marginal to an understanding of the region's past.

The content of these references further softened New England's complicity in slavery and revealed Palfrey's own antipathy to the institution by emphasizing the limits to slavery in New England. In one footnote commenting on the early laws regarding slavery in Massachusetts, Palfrey noted that, although these laws did allow for slavery under certain conditions, "[t]he being born of a slave mother is not mentioned among the causes of subjection to slavery; and in fact no person was ever born into legal slavery in Massachusetts." By specifying that slave status did not descend through the mother in colonial Massachusetts, Palfrey set up an implicit contrast to the South, where the condition of the mother determined an individual's status as slave or free. And so, even though he found it impossible to deny the existence of slavery in colonial Massachusetts, he suggested through this contrast that Massachusetts was far superior to the South in refusing to legalize natal slavery. In contrasting the mildness of New England's slave system to that of the South, Palfrey employed a common strategy used by New Englanders to minimize the role of slavery in their own history. He used the same strategy in another footnote when he observed, "From the reverence entertained by the fathers of New England for the nuptial tie, it is safe to infer that slave husbands and wives were never parted."[77] Here, Palfrey set up another implicit contrast to the South, for the inhumanity of southern slaveholders' refusal to legally recognize slave marriages and the consequent separation of slave families was a common refrain in abolitionist rhetoric. Through footnotes, then, Palfrey used a crucial mark of impartiality to at once condemn southern slavery in the present and palliate the character of slavery in colonial New England.

In his employment of primary sources, Palfrey used yet another attribute of impartiality to palliate New England slavery, for many of his references to slavery came as part of a passage quoted from a primary source. For example, he included a lengthy extract from Governor Bradstreet of Massachusetts in which Bradstreet noted that, except for one ship, "[t]here hath been no company of blacks or slaves brought into the country since the beginning of this plantation, for the space of fifty years. . . . Now and then two or three negroes are brought hither from Barbadoes and others of his Majesty's plantations, and sold here for about twenty pounds apiece, so that there may be within our government about one hundred, or one hundred and twenty."[78] By reproducing such passages with little or no direct comment of his own, Palfrey demonstrated his impartiality and detachment while at the same time evading the need to give any assessment of New England's responsibility for slavery. Instead, he used Bradstreet's words to suggest that slavery was not a significant presence in Massachusetts. In this way, primary sources enabled Palfrey to reconcile his desire for impartial truth with his desire to minimize the influence of slavery in New England's history, for, by letting his subjects speak for themselves in these passages, he could indirectly obscure their complicity in slavery without appearing to be biased in their favor.

If Palfrey's understanding of impartial truth furthered a racially exclusive definition of American identity, the desire to exclude slavery from his conception of the nation in turn shaped definitions of what constituted historical truth for Palfrey's New England colleague Lorenzo Sabine. Paradoxically, as he sought to exclude slavery from the New England's past and portray the history of his region as a story of the development of free white labor, Sabine heeded contemporary injunctions to broaden the scope of history to include an analysis of social and economic forces. Thus, in his biographical dictionary of the loyalists, Sabine offered an economic interpretation of the Revolution that questioned orthodox patriotic interpretations of the Revolution as a struggle for liberty. Published in 1847, this work provoked sharp controversy over its sympathetic portrayal of the loyalists. Questioning whether the principle of no taxation without representation really explained Revolutionary opposition to British taxation, Sabine was equally unconventional in his emphasis on the economic orientation of American objections to British taxation. For Sabine, the Revolution was a conflict over economic issues, whose main object was the achievement of free labor. For this reason, he took issue with the general tendency "to insist that questions of 'Taxation,' that points of 'Abstract Liberty,' produced the momentous struggle, which resulted in dismembering the British empire." Instead, he argued that "almost every matter brought into discussion was *practical*, and in some form or other related to LABOR, to some branch of COMMON INDUSTRY." Contrary to Revolutionary rhetoric, the real problem with British policy was not that it taxed the colonists without representation. Rather, "whoever has examined the acts of Parliament which were resisted, has found that nearly all of them inhibited Labor." In Sabine's view, British prohibitions and duties on colonial trade and manufacturing, such as the Sugar Act, were, by definition, opposed to free labor, for they restricted the American colonists from working in certain trades and deprived them of the full fruits of their labor. Therefore, Sabine concluded, "To me, then, the great object of the Revolution was to release LABOR from these restrictions."[79]

For this reason, Sabine located the "germs of the Revolution" in the Navigation Acts. Arguing that the Stamp Act "and other statutes of a kindred nature" had been given "too prominent a place" by conventional accounts as causes of the Revolution, he believed that the decision to enforce the Navigation Acts in 1761 precipitated American protests against British policy. Recognizing the importance of class to explaining such protests, he argued that, as the group whose interests were most directly harmed by British restrictions on trade, the "commercial class," by which he meant merchants and ship owners, took the lead in opposing British measures.[80] Sabine's class-based analysis then went on to break down the colonial population by occupation, explaining how and why certain professions such as lawyers were more likely to support the Revolution.[81] While his emphasis on economic motives challenged Bancroft's idealized view of the revolutionaries as motivated by disinterested principle, Sabine in the end, like Bancroft, still affirmed the legitimacy of American actions. He made this clear when he declared that American merchants and ship owners had been "entirely right" to resist the Navigation Acts, for "the barbarous code of commercial law, which disgraced the statute book of England" for the century before the Revolution, "was entitled to no respect whatever."[82] Sabine could view his interpretation of the Revolution as impartial in balancing a belief in the rightfulness of the Revolution with a recognition of the influence of self-interest on the revolutionaries. He thus reconciled impartiality with his nationalist purposes by making a nationalist vindication of the Revolution intrinsic to his understanding of this ideal.

Sabine's nationalist purposes were, at the same time, sectional in character, for, in emphasizing the role of free labor as a cause of the Revolution, he defined the nation very much in northern terms. A New England Whig, Sabine advanced this interpretation of the Revolution in the late 1840s, just as free labor ideology was gaining ascendancy over northern political discourse. This ideology served sectional purposes, for northerners used the idea of free labor to critique a southern society based on slavery. In free labor ideology, labor was supposed to be free in two senses—individuals should be free to work for whom they chose, and they should be free to keep the fruits of their own labor. Under such a system, diligent and frugal individuals would eventually be able to save enough money to purchase a farm or small business of their own, enabling them to achieve free labor in the ultimate sense, for they would be free from the control of any employer. The southern slave system threatened free labor ideals in two ways—by denying the slave the right to free labor and, more important for many northern whites, by denying nonslaveholding whites in the South the social mobility necessary to achieve the free labor ideal. Using free labor ideology to define northern society in opposition to the South, northern advocates of this ideology based their claims for the superiority of northern society on its ability to realize the free labor ideal.[83]

Accordingly, Sabine's interpretation of the Revolution differentiated between New England and the South on this basis. In an effort to be impartial, Sabine made little reference to slavery in his discussion of the southern colonies except for his comment that Virginia and North Carolina "were not able to provide troops according to their population, as compared with the States destitute of a 'peculiar institution.'" He noted that, in contrast, "more Whigs of new England were sent to her aid, and now lie buried in her soil, than she sent from it to every scene of strife from Lexington to Yorktown." Not only did Sabine deny the presence of slavery in New England as he contrasted the slaveholding South to a New England that was "destitute of a 'peculiar institution.'" He also attributed the South's inability to contribute as many troops to the Revolution as New England did to the "peculiar institution."[84] As part of his effort to be impartial, Sabine was careful to give credit to the South for its "more disinterested" exertions on behalf of the Revolution, reasoning that because its economy was predominantly agricultural, unlike the more commercially oriented economy of New England, southerners had less cause to resent British commercial restrictions, which did not impinge as much on the staple crops produced by southern planters. As he did so, however, he made clear that in characterizing the Revolution as a struggle for free labor, he was really speaking of New England. In turn, by emphasizing New England's deeply rooted commitment to the free labor ideal—a commitment that according to him dated from the passage of the Navigation Acts—Sabine further obscured the role of slavery in the region's history. Not only did his effort to provide an impartial economic interpretation of the Revolution serve nationalist purposes, then; through an impartial account that was balanced in recognizing both the limits to southern support for the Revolution and its more disinterested char-

acter, he also demonstrated how impartiality could further a sectional understanding of that nationalism.[85]

By identifying free labor with the Revolution, Sabine gave historical legitimacy to the ideal that defined New England and northern society, and he made
it an integral component of American nationality. Sabine's free labor interpretation of the Revolution thus at once allowed him to obscure the presence of slavery in New England's past, to define New England society as one based on free
labor, and to define the United States in terms of New England values. In doing
so, he implicitly criticized southern slaveholders who threatened and violated
the free labor ideal as not only misguided but un-American.[86]

"'Every brick in your houses is cemented by the blood of slaves'": A Nation Founded on Slavery

Although most New England historians shared Palfrey's and Sabine's desire to
erase slavery from their region's past, this tendency did not go entirely unchallenged, as some historians sought to apologize for and defend slavery against
abolitionist attacks through what they believed was an impartial analysis of
the centrality of slavery to America's history. Yet even those who most sharply
challenged the erasure of slavery by New England historians shared many of
the same assumptions as these historians, and, like Sabine and Palfrey, they
used impartiality in their own way for both sectional and nationalist purposes.
Southern physician and biblical scholar Samuel Cartwright revealed these
shared assumptions most clearly as he at once challenged a free labor interpretation of the Revolution and used that challenge to promote national unity.
Most important, as much as he differed from his New England opponents in his
treatment of slavery and his interpretation of impartiality, Cartwright, like his
opponents, expressed a firm commitment to exceptionalist ideology and used
the ideal of impartiality to further that commitment.

In one of the few—and sharpest—challenges to the vision of a historically
free New England, an anonymous pamphlet of 1850 published in response to
the theologian Moses Stuart's pamphlet *Conscience and the Constitution* demonstrated how an impartial and critical analysis of Puritan complicity in slavery could at once serve to vindicate the glory of the Puritan founders and discredit abolitionist attacks on slavery. Drawing on many of the same sources as
his contemporary New Englanders, and indeed on the works of New England
historians such as Benjamin Trumbull, Jeremy Belknap, George Bancroft, and
W. B. O. Peabody, the author of this pamphlet concluded from his research,

directly contrary to the intentions of most of these historians, that slavery was a generally accepted practice for much of New England's history. Refuting Stuart's (and Bancroft's) claim that slavery had been imposed on the colonists by the British, this writer argued that, on the contrary, the colonists—including the New England Puritans—had adopted slavery of their own accord and that slavery had existed in New England until the Revolution. Arguing that before the Massachusetts charter was annulled in 1684 the Massachusetts government had the authority to abolish slavery if it wished, the author of this pamphlet reasoned that its refusal to do so revealed that the Puritans saw nothing immoral about slavery. As "the men who admitted slavery in the first place," "without whose concurrence it could not have survived a single day," the Puritans, according to this pamphlet, "had the power to repeal the law by which it was established; a power they would not have been slow to exercise, had they thought its tendencies immoral or anti-scriptural. Had the owners proved contumacious, they could have been dealt with by a process as effective as that employed against Quakers, and Antinomians, and Anabaptists."[87]

According to this writer, slavery was so deeply rooted in the New England colonies that it continued unchallenged until the Revolutionary era. Consequently, even with the Revolution, Massachusetts was slow to act against slavery. Describing the slow and difficult process by which slavery and the slave trade were prohibited in Massachusetts, this pamphlet noted that not until 1788 was an act to abolish the slave trade passed in Massachusetts, "two and twenty years after the struggle is said to have commenced; some twelve years after the last vestige of British authority had vanished from the Old Bay State; and eight years after the citizens of the same" had begun to enjoy the benefits of "a government of the most popular cast, under the guarantee of a constitution, the fundamental article of which was that 'All men are born free and equal.'"[88] This pamphlet's exposé of New England complicity in slavery went beyond the Massachusetts Bay Puritans. While its analysis focused on Massachusetts, it argued that its claims about slavery applied "with but slight modification, to all the colonies of New England."[89] And so, commenting scathingly on Bancroft's glowing praise for Rhode Island as a "pure democracy" and for the prosperity that resulted from this system, the author pointed out that the real source of Newport's wealth was slavery. For this reason, he concluded, "the time was when it might have been said of Newport . . . 'Every brick in your houses is cemented by the blood of slaves.'"[90]

While acknowledging the wrongfulness of slavery, this writer did not condemn New Englanders for their acceptance of it. Instead, he argued that their commitment to slavery was understandable given their historical context.

Coming from a society in which feudalism and serfdom were not all that distant, this writer explained, the New England colonists could not be expected to recognize the wrongfulness of enslaving Africans. If they saw nothing wrong with virtually enslaving other Englishmen, it was even less likely that they would recognize the inhumanity of enslaving Africans. Reasoning that because "[n]o one doubted the rightfulness of villanage, and from villanage to slavery, and thence to the slave trade the transition was easy," "it might have been as much out of place to preach abolition in England as it is now in Mississippi."[91] The Puritans were, according to this writer, if anything, ahead of their contemporaries on the subject of slavery, for their laws at least limited the traffic in slaves to those who had already been enslaved elsewhere. In prohibiting the enslavement of those who were free, Puritan laws, for this writer, "displayed a benignity on the subject of slavery as much in advance of anything then existing at common law, or in the rolls of parliament, as the laws of Moses, in that respect, were superior to the polity of any nation in his time."[92] Thus, even as he acknowledged the presence of slavery in New England's history, this writer in the end, like Bancroft and Palfrey, still sought to vindicate Puritan greatness.

Where he differed from Bancroft and Palfrey was in his assumption that such a vindication did not require him to obscure Puritan complicity in slavery. Recognizing that his portrayal of the Puritans differed "from what imagination has sometimes cast about them," this writer did not think it necessary to embellish his account by exaggerating Puritan hostility to slavery, for the Puritans "require no adventitious aid. Never a set of men more ready than they to stand the gaze of truth, and with good reason; none had less to fear from her scrutiny." In disclaiming the "adventitious aid" of the imagination, this writer identified his account with a Rankean conception of truth as an unembellished account of fact. He saw no conflict between impartial truth in this sense and his desire to vindicate the Puritans because he believed that the Puritans were so admirable that their virtues did not require any embellishment by the historian, and even a recognition of their limits on slavery would not detract from their merits. And so, even while he sought to further the cause of truth by correcting the "false impression" that the Puritans were opposed to slavery, the author of this pamphlet was no less partial than those historians who sought to exclude slavery from New England's history, and like his opponents, he used his apparent impartiality to further his political purposes.[93]

Specifically, if his analysis appeared to be impartial in its effort to balance a recognition of Puritan limitations on the subject of slavery with an understanding of the reasons for those limitations (and truer to modern scholarly interpretations of the role that slavery played in New England), that recognition reflected and furthered his hostility to abolitionism. This writer made that hostility clear when he claimed that it was "a mistake" to think that the Puritans, whose goal was "to establish a religious commonwealth," "were imbued with many of the notions that constitute so large a portion of the stock in trade of a modern philanthropist. They were not Teetotallers, nor Non-resistants, nor Abolitionists. . . . On the contrary, they were valiant soldiers, temperate drinkers, and humane masters."[94] By differentiating between the Puritans and the "modern philanthropist," this writer criticized abolitionists and social reformers who sought to legitimize their activism by likening their moral zeal and their desire to purify society of the sin of slavery to the Puritans' religious fervor. This writer made his opposition to abolitionism even more explicit when he claimed that abolitionism would have been as "out of place" in Elizabethan England as it was in present-day Mississippi. And, as this comparison revealed, by trying to understand the Puritans in the context of their times, rather than condemning them for their acceptance of slavery, he hoped to encourage the same kind of understanding for southern slaveholders.

In an 1842 article for the *Southern Quarterly Review*, Samuel Cartwright—a southern doctor and apologist for slavery best known for his racial theories of disease—was even more explicit about how recognizing the centrality of slavery to the nation's history would serve as an antidote to abolitionist agitation. Combating abolitionism in this way was necessary for Cartwright not only because of his desire to further southern sectional interests but also because of his desire to preserve national unity. Thus he shared many of the same assumptions as his New England counterparts, especially their commitment to exceptionalist ideology; where he differed from them was in identifying the nation's future destiny with a South based on slavery rather than with a North based on free labor.[95] Hence, whereas *Slavery among the Puritans* focused on the role of slavery in colonial New England, Cartwright sought to demonstrate the importance of slavery to the Revolution. Consistent with his background as a doctor and a biblical scholar, he began his essay by appealing to the authority of his scientific and religious expertise as the basis for his claims about slavery, rooting those claims in both "inductions, made out in accordance with the rules of the Baconian philosophy," and his view of the Bible as "divine revelation."[96] In doing so, Cartwright revealed his assumption that a commitment to scientific fact (or at least what he considered scientific fact) and a providential perspective were not mutually exclusive. On the contrary, when he referred to the testimony of British parliamentary documents as "one of the clamps . . . of that scaffolding, aided by inductions from facts, . . . from the summit of which . . . infidelity itself may see God in his benevolence," he suggested that a scientific

approach based on induction from empirical evidence would provide the ultimate proof of a benevolent divinity.[97]

Cartwright took this assumption into his analysis of the Revolution as he at
once sought to demonstrate a scientific concern with fact by making claims to
scholarship in historical sources and affirmed his belief in a divine purpose to
history. Although his research was not as extensive as Bancroft's, he in this way,
like Bancroft, brought together a scientific ideal of impartiality with an exceptionalist framework. Thus he repeatedly spoke of his historical assertions as
"facts" and validated the factual basis for those assertions by citing—in the text
of the article and occasionally in rather rudimentary footnotes—influential
histories of the Revolutionary era such as Charles Botta's history of the American Revolution and John Marshall's *Life of George Washington*, as well as primary sources such as George Washington's writings. For Cartwright, the most
salient fact divulged by these works was that, far from being a hindrance to the
revolutionaries, as northern writers like Sabine suggested, slavery had strengthened the South during the Revolutionary War. Maintaining that "slave labor in
America is what money is in Europe, *the sinews of war*," Cartwright explained
that slaves had produced crops and goods necessary to fund and supply the
Revolutionary army; in addition, in freeing white men to fight against the British, slavery had enabled the southern states to provide "a larger number of soldiers, in proportion to their population, than any other people in the Union."[98]
Rather than a struggle effected by and for free labor, then, the Revolution, in
Cartwright's view, demonstrated how important slavery was to the nation's
prosperity and greatness.

To further substantiate these "facts," Cartwright also referred to "British
authorities," which he claimed drew on "parliamentary papers and British archives, inaccessible to the American public."[99] As he went into how the findings
of these sources buttressed his claims, he illuminated both his understanding
of impartiality and the political purposes that understanding served. According
to Cartwright, as they sought through such an "impartial examination of facts"
to understand why the British had "suffered such signal defeat and disgrace
in the slave-holding states of America" during the Revolution, "the despots of
England" had found, to their dismay, that "negro slavery is '*the accursed thing*'
which enabled the American colonies; without money or credit; to prosecute
successfully a seven years' war against the greatest power on earth."[100] For all of
what Cartwright considered to be their hostility to America, he believed that
these sources had demonstrated a certain kind of impartiality both in coming
to a conclusion directly at odds with their own hopes of using slave insurrection to divide and destroy America and in resting that conclusion on empirical

evidence derived from primary documents. In Cartwright's view, then, impartiality was a matter of subjecting partisan bias to the authority of "facts" independent of that bias, and like historians of his time, he based facts on the evidence of primary sources. In turn, by crediting the British sources he cited with impartiality, he at once demonstrated his own impartiality and gave his defense of slavery greater credibility as a pronouncement of truth; if even those individuals without any interest in defending slavery acknowledged its contribution to the Revolution, Cartwright suggested, then that was all the more proof of the truth of that contribution.[101]

If Cartwright in this way used impartiality to legitimize and defend slavery, he in turn hoped that such a defense would promote a more impartial attitude among contemporary southerners that would prevent them from being unduly provoked by antislavery rhetoric. By demonstrating how attached slaves were to their owners during the Revolution and how slavery actually strengthened the South's ability to fight the British, he hoped to alleviate southern fears that abolitionist agitation would incite slave insurrection and in this way to allay sectional tensions between North and South. As Cartwright explained, "Were the whole South fully apprized of its resources, its strength and security" "in a laboring peasantry, whom no temptations nor artifices can seduce from their allegiance, owing to this instinct in their nature, there would be but little danger" that British emissaries sent to the North "to stir up hostility against Southern slavery, could provoke the South to get entangled in angry and unprofitable collisions with the North."[102] Thus, for Cartwright, impartiality was both a cause and a consequence of recognizing the benefits of slavery, which would in turn promote national unity against British intrigues, for "a calm survey of facts" would demonstrate "that the South has nothing very seriously to fear from the direct action of Northern fanaticism, but that the whole country, North as well as South, has much to dread, lest the intrigues of a designing and interested class in England, should bring about *disunion, and disunion civil war.*"[103]

Preserving national unity was so important to Cartwright because of his commitment to exceptionalist ideology, and in his explanation for why southern slaves had remained so loyal to their owners during the Revolution, he embraced a southern variant of that ideology. Claiming that American history "abounds with instances, displaying the protecting hand of a superintending Providence, upholding the slave-holders in the darkest hours of trial, and leading them on to victory, to fame and to glory," Cartwright argued that Providence had exhibited its "protecting hand" both in giving black slaves an "instinctive attachment" to their owners and in dictating that the "race of Canaan" be enslaved in America. Not only did this "instinctive attachment" make southern resistance to the British—and hence for Cartwright the success of the Revolution—possible. But because "God had willed that the race of Canaan should be servants, and that they should act submissively," slaves in America were, according to Cartwright, far less oppressed than European laborers, who were not naturally destined to be servile.[104] Thus, like Bancroft, Cartwright used impartiality to reaffirm both a belief in America's providential destiny and its distinctiveness from Europe, but unlike Bancroft, he based that distinctiveness on slavery. And so, even as Cartwright's argument devalued blacks as racially inferior in its assumption that they were instinctively suited for slavery, it paradoxically acknowledged the value and importance of slave labor to the Revolution and, in doing so, made slavery integral to the nation's identity.

In making this argument, however, Cartwright in his own way contributed to the erasure of slavery from the North. The South, according to Cartwright, was able to contribute more soldiers to the Revolution than the North had because, unlike in the North, the presence of slavery in the South freed slaveholders to fight for their country without having to worry about who would protect the families they had left behind. No matter how brave and patriotic northern white men were, "while they are battling for their country, their families may be suffering,—their hired servants may desert them, or prove treacherous," whereas southern slaveholders could be certain that, regardless of what happened, "their families will not suffer, that their slaves will continue, to serve them, and be the first to give the alarm, in the event of the approach of an enemy, and help them to get out of his reach." Like his New England counterparts, then, Cartwright portrayed the North as a region based on free labor; where he differed from them was in seeing this quality as a disadvantage, rather than a source of strength.[105]

History "Unbedaubed with Patriotic Rouge": Richard Hildreth and the Political Function of Impartiality

If by acknowledging the role of slavery in the nation's history Cartwright resisted abolitionist efforts to eradicate slavery in the present, the historian Richard Hildreth demonstrated how the erasure of slavery from the nation's past could serve to aid in the elimination of slavery from the nation's future as he used his commitment to the ideal of impartiality to further his antislavery goals. And so, contrary to his reputation for scientific detachment, Hildreth, like other revisionists, used the ideal of impartial truth for social and political purposes and defined impartiality in racially exclusive terms. And like other re-

visionists, he interpreted impartiality to mean a more balanced and critical view
of both Puritan intolerance and the Revolution. Ultimately, what distinguished
Hildreth's history was not its commitment to impartial truth but its challenge to
the exceptionalist framework embraced by his fellow revisionists, for, although
Hildreth agreed with his contemporaries in his explanation for the Revolution,
he differed from them in his analysis of its outcome and purpose.

Hildreth's interests and activities were varied and wide ranging. Although
best known for his history, he was also a reformer and philosopher. Hildreth
began his reform career as a journalist, writing editorials for the Whig *Boston
Atlas*. Involved in a variety of antebellum reform causes, he was particularly
active in the antislavery movement, castigating slavery in his novel *The Slave:
Or Memoirs of Archy Moore* (1836) and his tract *Despotism in America* (1840).
In addition to the writing of polemical works against slavery, Hildreth's antislavery activities included organizing and speaking at antislavery meetings and
defending fugitive slaves. Even more controversial than his political views were
his philosophical ideas. A proponent of utilitarianism, Hildreth articulated his
philosophical theories in two treatises, the *Theory of Morals* and the *Theory
of Politics*. Following the publication of the *Theory of Morals* in 1844, Hildreth
devoted his attention to the first three volumes of his *History*, which appeared
in 1849. He published three more volumes in 1851–52, which continued the *History* up to 1821.[106] While far less popular and influential than Bancroft's history, Hildreth's work was, according to modern scholars, distinguished by its
scientific concern with objective truth, which stood in direct contrast to the
filiopietism of his contemporaries. By conventional accounts of American historiography, Hildreth's critical perspective on the nation's founders revealed his
commitment to a Rankean ideal of truth that required the historian to present
an unbiased account of the facts, detached from any social or political purpose.
Paradoxically, however, rather than representing a retreat from his political
activism, Hildreth's balanced analysis of American history both reflected and
furthered his political concerns.[107]

The conventional view of Hildreth as exceptional in his commitment to impartiality was rooted partly in his own description of his purposes, for in the
preface to his history, he differentiated himself from his contemporaries by emphasizing his concern with impartial truth. Complaining that "there are more
than enough" "centennial sermons and Fourth-of-July orations, whether pro-
fessedly such or in the guise of history," Hildreth sought instead "to present for
once, on the historic stage, the founders of our American nation unbedaubed
with patriotic rouge, wrapped up in no fine-spun cloaks of excuses and apology, without stilts, buskins, tinsel, or bedizzenment, in their own proper per-

sons, often rude, hard, narrow, superstitious, and mistaken, but always earnest, downright, manly, and sincere."[108] Often represented as the antithesis of—and even as directly reacting against—Bancroft in his "impartial" view of American history, Hildreth here, like Ellis, directed his criticism not against Bancroft but against Fourth of July orations. Indeed, it was unlikely that Hildreth had Bancroft in mind in his opening salvo, for Bancroft had published only the first three volumes of his history at this point, and his analysis had not yet covered the Revolution.[109] Thus, like Ellis, Hildreth defined truth in opposition to a "Fourth-of-July" version of history. In declaring that his purpose was to reveal the truth about American history by stripping it of the "patriotic rouge," "tinsel," and "bedizzenment" that these orations had imposed upon it, Hildreth made truth consist of an objective reality unembellished by the historian. Hence he wrote in a dry, colorless style that listed facts and events in an unemotional way, only occasionally relieved by the ironic humor and vivid prose of his caustic declamations against human bigotry and hypocrisy.[110] And, like his contemporaries, Hildreth defined impartial truth in masculine terms, for, in using terms with feminine associations like "rouge" and "tinsel" to describe the embellishment and distortion of truth, he characterized embellishment as feminine and, by implicit contrast, truth as masculine. Hildreth associated truth with manliness even more clearly when he argued that a true account of the nation's founders would not only reveal their flaws but also show them to be "manly, and sincere."[111]

As part of his effort to provide a more critical and impartial view of the nation's history, Hildreth challenged the idealization of the Puritans as flawless heroes. Although he did not go as far as Oliver in his attack on the Puritans, he was more critical of them than were revisionists like Motley, for he went beyond recognizing Puritan religious intolerance to argue that bigotry and fanaticism defined Puritanism.[112] Identifying impartiality with a scathing critique of Puritan intolerance, Hildreth portrayed Puritan society as a theocracy characterized by a "fierce, bigoted, domineering disposition," which the Puritans "had imbibed from the Old Testament."[113] In Hildreth's view, rather than a direct outgrowth of Puritanism, as Bancroft had argued, liberty was primarily the product of forces in conflict with Puritan ideals, and the struggle and eventual triumph of these forces against a powerful Puritan theocracy served as major organizing themes for the first two volumes of his history.[114] According to Hildreth, liberty—both political and religious—could emerge only when Puritanism had released its powerful grip over New England institutions and people. For this reason, in his narrative, the loss of colonial autonomy that came with the revocation of the original Massachusetts charter paradoxically furthered

the cause of American liberty, for "[i]f Massachusetts lost, under the new charter, the quasi-independence for which her theocratic rulers had so manfully
contended, she gained a commencement of religious freedom, and the extension to all her inhabitants of political rights."[115]
    As critical as Hildreth was of the Puritans, he, like most of his fellow New
Englanders, minimized their complicity in slavery. Although somewhat more
willing to acknowledge the role of slavery in New England's history than Bancroft was, he was far less critical of the Puritans for their acceptance of slavery
than he was of their religious intolerance. While he acknowledged that on the
eve of the Revolution slavery "existed as a matter of fact in every one of the
United Colonies," his analysis minimized the significance of slavery in New
England by contrasting the development of the southern colonies into a society based on slave labor with a New England where slavery "always remained"
"inconsiderable."[116] Attributing this difference to economic factors, Hildreth
explained that unlike in the southern colonies, where the large-scale production of staple crops created a demand for slave labor, "[t]he want in New England of any staple product" that required "hired or purchased labor . . . discouraged immigration and the importation of indented servants or slaves."[117]
Because of this difference, he believed that it was fortunate for the United States
that the "first collision" between the revolutionaries and the British "occurred
with the yeomanry of New England, freeholders who fought for their farms
and firesides, simple in their habits, inured to toil, but intelligent, not without
education, and full of the spirit and energy of freemen." A society defined by
these qualities would, he reasoned, be far more difficult to "subdue by force"
than one based on slavery.[118] In his praise for New England as a society of "freeholders," Hildreth not only characterized the region as a society based on free
labor but also revealed that he shared Sabine's assumption that the free labor
ideal of independence and self-sufficiency would stimulate "energy" and industry in its inhabitants. And, as Hildreth suggested when he described New
England's population as largely "home-born and home-bred," when he spoke of
free labor, he really meant white free labor.[119]
    Hence, like Sabine, Hildreth interpreted the Revolution as an economic
struggle to free the colonies from British commercial restrictions. Although
he believed that the revolutionaries were entirely justified in their opposition
to these restrictions, by emphasizing the economic, rather than the political,
character of British oppression, Hildreth, like Sabine, challenged patriotic mythology that portrayed the Revolution as a struggle for the abstract principle of
liberty. His account of the Revolution thus sought to be impartial by offering
a balanced view of the revolutionaries that defended their actions while ques-

tioning whether they were as idealistic as patriotic mythology claimed. And by emphasizing the economic origins of the Revolution, Hildreth, again like Sabine, broadened his understanding of historical truth to include economic as well as political forces. In Hildreth's account of the Revolution, economic self-interest was a driving factor on both sides. If, on the one hand, British trade regulations were designed to further British commercial interests at the expense of the colonies, or as he put it, "systematically to carry out the policy of rendering America completely subservient to the narrow views which then prevailed of the commercial interests of the mother country," the colonists, on the other hand, resented these restrictions as an obstacle to their own economic prosperity and development. Parliament foolishly provoked American resistance by extending its authority to include taxes for revenue just as the colonists' increasing self-confidence heightened their resentment of British trade regulations, for "as the colonies advanced in wealth and commercial enterprise, they grew more and more restless under the fetters on their trade and industry imposed by British legislation."[120]

But if other historians had already preceded Hildreth in challenging patriotic myths about American history, why did he portray himself as an iconoclast in debunking patriotic myths? What made him an iconoclast was not his commitment to impartiality or his critical view of the nation's founders but rather his assessment of the effects of the Revolution and its challenge to American exceptionalism. Contending that the Revolution had effected few discernible changes in American society, Hildreth argued that the Revolution "made no sudden nor violent change in the laws or political institutions of America beyond casting off the superintending power of the mother country; and even that power, always limited, was replaced to a great extent by the authority of Congress."[121] By itself, this assertion would have been unremarkable, for Bancroft's argument that the Revolution had simply consummated tendencies long present in American society also denied the radicalism of the Revolution.

But whereas Bancroft attributed the success of the Revolution, and its unique significance in history, to the social conservatism that distinguished it from other revolutions, Hildreth, in contrast, saw the conservative character of the Revolution as a limitation that diminished its achievement. Rather than embodying a turning point in the realization of democracy, the United States had, in Hildreth's view, yet to achieve the democratic principles associated with the Revolution. He made his doubts about the achievement of democracy clear as he deplored the sharply circumscribed practical effects of even the Revolution's greatest innovation, "the public recognition of the theory of the equal rights of man," which "encountered in existing prejudices and institutions many serious and even formidable obstacles to its general application, giving rise to several striking political anomalies." Influenced by his own concerns as an antislavery reformer, he singled out slavery as the "most startling" discrepancy in Revolutionary ideology, "inconsistent not only with the equal rights of man, but even with the law of England, as solemnly decided in the case of Somersett four years before the Declaration of Independence." Here, then, in direct contrast to Bancroft, Hildreth not only denied that the Revolution had set in motion the forces that would lead to the end of slavery but also suggested that, far from hindering emancipation, England was in advance of the United States in repudiating slavery. According to Hildreth, as long as slavery persisted in America, the Revolution would be incomplete, for it prevented, "more than all other causes, that carrying out of the principles of the Revolution, that assimilation and true social union toward which the states have constantly tended, but which they are still so far from having reached."[122] By emphasizing the unfulfilled promise of the Revolution in this way, Hildreth departed from orthodox and revisionist historians alike and challenged a basic axiom of American exceptionalist dogma— the belief that the Revolution had succeeded in transforming the course of human history.[123]

Despite these reservations about the ultimate consequences of the Revolution, Hildreth recognized the achievements of the revolutionaries. Indeed, like Bowen, who argued that a more impartial view of the Puritans would actually enhance their reputation, Hildreth believed that admitting the revolutionaries' faults would in the end deepen admiration for them by giving their descendants a better appreciation of the obstacles they had to overcome. Idealizing the revolutionaries as flawless heroes, he argued, led "to exaggerated historical estimates of the disinterestedness and public spirit of those times." In turn, these estimates "detract not a little from the real magnitude of the American Revolution, by giving the idea of a spirit of union and self-sacrifice that did not exist, and which cut off one chief source of intelligent admiration of the actors in it by diminishing the apparent difficulties they had to overcome." For Hildreth, the success of the Revolution appeared all the more remarkable and impressive after considering the folly and vice the founders had to overcome. As he explained, "Superhuman heroism being admitted, the accomplishment of any object becomes easy enough; the really difficult, the truly admirable thing, is to accomplish great objects by merely human means."[124]

Even as he celebrated the revolutionaries, however, Hildreth revealed the assumptions that distinguished his historical views from those of his contemporaries. By representing the Revolution as an exclusively human artifact and by making human agency the sole measure of its greatness, he offered an entirely naturalistic view of history that disavowed any appeals to providential design. Instead, influenced by utilitarian philosophy, Hildreth sought to explain historical events solely in terms of human action. Utilitarian thinkers based morality on utility, denying the existence of abstract standards of right and wrong. Therefore they advocated empirical methods of analysis and gave primacy to experience. As a result, they were skeptical not only of religion but also of any explanations that appealed to metaphysical forces.[125] Taking this positivist outlook into his history, Hildreth refused to look beyond the material world for higher causes. And in his refusal to interpret American history in terms of a larger providential design, he rejected another fundamental element of exceptionalist ideology.[126]

Yet if Hildreth did not share Bancroft's exceptionalist vision of the United States as an exemplar of democracy, he did share Bancroft's faith in democracy, and ultimately, he sought to further the advance of democracy in America through his skepticism about the consequences of the Revolution and its providential framework.[127] And so, rather than simply reflecting a disinterested concern with truth, his impartial and balanced view of American history served an important political purpose. Hildreth articulated that purpose in his *Theory of Politics* as he responded to critics who had disparaged his history for lacking any philosophical theory. Although this work was first published four years after his *History*, Hildreth had written most of it earlier in the 1840s. Prefacing this treatise with a sharp rejoinder to critics of his *History*, he commented sarcastically, "The author specially commends this treatise to the attention of such critics as have complained that his *History of the United States* has no 'philosophy' in it." The implication of this pointed declaration was that he had in fact written his *History* according to deeper philosophical principles, and critics who had overlooked these principles would find a more explicit elaboration in the work at hand.[128]

The philosophy that Hildreth presented in his *Theory of Politics* was his theory of democracy. As he outlined the obstacles to this ideal, he demonstrated how his understanding of impartiality would advance democracy. Hildreth was so hostile to metaphysical explanations because he viewed religion in general, or what he called "mystical ideas," as a threat to democracy. Disputing Alexis de Tocqueville's contention that religion had furthered the success of democracy in America, he attacked religion as a "foreign and even hostile ingredient" that was "more proper to a theocratic despotism than to a democracy, or even a civic aristocracy." For this reason, through what he considered to be an impartial analysis that eschewed metaphysical explanations and that recognized the harmful effects of Puritan bigotry and intolerance, he hoped to advance democracy by countering in his own time "that intolerant bigotry and bitter opposition to all freedom of inquiry" that, as a result of the growing influence of religion, he believed had become "no less characteristic of the United States than of Great Britain."[129]

Equally important, because for Hildreth slavery was by definition opposed to democracy, the nation would realize its democratic potential only when slavery was eradicated. Until then, he determined, "it will be in vain to look to this quarter for the full realization of that modern democratical system which had its very origin . . . in the repudiation of chattel slavery." By providing a balanced view of the Revolution that recognized both the limits and achievements of revolutionaries, Hildreth sought to further this goal. If, on the one hand, his criticism of the conservatism and limits of the Revolution served to remind his contemporaries of all the injustices that the Revolution had left unremedied, on the other hand, his acknowledgment of the revolutionaries' accomplishments provided his contemporaries with models of social activism that would spur them to take action against these injustices. And by portraying the revolutionaries' accomplishments as the products of unaided human action, Hildreth invalidated reliance upon divine intervention as a surrogate for human action in the present. Just as the revolutionaries had overcome British oppression without divine aid, implied Hildreth, so too did contemporary Americans need to recognize that social change depended on human initiative. In this way, rather than being an end in itself, Hildreth's quest for impartial truth served an important political function.[130]

Hildreth himself pointed to the political function of impartiality while elaborating on the threats to democracy. In theory, he argued, democratic institutions were the direct antithesis of "that excessive admiration which can discover nothing bad or wrong, and which is ready to pardon every thing in those who are the objects of it, and to that arrogant contempt which can see nothing good or right in those against whom it is directed, and which can make no excuses nor allowances for them."[131] This contrast implied that the filiopietistic admiration for the revolutionaries so widespread in his time endangered democracy. Yet countering this trend with a wholesale condemnation of the founders would also be misleading and antidemocratic. Because for Hildreth impartiality was, by definition, a democratic ideal, demystifying the founders while recognizing their merits was necessary to preserve and enlarge the very principles the revolutionaries had sought to establish. For all the differences between them, then, Hildreth, like Bancroft, in his own way identified democracy with the ideal of impartiality.

Democracy was so important to Hildreth because he, like Bancroft, identi-

fied democracy with progress, but unlike Bancroft, Hildreth based this conclusion on a utilitarian analysis of the pain and pleasure produced by different
types of government rather than on a transcendental view of democracy as an
eternal principle. After calculating the effects of democracy on "the increase and
diffusion of knowledge and wealth, and the elevation of the standards of taste
and morals," Hildreth concluded that democracy was the system that would
produce the greatest human happiness. Democracies, he claimed, "by reason
of the very principle of equality upon which they are founded, are decidedly
hostile to all monopolies, restrictions, or prohibitions." As a result, democracies
fostered "free competition," which was, in turn, he believed, the most important
factor in the "rapid advancement" of civilization, for competition maximized
the increase and diffusion of wealth, knowledge, and taste. Sounding much like
Adam Smith in his celebration of the benefits of free competition, Hildreth here
embraced the capitalist faith that competition would further progress. And so,
by using impartiality to advance democracy, Hildreth believed that he was ultimately contributing to the advancement of progress itself, for he identified
democracy with capitalism.[132]

"A naked record of facts"? Impartiality, Exceptionalism, and the Response to Hildreth's History

In the end, however, Hildreth failed in his goal of effecting social change through
his history, for this work achieved only limited popular success. Although his
history sold well enough for it to be reissued six times in the next thirty years,
it was far less popular than Bancroft's history, and by 1854, the proceeds of Hildreth's *History* were only $4,476.58, in contrast to the $50,000 that Bancroft's
early volumes had earned by that point. If the poor sales for his history revealed
that Hildreth's "impartial" perspective was certainly not representative of his
time, neither was it completely anomalous, for the mixed critical response to
his work demonstrated that at least some historians shared his concern with
impartiality.[133] Yet the conflict among Hildreth's critics was not one between
impartial and partial history, for even Hildreth's most favorable reviewers did
not fully share his understanding of impartiality and his critics were by no
means completely opposed to this ideal. Hildreth's reviewers disagreed with
Hildreth and one another not because they disputed the importance of impartiality but because they interpreted this ideal in different ways and used it for
sharply opposing social purposes. Where Hildreth's critics and admirers agreed
with one another—and disagreed with Hildreth—was in their commitment

to the ideology of American exceptionalism. And so, even as they argued over Hildreth's understanding of impartiality, they found different ways of reconciling his "impartial" analysis of American history with their belief in the nation's special mission. As they did so, Hildreth's reviewers demonstrated how they could genuinely view themselves as impartial, even while their understanding of impartiality furthered their political and social purposes.

One critic who shared Hildreth's commitment to impartiality was Daniel Curry, and in a favorable review of Hildreth's history for the *Methodist Quarterly Review*, he praised Hildreth specifically for this quality. Commending him for his "strict fidelity to the truth," Curry explained that Hildreth's "perceptions seem to be very little affected by his feelings: he considers things with entire impartiality." Unlike those historians who, "like portrait-painters," feel obliged "to make the best of their subjects" and "to fill in and colour up as the case may require," Hildreth "emulates the photographer,—for in his sketches of character one may recognize with equal clearness 'their faults as well as their virtues, their weaknesses as well as their strength.'"[134] For Curry, then, impartial truth required the historian to provide a balanced view of his subjects that recognized both their faults and virtues. Viewing the historian as a "photographer" rather than an artist, Curry believed that the historian's role was to represent his subjects exactly as they were, without allowing his portrayal to be colored by his own feelings or opinions. And, like a photograph, the more exact a copy of that reality, the truer the historian's depiction would be. In likening the historian to the photographer, Curry expressed a scientific understanding of truth as the recreation of an objective reality independent of the historian's interpretation— hence he could praise Hildreth for his success in presenting the "stern, unvarnished truth."[135] Here, while Curry's definition of truth conformed closely to Hildreth's, he accepted Hildreth's claims to impartiality at face value and failed to see how this conception of truth could itself further a social purpose.

In one of the most favorable reviews of Hildreth's history, transcendentalist and social reformer Theodore Parker revealed the social function of this ideal, as he, like Hildreth, used impartiality for antislavery purposes. Just like Hildreth, Parker was something of a maverick within the Brahmin elite. A direct descendant of Captain John Parker, renowned as the American commander at the battle of Lexington, Parker came from an illustrious Revolutionary lineage. Yet his unorthodox religious views and his antislavery activities turned him into an outcast in Brahmin circles.[136] But even while Parker shared in many ways both Hildreth's understanding of impartiality and his reform goals, Parker brought together these imperatives in a different way. Not only was he far more optimistic than Hildreth was about the status of democracy in America; on a more fundamental level, this optimism signified subtle but important differences in the character and function of impartiality for Parker. Praising Hildreth's history as a "work of much value and importance" in an 1850 review for the journal he founded—the *Massachusetts Quarterly Review*—Parker, like Curry, singled out Hildreth's impartiality as one of his greatest merits. For Parker, because Hildreth "writes in the interest of mankind, and not for any portion thereof," he "allows no local attachment, or reverence for men or classes of men, to keep him from telling the truth as he finds it." As a result, "[h]is work is almost wholly objective,—giving the facts, not his opinions about the facts."[137]

In declaring that "objective" truth required the historian to provide an account of facts without expressing his opinions about them, Parker, like Curry and Hildreth, offered a definition of truth that sounded much like Ranke's ideal of objectivity. For Parker, as for Ranke, truth was something to be discovered by the historian, rather than a matter of interpretation. At the same time, in contrast to the Rankean ideal, Parker did not believe that the objectivity required the historian to uncover the truth as an end in itself, detached from any social purpose. When he commended Hildreth for writing "in the interest of mankind," Parker suggested that objective history could and should serve a social purpose, as long as that purpose benefited all of humanity. To be partial was to favor a particular group, not to write history for a social cause.

For Parker, Hildreth had lived up to this definition of impartiality in his treatment of the Puritans, for he did not show a bias either in favor of or against the Puritans. Parker praised Hildreth for avoiding both the extremes of "unqualified praise and unqualified condemnation" and letting Puritan actions "speak for themselves."[138] In portraying the Puritans as an undemocratic society characterized by religious intolerance, Hildreth "is not misled by any reverence for the Puritans; he shows no antipathy to them; extenuates nothing, adds nothing, and sets down naught in malice."[139] Yet Parker offered, overall, a more favorable view of the Puritans than Hildreth did, revealing that they differed over what a balanced and impartial view of the Puritans meant in practice. With all their faults, Parker believed, the Puritans were still far superior to the southern colonists in their commitment to ideals over economic interest. Even while condemning the Puritans for their intolerance and fanaticism, he could still express admiration for their "hardy vigor," their "capacity for doing and enduring," and their "manly reliance on God and their own arm."[140]

Parker's unwillingness to repudiate the Puritans reflected in part his own sectional loyalties to New England. On a more fundamental level, Parker's ambivalence about the Puritans reflected his ambivalence about abolitionism. Although firmly opposed to slavery, Parker also rejected the radicalism of Garrisonian abolitionists. Instead, like Charles Sumner and Horace Mann, he hoped to eradicate slavery through electoral means within the existing political system. Just as he sought to articulate an impartial antislavery position that, unlike the Garrisonians, recognized problems in the existing social system without repudiating that system altogether, Parker offered a balanced and impartial view of the Puritans that recognized both their flaws and virtues. Indeed, these two imperatives were integrally related to each other. Through his criticism of Puritan intolerance, Parker could counter conservatives within the Brahmin elite who opposed contemporary efforts at social reform as threats to the greatness of New England's Puritan heritage. By challenging such an idealization of that heritage, Parker suggested that reformers who wished to effect changes in the social order would provide a much-needed remedy to the shortcomings of the Puritan legacy. At the same time, in his recognition of Puritan merits, Parker warned radical abolitionists against a wholesale repudiation of the established social order that would destroy all that the Puritans had achieved.[141]

Yet if Parker was similar to Hildreth in using an impartial view of the Puritans to further his antislavery purposes, he differed from Hildreth in his commitment to American exceptionalism. Accordingly, as much as he recognized the need for reform, Parker still celebrated America's greatness as a democratic nation. Implicitly dismissing Hildreth's own doubts about the realization of democracy in America, he prefaced his endorsement of Hildreth's history with a lengthy affirmation of America's importance as a unique and successful experiment with democracy—a central doctrine in American exceptionalist ideology. According to Parker, "political institutions were set agoing here radically unlike any others in the world." As a result, the United States now "present one of the most interesting and important political phenomena ever offered in the history of mankind," for the success of the American experiment with democracy could dispel the horror and suspicion surrounding the concept, making it "perhaps, the prophecy of what most of the others are destined to become."[142] While recognizing that slavery represented a "dreadful blot" on this experiment, Parker concluded that, overall, the nation's democratic achievements far outweighed its lapses. Indeed, the nation's special status as a democratic experiment made the abolition of slavery all the more imperative, for only in this way could the nation fully realize its democratic mission.[143]

Again in direct contrast to Hildreth's secular perspective, Parker explained the rise of democracy in America as the product of a divine plan. For this reason, Parker claimed that the American colonies had developed "as if there was a regular plan, and as if the whole was calculated to bring about the present result." He continued, "No doubt, there was such a concatenation of part with part, only the plan lay in God, not in the mind of Oglethorpe and Captain Smith, of Carver and Roger Williams." Thus, Parker converted a positive evaluation of Hildreth's *History* into an exposition on the nation's transcendental importance. In this way, ironically subverting Hildreth's own purposes, he yoked Hildreth's impartial perspective to one of the central premises of American exceptionalism—the belief that America's democratic mission was divinely ordained.[144]

Parker could do so because, although he agreed with Hildreth on the importance of impartiality, he differed from Hildreth in his understanding of the historian's role. Believing that it was the duty of the "philosophical historian" to tell the story of the unfolding and realization of the divine plan, Parker explained, "If a great idea appears in human affairs, founding new institutions and overturning the old," as was the case with the rise of democracy in America, it was incumbent on the philosophical historian "to refer it back to its origin in the permanent nature of man, or the accidents of his development; to show the various attempts to make the thought a thing, and the idea a fact." As Parker criticized Hildreth for providing "too little of the philosophical part of history" in his apparent concern with just giving the facts, he revealed how his understanding of the historian's role differed from Hildreth's.[145] While, contrary to Parker's criticism, Hildreth shared Parker's belief in the philosophical function of history, his definition of "philosophical history" differed from Parker's. Because, for Hildreth, all the "philosophy" or general principles revealed by history were the products of human action, the historian would make those principles evident simply by presenting the facts of history and describing what had happened in the past. In contrast, Parker assigned to the historian a more active role in interpreting the larger meaning of those facts because he located the meaning of history outside history; in other words, believing that the truth of history was ultimately to be found not in human action but in the unfolding of transcendent principles derived from providence, Parker concluded that only by looking beyond the surface of events could the historian uncover that truth.

Maintaining that impartiality was necessary but not sufficient for the "philosophical historian" to achieve this goal, Parker reconciled his belief that history was supposed to trace the development of the nation's democratic mission with his praise for Hildreth's impartiality by reasoning that "[h]is book is written in the spirit of democracy, which continually appears in spite of the author." For Parker, the fact that Hildreth's history revealed the advance of democracy in America despite his unwillingness to analyze this process or to express his own political sympathies was all the more proof that democracy represented a fundamental and inescapable higher truth embedded in the "permanent nature of man."[146] In this way, rather than seeing a contradiction between Hildreth's impartial perspective and his own commitment to exceptionalist ideology, Parker turned his commendation of Hildreth into a reaffirmation of what he believed was the higher truth of the nation's divine mission.

In another favorable review of Hildreth's history, a writer for the *Christian Review* in his own way used impartiality to reaffirm exceptionalist premises as he even more directly addressed the relationship between Hildreth's reassessment of the nation's history and the belief in America's divine mission. Like Parker, this writer found nothing intrinsically offensive about Hildreth's critical perspective on the nation's founders. What some reviewers criticized as Hildreth's "want of becoming national spirit" and "a patriotic sympathy with the rapidly developing greatness of our country," this critic considered "as on the whole a feature to be commended."[147] Less willing than Parker to disregard the secular bias of Hildreth's analysis, he did express misgivings that the "religious portion of the community may reasonably regret that a more distinct recognition of God's hand in our planting and progress is not here observable."[148] As he did so, he identified the distinguishing characteristic of Hildreth's history—its entirely secular orientation. Yet, instead of repudiating Hildreth's interpretation for this reason, he adroitly reconciled Hildreth's dispassionate analysis with a recognition of America's divine mission among the "increasing number who trace to the right, but high and hidden source of God's unmerited benignity, the influences which have made us to differ from most of the nations of the earth." He reasoned that their "pious thankfulness will not be less likely exercised in the perusal of these volumes, because they are not formally and frequently called to its utterance."[149] This reviewer saw no conflict between Hildreth's "impartial" perspective and the exceptionalist belief in America's divinely ordained mission because he was so confident of that mission that he did not consider it necessary for Hildreth to remind his readers of it.

Yet this reviewer, like Parker, evaded Hildreth's challenge to another tenet of American exceptionalism—the conception of the Revolution as a uniquely significant event in human history. Hildreth's most perceptive and, for that reason, most critical reviewer was Francis Bowen, who understood what made Hildreth's particular brand of revisionism so unique and subversive. Even while Bowen shared Parker's view of the historian's role and his belief in exceptionalist ideology, he was more critical of Hildreth's history than Parker was, for he repudiated the reform goals that Hildreth and Parker shared. On a more fundamental level, Bowen saw more clearly than Parker the threat that Hildreth's interpretation posed to exceptionalist assumptions because, unlike Parker, he recognized that Hildreth's very definition of impartiality was not entirely disinterested but contained an implicit challenge to the belief in a higher truth and meaning to history. A leading figure in the Brahmin establishment that Parker sought to challenge, Bowen edited the *North American Review* from 1843 to 1853. Although best known as a philosophical thinker, he also wrote extensively on history, contributing three biographies to Jared Sparks's *Library of American Biography* and numerous historical essays to the *North American Review* during the 1830s and 1840s.[150]

In one such essay reviewing Hildreth's history, Bowen took exception to Hildreth's work not because he disagreed with Hildreth and Parker on the importance of impartiality; on the contrary, the problem with Hildreth's history, in his view, was its failure to live up to that ideal. If, for Bowen, Palfrey had been too uncritical of the Puritans, Hildreth had gone too far in the other direction in his hostility to them. In Bowen's view, Hildreth's history was "quite as one-sided and deceptive" as the Fourth of July orations that Hildreth sought to challenge, and the "only difference is, that where the preacher and the orator have gone to the right, he has carefully gone to the left. The truth lies about half way between them."[151] Specifically, Bowen believed that Hildreth had emphasized the theocratic nature of the Puritan system at the expense of other qualities that characterized the Puritans. Through such an interpretation, according to Bowen, far from presenting the facts unadulterated by his own theories or opinions, Hildreth had attempted to use history as a vehicle for his own hostility to religion by demonstrating the "evils of a theocratic form of government, and the folly and hypocrisy of rulers who profess to act upon religious principles."[152]

Whereas Parker took Hildreth's claims to impartiality at face value, then, Bowen recognized that Hildreth's apparent impartiality itself served a social purpose, for he believed that it was impossible for the historian to divest himself of his own opinions and prejudices and provide a disinterested chronicle of the facts. As Bowen acknowledged, "[I]t is impossible to write history without seeking, either avowedly, or stealthily, or unawares, to verify some hypothesis, or establish some theory, which furnishes a reason and a guide for the selection and arrangement of the materials." According to Bowen, as much as the historian tried to avoid imposing his own theories on his history, he would still do so unconsciously simply through the facts he selected or emphasized. Thus, "[w]ithout one false assertion or positive misstatement, a writer may give any tone to a narrative that he pleases, simply by an artful choice of the events to which prominence is given, and a studied collocation of the circumstances. And he may do this unconsciously, or while sincerely striving to elucidate the truth." For this reason, Bowen concluded, "A naked record of facts must also be untrustworthy; it will be not merely incomplete, but deceptive. It will give rise to unfounded impressions, and create false judgments."[153] Hence, for Bowen, to present history as just an account of the facts was itself an interpretive choice, which was doubly misleading. Not only would such an approach provide an incomplete and therefore distorted view of the past. By assuming the appearance of impartiality, the historian would mislead readers into thinking that such distortions represented an unbiased account of the truth.

Bowen here revealed a certain tension in his understanding of impartiality. Even as he seemed to acknowledge that total impartiality was impossible for any historian, his criticism of both Hildreth and Palfrey for their lack of impartiality implied a belief in the existence and attainability of this ideal. Bowen revealed how he reconciled the tensions in his view of impartiality when he explained why presenting history as a "naked record of facts," as Hildreth had done, was so misleading. For Bowen, Hildreth's approach would give rise to "false judgments" because it did not look at historical actors in their own context, and he believed that the historian could free himself of bias only by entering into the feelings and assumptions of his subjects. Proclaiming that "[t]he men of the seventeenth century must not be tried by the same standard as the men of the nineteenth century," Bowen criticized Hildreth's condemnation of Puritan bigotry and tyranny for judging the Puritans according to the standards of his time rather than their own.[154] Instead, when "[t]he opinions and the sentiments of his own age and country cease to be a standard for judging those of every other," Bowen argued, "the biographer gradually conceives an affection for his hero, of whose character he had previously determined to be a rigid and impartial judge." In turn, once the historian allowed himself to be "imbued with their [his subjects'] spirit and animated by their enthusiasm," he would "live in the olden times of which he is to be the chronicler," and "[h]is mind" would "gradually lose its hold of the prepossessions and theories with which he began his task."[155] Paradoxically for Bowen, in contrast to Hildreth and Parker, the historian would come the closest to achieving true impartiality when he abandoned the guise of the "rigid and impartial judge" and allowed himself to become imbued with "affection" for his subjects; the historian could best transcend his own prejudices not by detaching himself from his subjects but by sharing their enthusiasm and biases.

For Bowen, impartiality in this sense was in turn necessary for the historian to achieve truth. For this reason, Bowen believed that, in his failure to take the different context for Puritan intolerance into account, Hildreth "commits high treason against truth," for truth entailed "a comprehensive view" of the facts that illuminated the relationship between those facts and the "the distinctive features" of their context.[156] As Bowen made clear in accusing Hildreth of committing "treason" against the truth, even as he questioned whether the historian could ever be completely unbiased, he firmly upheld a faith in the possibility of achieving historical truth. Such a "comprehensive view" was necessary for truth because, like Parker, Bowen believed that the historian's function was to provide more than just a record of facts. In his injunction that the historian had to provide "a large view of the facts" that would "not only chronicle the occurrences, but decipher their meaning, and point out the laws under which they take place," Bowen presented a view of the historian's role that sounded much like Parker's conception of the philosophical historian; like Parker, Bowen believed that there was a larger meaning to history beyond the surface of events and that it was the historian's role to discern and disclose that meaning. Yet Bowen was far more critical of Hildreth than Parker was: whereas Parker saw no conflict between this view of the historian's role and Hildreth's effort to provide an unbiased record of fact, Bowen believed that to define history as a "naked record of facts" was to deny the existence of a higher meaning and purpose to history.[157]

At the same time, Bowen agreed with the particulars of Hildreth's interpretation in many respects; where he disagreed with Hildreth was on the significance of these particulars. For example, although Bowen condemned Hildreth for being too critical of the Puritans, Bowen's interpretation of the Puritans actually resembled Hildreth's in many ways, and they both repudiated Bancroft's characterization of the Puritans as exponents of democracy. Hence, like Hildreth, Bowen emphasized the Puritans' religious motives for colonization and recognized that the Puritans had no intention of establishing a democracy. Agreeing with Hildreth that the idea of equality was completely alien to the Puritans, Bowen argued that this principle did not take hold in New England until well after the American Revolution. Attributing this development to the influence of the French Revolution, Bowen asserted, "The republican element did not begin to develop itself in New England till a much later day; and the theory of absolute equality, both political and social, was hardly so much as broached for some years after the establishment of American independence." Characterizing the principle of equality as a "dogma" that "was first preached by the speculative zealots of the French Revolution," Bowen concluded that to condemn the Puritans for their failure to live up to this principle was a "gross anachronism." As Bowen's use of terms like "dogma" and "zealots" revealed, rather than viewing the Puritans as intolerant religious fanatics, he believed that advocates of democracy were the ones guilty of a dangerous fanaticism rooted in speculation and theory, rather than in reality or experience.[158]

As this assessment made clear, Bowen, unlike Parker and Hildreth, did not see the Puritans' hostility to democracy as a defect. Rather than condemning the Puritans for their undemocratic views, Bowen used them to critique democracy. By dissociating the Puritans from democracy, he undermined the historical legitimacy of this principle, portraying it instead as a radical innovation, untested and unsanctified by tradition. And so, whereas Parker and Hildreth sought to promote social reform by acknowledging the undemocratic character of Puritan society, Bowen, deeply conservative in his social views even by the standards of already conservative Boston Brahmins, used this realization to defend the established social order. Bowen was even more explicit about his distrust of democracy and pointed to the contemporary sources of that distrust when he explained his motives for writing an essay that condemned the Dorr Rebellion of 1842, declaring, "I am a stanch conservative, and some anti-democratic notions had been working so long in my head, that they would have rent my skull open, if they had not found vent in some other way."[159]

This uprising occurred when Thomas Dorr and his followers organized the writing and ratification of a new state constitution and formed their own government under that constitution as part of their campaign to reform Rhode Island's charter government to allow for universal manhood suffrage. Although these measures were extralegal and were proscribed by the existing state government, Dorr and his supporters based their authority on the sovereignty of the people, the majority of whose support they claimed for their constitution. Although the existing government easily suppressed the rebellion, Dorr's appeal to popular sovereignty as a basis for overturning the established government and the violence that ensued aroused Whig fears of the destabilizing effects of a belief in popular supremacy. Consequently, like his fellow Whigs, Bowen condemned the rebellion as an illegitimate usurpation of the government by the people, or, as he termed them, "the unthinking and uneducated classes, whose passions had first been roused by false statements and heated declamation, and whose ardor was now sustained and even increased by the electric influences of a Revolutionary contest."[160] Further compounding Bowen's fear of democracy as a fanatical contagion that, once unleashed, threatened to engulf the social order in chaos and violence was the outbreak of the European revolutions of 1848. In an article on the revolutions of 1848 for the *North American Review*, Bowen expressed his fear of these "popular tumults" as he condemned the inflammatory spirit and senseless destruction of the French Revolution of 1848.[161] Bowen's effort to dissociate the Puritans from what he saw as the destructive fanaticism of democracy, then, did not just come from a fear of democracy in the abstract but was a response to tangible threats of social disorder in his own time.

Yet if Bowen did not share Parker's faith in democracy, he was as committed as Parker was to the belief in American exceptionalism. For this reason, while Bowen did not dispute the particulars of Hildreth's interpretation of the Revolution, he attacked this interpretation for divesting the Revolution of any larger meaning or significance. And so, even though Bowen acknowledged that there was nothing factually incorrect about Hildreth's account—"we know not that a single statement in it can be successfully impugned"—he concluded, "[I]t is not the truth, because it is not the whole truth."[162] Although clear and succinct, Hildreth wrote "in as cold-blooded a manner as if the writer had been engaged with an account of a long struggle between two tribes of savages in the heart of Africa. *Nil admirari* might be inscribed on the volume as its motto." Bowen exaggerated in his scathing summary, but he grasped the essence of Hildreth's iconoclasm; Hildreth saw the Revolution "as rather an insignificant affair," which "was only the violent separation from the parent country of thirteen feeble colonies, whose inhabitants, taken together, hardly equalled in number the present population of the State of New York or the city of London."[163]

According to Bowen, Hildreth, in his narrow perspective on the Revolution, had completely overlooked its broader ramifications, for, "[w]hen regarded in its broadest aspect, and when its causes, its general character, and its consequences are fairly estimated, the Revolution appears in its proper light, as one of the greatest events in the annals of nations. It was a turning point in the history of the world."[164] Thus, Bowen understood better than modern scholars the real nature of Hildreth's heresy. In Bowen's view, the problem with Hildreth's history was not his critical attitude toward the founders. Rather, Hildreth's most significant and disturbing departure was in detaching that skepticism from one of the foundations of American exceptionalism—the belief that the Revolution had transfigured the course of American and world history, making it an event qualitatively different from all others. Although taken alone, Hildreth's critical perspective on the nation's history was for Bowen misleading and false, Bowen in his own way reconciled an impartial view of the nation's founders that recognized their flaws with an exceptionalist framework by suggesting that a comprehensive—and hence for him true—account of American history would bring together these two perspectives.

Early nineteenth-century historians thus revealed the complex relationship between partiality and impartiality in their interpretations of American history as they expressed a deep commitment to the ideal of impartial truth. If even the most seemingly partial of these historians were genuine in their professions of impartiality, conversely, the most impartial of these historians sought to use their history for partial purposes. Therefore, although modern scholars have portrayed Bancroft and Hildreth as polar opposites, they were less different than this portrayal suggests. If Bancroft was more impartial than he seemed, Hildreth was more partial than he claimed. All these historians could claim to be impartial, despite the differences between their views of American history, because they differed in their interpretations and definitions of impartiality. Whereas for Bancroft impartial truth meant recognizing the democratic nature of Puritanism, Oliver believed that this ideal required acknowledging the brutality and hypocrisy of the Puritans.

Not only did these historians differ in their interpretations of what constituted an impartial account of American history; they also differed subtly in their views on the nature of impartial truth itself. While they subscribed to a Rankean ideal of truth that required the historian to present the facts undistorted by his prejudices and opinions, they did not believe that this ideal precluded speculation about the direction and purpose of history, or about what Peter Novick calls "larger questions of end and meaning."[165] Consequently, they could at once emphasize the need for a balanced and unbiased account of the nation's history and embrace the exceptionalist view of American history as the unfolding of providential design. But even though they agreed that history was supposed to serve a philosophical purpose, they differed over both the nature of that purpose and the historian's role in furthering that purpose. Whereas for Parker, Hildreth's view of history as an unbiased record of fact could advance democracy in spite of itself, for Bowen this prospect was impossible because there was no such thing as an unbiased record of fact.

Such conflicts and tensions were in turn a function of political divisions among antebellum historians. If for Bancroft an impartial history would reveal and further the advance of democracy, Motley and Bowen expressed their anxieties about the rise of democracy through their concern with impartiality. New England historians were more in accord over the marginalization of slavery from their accounts of Puritan and Revolutionary history, but the result was that they still defined impartial truth—and the nation—in sectional terms. Hence, despite their nationalist purposes, these historians actually contributed to sectional tensions in their efforts to be impartial as southern historical writers sharply challenged the sectional bias to their understanding of impartiality. Paradoxically, then, the more antebellum historians sought to be impartial, the more this ideal contributed to sectional conflict, and the next chapter examines how this could be the case by looking at antebellum interpretations of the loyalists, in which historians went even further in their quest for impartiality.

CHAPTER FIVE

THE "LOSERS" OF THE REVOLUTION

Loyalists, Indians, and the Ideal of Impartiality

In the third edition of his memoir of the loyalist Samuel Curwen, published in 1845, George Atkinson Ward declared, "Unfortunately for the loyalists of South Carolina, all the written testimony of the [Revolutionary] period is from the pens of their opponents, by whom their actions have been misrepresented, their motives misconstrued, and themselves vilified and abused." As a result, "the unflinching integrity of the Tories of the Revolution has, hitherto, been thought worthy only of execration; their conduct has been constantly attributed to the most unworthy motives, and their memory has been allowed to remain under the most unmerited reproach." Ward believed that such condemnation was undeserved, for the loyalists had acted out of genuine principle and concern for their country.[1]

Modern scholars have portrayed loyalist historiography in much the same way that Ward did. Like Ward, they have emphasized the hostility that characterized American perceptions of the loyalists. The loyalists were, as George Athan Billias puts it, "the first un-Americans." For this reason, according to modern scholars, American historians have, until the twentieth century, either vilified the loyalists or ignored them altogether. By this account, historians in Ward's own time were especially guilty of this tendency. Expressing the chauvinistic nationalism of this period, antebellum historians sought to promote a sense of national greatness by glorifying the revolutionaries at the expense of the loyalists. Their biased perspective was, for modern scholars, emblematic of the simplistic and filiopietistic character of American historical thought in this period.[2] Yet in criticizing his contemporaries for such prejudice, Ward revealed that views of the loyalists in his time were more complex than modern scholars have acknowledged. Although Ward was not typical, neither was he completely anomalous in his sympathy for the loyalists. While the prevailing view of the loyalists was as unfavorable as Ward claimed, a small but significant number of historical writers—whom I will call loyalist revisionists—had also begun to question this negative image of the loyalists by the 1820s. Like

Ward, these historians sought to revise orthodox patriot interpretations of the Revolution by offering a more sympathetic and balanced portrayal of the loyalists.

In this reappraisal of the loyalists, antebellum historians went even further than revisionist interpreters of the Puritans did in their commitment to impartiality. And as they sought to put this ideal into practice, they revealed the different dimensions to their conception of historical truth. But even as it reflected the desire for impartiality, loyalist revisionism served social and political purposes. As they reassessed the loyalists, these historians were also grappling with the advent of "Jacksonian democracy," the rise of party politics, and escalating sectional tensions. Loyalist revisionists differed among themselves in the nature and purpose of their reassessment, for they disagreed in their definitions of American identity. Despite these differences, they were similar in reconciling their sympathy for the loyalists with a fervent sense of nationalism. These historians could acknowledge the loyalists as Americans, despite loyalist opposition to the Revolution, because they did not define the nation solely in terms of ideals.[3]

In questioning the centrality of ideals to American identity, these historians did not question the ideology of American exceptionalism. On the contrary, rather than signifying a rejection of the nation, loyalist revisionism ultimately reflected and furthered exceptionalist doctrines. These historians' commitment to impartiality was thus integrally related to their belief in the nation's special mission, as reassessments of Native American opposition to the Revolution revealed most clearly. Hence, as they sought to acknowledge the perspectives of Native Americans who had opposed the Revolution, antebellum historians at once went even further than loyalist revisionists did in questioning orthodox patriot accounts of the Revolution and reaffirmed even more forcefully their attachment to exceptionalist ideology.

"A more fit instrument for the purposes of a corrupt court": The Loyalists in Revolutionary Historiography

The Revolutionary historians did, for the most part, live up to their reputation for hostility to the loyalists, displaying little sympathy or understanding for their loyalist opponents. For these historians, writing at a time when national bonds were still tenuous, it was necessary to portray the Revolution as a unanimous uprising against tyranny; only by demonstrating the presence of consensus and uniformity in the past could they use history to promote unity in the present. To do so, however, they had to ignore or obscure the role of loyalist dissent in the Revolution. This interpretation of the Revolution in turn denied the loyalists' identity as Americans, for it made American identity contingent on allegiance to Revolutionary ideals.[4]

While the Revolutionary historians agreed in repudiating the loyalists, they did so in different ways. Some of them marginalized the loyalists simply by omission, limiting their discussion of the loyalists to occasional allusions, at most. Thus John Lendrum in his history of the Revolution, and John Daly Burk in his history of Virginia, made only passing references to the loyalists.[5] When the Revolutionary historians did acknowledge the loyalists, they did so merely to vilify this group as the embodiment of the very traits and principles that had alienated the American colonies from Britain, as the dramatist and historian Mercy Otis Warren did in her condemnation of Thomas Hutchinson. In singling out Thomas Hutchinson, the loyalist governor of Massachusetts, for her most scathing criticism, she followed Revolutionary precedents. Because of his prominence in upholding royal authority, Hutchinson had, during the Revolution, become a special target for Revolutionary hostility. The revolutionaries vented their hatred for the loyalists onto Hutchinson, turning him into a symbol of all the qualities they most abhorred in the loyalists.[6] An active propagandist for the Revolutionary cause, Warren had taken part in this campaign, deriding Hutchinson as an unscrupulous villain in her plays. She took this hostility for Hutchinson into her history of the Revolution, published in 1805. Here, Warren grudgingly and indirectly acknowledged Hutchinson's private virtues, but for her these virtues paled in comparison with his public transgressions. Warren singled out Hutchinson as an example of "the deformed features" of her "own species," whose overweening ambition and self-interest led him to conspire with the British against the liberties of his fellow Americans. Because of these traits, Warren concluded "that few ages have produced a more fit instrument for the purposes of a corrupt court. He was dark, intriguing, insinuating, haughty and ambitious, while the extreme of avarice marked each feature of his character."[7]

One extenuating circumstance tempered Warren's indictment of Hutchinson. In her view, at least Hutchinson was "uniform in his political conduct. He was educated in reverential ideas of monarchic government, and considered himself the servant of a king who had entrusted him with very high authority." Accordingly, "[a]s a true disciple of passive obedience, he might think himself bound to promote the designs of his master, and thus he might probably release his conscience from the obligation to aid his countrymen in their opposition to the encroachments of the crown." While acknowledging that Hutchinson's personal background made his conduct understandable, Warren drew a contrast to the behavior of her contemporaries. She implicitly criticized Americans of her own time when she declared, "In the eye of candor, he may therefore be much more excusable, than any who may deviate from their principles and professions of republicanism, who have not been biassed by the patronage of kings, nor influenced in favor of monarchy by their early prejudices of education or employment."[8]

Here Warren referred to the corruption and social conflict that seemed so prevalent in her own time. To Warren, Americans of the 1780s and 1790s had betrayed republican principles by succumbing to the corrupting influence of self-interest. Specifically, at the time Warren wrote her history, partisan divisions between Federalists and Republicans were just beginning to emerge. A staunch Republican, Warren identified her Federalist opponents in particular as culprits in the degeneration from Revolutionary principles. What was more, Warren believed, their betrayal was far more reprehensible than Hutchinson's, for their Revolutionary background and professions of republicanism deprived them of even Hutchinson's excuse. If, in one sense, this analysis softened Warren's condemnation of Hutchinson, it was also the ultimate repudiation, for in it she severed Hutchinson from his claims to identity as an American. Warren's phrase "his countrymen" made clear her recognition of Hutchinson's American birth. Yet by emphasizing how Hutchinson's monarchical principles and heritage divided him from his fellow colonists, she highlighted his ties to Britain and characterized him as an alien in a nation founded on republicanism. In this way, Warren defined national identity in ideological terms and made American nationality contingent on allegiance to republican principles.[9]

Of all the Revolutionary historians, David Ramsay assessed the loyalists most sympathetically. Yet even as he acknowledged their sufferings, he alienated them all the more decisively from the nation. Like Warren, an active supporter of the Revolution, Ramsay published his influential and highly regarded history of the Revolution in 1789.[10] In this history, not only did he acknowledge the existence of considerable loyalist sentiment during the Revolution, but he also accorded the loyalists a certain degree of understanding. Recognizing that the Revolution was a civil war, Ramsay expressed his horror of the bitter bloodshed that Whig and Tory inflicted on each other. Rather than portraying the Whigs as the innocent victims of Tory aggression, he recognized the ruthless behavior of both sides. As he put it in his history, "Humanity would shudder at a particular recital of the calamities which the whigs inflicted on the tories, and the tories on the whigs."[11] There were strict limits to Ramsay's compassion for the loyalists, however, and in the end he repudiated them as Americans. While he acknowledged the complexity of loyalist motivation, his explanation for their opposition to the Revolution was unflattering overall. Whereas "[t]he young,

the ardent, the ambitious, and the enterprising, were mostly whigs," "the phleg-
matic, the timid, the interested, and those who wanted decision were, in general, favourers of Great Britain, or at least only the lukewarm inactive friends of
independence."[12] Significantly, Ramsay confined most of his discussion of the
loyalists to appendixes. In doing so, Ramsay implied that the loyalists and their
experiences were not an integral part of the Revolution. And by marginalizing
the loyalists from the event that had established the nation, Ramsay divested
them of any claims to identity as Americans.[13]

"The calm judgment of an impartial posterity": Loyalist Revisionism and Impartial Truth

As Americans developed an increasingly assertive and confident sense of nationalism in the wake of the War of 1812, the tone and character of their historical writing became, if anything, even more ardently nationalistic and filiopietistic than that of their Revolutionary predecessors. This kind of chauvinistic
nationalism made it all the more imperative for some historians to dissociate
the loyalists from the nation. Yet if many historians continued to marginalize the loyalists, others challenged this tendency by rehabilitating the loyalists
as members of the nation. Their revision of Revolutionary historiography was
admittedly halting and incomplete; hostility toward the loyalists persisted, and
even the most sympathetic chroniclers expressed considerable ambivalence
about them. Overall, however, not only did historians of this period display
a greater interest in the loyalists than did their Revolutionary predecessors;
they also portrayed the loyalists far more sympathetically. In doing so, these
revisionists sought to live up to their desire for impartiality. As they explained
how a reassessment of the loyalists would further this goal, they revealed the
dualities in their understanding of truth. Even as they prescribed detachment
and neutrality for the historian, loyalist revisionists recognized the subjective
element to historical interpretation. And while they regarded the historian as a
disinterested chronicler of truth, they firmly upheld a belief in the moral function of history.[14]

George Bancroft revealed the persistence of hostility toward the loyalists
in his popular and influential history of the United States. Because it was so
influential, this work has come to exemplify the self-congratulatory patriotism
associated with the antebellum period. Like his Revolutionary predecessors,
Bancroft gave the loyalists short shrift in his interpretation of the Revolution.
While recognizing that loyalist sentiment had been considerable, he referred

only occasionally and briefly to the loyalists in his history. When he did mention the loyalists, he generally spoke disparagingly of them. Thus, for example, Bancroft agreed with Warren in condemning Hutchinson as a corrupt conspirator against liberty. He concluded his discussion of Hutchinson by declaring, "To corrupt pure and good and free political institutions of a happy country, and infuse into its veins the slow poison of tyranny, is the highest crime against humanity. And how terribly was he punished! For what is life without the esteem of one's fellow-men!"[15] Nor did Bancroft look much more favorably on the loyalists as a group, as he revealed when he argued that the war would have been much shorter if the king had relied only on English troops. The British derived much of their support from the loyalists, and the army was "largely recruited from American loyalists; from emigrants driven to America by want, and too recently arrived to be imbued with its principles; from Ireland and the Highlands of Scotland; and from Germany." In identifying the loyalists with immigrants and foreigners, he suggested that the loyalists were somehow less American than the revolutionaries were. To be more precise, as recent immigrants, they supported the British because they had not yet developed an attachment to American principles. By emphasizing how unfamiliarity with these principles alienated the loyalists, Bancroft, like Warren, defined national identity in ideological terms. Thus Bancroft implied that allegiance was a voluntary matter, based on a commitment to certain principles.[16]

As Bancroft elaborated on their motives, he divorced the loyalists even more explicitly from claims to American identity. Although he attributed loyalism partly to self-interest, he also acknowledged that some of the loyalists had acted out of more disinterested considerations of honor. In the end, however, Bancroft set up an opposition between loyalism and nationalism when he spoke of the loyalists' exile to Nova Scotia, where they exchanged "the delight of a love of country for a paralyzing, degrading sentiment of useless loyalty." In choosing loyalty to Britain, the loyalists had forfeited their claims to be considered American, or even to be considered patriotic. It did not occur to Bancroft to view their loyalty to Britain as a form of patriotism or to think that they might have believed they were promoting American interests by opposing independence.[17]

While Bancroft's interpretation of American history was influential, it was by no means uncontested. Even as Bancroft and his adherents continued to disown the loyalists, other historical writers offered a more sympathetic perspective that rehabilitated the loyalists as members of the nation. Bancroft's fellow Brahmins took the lead in this reassessment. Unlike Bancroft, predominantly Federalist and, later, Whig in their political allegiances, these Brahmin revisionists were predisposed to sympathize with the loyalists as fellow "losers" who had, like the Federalists, been relegated to the margins of American politics.[18] The most tangible signs of interest in the loyalists were the numerous publications of works by and about them that appeared beginning in the 1820s. Histories written by loyalists were in particular demand. The Massachusetts Historical Society led the way when it helped sponsor the publication of the third volume of Thomas Hutchinson's history of Massachusetts in 1828. The next year, its New York counterpart followed suit by publishing William Smith's history of New York. The southern writer B. R. Carroll published selections from George Chalmers's *Political Annals* and Alexander Hewat's history of Georgia and South Carolina in 1836, and Jared Sparks edited and published Chalmers's *Introduction to the History of the Revolt of the Colonies* in 1845.

Interest in the loyalists intensified during the 1840s as a series of biographical works about them came into print, including the journal and letters of Samuel Curwen, a similar memoir of Peter Van Schaack, and the military journal of the partisan officer John G. Simcoe. This trend culminated with the appearance of Lorenzo Sabine's collective biography of the loyalists in 1847. Although later scholars have dismissed these works as marginal and ephemeral, their contemporaries took them seriously as significant works of scholarship. They deemed several of these works important enough to merit reviews by all the major periodicals, and the generally positive character of these reviews demonstrated the prevalence of revisionist tendencies. Even histories on more general subjects discussed the loyalists at length, often drawing both factual information and interpretations directly from this body of scholarship.[19]

Prizing impartial truth as their ultimate objective, antebellum revisionists believed that achieving this goal required them to acknowledge and understand, not condemn, the loyalists. For these historians, impartiality meant a balanced assessment of the Revolution that took into account the perspectives of both its supporters and its opponents. By resisting nationalist prejudices against the loyalists, the historian would, in their view, demonstrate his ability to be dispassionate and to overcome bias—the defining characteristics of impartiality. In a favorable review of Lorenzo Sabine's biographical dictionary of the loyalists for the *Southern Literary Messenger*, Benjamin Blake Minor made this concern with impartiality explicit when he declared that "it may well be admitted that much may be said in defence, or extenuation of the tories or loyalists of our Revolution; and that sufficient time has elapsed for them now to be treated with justice and with impartiality." For this reason, he praised Sabine's balanced treatment of the loyalists, which "appears to us a specimen of original, independent and impartial historical writing,—such as is *rarely* to be met with." Although Sabine's own sympathies were clear, in Minor's view, those sympathies had not prevented him from recognizing opposing points of view. As a result, Minor believed that his analysis had been remarkably evenhanded: "Written by a decided Whig, it yet does justice to the Tories; by a northern man, it yet shows no invidious spirit towards the South."[20]

Minor recognized that impartiality was difficult to achieve. As he explained, although "[i]mpartiality in History is what all profess to admire, as they do candor and independence in individuals," these qualities were themselves contested. Minor elaborated, "[S]o universally applauded in the abstract, [they] are often unobserved, disputed, or censured, when particular applications of them are made that do not accord with our preconceived notions of what impartiality, candor, and independence require, and in what they consist."[21] By emphasizing the conflict between "preconceived notions" of impartiality and "particular applications" of this ideal, Minor implied that deviations from truth did not necessarily result from the willful abandonment of impartiality by one party. Rather, each individual interpreted and applied this ideal differently, according to his own personal circumstances and prejudices. Hence, for Minor, the unconscious influence of individual perspective, not purposeful deception, was the most important obstacle to impartiality.

This understanding of the obstacles to impartiality encouraged sympathy for the loyalists, as Jared Sparks demonstrated. Notorious for bowdlerizing Washington's letters to protect his subject's dignity, Sparks would seem to be the last historian to favor a more balanced and impartial view of the loyalists. Yet Sparks was a more sophisticated historian than his reputation suggests. Even while he revered the revolutionaries, he criticized the tendency to vilify the loyalists and firmly advocated the need to understand their point of view. For this reason, he was pleased by the success of George Atkinson Ward's edition of the loyalist Samuel Curwen's journal and letters. As Sparks explained to Ward in 1845, the success of his work "shows a disposition to inquire into the whole subject of our Revolutionary contest, and no cause, that is, no good cause will suffer by knowing the whole truth." For Sparks, only by including the loyalists' perspective would the historian comprehend the "whole truth" about the Revolution.[22]

Until American historians incorporated this perspective, they would have only a partial and distorted view of the Revolution, for, as Sparks explained, "In all wars particularly in civil wars, there are outrages on both sides, and the conquering party tells its story in its own way, concealing or excusing its own faults, and exaggerating those of its opponents. Witness the accounts which the Romans have given of the Carthaginians, and the manner in which our writers have described the Indian wars. If Hannibal or Sassacus had written histories, we should now see important portions of history under a different aspect."[23] For Sparks, because the revolutionaries had been the winners in their conflict with the loyalists, their interpretation of the Revolution had prevailed. And because they were naturally disposed to put their own side in the most favorable light, their view of the Revolution was necessarily biased and one sided. Retrieving the loyalists' side of the story would provide a valuable corrective to these distortions, for, as the losers in this conflict, the loyalists would have given a very different account of the same events. In making historical interpretation a function of success or defeat, Sparks recognized the subjective element to historical understanding; because the circumstances of the observer always shaped perceptions of an event, individuals would vary in their interpretations of the truth.

As Sparks's use of the term "good cause" indicated, his willingness to recognize the loyalists' perspective did not mean that he questioned the legitimacy of the Revolution. He could understand the loyalists' point of view, but he still judged it wrong. Nor did his recognition of the subjective element in history mean that he jettisoned a faith in the possibility of impartial truth. Sparks affirmed his belief in this ideal and explained how an acknowledgment of the loyalists' perspective would further truth as he himself contributed to this endeavor by publishing an edition of the loyalist George Chalmers's *Introduction to the History of the Revolt of the Colonies* in 1845. Although Sparks acknowledged in his preface that the "the subject is thus presented under one aspect only, the picture being exhibited as it was sketched by the partisans of the British government in America," he still believed that Chalmers's history was valuable. He argued that Chalmers's history would contribute to truth not despite but because of its bias, for only by understanding opposing points of view could the historian arrive at the truth. He reasoned, "[I]n all party conflicts involving the political condition and welfare of nations, the truth of history requires that each party should be permitted to state its own case, and then leave the merits of the controversy to be decided by the calm judgment of an impartial posterity."[24]

For Sparks, impartiality did not preclude moral judgment by the historian. On the contrary, when he spoke of the "calm judgment of an impartial posterity," he made such judgments a requisite of impartiality. When he declared that "each party" should be allowed "to state its own case," Sparks likened history to a trial, with the historian presiding as a judge. Just as a judge needed to hear testimony from both sides to reach a just verdict, the historian could make a fair and true judgment about historical actors only if he had both sides of the story. And so, while Sparks admitted that it was impossible for historical actors to be unbiased, he did believe it was possible for a future historian, more distant from the events he described, to view these events dispassionately, without favoring one side or the other. Sparks saw no conflict between this view of the historian as a disinterested chronicler of truth and his belief that the historian was supposed to make moral judgments because he believed that in making such judgments the historian was conveying larger moral truths to the reader. The more unbiased and dispassionate the historian, the more likely he would be to make correct moral judgments that expressed and conformed to those larger truths.[25]

Lorenzo Sabine, one of the most influential and prolific loyalist revisionists, made this view of the historian's role explicit in a review of Chalmers's history when he declared that the historian "should sift testimony as thoroughly and weigh it as accurately as a judge upon the bench, and should know no sect in religion, and party in politics." The historian, like the judge, could view the evidence impartially only if he transcended sectarian and partisan interests. For Sabine, the historian's purpose in divesting himself of such influences was not to eschew judgment but to correct false judgments. Firmly adhering to the belief that it was the historian's function to commend the worthy and condemn the profligate, Sabine believed that truth required the historian to revise these judgments in cases in which individuals had been undeservedly exalted or defamed. Because, invariably, the historian "will find that some good men have been given over to obloquy and shame, and that some bad men have been elevated to distinction, he should not hesitate to declare the truth, and the whole of it, in relation to both." In recognizing that the loyalists were not the villains of patriotic myth, while the revolutionaries were not all flawless heroes, as they had been traditionally portrayed, Sabine sought to correct what he believed were fallacious judgments in just this way.[26]

Finally, Sabine instructed the historian, as he went in pursuit of truth, "[t]o popular opinion, whether past or present, he should not listen; . . . since to correct that opinion, whenever wrong, is an important part of his duty." For Sabine, because truth was an objective entity independent of public opinion, the historian would achieve truth only by refusing to heed the dictates of that opinion. Sabine urged the historian to disregard public opinion at a time when the rise of democratic politics and the commercialization of literature made popular opinion an increasingly powerful force in American society. As this injunction demonstrated, Sabine was not just interested in achieving impartial truth for its own sake; in his very definition of truth, he expressed his distrust of democracy and sought to establish a new basis for elite authority at a time when that authority was increasingly threatened by the rise of democracy. If, with the advent of democratic politics, it was more and more difficult for the elites to demonstrate their superior capacity for virtue and disinterestedness in the political realm, Sabine suggested that they could now display those qualities in the historical realm by being impartial.[27]

"We pity, while we pronounce the decree": Jacksonian Democracy and the Political Function of Impartiality

Charles Francis Adams revealed even more clearly how anxieties about the rise of democratic politics contributed to a reassessment of the loyalists as he revised conventional interpretations of Thomas Hutchinson. Adams's disaffection from contemporary politics did not mean that he repudiated the Revolution or the nation it created. Using his sympathy for the loyalists to reinforce exceptionalist assumptions, he sought to reassess the loyalists, ironically, because of, not despite, a belief in national greatness. Adams could claim Hutchinson as an American without threatening this belief because he did not believe that ideals alone determined who was American. Yet, in the end, Adams would only go so far in his reassessment of the loyalists, not only because of his commitment to exceptionalist ideology but also because of his belief in the moral function of history.

As a descendant of the Adams family, Charles Francis came from an illustrious political lineage. He carried on this heritage by entering politics himself, and he played a leading role in forming the Conscience Whigs during the 1840s. Adams's desire to maintain his family heritage also contributed to his interest in history. He wrote extensively on this subject, editing collections of John and Abigail Adams's letters and publishing historical essays in the *North American Review*. He took a particular interest in the loyalists, and he wrote a series of articles about them for the *North American Review* during the 1830s and 1840s. Adams was especially fascinated by Thomas Hutchinson, alluding repeatedly to Hutchinson in his diary. Adams's choice of Hutchinson—the embodiment of loyalist infamy—as an object of sympathy was particularly revealing, for it demonstrated the extent to which he was willing to revise conventional interpretations of the loyalists. As he demonstrated in his characterization of Hutchinson, Adams, like other Brahmins, felt increasingly marginalized by the democratic tendencies of the 1820s and 1830s, which they believed threatened elite claims to authority by virtue of their superior education and social background. Compounding these anxieties, the defeat of his father, John Quincy Adams, at the hands of Jackson in the presidential election of 1828 gave Charles Francis personal reason to deplore the power of these democratic currents.[28]

Adams could identify with Hutchinson because of his own disaffection from

popular politics, for he believed that they had both suffered the effects of defying public opinion. Writing in 1833, Adams "did not much wonder" at Hutchinson's complaints about popular politics, remarking sympathetically, "To struggle
with popular feeling, hard as it is everywhere, becomes harder in a Community
in which there is so rigid a compliance expected with public opinion." Adams
could speak from his own experience, since "[m]y Grandfather and my father
have done it all their lives. The consequences have reflected upon me, who am
myself exactly such another in disposition although not in talent." Adams concluded gloomily, "I have the spirit to be independent without the capacity to
keep myself above water. I am therefore doubly unfortunate."[29] In his desire to
stand up to the influence of public opinion, Charles Francis sought to emulate
his illustrious forebears John Adams and John Quincy Adams and live up to
their standards of political independence and integrity. At the same time, Adams feared that he lacked their ability to surmount the power of popular opinion, a fear that would have been compounded as the increasingly democratic
character of American politics made it even more difficult for him to follow
their example. Here, then, Adams's personal insecurities about his ability to live
up to his venerated family heritage and his anxieties about Jacksonian democracy reinforced each other. Initially uncertain about whether to enter politics
as a member of the Massachusetts Antimasonic Party because of his anxiety
to establish both to himself and to others that he was really following the most
principled course, Adams would have felt such insecurities about his ability
to maintain his political independence and integrity especially acutely in 1833,
just one year after he made the decision to support the Antimasons and before
he had had a chance to prove himself politically.[30]

Adams's sympathetic portrayal of Hutchinson did not mean that he questioned
the legitimacy of the Revolution. Nor did it mean that he was any less nationalistic than Bancroft was. On the contrary, as the grandson of John Adams, one
of the leading figures in the Revolution, Charles Francis had a personal stake in
vindicating the Revolution. Paradoxically, his compassion for Hutchinson—one
of his grandfather John's leading opponents—furthered this imperative, serving
to underscore the greatness of the Revolutionary achievement and, by extension,
of the nation that the Revolution established. The inability of ordinary men such
as Hutchinson to comprehend the Revolution simply confirmed for Charles
Francis the extraordinary nature of what the revolutionaries—especially his
grandfather John Adams—had accomplished. As Adams wrote in an 1834 review of Hutchinson's history, Hutchinson's "capacity exerted itself well in the
ordinary paths of human action. . . . Nor would the worldly disposition which
often attends this union of qualities, have been in him an obstacle to fortune,
had he not fallen upon a moment when the standard of human conduct soared

far above the level of its ordinary elevation. He was tried by that standard, and he failed. We pity, while we pronounce the decree."[31] Adams's reassessment of Hutchinson thus combined anxieties about the democratic tendencies over-taking American society with a fervent affirmation of national greatness. Ultimately, by using Hutchinson to affirm the extraordinary nature of the Revolution, Adams reconciled his sympathy for the loyalists with one of the basic assumptions of American exceptionalism—the belief that the Revolution was an unsurpassed achievement that set America apart from other nations.[32]

Even as he differentiated between Hutchinson and the revolutionaries, Adams, unlike Bancroft or Warren, still acknowledged Hutchinson as American. Hence, Adams offered an incisive but temperate critique of Hutchinson's character in his 1834 review of Hutchinson's history. In that review, Adams gave Hutchinson credit for good intentions while pointing to his limitations. Whereas Warren had emphasized Hutchinson's greed and ambition, Adams acknowledged that Hutchinson had acted from motives more complex than avarice or malevolence. And unlike Warren, who had denied Hutchinson any real sense of allegiance to his country, Adams believed that Hutchinson was sincere when he claimed to be serving the liberties and interests of his fellow Americans. In making this claim, Adams implied that he still considered Hutchinson in some sense an American. Because he had acted out of patriotic motives, Hutchinson had not renounced his identity as an American by choosing loyalty to Britain. Unlike Bancroft, then, Adams did not think that loyalty to Britain and patriotic attachment to America were mutually exclusive. However, Hutchinson's "mental vision could penetrate no farther, than to see Massachusetts forever dependent on Great Britain. He considered it better to temporize, and even sacrifice some rights, than risk all in maintaining them." For this reason, Adams concluded, "We will not condemn him too harshly for opinions often held very successfully in more peaceful times, but we can award him no praise."[33]

This analysis revealed the limits to Adams's sympathy for Hutchinson, and he became even more hostile to Hutchinson in his essays of the 1840s. Accordingly, in an essay published in 1842, Adams offered a far harsher judgment of Hutchinson than before, and he denied Hutchinson even the merit of good, if misguided, intentions. Contrasting Hutchinson with those loyalists who had acted from principle and concern for the nation, Adams classed Hutchinson among those who "cared nothing for the question at issue except as it affected their bread and butter" and inflamed the British against the colonists out of self-interest.[34] Consequently, the next year, in a review of George Atkinson Ward's memoir of the loyalist Samuel Curwen, he disputed Ward's "exalted opinion" of Hutchinson, arguing that Hutchinson was "selfish, grasping, and profligate, as a politician."[35]

More secure now about his political identity and the moral righteousness of his political program, as he had, by the early 1840s, become increasingly active in the antislavery movement as a Whig representative to the Massachusetts state legislature, Adams was less inclined to identify with Hutchinson as a loser in the struggle against the force of popular opinion and had instead become increasingly mindful of what he perceived as Hutchinson's willingness to sacrifice principle for the sake of practical interest.[36]

Even as Adams condemned Hutchinson on this basis, he made explicit his belief in Hutchinson's American identity. Adams found Hutchinson's actions all the more reprehensible because of his American birth and upbringing. For Adams, this circumstance was the most compelling rebuttal to Ward's attempt at salvaging Hutchinson's reputation: "Above all, we know that he was born an American, had been cradled in the nursery of republican principles, had raised himself to general consideration among his fellows by the support of them, and that he sacrificed them for a mess of pottage." Adams felt no indignation against "imported governors" for their role in the Revolution, "but that a child of our own raising should have courted favor with the minister by advising restrictions upon the liberty of his brethren, is altogether too much for our philosophy."[37] Adams could claim Hutchinson as an American because he did not define American identity solely in terms of ideals. As his characterization of America as the "nursery of republican principles" suggested, he did believe that American identity was partly a matter of allegiance to certain ideals. But Adams could still characterize Hutchinson as an American despite Hutchinson's repudiation of those principles because Hutchinson had been born American. Here, Adams advanced a nonvoluntary conception of allegiance that made American nationality a matter of birth and blood, as well as ideology.[38]

Adams was even clearer about both his commitment to exceptionalist assumptions and the limits to his reassessment of the loyalists as he critiqued Ward's portrayal of the loyalists more generally. The great-grandnephew of the loyalist Samuel Curwen, Ward went much further than did Adams or other loyalist revisionists in asserting the loyalists' American identity when he suggested that the loyalists were as true, if not more so, to American principles as their Revolutionary opponents were. Pointing to how Revolutionary persecution of the loyalists violated the very ideals that defined the nation—freedom of thought and hostility to tyranny—Ward attributed the opposition of loyalist partisans to the failure of the revolutionaries to uphold the principles they claimed to defend. For Ward, then, the only real difference between the loyalists and the revolutionaries was that the revolutionaries had won. But if, as Ward suggested, there was nothing intrinsically superior about the Revolu-

tionary cause, then only success legitimized the Revolution, a conclusion he
made explicit when he declared that "[r]evolution is, after all, only successful
rebellion."[39]

Had Ward confined himself to the contention that genuine, but different,
principles motivated loyalist opposition to the Revolution, Adams would have
found little to dispute in his analysis. Adams astutely recognized, however, that
Ward was making a far more dangerous and radical claim when he asserted the
equal moral validity of the ideals maintained by the revolutionaries and their
opponents. For this reason, he took particular exception to Ward's contention
that the loyalists were "actuated by principles not less *lofty* than those who embraced the popular opinions of the day."[40] Because "[t]he question was one of
liberty or servitude," Adams recoiled from an argument that judged Revolutionary principles according to success or defeat. Instead, Adams asserted that
"misfortune could have done nothing to tarnish their intrinsic purity."[41]

Adams found Ward's interpretation so abhorrent because it went directly
counter to his view of the Revolution as a conflict between right and wrong
and, in doing so, threatened the basis for his belief in American exceptionalism.
For Adams, unlike for Ward, the revolutionaries were struggling to defend eternal moral verities, which would have been valid no matter what the outcome.
The problem with Ward's interpretation, in Adams's view, was that in divesting
the Revolution of its transcendental significance, Ward was repudiating the basis for America's standing as an exceptional nation. If only success legitimized
the Revolution, as Ward suggested, then Americans could no longer claim that
their nation was exceptional by virtue of its allegiance to a set of timeless moral
principles effected by the Revolution. Rather than a uniquely transformative
event that had changed the course of human history by enacting and bringing those principles to fruition, as Adams believed, the Revolution appeared in
Ward's account to be simply a rebellion that happened to be successful.[42]

Adams rejected Ward's interpretation not only because of his commitment
to exceptionalist assumptions but also because it threatened his moral conception of truth. By making historical judgment a function of success or failure,
Adams believed, Ward threatened standards of morality altogether. For Adams,
Ward's doctrine, "if adopted, would destroy the standard of right and wrong in
public conduct completely. If the only fault of the loyalists was, that they had to
contend with adverse circumstances, and the injustice of a popular excitement
against them . . . , then it must follow, that the chief merit of their persecutors,
as he styles them, consisted in their power and their ultimate success in doing
wrong."[43] In turn, without fixed standards of right and wrong, Adams argued,
the historian could not carry out his moral function, for this understanding of

the historian's role was based on the assumption of unchanging moral principles. Adams reasoned, "Even though we may not incline to doubt the purity
of the motives under which they [historical personages] act, yet, in awarding
praise or blame, we must try their conduct by some positive standard of excellence previously existing in our own minds."[44] As Adams recognized, in order
to make judgments about the virtuous and the profligate, the historian needed
to measure historical actors against immutable and absolute standards of virtue. Without such standards, the historian's judgments would lose their validity as impartial pronouncements of eternal truth, becoming merely subjective
expressions of opinion.

"Whatever the guilt of the Tories, the Whigs disgraced their cause and the American name": The Loyalists and American Destiny

Ultimately, then, even while it was inclusive in its acknowledgment of dissent,
Adams's reassessment of the loyalists signified a chauvinistic and restrictive conception of nationalism. Lorenzo Sabine revealed these two sides of loyalist revisionism even more clearly in his reappraisal of the loyalists. On the one hand,
Sabine could reclaim the loyalists for the nation because he respected political
opposition itself as American. This inclusive understanding of American nationality reflected Sabine's own involvement in party politics. On the other hand, Sabine appealed to a racially exclusive definition of American identity when he, like
Adams, acknowledged the loyalists as American because of their birth and blood.
And as he used this understanding of national identity to promote a sense of
American destiny, Sabine demonstrated how loyalist revisionism could actually
further a belief in American exceptionalism.

Although he belonged to the same literary circles as Adams and Bancroft,
Sabine occupied a somewhat marginal status in those circles. Based in Maine,
rather than Massachusetts, Sabine lived on the periphery of the Boston literary
elite. Nor did he share the patrician family background of Boston Brahmins like
Charles Francis Adams. Sabine's father died when Sabine was fifteen, leaving
his family in straitened financial circumstances. From a young age, then, Sabine
had to make his own living. In 1821, he settled in Maine, where he turned to
commerce for his livelihood and eventually succeeded in establishing his own
fishery business. Sabine's residence in Maine sparked his interest in the loyalists. He lived near the Canadian border and so came into direct contact with
descendants of the loyalists who had settled in Canada. As he informed Jared

Sparks in 1845, although he had been "revolution-mad" since he was a child, it was not until he moved to Maine that "the fact that there was more than *one* side to the Revolution crossed my mind. Every 'Tory' was as bad as bad could be, every 'son of Liberty' as good as possible." In turn, Sabine's own peripheral status within the Brahmin elite would have made him more inclined to sympathize with loyalists who had been marginalized from national consciousness.[45]

Paradoxically, he made his name as a historian and established his status as part of the New England intellectual elite through his reassessment of the loyalists. Sabine first challenged traditional portrayals of the loyalists in a series of articles for the *North American Review* during the 1840s. He expanded on these articles with his biographical dictionary of the loyalists, published in 1847. Sabine's best-known and most influential work, the biographical dictionary offered the most comprehensive study of the loyalists to that point, with biographical entries on a wide range of figures. Sabine used this exhaustive analysis to challenge the myth that the Revolution had represented a unanimous movement for independence. Rather than a marginal and alienated minority, the loyalists "were powerful in all the thirteen Colonies," and, "in some of them, they were nearly, if not quite, equal in number to its friends, the Whigs."[46] For Sabine, the result was a bloody civil war that inflicted untold suffering on both sides, and he dwelled in gory detail on the horrific violence that ensued. While recognizing the outrages committed by the loyalists, he emphasized that the Whigs bore a large share of the responsibility for wartime atrocities as well. After noting that it was difficult to determine "which party was guilty of the greatest barbarities," he could only conclude that "whatever the guilt of the Tories, the Whigs disgraced their cause and the American name."[47] For this reason, Sabine deplored the tendency to glorify the revolutionaries at the expense of the loyalists. Furthermore, he believed that this tendency slighted the many loyalists who had acted from patriotic and disinterested motives. As Sabine summed up, "all who called themselves Whigs were not *necessarily and on that account* disinterested and virtuous, and the proper objects of unlimited praise," while "*the Tories were not, to a man, selfish and vicious*, and deserving of unmeasured and indiscriminate reproach."[48]

Sabine could recognize the merits of loyalist opposition to the Revolution because the entire concept of organized political opposition had become more acceptable with the rise of party politics. Although parties quickly became a fixture in the politics of the new republic, hostility to the idea of a party system was deeply rooted in American political culture and persisted into the early nineteenth century. According to republican theory, parties and factions were, by definition, opposed to the public good. Concerned only with furthering their own interests, parties and factions would bring destructive strife in their wake.

By the 1830s, however, Americans had begun to accept the idea of a party system and its corollary—the belief in the possibility of a legitimate opposition.
Rather than automatically attributing malicious designs to party opponents,
they acknowledged the patriotic intentions of each side. They interpreted party
conflicts as disagreements over the best means of protecting national interests.
Indeed, they came to believe that healthy competition between parties was necessary to the preservation of liberty.[49]

Sabine participated directly in this system, serving as a Whig congressman
as well as holding various local posts in Maine and Massachusetts. Following
his successful election to Congress in 1852, he acknowledged the value of party
opposition in a letter to his Democratic opponent, Charles Hazewell. He expressed gratitude to Hazewell for his generous conduct during the election campaign, declaring, "The great bulk of our countrymen of all parties, are sincere
in their professions of attachment to our institutions, and desire only an honest
and faithful administration of our public affairs. We differ simply, after all our
abuse of each other, as to the surest and best means to develope [sic] our resources, and to advance our prosperity and happiness." While "you democrats
go too fast, and would progress too rapidly," "we Whigs, on the contrary, move
too slow, while some among us, would stand still forever." As a result, "[t]he
two parties correct each other, and thus keep every thing safe."[50] Sabine took
this respect for political differences into his analysis of the loyalists and the
revolutionaries, for he portrayed the conflict between them in similar terms.
Just as he believed that Whigs and Democrats differed only over how to further the nation's best interests, so too did Sabine, like other revisionists, recognize the patriotic motives of both loyalist and revolutionary. Like political parties, the loyalists disagreed with the revolutionaries over how to achieve this
goal. Sabine even used the term *party* to speak of the loyalists and revolutionaries, calling them the "*last* Colonial parties." In this way, he turned the conflict
between the revolutionaries and the loyalists into a conflict between two opposing political parties, rather than one between patriots and traitors.[51]

Yet there were limits to Sabine's acceptance of loyalist dissent. For all his recognition of the loyalists' patriotic and disinterested motives, Sabine did not put
them on the same moral plane as the revolutionaries. In the end, he fervently
maintained the intrinsic superiority of the Revolutionary cause, just as he believed that the Whig Party more truly represented the public good than the
Democrats did. In his view, current resistance in Canada against British colonial
rule offered the best vindication of the inherent moral legitimacy of the Revolution. Indignantly repudiating the suggestion that only success legitimized
the Revolution, Sabine saw in British concessions made to Canadian descendants of the loyalists "an approval of the principles on which the Revolutionary

contest hinged, and an entire abandonment of the charge, that the Whigs were but successful rebels and traitors."[52] Sabine could express understanding for the loyalists not despite but because of this confidence in American superiority. He believed that Americans could now afford to be magnanimous toward the loyalists precisely because they were secure enough in their victory to acknowledge the loyalists without any danger to the nation. Thus, he observed grandly, "While intending to be just, I have felt that I might also be generous. The *winners* in the Revolutionary strife are now twenty millions of people; and, strong, rich, and prosperous, can afford to speak of the *losers* in terms of moderation." Sabine thus turned his acknowledgment of the loyalists into a forceful assertion of national greatness by using it to underscore the magnitude and completeness of the Revolutionary triumph.[53]

If this self-confident nationalism was in one sense inclusive, by allowing for the possibility of dissent, it was in another sense highly restrictive. In his emphasis on birth and blood, Sabine narrowed the nation's boundaries to exclude those who lacked the birth and background shared by both the revolutionaries and their opponents. He revealed the exclusionary side of loyalist revisionism and the influence of Anglo-Saxon racialism on this conception of nationalism in a review of John G. Simcoe's *Military Journal.* Sabine's article appeared in 1844, just as Anglo-Saxon racialism was on the rise in America. This ideology held that America's innate racial superiority as a white Anglo-Saxon nation destined it for greatness. This doctrine possessed special appeal for Americans of the 1840s, for it justified the rampant expansionism of the period. Anglo-Saxon racialism in this way reflected and encouraged a growing sense of national assertiveness. At the same time, this ideology stemmed partly from fears and anxieties about the influx of Irish and German immigrants who made their way to America in the same period.[54]

Sabine appealed to this sense of Anglo-Saxon destiny and revealed his sympathy for the loyalists in his critique of Revolutionary reprisals against them. For Sabine, this policy had been misguided because it had created an unnatural separation between loyalists and revolutionaries sharing the same racial origins. Driven from the nation by patriot persecution, many loyalists found refuge in Canada, and, Sabine believed, Americans were now suffering the pernicious consequences of their earlier severity. Sabine lamented that this policy had created a rival nation composed largely of fellow "countrymen," whereas "had we pursued a wise course, people of our own stock would not have become our rivals in ship-building, in the carriage of our great staples, and in the prosecution of the fisheries." By "our own stock," Sabine meant Anglo-Saxon stock, giving his conception of Americanness a racially exclusive meaning.[55]

Precisely because of their shared racial origins, Sabine could express cautious optimism that "[t]he doctrines of the Whigs may yet be embraced, before the century closes, by their opponents of whom we have discoursed," for "[c]olonies become nations as surely as boys become men; and of all races, the Saxon learns to rule itself the soonest." Sabine's faith that the revolutionaries would be vindicated was thus based on a belief not just in the superiority of the principles they espoused but also in Anglo-Saxon racial superiority. And so he was even more explicit about the racial boundaries to national identity while defending the necessity for independence from Britain. In his view, "without a dissolution of the connection, the Saxon race in the New World could neither have developed their own character or the resources of the continent they occupied." Sabine here affirmed a faith in America's mission as an Anglo-Saxon nation and its capacity, as such, for expansion and progress in the future. In making this argument, he revealed his ambivalence about America's relationship to England—an ambivalence that was widely shared by Americans of his time. Comprising a mixture of Anglophilia and Anglophobia, Sabine's conception of Anglo-Saxon destiny at once exalted America's English origins and asserted the nation's superiority to England. It was now America's turn, he believed, to carry on the mission of strengthening and expanding the influence of the Anglo-Saxon race. And in his claims for America's special mission, Sabine embraced a basic tenet of American exceptionalism—the belief that the nation was ordained to fulfill a unique destiny.[56]

Yet Sabine's lofty predictions of American greatness came at a time of escalating sectional tensions between North and South. These tensions had become increasingly acute during the 1840s, partly because of the expansionist impulses that Sabine embraced so fervently. Northerners and southerners polarized over the status of new territories acquired in this period—specifically over whether they should be admitted as free or slave states. Hence, anxieties about the fragility of national unity went hand in hand with a sense of assertive nationalism.[57] Such anxieties gave Sabine's reassessment of the loyalists added significance, as he used his invocation of national destiny to bring Americans together in a shared sense of national greatness. In reaffirming confidence about the nation's prospects, then, Sabine could combat sectional threats to national unity, as he did in an essay for the *North American Review*, published the year after his biographical dictionary. As part of a larger analysis of how much the nation had progressed since the Revolution, Sabine pointed to the sectional tensions that divided the revolutionaries in order to dispel contemporary fears that the "increased sectional feeling" of the present was a sign of the "decline of public virtue," arguing that this "sectional feeling" was no worse in his time than it

was during the Revolutionary era. In doing so, Sabine sought not only to refute
current fears about degeneration and decline but also to allay contemporary
anxieties about the disintegrating effects of sectional conflict. If the nation had
not dissolved amid all the sectional conflicts that divided the Revolutionary
generation, it was unlikely that such conflicts would now lead to national dissolution, for, as Sabine put it, "flippant paragraphs, resolves of associations, and
oratorical flourishes do not always portend the separation of states and the division of a nation."[58] Even while dismissing the possibility of secession as an
imminent danger, Sabine—through his graphic account of the Revolution as a
bloody civil war—warned against the horrors that would ensue if such a dissolution did occur. In this way, his work served to promote national unity by offering hope of sectional conciliation through his acknowledgment of sectional
dissension among the revolutionaries and, at the same time, warning against
the horrors of civil discord through his account of the divisions between loyalist and revolutionary.

"Sumner properly owes his cudgelling to you": Sectional Conflict and American Nationality

Sabine's reappraisal of the loyalists backfired, however, as a vehicle for unity; his
work actually had the opposite effect, provoking one of the key events in the
sectional crisis—Preston Brooks's famous attack on Charles Sumner in 1856. In
a debate over Kansas statehood, Sabine's fellow New Englander Charles Sumner drew on Sabine's work to attack Senator Andrew Butler of South Carolina,
using Sabine's discussion of loyalist sentiment in South Carolina to cast aspersions on the patriotism of Butler's home state. In retaliation for this insult, Butler's nephew Preston Brooks caned Sumner, which in turn outraged Sumner's
fellow northerners, further escalating sectional tensions. The southern writer
William Gilmore Simms pointed to the role that Sabine's book played in this
dispute when he told Sabine, "Sumner properly owes his cudgelling to you!"[59]
Even before this incident took place, Simms himself had responded angrily to
Sabine's work, interpreting it as an attack on the South. For all his anger with
Sabine, Simms was also fascinated by the loyalists, and he agreed with Sabine
in his analysis of the extent, motives, and effects of loyalist opposition to the
Revolution. As a southerner, however, he felt marginalized and excluded by New
England historians like Sabine. Hence he employed that analysis for different
purposes—to challenge what he considered northern sectional dominance. Yet
in doing so, he did not repudiate the nation, and his analysis of the loyalists also

demonstrated his deep sense of nationalism. Simms saw no conflict between his sectional purposes and his sense of nationalism because he differed from Sabine in his definition of American nationality itself. As he used his analysis of the loyalists to reconcile his sectional concerns with his nationalist loyalties, Simms, like Sabine, ultimately expressed and furthered exceptionalist doctrines.

Best known as a novelist and as an exponent of southern sectional inter-ests, Simms also wrote extensively on history.[60] Writing a scathing indictment of Sabine's book for the *Southern Quarterly Review* in 1848, he began by criti-cizing Sabine for devoting too much attention to the loyalists. Because the loy-alists were, for the most part, mediocre figures, he believed that few of them had accomplished enough to warrant a biography, "and the misfortunes of still fewer deserve to be regarded, apart from the errors and offences in which they originated mostly." For this reason, Simms believed that such a study could serve little useful purpose, and he concluded of Sabine's book, "It is a good rule in liter-ature, which we commend to Mr. Sabine, that, when you have nothing to write about, you should write nothing."[61] Yet in both his fictional and nonfictional works, Simms had himself spent considerable time and energy on the subject of the loyalists. He wrote a whole series of reviews of books on the loyalists, made the partisan conflict between Whig and Tory a central theme in his historical novels, and offered a lengthy discussion of the loyalists in his general history of South Carolina. Thus, for all Simms's protestations to the contrary, Sabine's choice of subject matter was not in itself offensive to Simms, for Simms actually shared Sabine's interest in the loyalists.[62]

Nor did Simms differ all that greatly from Sabine in his interpretation of the loyalists. He criticized Sabine, however, for distorting the significance of loyal-ist sentiment in South Carolina, and he took such distortions as an attack on his own state. As Simms told Sabine in a letter of 1856 explaining his hostile reac-tion to the book, "You assailed my country, as I thought, & still think, unjustly, and in a bad temper: and I defended her, as well as I could."[63] Even while at-tacking Sabine, he revealed the similarities in their view of the loyalists. Simms agreed with Sabine in admitting that opposition to the Revolution in South Carolina had been considerable. Simms objected to the conclusion that he be-lieved Sabine drew from this revelation—that the prevalence of loyalist senti-ment reflected unfavorably on South Carolina's patriotism. Simms defended his state from such aspersions by reasoning that numbers were irrelevant to an as-sessment of the state's contribution to the Revolution. Instead, South Carolina's claims to distinction "are necessarily based upon the achievements of those who strove for her independence, and not upon the hostility of those who strove against it." Indeed, the additional difficulties created by their numerical disadvantage, and their ability to overcome them, simply redounded all the more to the glory of South Carolina's patriots. Simms concluded, "[A]nd in due proportion to their [loyalist] numbers, the claims of merit are necessarily increased, on the part of those by whom they were overcome."[64]

But, though by no means entirely devoid of sectional bias, Sabine's analysis of the loyalists was more even handed than Simms acknowledged. While declaring that "the adherents of the crown were more numerous at the South, and in Pennsylvania and New York, than in New England," Sabine was not trying to single out the South for obloquy, as Simms believed. Sabine made this statement as part of his larger argument that loyalist sentiment was considerable throughout all the colonies, including New England. Furthermore, Sabine argued that southerners' reluctance to support the Revolution was understandable, given that British colonial regulations did not directly threaten their interests. Indeed, he concluded that this circumstance added to the credit of those southerners who did support the Revolution, for "[i]f, therefore, the war of the Revolution had its origin in a long course of aggression upon the rights of the North, its successful issue was due in some measure to the more meritorious, because more disinterested, exertions of the South"—a conclusion not all that different from Simms's own assessment.[65]

In his reaction to Sabine, then, Simms was not just responding to what Sabine was saying about the loyalists. In his attack on Sabine, Simms was also expressing a widespread southern concern about the threat of northern cultural hegemony, as both cultural and political developments put the South increasingly on the defensive. With the advantage of a more developed infrastructure, northern literary productions had proliferated at the expense of southern publications. Northern cultural dominance made itself felt above all in the writing of history, as George Bancroft and his New England colleagues gave a distinctly sectional cast to their interpretation of American history. They used their histories to portray America as New England on a larger scale, thus nationalizing their sectional values, as Sabine did in his free labor interpretation of the Revolution. By turning the Revolution into a struggle over free labor—the very ideal that northerners used to differentiate themselves from the South—Sabine would have given Simms cause to believe that he was trying to usurp all the glory of the Revolution for New England.[66]

Consequently, southerners were especially sensitive to any aspersions on their history, interpreting such attacks as part of a larger tendency to magnify New England at their expense. Simms himself identified what he believed was Sabine's attempt to usurp all the glory of the Revolution for New England with this tendency when he asserted that Sabine's parochial perspective "is the common misfortune with New England writers and New England politicians." He remarked scathingly on the pleasure that New England took in its propensity "to regard her children as the saints, to whom the possession of the earth has been finally decreed." For this reason, Simms concluded, it was not surprising "that the inheritors of so goodly a faith and fortune, should naturally assume that they are the proprietors of all the good deeds that are done within its bounds. They have all the talents, all the virtues, and perform all the achievements. Even Mr. Webster tells us, that Bunker Hill was the Revolution." As Simms's reference to New England politicians revealed, this kind of assault represented, for him, an extension of northern attempts to establish political hegemony over the South. Therefore, in challenging northern claims to primacy in the historical domain, Simms sought to resist northern efforts at domination in the present.[67]

Yet in defending the South against such attacks, Simms was not rejecting the nation in favor of his own region. In his eyes, New England writers were the ones who were guilty of a narrowly sectional perspective. He believed that they were merely using nationalism to disguise their sectional agenda. Simply in making their sectional values representative of the nation as a whole, northern writers revealed their own parochialism and bias. Because of this belief, he could tell Sabine in 1856, "I think you [are] still altogether wrong in certain matters of Revolutionary history, and can only [ascribe] it to the bias of that narrowing N.E. education, which in fifty years, at least, has been training all its people in a common disparagement of all other sections."[68] And by criticizing New England for such provincialism, Simms demonstrated, by implicit contrast, his own nationalist perspective. As he defined national identity in opposition to New England writers like Sabine, he could at once defend his own state and establish his sense of nationalism.[69]

Simms reconciled these two objectives through his recognition of the loyalists, for he, like Sabine, used this recognition to magnify the achievements of the revolutionaries. By emphasizing how much opposition South Carolina's revolutionaries had faced, he made their support for the Revolution seem all the more remarkable. If Simms's defense of South Carolina's contribution to the Revolution revealed his deep sense of sectional pride, it also highlighted his patriotic attachment to the Revolution. His concern with affirming his state's achievements for the Revolution demonstrated his own commitment to the Revolution and, by extension, to the nation that the Revolution had created. The task of establishing the patriotism of South Carolina's revolutionaries took on added urgency in this period, as southern assertions of the primacy of states' rights over federal authority exposed southerners to charges of disloyalty and treason. In asserting the patriotism of his Revolutionary predecessors, Simms implicitly refuted these slurs on the patriotism of present-day South Carolinians. Further, by affirming South Carolina's contribution to the Revolution, he sought to refute what he believed was Sabine's slur against slavery, for he contended that Sabine's purpose in pointing to the limits to South Carolina's support for the Revolution was to show how slavery, "as a source of our assumed military weakness," had prevented the state from fighting as vigorously for the Revolution as the New England states. On the contrary, Simms argued, far from being a source of weakness, slavery was actually "a source of superior strength," providing "an abundant agricultural supply" while freeing white men from agricultural labor so that they could fight for the Revolutionary cause.[70] Here, then, Simms sought to legitimize slavery by making it integral to the success of the Revolution and therefore to the creation of the nation itself. Thus, by using the Revolution to vindicate and exalt his own state—and its commitment to slavery—Simms employed nationalism for sectional purposes, while his efforts at sectional vindication revealed his nationalist perspective.[71]

Simms saw no conflict between these imperatives because he defined national identity in terms of his sectional interests. For this reason, he was less willing than Sabine and Adams to claim the loyalists as Americans. Simms suggested that the loyalists could not really be considered part of the nation when he argued that it would be misleading to draw any conclusions about South Carolina's character from the prevalence of loyalist sentiment among its inhabitants. The loyalists did not represent South Carolina, in Simms's view, because national character was not necessarily based on the views of the majority. As Simms explained, "[T]he character of a country does not depend upon the opinions of the mass." As this pronouncement revealed, Simms shared the elitist assumptions of his New England counterparts, and he, like Adams, discountenanced the authority of popular opinion. But unlike Adams, who portrayed the loyalists as dissidents defying the majority, Simms characterized the revolutionaries in this way because, according to him, the loyalists had represented the majority in South Carolina. And whereas Adams sought to maintain the preeminence of the New England elite, Simms's repudiation of popular authority reflected another concern—his desire to justify southern resistance to a northern majority. By defining national character in this way, then, Simms implied that although the South might represent a minority within the Union, it could still claim to stand for the nation. Those individuals who supported the principles identified with the South might be outnumbered, but that did not make them any less true to the nation.[72]

As he elaborated on why he could not consider the loyalists true Americans, Simms revealed how he differed from Sabine in his definition of national identity. His explanation for loyalist opposition to the Revolution was actually quite similar to Sabine's, as he demonstrated in a review of Samuel Curwen's journal and letters, published for the *Southern Literary Messenger* in 1846. Like Sabine, Simms offered a comparatively sympathetic portrayal of loyalist motives. He believed that these motives, while not altogether admirable, were at least understandable. Simms agreed with Sabine that, for the most part, the Tories were motivated by a sincere, if misguided, concern for their country. Simms agreed "that there were many among them, who really sympathized with their country, though they denied the propriety of the movement, we are sure; and that many were only timid, and not treacherous." He went further to argue that the loyalists and revolutionaries shared the same principles. For Simms, the loyalists differed with the revolutionaries not over principle, or in their attachment to their country, but simply over whether independence was practicable. He argued, "[I]t does not appear that the arguments of the loyalists amounted to any thing more than objections on the score of safety and expediency. It was not the right divine of kings by which they were restrained, but whether they could stand in safety before the wrath of kings."[73]

Yet because Simms considered national allegiance more than a matter of shared ideals and emotions, he could not view the loyalists as true patriots and citizens. Although he was willing to grant that many of the loyalists "were pure of motive, were not wanting in love of country, were free from the narrow selfishness that cares only for its safety and its substance," in his view, "there still lacks something without which the essentials of character and patriotism are incomplete." He elaborated: "The good citizen is required to keep pace with the progress of the country—to prepare himself for her exigencies,—to demand that she have her true position in due degree with her endowments of mind and wealth,—to feel keenly the hurts which she suffers; and in the remedy of these hurts, to surrender his own notions of expediency in compliance with those, which are urged by the prevailing voice, and which are addressed to the repair of her injuries." And when any force threatened to deprive the nation of its due, it was necessary that "that the good citizen set down his foot firmly, like a man, and resent and resist the danger at the last peril to himself." Simms here made citizenship and patriotism a matter of active allegiance. Unlike Adams or Sabine, he did not believe it was enough that the loyalists shared the same birth and background as the revolutionaries; they also had to be willing to act against any threats to national development. In allowing considerations of expediency to deter them, then, the loyalists forfeited their claims to be considered patriotic citizens.[74]

By defining nationality in this way, Simms encouraged southern opposition to northern domination, for he was here offering a commentary on the relationship between North and South. For Simms, northern efforts to dominate and claim superiority over the South represented an affront to southern greatness, just as the British had stood in the way of American potential when they sought to squelch the rising power and strength of colonies. And to be true citizens, southerners had to act against northern encroachments on their rightful position, just as the revolutionaries had against the British. Thus, like northerners who expressed both hope and fear about the direction the nation was taking, Simms betrayed a mixture of anxiety about southern marginality and confidence about the region's prospects for greatness. And when he suggested that by resisting infringements on its "true position" the South would fulfill its destiny as a great nation, Simms extended the exceptionalist belief in American destiny to his own region; it was now the South's turn, he implied, to follow the example of the revolutionaries and carry on the mission that they had begun.[75]

In Simms's view, there was yet another ingredient in American nationality— bloodshed and civil war—as he revealed in his discussion of the partisan conflict that took place during the Revolution. For Simms, the division between Whig and Tory turned the Revolution into a bloody and bitter civil war, and like Sabine, he was fascinated by this civil war. The war between loyalist and revolutionary provided the backdrop for many of his historical novels about the Revolution, serving as an important plot device and source of dramatic tension. Simms dwelled on this subject in nonfictional works like his history of South Carolina as well. The horrors of "that dismal civil war, which desolated the fair fields of Carolina, and deluged her dwellings with the tears and blood of her children," wrote Simms in the 1842 edition of his history, were beyond the powers of human description. He then went on to detail its terrible consequences: "The ties of nature, of society, of neighborhood, were torn apart and trampled. Friendships and fellowships were sundered with the sword. Father and son stood with confronting weapons in opposite ranks, and brothers grappled in the gladiatorial embrace of the savage, goaded to constant strife by the shouts and rewards of the British conqueror."[76]

And like Sabine, Simms expressed compassion for the sufferings that this conflict had inflicted on the loyalists. As in Sabine's case, Simms's vivid recital of the loyalists' downfall and their consequent sufferings contained a somber warning about the disastrous consequences of division. Whereas Sabine's warning was national in scope and purpose, serving as an antidote for sectional divisions, Simms's appeal for unity was a specifically regional one—directed to his fellow South Carolinians rather than to the nation at large. Thus his history described the Tories on the eve of the British retreat: "[P]iteous, indeed, was the misery of the wretched loyalists whom this abandonment virtually surrendered to the rage of the long persecuted patriots. A fearful day of retribution was at hand, which they did not venture to await." The condition of the loyalists became even more pathetic once their retreat began, "and with a last look upon their homes, a mournful cavalcade of men, women and children, prepared to abandon the fields of equal beauty and plenty, which their treachery to their country had richly forfeited, but for which they were still willing to perish rather than depart. . . . How bitterly in their ears, at such a moment, must have sounded the notes of that drum and trumpet which had beguiled them from the banners of their country to those of its invader." Simms's concluding statement made clear that their fate held a lesson for his contemporaries, and he expressed the hope that "[s]urely, when the barbarian drum again sounds to war in Carolina, her children will find themselves all, with one heart, united under the same banner."[77] Here, Simms revealed that he was prepared for the possibility of disunion and another civil war. More willing than Sabine to entertain this possibility, he suggested that sectional differences between North and South might prove intractable. If this should occur, Simms warned, his fellow South Carolinians had to stand united against northern aggression or face the same tragic fate that the loyalists of the Revolution had suffered. Such a warning seemed all the more necessary as escalating sectional tensions in the 1840s made Simms and many of his fellow southerners feel increasingly marginalized from the rest of the nation.[78]

Yet even at his most forceful in defense of southern interests, Simms still sought to reconcile his sectional loyalties with his sense of nationalism. As he revealed when he described the final outcome of this war for the loyalists, if he wished to unify South Carolinians in the event of a civil war, he also desired to show that civil war did not preclude national unity. In his view, both the loyalists and the revolutionaries shared responsibility for the tragedy of this bloody civil war, for "[i]f the patriots were too warm, they [the Tories] were too cold," and "[u]nhappily, the indiscretion of individuals of both parties, increased the differences between them, and the gulf through which they had to wade, to sympathy and union in the end, was one that dyed their garments in blood, the stains of which to this day are scarcely obliterated." While Simms deplored such bloodshed, he also made clear that the end result was "sympathy and union." In this way, he suggested that the loyalists had not irrevocably alienated themselves from the nation, for the two sides had ultimately reunited.[79]

In reclaiming the loyalists as Americans, Simms was commenting not just on the relationship of South Carolinians to one another but also on the relationship between the South and the rest of the nation. Even while warning against the horrors of civil war, he suggested that such horrors had not prevented Amer-

icans from achieving national unity. Indeed, his language here suggested that
civil conflict had in some sense contributed to the establishment of the nation.
By speaking of how "sympathy and union" had emerged from bloodshed, he
implied that national unity had come about not just despite such divisions but
because of them. Even though they had fought against each other, this internal
conflict had provided Americans with a common experience that could unify
them, for both sides had shared in the horror of civil bloodshed. In this way,
he made conflict an integral part of what it meant to be American. By defining
American identity in this way, Simms could reconcile his support for secession
with his sense of nationalism. If it should come to secession and civil war, he
suggested, such a drastic measure was actually consistent with and true to the
nation's origins. The nation, after all, was itself founded on civil war and bloodshed.[80] And by emphasizing how unity had come out of civil war, he even held
out the hope that civil war between North and South could ultimately result in
the reunion of the two sections.

"The Indians have not been the sculptors": Reassessing Indian History

Historical writers in this period took their commitment to impartiality to its furthest extreme in their reassessment of an even more maligned group—Native
Americans who had opposed the Revolution. Just as loyalist revisionists sought
to rehabilitate the loyalists from their reputation as villainous traitors, a small
but significant number of historical writers during the 1830s and 1840s began to
challenge the conventional view of Indians as brutal savages by offering a more
sympathetic and balanced analysis of their history. As William Leete Stone—a
leading figure in this movement—explained why such a revision was necessary,
he went even further than Sparks and other loyalist revisionists in acknowledging that perceptions of historical truth were contingent on success or failure.
Yet Stone's recognition of the subjective nature of historical interpretation did
not signify a repudiation of the ideal of impartial truth. On the contrary, in
his assumption that such a recognition would ultimately further truth, Stone
demonstrated how a greater awareness of the contingent character of historical
understanding could actually strengthen a faith in the possibility of objective
knowledge about the past. And, for all the apparent relativism of his desire to
understand the perspectives of his subjects on their own terms, Stone firmly
maintained a belief in the historian's moral function and in America's destiny
to advance the cause of Anglo-American civilization and progress. In this way,
whereas for Charles Francis Adams the very idea that historical judgment could

be a function of success or failure threatened the belief in transcendent moral truths that constituted the basis for both the historian's moral office and exceptionalist ideology, Stone revealed that these assumptions were not necessarily opposed to one another.

From the earliest settlements, the American colonists had embraced a dual image of Native Americans. One side of this image demonized Native Americans as barbaric and cruel savages who stood in the way of civilization and deserved extermination. Already reviled as savages, those Native Americans who had opposed the Revolution were the subjects of particular hostility, as they compounded the enmity of Revolutionary Americans by allying with the British. At the same time, however, a conflicting view of the American Indian as a noble savage developed alongside this hostile image. The myth of the noble savage portrayed the Indian's lack of civilization as a positive attribute, rather than a failing. This myth idealized the Indian as an innocent and untamed child of the wilderness. Uncorrupted by the materialism and vices of society, the Indian represented man in his natural state of moral purity and goodness.[81]

By the early nineteenth century, American ambivalence toward Native Americans had deepened even further. Even as novelists like James Fenimore Cooper revealed a growing fascination with them, these novelists all the more forcefully defended the destruction of Native Americans as necessary and inevitable. Cooper in turn drew on the work of the missionary John Heckewelder, whose "Account of the History, Manners, and Customs of the Indian Nations Who Once Inhabited Pennsylvania and the Neighboring States" (1819) helped lay the basis for the emergence of the field of ethnography in the United States in the 1830s and 1840s. Although Heckewelder would not have described himself as an ethnographer, for the word was not even used in English until the 1830s, his effort to study Native American culture through direct observation and experience anticipated ethnography in both its subject matter and its methods, particularly his emphasis on the importance of language and the need for what would later be termed fieldwork. The emergence of ethnography as a field devoted to the systematic description of the social customs and institutions of particular cultures both reflected and furthered the growing interest in Native Americans as nineteenth-century American ethnographers—led by Lewis Henry Morgan with the publication of his *League of the Ho-dé-no-sau-nee, or Iroquois* in 1851—sought to place the study of Native American culture on a more scientific and empirical basis. Yet even as some of these ethnographers expressed a certain degree of sympathy for and understanding of Native Americans, they ultimately helped legitimize the marginalization and dispossession of Native Americans by writing them out of the realm of history and into that of science and nature.[82]

The exclusion of Native Americans from American historical consciousness would not come to fruition until the end of the century, however. And so, even while this process of marginalization had roots in the 1830s and 1840s, historical writers in this period showed more of an interest in Native American history and portrayed their Native American subjects more sympathetically than their Revolutionary predecessors had. Indian revisionists (as I will call these historians for the sake of convenience) fixed upon the Mohawk chief Joseph Brant (Thayendanegea)—who, until this period, had been the embodiment of Indian infamy and savagery—as the centerpiece for their reassessment of Native Americans in the Revolution. William Leete Stone took the lead in revising conventional interpretations of Brant when he published a biography of the Mohawk leader in 1838. A prolific author and journalist, Stone edited the *New York Commercial Advertiser* and wrote on a wide range of literary and political subjects. Born and bred in New York, he took a deep interest in the history of his own state. Also fascinated by Native American history, Stone published many works on this topic, including a biography of Red Jacket, a history of the border wars of the Revolution, and a study of Uncas and Miantonomoh. Stone's biography of Brant combined these two interests. Brant was one of the Revolution's most prominent Native American opponents, leading and coordinating Iroquois attacks on American settlements along the frontier of New York and Pennsylvania. In particular, he gained notoriety for leading the raids on American settlements at Wyoming and Cherry valleys. Horrified at the losses they suffered in these two attacks, Americans branded the raids as massacres. As a result of the devastation inflicted by such raids, conventional interpretations of Brant vilified him as the epitome of Indian savagery and cruelty.[83]

Responding specifically to Thomas Campbell's portrayal of Brant in his poem "Gertrude of Wyoming," Stone challenged this one-sided depiction. First of all, he denied that Brant had even been present at the Wyoming Valley expedition. On a more fundamental level, Stone revised orthodox accounts by portraying Brant as a humane and civilized statesman who had opposed the Revolution out of patriotic necessity. As Stone summed up Brant's character, "Brant was no less humane than he is on all hands admitted to have been brave. He was an Indian, and led Indians to the fight, upon their own principles and usages of war."[84] Stone's reassessment generated sharp controversy. Hostility to Native Americans persisted in this period, as demonstrated by Stone's critics, who strenuously objected to Stone's effort to rehabilitate Brant and his followers. Yet the many favorable reviews of Stone's biography also indicated considerable support for his interpretation.[85] In one such review, James Waddel Alexander summed up the purpose and character of Stone's reassessment as he praised Stone for the "impartial, independent judgment" that he had demonstrated in his work. As a result, Alexander believed, Stone "has vindicated the Indian race from undeserved obloquy, as it regards their mode of warfare: and he has not shielded from merited reproach, men who, under the name of civilization and Christianity, have been guilty of deeds of cold blooded cruelty, at which even the savages stood aghast." For Alexander, then, by redeeming the Indians from their reputation as cruel savages and condemning white brutality against them, Stone had succeeded in providing an impartial and unbiased view of this subject.[86]

Stone was careful to place his analysis of Brant within a broader historical context, and he devoted much of the biography to a more general account of the border wars in which Brant had played such an important role. Like loyalist revisionists, Stone characterized the Revolution as a bloody and divisive civil war. Stone implicated loyalist, revolutionary, and Indian alike in the countless atrocities that occurred during these conflicts. Rather than romanticizing Native Americans as innocent victims, then, Stone admitted their capacity for brutality and cruelty. He argued, however, that such atrocities were no worse than those committed by their supposedly more civilized opponents. Stone conceded, "Cruel they were, in the prosecution of their contests; but it would require the aggregate of a large number of predatory incursions and isolated burnings, to balance the awful scene of conflagration and blood, which at once extinguished the power of Sassacus, and the brave and indomitable Narragansets over whom he reigned."[87]

Furthermore, Stone explained, "Nor does it seem to have occurred to the 'pale-faced' writers, that the identical cruelties, the records and descriptions of which enter so largely into the composition of the earlier volumes of American history, were *not* barbarities in the estimation of those who practised them. The scalp-lock was an emblem of chivalry." In Stone's view, practices like scalping, which appeared barbaric by the colonists' standards, were, by Indian standards, actually badges of civilization. Stone made the same argument in defense of Brant's wartime conduct, urging the need to understand Brant's identity and perspective as an Indian. Brant's ruthless tactics, he explained, followed Indian customs of war. And from the Indians' point of view, these seemingly savage methods were honorable and necessary for survival. Stone here suggested the importance of understanding Indian culture on its own terms. Instead of judging the Indians according to absolute standards of civilization and barbarism, then, Stone suggested that such standards were themselves relative and varied from culture to culture.[88]

Because of this belief, Stone believed that a truly impartial account of the Revolution had to incorporate the Indians' point of view; only in this way could the historian judge them by their own standards. According to Stone, the reason why the Indians had been vilified as cruel savages was because "the Indians have not been the sculptors—the Indians have had no writer to relate their own side of the story." Stone here referred to Aesop's fable of the lion and the sculptor. In this fable, as Stone recounted it, a forester points to a statue of a man standing over a vanquished lion as proof of human superiority over lions. The lion responds by saying that if lions had been the sculptors, the positions of the lion and the human in the statue would have been reversed. For Stone, the moral of this fable was that the belief in the superiority of white Americans had grown simply out of this group's control over the writing of the past. As the victors in the struggle against the Indians, whites had written all the histories of the subject to this point. Written from their perspective, these histories naturally favored whites over the Indians. Thus, Stone implied, conventional portrayals of the Indians as uncivilized savages had no real basis in fact, and a very different picture would have emerged if Indians themselves had recorded their history.[89]

In making this argument, not only did Stone question the truthfulness of historical portrayals of Native Americans; he also raised questions about whether objective historical truth was possible at all. His reasoning suggested that written history merely represented the point of view of the winners, rather than any kind of objective reality. Even more dangerous for the belief in objective truth, the fable of the lion and the sculptor suggested that neither side could claim to represent truth, for both the victors and the vanquished would interpret events to suit their own circumstances and experiences. But if interpretations of the truth always varied according to the individual's perspective, then how could the historian free himself from that perspective and discern the objective reality of the past? Equally important, in making historical interpretation a function of success or failure, and in failing to privilege either perspective as more valid than the other, Stone seemed to embrace the very doctrine that Adams had condemned as so threatening to the historian's moral function in his assessment of Ward.[90]

Rather than abandoning a faith in the possibility of historical truth, however, Stone firmly maintained a belief that the historian could access the objective reality of the past. Hence, after recognizing the difficulties inherent in his subject, Stone could still claim for himself, "[B]ut tangled as was the web, the author has endeavoured to unravel the materials, and weave them into a narrative of consistency and of truth."[91] He explained how he had been able to achieve this goal as he elaborated on why previous historical accounts had been so hostile to the Indians. Stone reasoned that both English and American historians had been unable to do justice to the Indians because of their emotional engagement in the events they described. Writing "too near the time when the events they were describing occurred, for a dispassionate investigation of truth," Stone explained, "[t]heir passions had not yet become cooled, and they wrote under feelings and prejudices which could not but influence minds governed even by the best intentions."[92] Later historians, more distant from the events they described, had proved no more reliable, for they had simply perpetuated and copied the distortions of their predecessors. But, as his reference to the "dispassionate investigation of truth" suggested, Stone did believe that historians should and could eventually overcome these prejudices and provide a more balanced—and hence, more truthful—view of the Indians.

In suggesting that it was possible for the historian to transcend his own biases, Stone revealed a tension in his understanding of historical truth, for this claim went counter to the moral of the fable of the sculptor and the lion, which implied that interpretations of historical events always depended on the individual's perspective and circumstances. No matter how distant they were from the events they described, historians on the winning side would necessarily interpret these events differently than would those on the losing side. In his own approach to Brant, Stone revealed his awareness of this problem, for his biography of Brant included lengthy extracts from the letters and speeches of his historical subjects—the very sources that, by Stone's reasoning, were most prone to distortion and bias. For Stone, this approach had the advantage of "allowing the actors in the scenes described to tell their own stories." In this way, Stone provided his own solution to the problem of the sculptor and the lion. If truth varied according to the individual's perspective, and if historians themselves were bound by their own perspective, then presenting the accounts of contestants from all sides, unmediated by the historian, was necessary for a truly impartial understanding of the past. According to Stone, then, the obstacles to impartiality and the solution to these problems were one and the same, for, paradoxically, he suggested, the partiality of the historian's subjects could advance the cause of impartial truth.[93]

In this way, the development of history into an autonomous discipline defined by the critical study of written documents did not necessarily mean the exclusion of Native Americans from American historical understanding, as Steven Conn suggests was the case in the nineteenth century. If, as Conn has argued, American historians over the course of the nineteenth century sought to establish the authority of history as a formal discipline by relegating Native American history, based as so much of it was on oral tradition, to the realm of myth and defining themselves in opposition to that realm, Stone, in contrast, believed that the historian could liberate historical truth from myth only by including Native American perspectives. And rather than disqualifying Native Americans from inclusion in the historical record, the primacy given to primary documents as a basis for truth would, for Stone, actually further that inclusion (at least in Brant's case).[94]

In his desire to allow historical actors to tell their own stories, Stone also revealed his firm commitment to the historian's moral function. Although he appeared to abdicate the historian's role as a moral judge by allowing his subjects to speak for themselves, Stone believed that such an approach would actually further the historian's moral purpose, for the historian could make proper moral judgments only if he knew the circumstances that had influenced his subjects. For this reason, he approvingly quoted an English writer from the *London Quarterly Review* on the value of documentary extracts. Stone wrote, "Speaking of the maxim that 'history is philosophy teaching by example,' he [the English writer] remarks, 'In morals, all depends on circumstances. An example, whether real or fictitious, can teach us nothing, if it contains only dry facts.'" The passage that Stone quoted went on to argue, only by examining the letters and words of historical actors themselves was it possible for the historian "'fully to appreciate the temper and spirit in which the acts commemorated in history were done,'" for these letters "'must be written, to a great extent, in the spirit of the age in which their writers lived.'" In particular, according to this writer, the historian had to know "'the writers' feelings toward their neighbours, and their neighbours' feelings toward them—their comments on the ordinary course of things around them'" before he could draw moral lessons from history.[95] And so, Stone suggested, the historian could not make moral judgments in the abstract, for morality depended on the individual's context and circumstances. In this way, Stone reconciled his recognition of the subjective element to history and the need to understand historical actors on their own terms with the traditional belief in the historian's moral function.

Even while he recognized in the fable of the sculptor and the lion that perceptions of superiority were relative, Stone ultimately affirmed his belief in Anglo-American superiority, for he was no less committed than Adams and Sabine were to the exceptionalist belief in America's special mission as both an exemplar and agent of liberty and progress. Thus, for all his emphasis on understanding the Indians' perspective, he still placed that perspective within a framework of Anglo-American civilization and progress. In fact, Stone and his adherents found Brant such an appealing figure partly because Brant seemed to live up to Anglo-American standards of civilization in many ways. Educated at a charity school in Connecticut, Brant was fluent in English and conversant with Western history and literature. He converted to Anglicanism and visited England twice. As a result, Stone could proclaim, "Combining with the native hardihood and sagacity of his race the advantages of education and of civilized life," Brant "became the most formidable border foe with whom the Provincials had to contend, and his name was a terror to the land."[96]

Stone revealed his attachment to Anglo-American ideals of civilization even more clearly as he discussed the final years of Brant's career. During this period, according to Stone, Brant faced particular challenges in governing his followers, for Mohawk society was "in a transition state—being neither the hunter nor the agricultural but partaking in part of both." Stone praised Brant for recognizing that religion and education were necessary for "the moral and social improvement of his nation."[97] As his language here demonstrated, Stone embraced the four-stage theory of history associated with the Scottish conjectural historians. Scottish conjectural theory provided a scientific framework and foundation for the belief in progress, contending that human societies followed certain natural laws of development. Most important, according to this theory, in the course of progress, societies went through four different stages—the hunter, pastoral, agricultural, and commercial—each more advanced and civilized than the one before it. This theory was used to justify the destruction of Native Americans as a necessary stage in the progress of humanity, for, as "savages" still in the hunter stage, Native Americans were, according to this theory, in a more primitive stage of development than were Anglo-Americans, who had advanced to the agricultural and commercial stage. For proponents of this theory, to interfere with this process would not only be wrong; it would also be fruitless, for it would go against the natural course of human development.[98]

Stone criticized General John Sullivan's 1779 expedition against the Iroquois precisely because it had destroyed Indian villages that had advanced to what he believed was a more civilized, agricultural stage of development. Lamenting that few of his contemporaries "are thoroughly aware of the advances which the Indians, in the wide and beautiful country of the Cayugas and Senecas, had made in the march of civilization," Stone pointed out that "[t]hey had several towns, and many large villages, laid out with a considerable degree of regularity. They had framed houses, some of them well finished, having chimneys, and painted. They had broad and productive fields." As this analysis revealed, Stone was as committed to the conjectural theory of progress as were those historians who vilified the Indians; where he differed from them was in arguing that at least some Indians had progressed beyond the more primitive hunter stage of development.[99]

Whatever the costs the Revolution had exacted from the Indians, Stone did not, in the end, question the legitimacy of the Revolution or the belief that the Revolution had advanced the cause of human liberty. He made this assumption clear as he discussed loyalist resistance to independence in New York. Rather than retarding the spread of Revolutionary principles, such resistance actually strengthened and furthered them, for, "like the bitter plant in the vegetable phar-macopoeia, the principles of liberty only thrive more rapidly beneath a pressure, and the spark which had been struck in the Palatine district, they not only found it impossible to extinguish, but a measure of their own adoption had the effect of kindling it into a blaze—and, once kindled, the fire of liberty is as inextinguish-able as the Greek."[100]

And so, as much as he sympathized with the Indians and condemned white brutality toward them, he in the end accepted the consequences of such brutal-ity—the displacement and eventual extermination of the American Indians—as a necessary and inevitable stage in the advance and progress of civilization. Indeed, in recognizing the need to recover the perspective of Native Americans, he underscored the finality and completeness of their defeat, just as Sabine used his sympathy for the loyalists to emphasize the magnitude of the revolutionar-ies' success over them. According to Stone, the reason that it was so important to recover the Indians' perspective was because "that brave and ill-used race of men" was "now melting away before the Anglo-Saxons like the snow beneath a vertical sun."[101] Reasoning that the Indians would soon be entirely extinct, Stone believed that it was imperative for the historian to preserve "memorials of a people,—once a noble race—numerous and powerful—now fast disappearing from the face of the earth" before it was too late. In this depiction of the Indians as a noble but doomed race, Stone reaffirmed the belief that it was the destiny of white Americans to take over the continent. As noble as the Indians were, according to Stone, they were still no match for "Anglo-Saxons," whose superior civilization had enabled them to surpass and overpower the Indians. And so, Stone suggested, while tragic, the destruction of the Indians was necessary for white Americans to carry out their special mission to spread civilization and liberty throughout the world. Whatever the costs of this process to the Indians, the benefits far outweighed these costs, in Stone's view, for not only did the fate of white Americans hang in the balance—also at stake was the progress of hu-manity in general.[102]

"The historian consummates, more than he celebrates, the career of his heroes": The Impartial Historian as Agent of American Destiny

Not only was a reassessment of Native American history compatible with ex-ceptionalist assumptions; Benjamin Bussey Thatcher demonstrated how such a reassessment could actually further those assumptions as he, like Stone, urged the need for a more balanced and impartial account of Indian history. Even while recognizing the injustices that white colonists had committed against Native Americans, Thatcher could defend white colonial conquest as the necessary and inevitable triumph of civilization not despite but because of his sympathy for the Indians. Thatcher saw no conflict between these imperatives, for he believed that impartiality and commemoration were integrally related objectives for the historian. Hence, in his understanding of the relationship between the historian and his subjects, not only did he express and promote exceptionalist doctrines; he also assigned to the historian a crucial role in carrying out the nation's special mission. And so, ultimately for Thatcher, by being impartial, the historian would himself help fulfill and prolong the nation's exceptionalist destiny.

Thatcher made his own contribution to a reappraisal of Native American history with the publication in 1832 of his *Indian Biography*, a two-volume collective biography of prominent Native Americans in North American history, ranging from Powhatan to Tecumseh. Thatcher, like Stone, sought to redeem Indians from their reputation as cruel savages, but his analysis extended beyond the Revolutionary era to span from the colonial period to his own time. Indians were not, in Thatcher's view, the ruthless barbarians of patriotic myth. Instead, he acknowledged the many provocations given by white settlers and the unjust sufferings that whites had inflicted on the Indians. Many instances of so-called Indian savagery were, by his account, retaliation for cruelties inflicted by whites. Above all, Thatcher emphasized the patriotism of his native subjects and in this way echoed loyalist revisionists on the patriotic motives of their subjects. In their many bloody conflicts with white settlers, Thatcher argued, Indians acted not out of savage hatred for whites but out of a patriotic desire to defend their nation from white encroachments.[103]

This appreciation for the Indians' patriotic motives was part of a more widespread trend, as demonstrated by the favorable reviews Thatcher's work received. In one such review for the *Christian Examiner*, William Joseph Snelling used Thatcher's reassessment to express his ambivalence about white expansion, praising Thatcher for providing a much-needed corrective to traditional portrayals of the Indians. A satirist and social reformer from Boston, Snelling had lived in the West and had encountered Native Americans firsthand. Even as he, like Thatcher, recognized the principled and patriotic character of their resistance to white encroachments, he asserted the inevitability and legitimacy of their conquest. Accordingly, for Snelling, while "[i]t may not be a matter of regret that their noble qualities availed them not; we may rejoice that their patriotism and valor had no effect; we may, perhaps, feel no sorrow that their race has wasted utterly away," the valiant struggles of the Indians deserved sympathy and recognition.[104] And as he expressed such sympathy, Snelling, like Stone, underscored the completeness of the white victory over the Indians. Indeed, as New Englanders, Thatcher and Snelling could lament the fate of Native Americans precisely because they had all but disappeared from the Northeast by this point. It was easier for Thatcher and Snelling to sympathize with their ancestors' Native American opponents, now that they were no longer in direct conflict with the Indians or in imminent danger from Indian attack.[105]

Snelling revealed the sectional bias to his reassessment of Native American history even more clearly as he used Thatcher's history to criticize the policy of Indian removal. Applying Thatcher's historical critique to present-day treatment of the Indians by the West and South, Snelling expressed his hope that westerners and southerners would read Thatcher's work, for it "may, perhaps, teach them more humanity than they are wont to display in their intercourse with Indians." The South and West, he suggested, were guilty of the same brutality and injustice toward the Indians that his New England ancestors had displayed in Thatcher's historical account. Here, Snelling was commenting on the expansionist tendencies that were so prevalent in these regions. To white Americans in the West and South, unlike in New England, Native Americans still represented an immediate threat. As white settlers of these regions moved westward, they came into direct conflict with the Native American inhabitants of these areas and showed little compunction about removing any of them who stood in their way.[106]

The most glaring instance of white inhumanity toward Native Americans in Snelling's time was the conflict between Georgia and the Cherokee Indians. Snelling published his review just as this conflict brought the question of Indian removal to the fore. One of the "Five Civilized Tribes," the Cherokees of Georgia had adopted many "civilized" practices. The Cherokees had learned English, settled on farms, and established a constitutional republic. Desiring Cherokee lands for white settlers, the state of Georgia claimed authority over this tribe and its lands in 1828. The Cherokees protested, but to no avail. A fervent advocate of Indian removal, Jackson sided with Georgia in the dispute with the Cherokees, and Congress added its support for removal by passing the Indian Removal Act in 1830. In 1832, the year before Snelling published his review, the Supreme Court ruled in favor of the Cherokees, but Jackson refused to enforce its decision. The outcome of this conflict was the forced removal of thousands of Cherokees from the South by the end of the 1830s. Although Georgia prevailed in its quest for Cherokee lands, the state's treatment of the Cherokees provoked strenuous opposition from critics—especially in the Northeast—who considered this removal policy inhumane and unjust.[107]

Snelling referred directly to the Cherokees in the closing passages of his review, indicating that sympathy for their plight had inspired his admonition to the West and South. He concluded by expressing the hope that those Americans "who have treated the Cherokees or Saques with rigor may be made to see the exceeding ugliness of their conduct, and peradventure, to change it." By recognizing the merits of Indians in the past and condemning the brutality of their white opponents, Thatcher's reappraisal would, Snelling hoped, discourage Americans of his own time from inflicting the same inhumanities as their ancestors. In this way, Snelling revealed his ambivalence about the process of American expansion.[108] Although he gloried in the nation's past conquests and the spread of American civilization, he did express qualms about the nature of white expansion in the present.

Thatcher himself vindicated the necessity of white colonial conquest as firmly as Snelling did. And so, even as Thatcher criticized white Americans for their treatment of Native Americans in the past, he used his reassessment to defend and legitimize the results of this process. Thatcher's concern with demonstrating the Indians' patriotic motives came through most clearly in his analysis of Metacom, better known as King Philip. As the leader of a war that nearly destroyed the English colonists, Philip had long been vilified as the epitome of Indian savagery and brutality. Directly challenging this characterization of Philip, Thatcher interpreted King Philip's War as a patriotic struggle by Indians to resist white encroachments on their land. Rather than a brutal savage, Philip was, for Thatcher, the embodiment of self-sacrificing patriotism. Despite his tragic end, Thatcher believed, "Philip did and endured enough to immortalize him as a warrior, a statesman, and we may add, as a high-minded and noble patriot." Thatcher elaborated, "He fought and fell,—miserably, indeed, but gloriously,— the avenger of his own household, the worshipper of his own gods, the guardian of his own honor, a martyr for the soil which was his birth-place, and for the proud liberty which was his birth-right." While Thatcher's emphasis on Philip's nobility and desire for liberty was consistent with the myth of the noble savage, his depiction of Philip as a patriotic statesman departed from this image by attributing to Philip qualities associated with civilization.[109]

Hence, rather than idealizing his subjects as pure and simple beings, uncorrupted by the evils of society, Thatcher characterized Philip and his successors as realistic and farsighted statesmen, who resorted to violence only after a rational calculation of their best interests. In Thatcher's account, the provocative behavior of white colonists, the growing power of their settlements, and previous white encroachments on Indian territory all convinced these Indian leaders that violent resistance was their only hope for survival. Thus Thatcher explained the reasoning behind Pontiac's decision to organize an uprising against the English in 1763: "[Pontiac] reasoned as Philip had done before him, and as Tecumseh will be found to have done since. He had begun to apprehend danger from this new government and people; danger to his own dominion and to the Indian interest at large; danger from their superiority in arms, their ambition, their eagerness in possessing themselves of every military position on the Northern waters." According to Thatcher, Pontiac recognized the expansionist designs of the English and saw that English expansion, if unchecked, could only result in the destruction of the Indians. He sought to preempt this long-term danger by uniting the Indians against the English before the English had consolidated their power.[110]

In this depiction of Philip and Pontiac, Thatcher made them seem much like the white Americans they fought. Just as Pontiac anticipated and sought to resist the threat that the English colonists posed to the Indians, Thatcher suggested, the revolutionaries recognized that they had to resist English encroachments on their liberties before it was too late. On a more fundamental level, in his emphasis on their patriotism, Thatcher projected onto Native Americans the same kind of patriotic devotion that white Americans claimed for themselves. And by pointing to Philip's love of liberty, Thatcher suggested that he embraced the same principles that white Americans did. By identifying Philip with the ideals that defined the nation, Thatcher, as Richard Slotkin puts it, turned Philip into a "kind of Indian George Washington." And so, in praising the virtues of his Native American subjects, Thatcher was celebrating Americans themselves. His sympathy for Native Americans thus both reflected his own deep sense of nationalism and legitimized that nationalism. If the Indians were justified in using any means necessary to defend their nation, then, Thatcher implied, so too were white Americans. In this way, paradoxically, Thatcher used his sympathy for Native Americans to legitimize the very forces that had helped bring about their destruction, and he revealed how the chauvinistic nationalism of this period could at once serve as a bridge for understanding dissent and further the exclusion and dispossession of those people who opposed the nation's progress. Ultimately, then, Thatcher still came down on the side of the white settlers and believed that their success was necessary to further the progress of civilization, as he revealed in his assessment of Sassacus. Provoked by the English colonists' attacks on the Pequots, Sassacus "began a war of extermination; and then indeed it became necessary that one of the two nations at issue should be completely disabled. No civilized reader entertains a doubt as the result which, under such an alternative, was most to be desired."[111]

Thatcher admitted that the colonists were to blame in bringing about this destruction, for they had incited Indian hostility and suspicion in the first place.

Arguing that the "rashness of the civilized party was the ultimate cause of the ruin of the savage," Thatcher urged, "let that injustice be acknowledged, though it should be with shame and with tears." For Thatcher, it was now up to the historian to make up for this injustice by exposing "the whole truth" about these conflicts, and he exhorted, "Let it be atoned for, as far as it may be—in the only way now possible—by the candid judgment of posterity and history, upon the merits and misfortunes of both." In this way, even as he condemned the colonists for contributing to the extinction of the Indians, he made that development seem irreversible. As unjust as it was, there was nothing that his contemporaries could do to make up for that injustice except for historians to acknowledge it as injustice. In turn, by assigning this duty to the historian, he absolved his contemporaries from the responsibility of atoning for that injustice in more concrete and material ways.[112]

As he at once defended white expansion and recognized its costs, Thatcher expressed a dual understanding of the historian's role. Indeed, his views of expansion and of the historian's role were integrally related to each other, as he made clear in a review of Stone's biography of Brant. In this review, Thatcher made his commitment to impartiality explicit and explained how a reassessment of the Indians would further this ideal. Believing that impartial truth required the historian to acknowledge and understand opposing points of view, he praised Stone's revisionist account as a necessary corrective to the overwhelming bias that other writers had displayed against the Indians. Like Stone, Thatcher attributed this one-sided perspective to the lack of any accounts by the Indians themselves. He explained why this deficiency was so detrimental to an understanding of Indian-white relations by drawing a contrast to other historical controversies. In most historical disputes, the historian could draw on testimony from both sides, each of which was biased in its own way. Thatcher observed, "In the case of most differences between great parties like these,—as between political factions, or contending communities,—there are sure to be two sets of prejudices, exaggerations, and fabrications, the one of which does tolerably well as an off-set against the other." Although he thus recognized that both sides would interpret and distort events in their own favor, Thatcher did not abandon the hope of achieving historical truth. On the contrary, again like Stone, Thatcher argued that the historian could ascertain truth by taking all these conflicting perspectives into account. Reasoning that the prejudices of both sides would counteract each other, he argued that "putting both together, and weighing well, at the same time, the strictures with which everything advanced by one party is sure to be met by the other, an observer or reader, who is really disposed to get at the truth, may be able to do so, in due course of time."[113]

By referring to historical disputants as "great parties" and comparing them to "political factions," Thatcher demonstrated how the rise of party politics contributed to his understanding of impartiality. He did not see historical partisanship as harmful or undesirable. On the contrary, just as Americans in this period had come to accept the legitimacy of party politics, Thatcher believed that such partisanship in history was both inevitable and valuable. For him, just as healthy competition between political parties would benefit the cause of liberty, the clash between competing historical interpretations would advance the quest for impartial truth. Thatcher linked partisanship and impartiality even more directly when evaluating Stone as a historian. As Thatcher put it, the leading characteristic of Stone's book, and "in our eyes almost its first merit, and that a very rare and high one, is his *partiality*, we were going to say, for the Indians; his *impartiality*, however, we mean." For Thatcher, such "partiality" was compatible, and almost synonymous, with impartiality. Hostility against the Indians was so prevalent that any effort to do them justice appeared partial by comparison. And because of this hostility, an account that was prejudiced in favor of the Indians was necessary for truth, for only in this way could the historian counteract the bias against the Indians.[114]

Stone's enthusiasm for his subject had, according to Thatcher, carried him away in one respect—by leading him to include far too many extracts from Indian speeches. According to Thatcher, the problem with this approach was that it would take away from the popularity of Stone's work, for, "[v]ery much the larger part of this talk is, to speak plainly. . . intolerably stupid and tedious; as unimportant to the public or to posterity in all cases, as the ordinary daily speechifying of *caucuses* among the whites; and very much more so in many." Here, then, even as Thatcher praised Stone for his impartiality, he criticized him for the very practice that Stone claimed would ensure his impartiality. And so, while they agreed that a reassessment of the Indians was necessary for impartiality, Stone and Thatcher differed over how to carry out that ideal.[115]

For Thatcher, whatever the limitations of Stone's history, they were the product of Stone's pioneering role as a historian. As he likened the historian to the pioneer, Thatcher revealed the dualities in both his view of white expansion and his understanding of the historian's role. In his admiration for western pioneers, not only did he celebrate the very people who had committed the brutalities he condemned; even as he prescribed the need for impartiality, he revealed his belief that the historian was supposed to commemorate his subjects. Because so little had been written about American history up to that point, Thatcher viewed this subject as "new ground," or "as it were historical *forest*." Likening American history to wilderness that still needed to be conquered, he declared,

"We look upon men like Mr. Stone as Boones or Putnams, first settlers and surveyors of the wild land of literature. The spirit, which makes men pioneers in the one case as in the other, is a spirit to which America owes a vast debt, and must owe a greater one still." "[J]ust as it was and is necessary that the literal wilderness, which covers a great portion of the face of the country, should be cleared away for the advancement of civilization," it was now the historian's turn to conquer the wilderness of the American past.[116]

As much as he pitied the sufferings of the Indians who had been marginalized by white settlement of the continent, Thatcher's language here glorified the very pioneers who had dispossessed the Indians of their land. And, as Thatcher made clear, he, like Stone, believed that this process of conquest was a "necessary" stage in the "advancement of civilization." Indeed, in using the term "wilderness" to speak of this land, he suggested that it was empty, revealing his assumption that Native Americans could not be considered real inhabitants of those areas. And, as he glorified the spirit of the pioneer, Thatcher celebrated the uniqueness of the American character. While that spirit had enabled the pioneers to conquer the American wilderness, the vast expanse of land in America had in turn fostered this spirit of "enterprise and energy" by providing white Americans with opportunities to exercise that spirit. In this way, Thatcher embraced the myth of the frontier hero, identifying this quality as one of the forces that set the nation apart.[117]

The likeness between the historian and the pioneer was more than metaphorical for Thatcher, for he believed that there was a close affinity between the writing of history and the making of history. The "drudgery" involved in Stone's research was "peculiar to history-making in this country, and such as this;—very similar, as we said before, to the drudgery of *making* the country itself."[118] Not only did the historian engage in the same kind of activities as his subjects; ultimately for Thatcher, in writing about history, the historian played a role in the making of history. For this reason, he believed that the chronicler of heroic deeds "deserves the privilege he secures, of connecting his own memory with *theirs*," for the "'bene-dicere'" is "not so much the preservation, as it is the sequel, of the 'bene-facere' of the act. The historian consummates, more than he celebrates, the career of his heroes."[119] Thus, he suggested, the actions of his subjects would be incomplete without the historian to record and consecrate them.

Thatcher saw no conflict between his commitment to impartiality and his desire to commemorate the heroic deeds of his subjects, for he believed that all the historian needed to do to display their heroism was to present the truth about their actions. The historian did not have to embellish or even commend these actions because their heroic character would be apparent to all. Thatcher made this assumption explicit when he declared that "the best compliment, the most generous justice, the worthiest monument" that the historian could confer on the Pilgrims "is the strictest, plainest, and fullest statement, as far as possible, of what they did, and who they were." He reasoned, "The task of mere eulogy, compared with this, if it be true, or founded on truth, is but a vain effort to construe actions which speak better for themselves." In fact, the more the historian recognized the faults of his heroes, the more his readers would admire them, for "[i]t was not only what they were, but what they did despite of what they were and what the age was with them, which gives them a title to our admiration," and "[t]his we magnify in proportion as we magnify their faults and their misfortunes." For Thatcher, the accomplishments of his heroes would appear even greater if readers understood the obstacles they overcame—and those obstacles included their own limitations. Thus, by recognizing the wrongs that white Americans had committed against Native Americans in the past, Thatcher in the end sought to heighten admiration for what they did achieve in spite of their shortcomings.[120]

In this way, for Thatcher, by being impartial the historian would not only reveal the exceptional nature of what white Americans had accomplished in conquering the "wilderness"; in doing so, he would also further the mission they had begun, for when Thatcher argued that historians actually consummated the actions of the individuals they described, he suggested that historians themselves played a role in the historical events they related. Now that the conquest of the American wilderness seemed assured, Thatcher implied, it was time for the historian to complete that process by writing about and commemorating it. As Thatcher concluded, "The fighting duty, at least, of this community has, we trust, been chiefly performed; the writing service largely remains to do. The age of the historian here, as in Rome, has succeeded the age of the hero."[121]

Although, in this understanding of the historian's role, Thatcher confidently affirmed his faith in the nation's prospects for greatness, he also expressed anxieties about the implications of exceptionalist ideology. If, according to exceptionalist doctrine, the American Revolution was an event of unparalleled importance and heroism, then how could Americans of the post-Revolutionary generation ever match the heroic deeds that their Revolutionary predecessors had achieved? Thatcher himself recognized that the opportunity for this kind of greatness had passed and expressed what George Forgie has termed the anxieties of living in a "post-heroic" age when he declared that the "age of the hero" was over. With the passing of the "age of the hero," it was incumbent on Americans of Thatcher's generation, as successors to the revolutionaries, to revere and preserve their accomplishments. At the same time, they desired to emulate their predecessors and achieve the same heroic status for themselves. Yet these two goals conflicted with each other. Whereas the task of founding a new nation had provided the revolutionaries with a chance to perform heroic deeds, Americans of the post-heroic generation lacked the same opportunities for fame. If all that was left for them to do was to preserve the Revolutionary achievement, post-Revolutionary Americans would have little occasion to display the kind of heroism that had entitled their ancestors to remembrance by posterity. Consequently, Americans of the post-heroic generation could obtain fame only by endangering the legacy they sought to preserve. Thatcher's definition of the historian's role offered one solution to this problem—by equating the act of commemoration with the very deeds it commemorated, he allowed his contemporaries to preserve the legacy of their predecessors and achieve the heroic status their subjects possessed.[122]

Thatcher's analysis raised another question: What were Americans to do when they had conquered and civilized the "wilderness"? In order to realize their exceptionalist destiny, Americans had to expand across the continent. By expanding through space, Americans would not only spread the principles that made the nation unique; such expansion would also protect the United States against the corruption and decay that had destroyed other republics, for another tenet of exceptionalist ideology was the assumption that, as the basis for virtue and independence, land would enable Americans to escape time. But in proclaiming that all that remained for Americans to do was the "writing service" of the nation, Thatcher suggested that it would not be long before the very force that had made the nation exceptional—its vast expanse of land—came to an end. Yet if the nation could no longer be unique by virtue of its ability to escape history, Thatcher believed, it could still claim to be exceptional by virtue of its ability to record history. Just as the pioneers had unique opportunities for prosperity and success because of the vast "wilderness" available to them, the historian possessed unprecedented opportunities for historical knowledge because of the nation's unique abundance of documents. Unlike "other countries," where "the material of history has been comparatively used up long since," Thatcher asserted, "[t]his country is richer even than any other ever was in historical material." Because of this wealth of material, historical collectors "are traversing, as first explorers, a complete El Dorado of a region, whose soil everywhere breaks out with shining ores." Here, then, even as Thatcher sug-

gested the limits on America's ability to exempt itself from history, he explained
how Americans could prolong their status as an exceptional nation.[123]

As they reassessed both the loyalists and Native Americans, historians revealed
the contradictory and paradoxical uses and meaning of the ideal of impartiality
in this period. In revising orthodox portrayals of the loyalists and Native Americans, historians simultaneously used history to further their social purposes
and displayed a genuine commitment to impartial truth. Thus, for these historians, partisanship could promote impartiality, and impartiality could serve
partisan purposes. Hence, even as they used impartiality to promote national
unity, this ideal further divided them. While they agreed in using this ideal to
reaffirm their belief in America's character as an exceptional nation, they differed in their understanding of what the nation represented. And so, even while
Sabine and Simms largely agreed in their assessment of the loyalists, Simms
took Sabine's analysis as an attack on the South. Antebellum revisionists in turn
revealed the internal tensions and dualities in their sense of nationalism as they
expressed both anxiety and confidence about the nation's future and offered a
conception of national identity that was at once inclusive and exclusive.

Likewise in their definitions of what impartiality entailed, these historians
reconciled seemingly contradictory assumptions about the nature of truth and
the historian's role. Thus these historians could at once privilege detachment
for the historian and recognize the subjective character of historical interpretation. Rather than seeing these qualities as mutually exclusive, however, they
believed that understanding the influence of bias on perceptions of truth would
actually enable the historian to achieve impartial truth. Nor did antebellum
revisionists see a conflict between either of these assumptions and their firm
belief in the moral function of history. If for Stone letting historical actors "tell
their own stories" was necessary for the historian to carry out his moral function, Sparks believed that the historian would arrive at correct moral judgments
only if he divested himself of bias. Thatcher went the furthest in bringing together seemingly opposed views of the historian's role, calling for the historian
to serve at once as a disinterested chronicler of the historical process and as
a participant in that process. As he did so, he turned the historian's quest for
impartiality into an instrument and expression of the realization of the nation's
exceptionalist destiny.

Conclusion

Contrary to their own belief that they would achieve fame and remembrance through their historical writing, antebellum historical writers have largely been dismissed or forgotten by their successors. Ironically, antebellum historians were responsible for developing the very ideals—impartiality and originality—that were used to marginalize them, as the "scientific" historians at the turn of the century sought to demonstrate their own commitment to these ideals by defining themselves against the uncritical filiopietism of their early nineteenth-century predecessors. By setting up an opposition between themselves and their antebellum predecessors, turn-of-the-century American historians could at once demonstrate their own objectivity and make that objectivity seem new and original. In turn, such an opposition served to legitimize the development of history into a professional discipline defined by a commitment to objective truth. Even though antebellum historians in many ways laid the basis for this development, then, the process of professionalization would come to fruition only through the erasure of their role in it. That erasure would persist to the present day, as modern historians have continued to identify the origins of professional history in the United States with the scientific historians of the late nineteenth century.[1] Thus, not only can a reexamination of antebellum historiography contribute to a better understanding of the history of the discipline of history; it can also illuminate some of the central issues that confront historians today, for antebellum historians were grappling with many of same problems and dilemmas as their modern-day successors.

Most important, then, as now, the ideal of historical truth was uncertain and precarious, though for different reasons. If the ideal of impartial truth was precarious for antebellum historians because they were just in the process of beginning to define this ideal, today the ideal of objective truth faces new threats and challenges. These challenges have come on three fronts, which are at once interrelated and in tension with one another—concerns about declining popular interest in history, the emergence of postmodernism, and the rise of the "new" social history—but in all three of these areas, modern debates have analogues in the debates of antebellum historians about truth.

Writing at a time of growing concern that academic history has become too

specialized and inaccessible to popular audiences, modern historians have begun to search for new ways of broadening the appeal of their works. The shrink-
ing size of library and university press budgets has added to the pressures on
historians to make their works more accessible—and hence salable—to the
general public.[2] In their quest for popular appeal, modern historians have, like
their antebellum predecessors, become increasingly concerned about footnotes
and citation. Fears that footnotes might discourage popular interest in history
contend with the desire for scholarly integrity and precision now, just as they
did for historians in the early nineteenth century. Seeking to make their works
more popular, modern historians have begun to reassess and question the need
for footnotes. For this reason, the historian Gordon Craig could say, "Now I've
written several books with no footnotes at all" because "I figure I'm writing for
the cultivated lay public, and they're not interested in footnotes."[3] This trend has
in turn provoked a reaction from scholars who bemoan the abandonment of
footnotes as a threat to the very idea of truth. In her lament "Where Have All the
Footnotes Gone?" Gertrude Himmelfarb, for example, argues that the problem
with discarding footnotes is that "[t]he indifference to form inevitably engen-
ders an indifference to content," for "the author is tempted to be careless about
such details as accuracy and relevance." Hence, Himmelfarb concludes that the
turn away from footnotes is part of a "slippery slope" toward a school of thought
that seeks to "deride 'facticity' and exalt 'invention.'"[4] For Himmelfarb, then, the
abandonment of footnotes would not only undermine truth by making factual
mistakes more likely but, in doing so, would contribute to and signify acceptance of postmodern challenges to the very idea of truth. The recent discovery
of substantial plagiarism in the works of eminent popular historians Stephen
Ambrose and Doris Kearns Goodwin, despite their own professed commitment
to the ideal of objective truth, has only fueled concerns among academic historians that popular success necessarily comes at the expense of scholarly integrity. For Ambrose's and Goodwin's critics, their plagiarism did not just denote
careless scholarship but was also emblematic of the derivative and superficial
character of popular history.[5]

Antebellum historians too were concerned with accommodating popular
audiences. And, no less than modern scholars like Himmelfarb, they viewed
footnotes as a sign of scholarly integrity and truth, as the reviewer for Charles
Campbell's history made clear when he commented on how Campbell's detailed
footnotes "savour of exactness."[6] Yet they did not see popularity and scholarly
integrity as mutually exclusive. On the contrary, seeking to balance the "popular aspect" of his *Library of American Biography* with his desire for "care and
accuracy," Jared Sparks demonstrated how footnotes could actually reconcile

these competing imperatives when he told contributor Charles Upham, "Brief & pointed notes will often be valuable, & frequent references to original authorities, but not to recent compilations, which seldom contain anything new, and for the most part are much given to dullness and blunders. Notes of this sort will be a proof of research, & a guide to further inquiry, which many readers will prize & none will dislike." Nor did Sparks here see original scholarship and popularity as mutually exclusive goals, as some critics of popular history today have assumed. On the contrary, he suggested in his disparagement of "compilations" that histories that were unoriginal and based solely on other secondary sources would be less likely to engage the interest of popular audiences.[7]

Modern scholars have attributed the increasingly specialized and esoteric character of history to the influence of postmodernism and the rise of the new social history, two developments that have in their own way contributed to doubts about historical truth. With the postmodern attack on the very idea of objective reality, scholars have begun to question the existence and possibility of historical truth. Because, according to postmodern theory, historical texts are simply literary constructions, rather than representations of objective reality, there can be no real difference between history and fiction. In their response to the novel, antebellum historians revealed striking parallels to modern debates about postmodernism, for, just as postmodernism has undercut the belief in historical truth by blurring the distinction between history and fiction, the rise of the novel threatened this belief by contributing to uncertainty about the relationship between history and fiction. Hence, when, in one of the most controversial and best-known challenges to the ideal of objective truth, Hayden White likened history to fiction—arguing that historical narratives are "verbal fictions, the contents of which are as much *invented* as *found* and the forms of which have more in common with their counterparts in literature than they have with those in the sciences"—he sounded much like Simms when he declared that "it is the artist only who is the true historian" because most history "is built upon conjecture," which, "assuming bolder privileges, becomes romance."[8]

Influenced partly by postmodernism and seeking to make history engaging and accessible to readers, modern historians have incorporated fictional techniques and the use of the imagination in what Lawrence Stone has termed "the revival of narrative," just as antebellum historians sought to achieve popularity by emulating the novel in their historical writing.[9] And like their antebellum predecessors, modern historians have been deeply ambivalent about blurring the boundaries between these two genres because of its implications for truth.[10] In their appeals to the imagination, practitioners of the "new" narrative history—most notably and controversially Simon Schama in his *Dead Certain-ties*—have both reflected and contributed to doubts about the nature and exis-tence of historical truth. For this very reason, the "new" narrative history has provoked sharp criticism from other historians concerned with upholding the ideal of objective truth.[11] Thus, for example, in his attack on Schama's "nar-rative experiment" for putting "the integrity of the discipline at risk," Gordon Wood sounds much like Simms's critics, who denounced Simms's "mania for fiction" as "at war" "with the cause of truth."[12] For Wood, as for Simms's critics, Schama's use of the imagination threatened the integrity of history specifically because of its challenge to truth. Arguing that the "conventions of objectivity and documentary proof" should "not to be abandoned without a fight either to postmodern skepticism or to Schama's playful experiments in narration," Wood concludes his review of Schama's work with the affirmation that, while recognizing the interpretive character of history, one "can still believe intel-ligibly and not naively in an objective truth about the past that can be observed and empirically verified."[13]

Yet antebellum historians were no less committed than Wood to the belief in objective truth. Hence, sounding much like Schama in his disclaimer "This is not to say, I should emphasise, that I scorn the boundary between fact and fiction," Simms—for all his apparent relativism—was careful to emphasize that he was "not disparaging the history which is known."[14] But as the works of Romantic historians like William Prescott revealed, early nineteenth-century historians had more faith than many of their modern-day successors in their ability to achieve the popularity and vitality of fiction without taking away from their claims to truth. Where antebellum historians differed most dramatically from modern historians was in their firm belief in the moral function of truth. Prescott and Simms could appeal to the imagination in their historical works without fearing that they were undermining the integrity of history because of their assumption that their ultimate purpose was to convey higher moral truths to their readers.

Yet even in this respect, antebellum and modern historians were not as dif-ferent as they might appear. While most modern scholars would reject the moral absolutism of their early national predecessors, both postmodernism and the rise of the new social history have contributed to a revival of the belief in the historian's moral function. Thus Hayden White in his own way assigned a moral function to history when he argued that, because no interpretation was more truthful or objective than another, the only criteria for choosing be-tween different interpretations were moral and aesthetic. Or, as White put it, sounding much like Simms and Theodore Parker in their reviews of Prescott, "there can be no 'proper history' which is not at the same time 'philosophy of history.'"[15] If, as even today's most staunch defenders of objectivity would admit, the historian's interpretation of the past is inevitably conditioned by his or her own social bias, then for some modern scholars the solution is not to deny that bias but to be more self-conscious and open about acknowledging the historian's social and moral purposes, as John Lewis Gaddis has urged in his injunction that "[y]ou can't escape thinking about history in moral terms. Nor, I believe, should you try to do so," for "we are, unlike all others, moral animals."[16] And in their view of history as an instrument of social change and reform, it could be argued that many of the new social historians have simply embraced an updated version of the antebellum belief in the historian's role as an agent of progress and moral improvement.

In doing so, these historians have contributed in yet another way to current uncertainties about the status of historical truth, for the rise of the new social history has been part of a larger transformation in both the interpretation and subject matter of American history, which has had mixed implications for the belief in objective truth. Here, again, antebellum historians revealed surprising similarities to modern scholars in their views on what constituted an impartial and truthful account of American history. Specifically, in their desire to revise and challenge patriotic myths about the Revolution as an idealistic struggle for liberty, antebellum historians anticipated modern debates about the origins and character of the Revolution—especially in their portrayal of the motives and treatment of the loyalists. Thus Charles Francis Adams's portrayal of Thomas Hutchinson as a man whose "capacity exerted itself well in the ordinary paths of human action" and whose "worldly disposition" would not have been "an obstacle to fortune, had he not fallen upon a moment when the standard of human conduct soared far above the level of its ordinary elevation" sounded remarkably like Bernard Bailyn's characterization of Hutchinson as a tragic figure, who, for all his good intentions and genuine attachment to America, "could not respond to the aroused moral passion and the optimistic and idealist impulses that gripped the minds of the Revolutionaries" because of his commitment to "small, prudential gains through an intricate, closely calibrated world of status, deference, and degree."[17] And like antebellum historians who believed that their reappraisal of the loyalists was necessary to understand the "whole truth" about the Revolution, Bailyn identified his "tragic" view of the loyalists with the shift to a more comprehensive and neutral perspective in which the historian "is no longer a partisan" and "can now embrace the whole of the event, see it from all sides."[18]

In their effort to provide a more comprehensive and true account of the past, antebellum historians not only revised interpretations of the loyalists but also sought to broaden the boundaries of history. And in their concern with expanding the boundaries of history to include ordinary people and "domestic" life, antebellum historians anticipated the "new" social historians of the 1960s and 1970s. And so, when Theodore Parker complained that "there are no pictures from the lives of the humble" in Prescott's history, he sounded much like Jesse Lemisch—one of the pioneers of the "new" social history—in his famous injunction calling on American historians to look at history "from the bottom up."[19] Admittedly, antebellum historians made a much more limited effort than the new social historians to put this injunction into practice. But even in their unwillingness to write social history, they shared many of the same concerns that have divided modern historians about the value of the new social history, for, then, as now, historians were ambivalent about social history because of its mixed implications for the ideal of impartial truth. While the new social history emerged out of a desire to make history more scientific, and thus more true, by applying the techniques of social science to the study of the past, this trend has also undermined faith in the possibility—and indeed the desirability—of objectivity, as many of its practitioners have self-consciously used history to further their political goals. As a result, the new social history has been sharply attacked by other historians who not only disagree with its specific political objectives but also fear more generally the politicization of history as a threat to the ideal of objective truth itself.[20]

Likewise, for antebellum historians, a redefinition of the subject matter of history at once reinforced and undermined the belief in impartial or objective truth. Like many of the new social historians, antebellum historians believed that "domestic" or social history would further truth by providing a fuller and more scientific view of the nation's past. Thus, when Lemisch argued that what he considered the unscientific neglect of social history had "distorted" "past reality" and that a "sympathy for the powerless brings us closer to objectivity," he sounded much like Benjamin Bussey Thatcher in his injunction that only by applying "a scrutiny almost as rigid as a chemical analysis" to the details of everyday life, or to use his words, the "gossip of history," could the historian "see men and things,—worth seeing,—as they were, and are."[21] At the same time, antebellum historians made only a limited effort to carry out Thatcher's prescriptions for social history because of the difficulty of obtaining primary sources on this subject. And so, like modern critics of social history, who have attacked the use of speculation and theory by social historians to fill the gaps in the documentary record as inimical to truth, antebellum historians found it difficult to reconcile the study of social history with their assumption that truth had to be derived from primary documents.[22]

One area in which antebellum historians did, like the new social historians, make an effort to write about history "from the bottom up" and give more attention to the perspectives of marginalized groups was their reassessment of Native American history. While antebellum "revisionists" like Thatcher and William Leete Stone believed that they could provide a more impartial and balanced view of American history by incorporating Native American perspectives, in their rationale for why such alternative perspectives were necessary, they recognized the contingent and subjective character of historical truth. In using the fable of the sculptor and the lion to explain why the Indians had been vilified as savages by American historians and in attributing such vilification to the fact that the Indians "have not been the sculptors," Stone anticipated postmodernists not only in his recognition of how much accounts of historical events varied according to the individual's perspective but also in his recognition of how relations of power determined which perspective would prevail.[23]

Like many of the new social historians, antebellum historians also used history to further their social purposes—where they differed most sharply from their modern counterparts was in the nature of those purposes. If for most of the new social historians history was supposed to be an instrument of social criticism and reform, their antebellum predecessors for the most part used history to uphold the established social order. Thus, contrary to conservative attacks on the new social history today, which criticize the "revisionist" history of the new social historians as unpatriotic, antebellum historians demonstrated that there was nothing inherently unpatriotic about revisionist history; far from being unpatriotic, antebellum historians used their reassessment of loyalist and Native American history to reaffirm their belief in American exceptionalism.[24] And, as they simultaneously furthered truth and their social purposes in their historical writing, antebellum historians revealed that, contrary to critics of the new social history, using history for social purposes was not necessarily opposed to truth. Antebellum historians saw no conflict between these two imperatives because, as they well understood, to use Thomas Haskell's phrase, "objectivity is not neutrality."[25]

Thus, both the belief in historical truth and anxieties about that ideal coexisted uneasily in the nation's early years, just as they do today. Modern historians divided over this ideal can thus look to their predecessors of the early nineteenth century for a way to resolve their uncertainties about truth. Modern historians concerned about the viability and integrity of their own discipline should take heart from the knowledge that such uncertainties are not new to the twentieth century. Not only did the discipline survive the earlier threats to truth posed by forces like the novel, but such threats actually contributed to the development of history as an autonomous discipline by encouraging historians

to solidify and define more clearly the basis for historical knowledge. Therefore, modern historians should view recent challenges to the ideal of historical
truth as an opportunity to redefine and strengthen discipline, rather than as a
danger.[26] As the efforts of historians like Joyce Appleby, Margaret Jacob, Lynn
Hunt, James Kloppenberg, and Thomas Haskell reveal, modern scholars have
already embarked on the process of redefining and establishing a new basis for
historical knowledge in response to current threats to truth. In doing so, these
scholars are part of a tradition that goes back to the early nineteenth century.
Although the specific solutions they have proposed are new, their efforts to establish a workable foundation for historical knowledge, while recognizing the
obstacles and limits to truth, are not.[27]

NOTES

Introduction

1. A note on terms: modern historians differ somewhat in their usage of the terms *early national, early republic,* and *antebellum.* The historical writers I discuss fall roughly into two chronological categories—those who themselves experienced and took part in the Revolution, and the descendants of the Revolutionary generation. For the sake of clarity and convenience, I refer to the first group as the Revolutionary historians and to their successors as antebellum historians, using the 1820s as the chronological dividing line between these two groups. I use the terms *early national* and *early republic* to refer to the whole period covered by my work, extending from 1783 to the 1850s.

2. Fisher, "Legendary and Myth-Making Process," 55–56.

3. The other figure most influential in establishing this myth was Fisher's contemporary Orin Libby. Like the title of Fisher's essay, the title of one of Libby's most cited articles, "Some Pseudo Histories of the American Revolution," revealed Libby's disdain for his early national predecessors and his refusal to take them seriously as historians. But whereas Fisher criticized the interpretations of these historians, Libby focused on their methodology, condemning them for copying from secondary sources without attribution.

4. On the importance and purpose of history in this period, see especially Cohen, *Revolutionary Histories;* Shaffer, *Politics of History;* Van Tassel, *Recording America's Past;* William Raymond Smith, *History as Argument;* Callcott, *History in the United States;* Danzer, "America's Roots in the Past"; Hoffer, *Liberty or Order;* and Messer, *Stories of Independence.* On the more general importance of history to the Revolutionary generation, see Colbourn, *Lamp of Experience;* Wood, *Creation of the American Republic,* 13–90; and Hoffer, *Revolution and Regeneration.*

5. In different ways, both Henry Steele Commager and Harlow Sheidley, for example, at once emphasize the important uses that Revolutionary and early national Americans assigned to history and point to how those uses simplified their understanding of the past. See Commager, "The Past as an Extension of the Present," and Sheidley, *Sectional Nationalism,* 258–356. On how the nationalist purposes of these historians limited their historical consciousness and their scholarly integrity, see Hoffer, *Past Imperfect,* 17–31. While pointing to the concern of George Bancroft and other Romantic historians with documentary research and scholarship, Joyce Appleby, Lynn Hunt, and Margaret Jacob, *Telling the Truth about History* (112–14), and Ann Douglas, *The Feminization of American Culture* (174–80), ultimately emphasize how these historians' desire to celebrate and

commemorate their historical subjects took precedence over scholarly imperatives. Even while recognizing the complexity of American attitudes toward the past, Michael Kammen, in both his *Mystic Chords of Memory* (17–90) and his *A Season of Youth* (3–14), emphasizes the weakness of tradition and the shallowness of American historical consciousness during this period. Likewise, while recognizing the widespread American interest in the past, Lewis Perry, *Boats against the Current* (47–78), at the same time points to the limits on American historical consciousness in the nineteenth century.

6. Influential surveys of American historiography that laid the basis for this narrative and that continue to be cited as standard authorities on the history of American historical writing include Jameson, *History of Historical Writing in America*, and Bassett, *Middle Group of American Historians*. While Michael Kraus recognizes that Fisher's attach on Bancroft was "excessively harsh," he still in the end perpetuates this narrative by characterizing Bancroft and his contemporaries as the "filiopietistic historians" and differentiating their view of history as literature from that of the scientific historians of the late nineteenth century. See his *Writing of American History*, 126–27, and Kraus, *History of American History*, 4–6. On the nineteenth-century Romantic historians' view of history as a form of literary art, see especially Levin, *History as Romantic Art*. Higham, *History*, and Novick, *That Noble Dream*, briefly acknowledge that certain features of modern critical scholarship had emerged among earlier nineteenth-century historians. Both of them, however, focus on the professionalization of history and start with the late nineteenth century, perpetuating the myth that the ideal of objectivity in American historical writing originated during this period. Even Van Tassel, *Recording America's Past* (121–34), who recognizes the earlier precursors of a critical approach, goes back only to the 1850s for this development. While recognizing the exaggerated character of Fisher's attack on early national historians and Bancroft's commitment to the methods of critical scholarship and the ideal of objectivity, Page Smith, "David Ramsay and the Causes of the American Revolution" (60–62), still in the end perpetuates Fisher's characterization of Bancroft's generation of historians by unfavorably contrasting Bancroft's idealized view of American history to that of his Revolutionary predecessors and indeed calls him an "unconscious myth-maker." Partly as a result of the perception of early nineteenth-century historical writing as simplistic and filiopietistic, recent scholarship on American historiography has given little attention to this period, focusing instead on the late nineteenth and early twentieth centuries. See, for example, Fitzpatrick, *History's Memory*; DesJardins, *Women and the Historical Enterprise in America*; and Tyrrell, *Historians in Public*. In recognizing that the ideal of objectivity had already begun to develop in the early nineteenth century, Casper, *Constructing American Lives*, offers an important exception to this tendency, though he focuses specifically on the implications of this ideal for biography.

7. On the concept of the autonomy of history and its importance to the development of modern historical writing, see Joseph Levine, *Autonomy of History*, vii–ix, and Collingwood, *Idea of History*, 201–3.

8. Novick, *That Noble Dream*, 7–9. Valuable and insightful works that exemplify

this "great man" tendency include, for example, Levin, *History as Romantic Art*; Wish, *American Historian*; and Vitzthum, *American Compromise*. Kraus, *Writing of American History*, offers a more comprehensive treatment of historians in this period but still follows a biographical approach. For important recent works on historiography that depart from this "great man" approach, see Phillips, *Society and Sentiment*; Fitzpatrick, *History's Memory*; DesJardins, *Women and the Historical Enterprise in America*; and Tyrrell, *Historians in Public*. For examples of works that use Bancroft to exemplify antebellum historical writing, see Appleby, Hunt, and Jacob, *Telling the Truth about History*, 112–14; Ross, "Historical Consciousness in Nineteenth-Century America," 915–19; Noble, *Historians against History*; and Page Smith, "David Ramsay and the Causes of the American Revolution," 60–62.

9. For this reason, I use both the term *historian* and the broader term *historical writer* interchangeably to refer to the historians I examine.

10. See, for example, Sheidley, *Sectional Nationalism*, 229n3; Van Tassel, *Recording America's Past*, 34n5; Bernard Bailyn, "The Losers: Notes on the Historiography of Loyalism," in *The Ordeal of Thomas Hutchinson*, 397; Franklin, "The North, the South, and the American Revolution," 6; Wood, "Rhetoric and Reality in the American Revolution," 15; Wish, *American Historian*, 51, 352n1; and Appleby, Hunt, and Jacob, *Telling the Truth about History*, 112n17.

11. Fitzpatrick, *History's Memory*, 192. On this point, see also Novick, *That Noble Dream*, 12–13; Phillips, *Society and Sentiment*, xiv; and Tyrrell, *Historians in Public*, 21.

12. Novick, *That Noble Dream*, 13. On this Whig tendency, see also Woolf, "Disciplinary History and Historical Discourse," 2–4. The term "Whig" interpretation comes from Herbert Butterfield's classic *The Whig Interpretation of History*. For examples of such surveys, see Wish, *American Historian*, and Kraus, *Writing of American History*.

13. See Levin, *History as Romantic Art*, and Gould, *Covenant and Republic*. For other examples of the growing interest in historiography among historians, see Phillips, *Sentiment and Society*; Cañizares-Esguerra, *How to Write the History of the New World*; Klein, *Frontiers of Historical Imagination*; and Bonnie Smith, *Gender of History*. On American historians' lack of interest in epistemological issues and in the philosophy of history, and on how the founding of *History and Theory* in the 1960s further "ghettoized" such questions as "an esoteric concern," see Novick, *That Noble Dream*, 593–94. On this view of historiography and the theory of history as separate from other kinds of history, see also Appleby, Hunt, and Jacob, *Telling the Truth about History*, 9–10, and Evans, *In Defense of History*, 8–9.

14. Phillips, *Society and Sentiment*, ix.

15. Quoted in ibid., xiv.

16. On the importance of the distinction between primary and secondary sources to the discipline of history, and on postmodern challenges to this distinction, see Evans, *In Defense of History*, 80–87.

17. Haskell, "Objectivity Is Not Neutrality." Although Novick himself disavows any such intention (see especially 6–7, 15–17, in *That Noble Dream*), he has been interpreted

as questioning the validity and continued viability of the ideal of objectivity by Haskell and many of his reviewers (see n. 19 in this chapter for references to such reviews). Historians of science have proved more willing than other historians to historicize the idea of truth by looking at its social function, as demonstrated by Shapin, *Social History of Truth*; Daston, "Objectivity and the Escape from Perspective"; Daston, "Baconian Facts, Academic Civility, and the Prehistory of Objectivity"; and Daston and Galison, "Image of Objectivity."

18. In taking a historical approach to this subject, I follow the lead of Daston, "Objectivity and the Escape from Perspective." For a useful interdisciplinary collection of essays on the debate over objectivity, see Megill, *Rethinking Objectivity*. For a useful response to and overview of current debates about historical truth, see Evans, *In Defense of History*.

19. Novick has been interpreted by many of his reviewers as making such a prediction, although he disclaims such an intention. On the debate over this point, see Hollinger, "Postmodernist Theory and Wissenschaftliche Practice," 690; Megill, "Fragmentation and the Future of Historiography," 693; and Novick, "My Correct Views on Everything," 702. On Novick's pessimism about the future of history as a discipline, see also Kloppenberg, "Objectivity and Historicism," 1026–27, 1029. On the sense of crisis among historians created by attacks on the idea of objective truth, see Evans, *In Defense of History*, 3–4. On the other forces contributing to this sense of crisis and on how a better understanding of the historical roots of contemporary threats to the profession can demonstrate the exaggerated character of such threats, see Tyrrell, *Historians in Public*, 1–24, 252–55.

20. See, for example, Bodnar, *Bonds of Affection*; Waldstreicher, *In the Midst of Perpetual Fetes*; O'Leary, *To Die For*; Grant, *North over South*; and Purcell, *Sealed with Blood*. Other influential works that have contributed to this reassessment of nationalism include Anderson, *Imagined Communities*, and Colley, "Whose Nation?" On how the professionalization of history and the ideal of scientific objectivity enabled nineteenth-century European historians to legitimize their nationalist purposes, see Iggers, *Historiography in the Twentieth Century*, 28.

21. See Ross, "Historical Consciousness in Nineteenth-Century America," 909–28; Ross, *Origins of American Social Science*, esp. 22–50; and Noble, *Historians against History*. See also R. W. B. Lewis, *American Adam*, and Somkin, *Unquiet Eagle*, 55–90, on how Americans in this period turned to nature over history, and on how the association between America and nature limited American historical consciousness. On how exceptionalist assumptions shaped and simplified women's interpretations of American history in this period, see Baym, *American Women Writers and the Work of History*.

22. Conn, "Who You Callin' an Intellectual?" 65.

23. For an early and influential critique of America's cultural backwardness, see Tocqueville, *Democracy in America*, 327–32, 347–53. More recently, Stanley Elkins and Eric McKitrick, *Age of Federalism* (163–93), have perpetuated a critical view of American culture in their analysis of the effects on American cultural development of the deci-

sion to locate the national capital in Washington, D.C. For a more celebratory view of the intellectual gap between America and Europe that emphasizes how American practicality and hostility to abstract ideas set the United States apart from Europe, see Boorstin, *Genius of American Politics*. Recent scholarship on classical republicanism has recognized the importance of European intellectual developments to American political thought. Scholars of republicanism have, however, confined their analysis to the political arena, paying little attention to other areas of American intellectual development. For important and notable exceptions to this trend, see Daniel Walker Howe, *Making the American Self*, and Foletta, *Coming to Terms with Democracy*.

24. Specifically on how the development of American historical consciousness lagged behind that of Europe, see Ross, "Historical Consciousness in Nineteenth-Century America," and her *Origins of American Social Science*. For a discussion of the failure of Puritan historians in colonial America and their isolation from contemporaneous European developments, see Gay, *Loss of Mastery*. Donald Kelley recognizes the connection between European and American historiographical developments by allotting a chapter to American historical writing in his recent study of nineteenth-century Western historiography, but, in contrast to his treatment of European historians, he focuses primarily on a few leading American historians like George Bancroft and John Lothrop Motley, and because he devotes only one chapter to them, he does not discuss their ideas in great depth. See his *Fortunes of History*.

25. While Steven Conn, *History's Shadow* (esp. 1–34, 198–229), also examines the integral relationship between the development of history into an autonomous discipline and the development of America's identity as an exceptional nation, he in his own way perpetuates the view of American exceptionalism as a force that limited American historical consciousness by pointing to how this process contributed to the exclusion of Native Americans as historical subjects. For a useful overview of the debate over American exceptionalism that challenges the perception of this ideology as unreflectively chauvinistic, see Kammen, "Problem of American Exceptionalism." In focusing on my subjects' belief in and perception of American exceptionalism, I follow the approach taken by Greene, *Intellectual Construction of America*, 6–7.

26. Novick, *That Noble Dream*, 7.

27. On the importance of impartiality as an ideal in early modern English historical writing and the contested character of this ideal, see Shapiro, *Culture of Fact*. On how Robertson's conception of impartiality differed from that of other eighteenth-century British historians such as Hume and Gibbon, see Smitten, "Impartiality in Robertson's *History of America*." Mark Kamrath, "Charles Brockden Brown and the 'art of the historian'" (237–38), briefly notes the concern of eighteenth-century British and American Revolutionary historians with impartiality but emphasizes the limits to that concern. For more on the Revolutionary historians' understanding of impartiality, see Cohen, *Revolutionary Histories*, 163–84.

28. On the changing meaning of the terms *objectivity* and *objective*, see the *Oxford*

English Dictionary. While Novick, *That Noble Dream* (25), dates the usage in English of *objectivity* in the modern sense somewhat later, to the last part of the nineteenth century, Daston, "Baconian Facts, Academic Civility, and the Prehistory of Objectivity" (37–38), argues that the modern meaning of the term *objective* had become widely accepted by the 1850s.

29. *Webster's American Dictionary of the English Language* (1828), http://1828.mshaffer .com (26 Aug. 2007), s.v. "impartial," "indifference." On the association of impartiality with judges and judgment in early modern English historical writing and its roots in the legal system, see Shapiro, *Culture of Fact*, 26–30, 43–44, 56–58. On the association of impartiality with indifference and disinterestedness, see Shapiro, *Culture of Fact*, 56–57; Smitten, "Impartiality in Robertson's *History of America*," 56–57; and Daston, "Baconian Facts, Academic Civility, and the Prehistory of Objectivity," 38.

30. On the earlier development of this exemplary theory of history among the Revolutionary historians, see Cohen, *Revolutionary Histories*, 185–211. A note on terms: I use masculine pronouns here and throughout the book when speaking of Revolutionary and antebellum views on the role of the historian in the abstract. I do so because these are the pronouns most historians at that time would have used. Although there were some women historians who wrote at this time, as I will discuss, the public realm of history was still predominantly considered a male domain, and truth itself was defined in masculine terms. Thus most historians of this time would not have used *he* or *him* in the generic sense; by these pronouns, they would have meant men. See Kerber, *Women of the Republic*, 15, on the gender-specific connotations of the pronoun *he* in political writing of this period.

31. On how Hume embraced this understanding of impartiality, see Smitten, "Impartiality in Robertson's *History of America*," 72–74.

32. For precursors to this understanding of impartiality in early modern English historical writing, see Shapiro, *Culture of Fact*, 57–58. On the meaning of impartiality in seventeenth-century English scientific discourse and the forerunners of the concept of objectivity as an unbiased account of facts, see Daston, "Baconian Facts, Academic Civility, and the Prehistory of Objectivity." For earlier expressions of this understanding of impartiality by Revolutionary American historians and the limits to their willingness to put that understanding into practice, see Cohen, *Revolutionary Histories*, 163–67, 183–84. Smitten, "Impartiality in Robertson's *History of America*" (57), portrays this conception of truth as a nineteenth-century development when he distinguishes it from eighteenth-century definitions of impartiality.

33. For a definition of the ideal of objectivity, see Novick, *That Noble Dream*, 1–2. For a summary of the Rankean ideal, see Krieger, *Ranke*, 2–7, though, as Krieger and other scholars of Ranke have demonstrated, Ranke's conception of truth was actually more complex than the ideal he came to represent.

34. On how Ranke himself reconciled his belief in impartiality with his moral conception of history, see Iggers, *Historiography in the Twentieth Century*, 25–26.

ONE. "To become a historian"

1. Francis Bowen to Lorenzo Sabine, 31 Oct. 1845, Lorenzo Sabine Papers, New Hampshire Historical Society, Concord (hereafter cited as Sabine Papers).

2. On the social backgrounds and purposes of the Revolutionary historians, see Shaffer, *Politics of History*, 1–10, 123–31, and Wish, *American Historian*, 39–41. See Messer, *Stories of Independence*, 139–82, 193–97, for a biographical overview of the Revolutionary historians and for an analysis of both the exclusionary and the democratic elements to their histories.

3. On the nationalist purposes of the Revolutionary historians and the relationship between their local and national loyalties, see Shaffer, *Politics of History*, esp. 9–29, and Van Tassel, *Recording America's Past*, 31–59. See Messer, *Stories of Independence*, 3–13, 105–69, on how the Revolutionary historians used history to define national identity, though he points to how they defined that identity in such a way as to allow some room for dissent and conflict.

4. On classical republican ideology, see Bailyn, *Ideological Origins of the American Revolution*; Pocock, *Machiavellian Moment*; Wood, *Creation of the American Republic*; and Wood, *Radicalism of the American Revolution*, 95–225. On the relationship between classical republican ideals and the moral purposes of the Revolutionary historians, see Cohen, *Revolutionary Histories*, esp. 161–211. See also Shaffer, *Politics of History*, 31–48, 96–102, on the sources of the Revolutionary historians' commitment to the political function of history and on their desire to promote republican ideals. On how the Revolutionary historians used history to promote and redefine the very meaning of republican virtue, and the complex relationship between republican ideology and American identity in their work, see Messer, *Stories of Independence*, 3–13,105–38.

5. On the debate over the influence of republicanism and liberalism in this period, see Shalhope, "Toward a Republican Synthesis"; Rodgers, "Republicanism"; and Appleby, *Liberalism and Republicanism in the Historical Imagination*. On the emergence of liberal capitalist ideals in this period, see Appleby, *Capitalism and a New Social Order*. See Wood, *Radicalism of the American Revolution*, 124–45, on the growing importance of trade and consumption in the eighteenth-century American colonies.

6. Jeremy Belknap to Ebenezer Hazard, 1 Aug. 1792, "Belknap Papers," 3:373. On how the Revolutionary historians incorporated and adapted to liberal assumptions in the content of their histories, see Messer, *Stories of Independence*, 105–82.

7. See Michael T. Gilmore, "Literature of the Revolutionary and Early National Periods," in Bercovitch, *Cambridge History of American Literature*, 1:551–52, on the unspecialized and unprofessional character of literature in this period.

8. On the transitional state of American publishing and the conditions for authorship in this period, see Davidson, *Revolution and the Word*, 16–37; Casper, *Constructing American Lives*, 21–25; Charvat, *Literary Publishing in America*, 17–60; and Tebbel, *History of Book Publishing in the United States*, 51–170.

9. Shaffer, *Politics of History*, 161, and Shaffer, *To Be an American*, 103–4.

10. Frank Mevers, "Jeremy Belknap," in *American Historians, 1607–1865*, 32.

11. On the impact of the Revolutionary historians and the reasons for their lack of popular success, see Shaffer, *Politics of History*, 161–63. See also Van Tassel, *Recording America's Past*, 52–54, on the publishing difficulties that the Revolutionary historians encountered.

12. In emphasizing the nationalist purposes of antebellum historians, I depart from Shaffer, *Politics of History* (174–75), who argues for how the more secure nationalism of this period enabled them to write history more for its own sake than for a political purpose. And in characterizing this period as a transitional one in the professionalization of history, I depart from Callcott, *History in the United States* (69–82), who emphasizes the nonprofessional character of history in the early nineteenth century.

13. See Roger Brown, *Republic in Peril*, and John William Ward, *Andrew Jackson*, 3–29, on the impact of the War of 1812 on American national identity. On the development of American nationalism immediately following the War of 1812, see Dangerfield, *Awakening of American Nationalism*. On how a growing sense of national confidence affected American literature, see Spencer, *Quest for Nationality*, 102–55.

14. Greene, *Intellectual Construction of America*, 207–8.

15. On American exceptionalism and the belief in America's special destiny, see Welter, *Mind of America*, 45–74; Tuveson, *Redeemer Nation*, 91–186; Merk, *Manifest Destiny and Mission in American History*, 3–60, 261–66; Bercovitch, *Rites of Assent*, 147–67; Ross, *Origins of American Social Science*, 23–26; and Ross, "Historical Consciousness in Nineteenth-Century America." On the rise of Anglo-Saxon racialism in this period and the increasingly exclusionary character of the belief in America's special destiny, see Horsman, *Race and Manifest Destiny*. See Noble, *Historians against History*, and Somkin, *Unquiet Eagle*, 55–90, on how Americans in this period believed that they could escape historical development through nature and westward expansion. See McCoy, *Elusive Republic*, on the importance of westward expansion to republican ideology.

16. Motley, "Polity of the Puritans," 493–95. See Ross, "Historical Consciousness in Nineteenth-Century America," 909–28; Ross, *Origins of American Social Science*, esp. 22–50; Noble, *Historians against History*; R. W. B. Lewis, *American Adam*; and Somkin, *Unquiet Eagle*, 55–130, on the antihistorical character of exceptionalist ideology.

17. Callcott, *History in the United States*, 71.

18. On the subject matter for history in this period, see ibid., 83–101.

19. On the importance of the Revolution to antebellum definitions of national identity, see Grant, *North over South*, 24–25. See also Wood, *Radicalism of the American Revolution*, 336, on the importance of the Revolution to American national identity in the early republic. On the growing fascination with the Revolution during the 1820s and the role of Revolutionary War veterans in this fascination, see Young, *The Shoemaker and the Tea Party*, 132–54, and Purcell, *Sealed with Blood*, 171–209. See also Kammen, *Season of Youth*, 15–27, 41–49, on the centrality of the Revolution to American culture and on the 1820s as a turning point in American attitudes toward the Revolution.

20. William Prescott to Washington Irving, 10 May 1842, in Wolcott, *Correspondence of William Hickling Prescott*, 303.

21. On how the duty to preserve the Revolutionary legacy created anxieties about fame for post-heroic Americans, see Forgie, *Patricide in the House Divided*, 3–12, 55–87. See also Sheidley, *Sectional Nationalism*, 30–33, on the ambivalence of the post-Revolutionary Massachusetts elite toward the Revolutionary generation.

22. Callcott, *History in the United States*, 61.

23. On the sectional character of their nationalism, see Sheidley, *Sectional Nationalism*, 118–47. On the sectional character of antebellum northern nationalism in general, and on the way northerners defined themselves in opposition to the South, see Grant, *North over South*.

24. For this usage of the term, see Nye, *George Bancroft: Brahmin Rebel*; Tyack, *George Ticknor and the Boston Brahmins*; and Lader, *Bold Brahmins*. Field, "Birth of Secular High Culture" (576) and *Crisis of the Standing Order* (8–9, 52–54), comments on the tendency to associate this term with the antebellum Boston elite but offers an alternative definition. On Oliver Wendell Holmes's definition of the Brahmin, see Darnell, *William Hickling Prescott*, 15–16. On the origins and uses of the term *Brahmin*, see Story, *Forging of an Aristocracy*, xii–xiii, 4–7, 196. In my terminology, I at once depart from and follow Story's usage. While, as Story rightly notes, characterizing this elite group as the "Brahmins" before the 1850s is anachronistic, for the sake of convenience, I use this term loosely as a shorthand for the antebellum New England elite whom I describe in this paragraph. Following Story's lead, however, I use the term *elite* rather than *upper class* to describe this group, for, as he points out, its members were still in the process of consolidating themselves as a class during this period and were not yet fully conscious of themselves as a class. The term *elite* thus better reflects the varied and fluid basis for this group's claims to superiority than does the term *class*, which implies a greater sense of cohesion and self-consciousness based on shared economic interests (Story, *Forging of an Aristocracy*, xii, 3–4, 196).

25. On the composition of and basis for membership in the Brahmin elite, see Sheidley, *Sectional Nationalism*, 4–9, and Story, *Forging of an Aristocracy*, 3–10.

26. See Story, *Forging of an Aristocracy*, 10–23, on the role of cultural institutions in the formation of the nineteenth-century Boston elite. On the fluidity of the Brahmin elite and its openness to men of letters, see Sheidley, *Sectional Nationalism*, 21–29. On the interconnection of high culture and mercantile wealth as determinants of Brahmin status, see Field, "Birth of Secular High Culture," 587–95, and Field, *Crisis of the Standing Order*, 80–110. See Foletta, *Coming to Terms with Democracy*, 57–58, and Michael Stevens, "Jared Sparks," in *American Historians, 1607–1865*, vol. 30 of *Dictionary of Literary Biography*, 299–300, on Sparks's humble beginnings. On Bowen as a "self-made man," see Daniel Walker Howe, *Unitarian Conscience*, 309–10. See Kirk Wood, "George Bancroft," in *American Historians, 1607–1865*, vol. 30 of *Dictionary of Literary Biography*, 16, and Handlin, *George Bancroft*, 22–23, 84–112, on Bancroft's early financial difficulties.

27. Lorenzo Sabine to Jared Sparks, 11 Dec. 1848, Jared Sparks Papers, Houghton

Library, Harvard University (hereafter cited as Sparks Papers), MS Sparks 153. By permission of the Houghton Library, Harvard University.

28. On Unitarian thought in this period, see Daniel Walker Howe, *Unitarian Conscience*; and on the appeal of Unitarianism to Sparks's generation of Federalist intellectuals, see Foletta, *Coming to Terms with Democracy*, 61–64. On the relationship between Unitarianism and the social purposes of the Brahmin elite, see Sheidley, *Sectional Nationalism*, 91–96. On the importance of those social purposes to the conflict over the Hollis professorship and the rise of Unitarianism, see Field, *Crisis of the Standing Order*, 47–81, 111–40.

29. On the relationship between religion and culture for Brahmin intellectuals, see Field, "Birth of Secular High Culture," and Field, *Crisis of the Standing Order*, 82–110. See Douglas, *Feminization of American Culture*, 169–80, on how these historians turned to history as a substitute for religion and theology and on the quasi-religious character of their interest in history. On Sparks's decision to leave the ministry, see Stevens, "Jared Sparks," 301.

30. On how this generation of New England intellectuals combined a greater sense of cosmopolitanism with a heightened sense of nationalism, see Foletta, *Coming to Terms with Democracy*, 81.

31. For a discussion of the connections between European and American historiographical developments in the nineteenth century, see Donald Kelley, *Fortunes of History*, 280–303. Specifically, on the European connections that Bancroft made as ambassador to England, see Nye, *George Bancroft: Brahmin Rebel*, 163–83. On Guizot's and Mignet's aid in giving him access to French archives, see Jared Sparks to Henry Wheaton, 29 Jan. 1844, Sparks Papers, MS Sparks 147h. By permission of the Houghton Library, Harvard University. On Gayangos's relationship with Prescott, see Wolcott, *Correspondence of William Hickling Prescott*, xvi. See Douglas, *Feminization of American Culture*, 180–81, on European respect for American Romantic historians like Prescott and Motley. On the importance of European historiography to southern historical writers, see Michael O'Brien, *Conjectures of Order*, 593–97.

32. Lord Mahon to George Bancroft, 24 Jan. 1852, George Bancroft Papers, Massachusetts Historical Society, Boston (hereafter cited as Bancroft Papers).

33. See Donald Kelley, *Fortunes of History*, 288–90, and Owen Dudley Edwards, "John Lothrop Motley," in *American Historians, 1607–1865*, vol. 30 of *Dictionary of Literary Biography*, 186, on translations of Prescott's and Motley's histories. For translations of Prescott's histories, see *Storia del regno di Ferdinando e Isabella sovrani cattolici di Spagna di H. Prescott, recata per la prima volta in italiano da Acanio Tempestini* (Florence: Per V. Batelli e compagni, 1847–48), and *Histoire de la conquête du Mexique avec un tableau préliminaire de l'ancienne et civilisation mexicaine la vie de Fernand Cortés* (Paris: Librairie de Firmin Didot Frères, 1846). On translations of Sparks's work, see Stevens, "Jared Sparks," 307. For European translations of Sparks's *Writings of Washington*, see, for example, *Leben und Briefwechsel Georg Washington* (Leipzig: F. A. Brockhaus, 1839), and *Vie, correspondance et écrits de Washington* (Paris: Charles Gosselin, 1840).

34. Stern, *Varieties of History*, 39. On the transitional status of history during the eighteenth century and its complex relationship to philosophy and erudition, see Donald Kelley, *Fortunes of History*, 6–9. On the distinction between historians and antiquaries, see Momigliano, "Ancient History and the Antiquarian"; Iggers, *New Directions in European Historiography*, 12–13; and Iggers, *Historiography in the Twentieth Century*, 23. On this distinction and efforts to bridge it in Renaissance England, see Woolf, "Erudition and the Idea of History in Renaissance England." On Gibbon's role in bridging the gap between the philosophes and the *érudits*, see Joseph Levine, "Strife in the Republic of Letters," in *Autonomy of History*, 122–26, and Momigliano, "Gibbon's Contribution to Historical Method."

35. Den Boer, *History as a Profession*, 118–19.

36. On the importance of the Göttingen school as predecessors to Ranke, see Butterfield, *Man on His Past*, 36–61; and on its specific contribution to the development of history as a science, see Iggers, *New Directions in European Historiography*, 12–17. On the impact of philology on early nineteenth-century German historical writing in general, see Donald Kelley, *Fortunes of History*, 112–17.

37. On Niebuhr's importance and influence, see Gooch, *History and Historians in the Nineteenth Century*, 14–23; Donald Kelley, *Fortunes of History*, 117–24; and James Westfall Thompson, *History of Historical Writing*, 2:153–57.

38. On Ranke's scientific conception of history and its importance to the professionalization of history, see Iggers, *New Directions in European Historiography*, 17–24, and Iggers, *Historiography in the Twentieth Century*, 24–26. On Ranke, see also Donald Kelley, *Fortunes of History*, 132–40; Gooch, *History and Historians in the Nineteenth Century*, 72–97; James Westfall Thompson, *History of Historical Writing*, 2:168–86, and Krieger, *Ranke*.

39. For works that trace Ranke's influence in the United States back to the late nineteenth-century American historians, see Iggers, "Image of Ranke in American and German Historical Thought," and Novick, *That Noble Dream*, 26–31.

40. On Niebuhr's popularity in the United States, see Callcott, *History in the United States*, 10. For the particular influence of Niebuhr on southern historical writing, see Michael O'Brien, *Conjectures of Order*, 604–605. For reviews of Niebuhr, see "Niebuhr's Roman History"; Howes, "History of Rome"; "Niebuhr's Lectures on Roman History"; Edward Everett, "Niebuhr's Roman History"; and "Ante-Roman Races of Italy." For translations of Ranke's histories published in the United States, see Leopold von Ranke, *The Ecclesiastical and Political History of the Popes of Rome during the Sixteenth and Seventeenth Centuries*, trans. Sarah Austin (Philadelphia: Lea and Blanchard, 1841); Ranke, *History of the Reformation in Germany*, trans. Sarah Austin (Philadelphia: Lea and Blanchard, 1844); and Ranke, *Civil Wars and Monarchy in France*, trans. M. A. Garvey (New York: Harper and Brothers, 1853). For American works that refer to Ranke, see, for example, Bancroft, *History of the United States*, 4:280n1; Motley, *Rise of the Dutch Republic*, 2:228, 231n, 233n; Prescott, *History of the Reign of Philip the Second*, 1:67n28; Palfrey, *History of New England*, 1:239n1; Perkins, "Gregory the Seventh and His Age";

and "Reading of History." For reviews and notices of Ranke's works in American periodicals, see Review of *Princes and Nations of the South of Europe in the Sixteenth and Seventeenth Centuries* by Leopold von Ranke; "Editorial Notes: Literature," *Putnam's Monthly Magazine of American Literature, Science, and Art* 2 (August 1853): 220; and "Literary Notices," *New Englander and Yale Review* 11 (November 1853): 643.

41. On the impact of their Göttingen experiences on these thinkers, see Foletta, *Coming to Terms with Democracy*, 51–57. On these thinkers' desire to import what they had learned in Germany to the United States, see Callcott, *History in the United States*, 10. On the influence of German critical scholarship on these historians, see Donald Kelley, *Fortunes of History*, 285–90. On Bancroft's relationship to German philosophy and thought and his admiration for Heeren in particular, see Handlin, *George Bancroft*, 65–66, 100–101; Nye, *George Bancroft: Brahmin Rebel*, 32–58; Wish, *American Historian*, 71–75; and Rathbun, "George Bancroft on Man and History," 51–56, 62–66.

42. On the differences between Germany on the one hand and the rest of Europe and United States on the other in the status of history as a profession, see Iggers, *Historiography in the Twentieth Century*, 27, and Iggers, *New Directions in European Historiography*, 25.

43. Kenyon, *History Men*, 60–61, 148–54; Donald Kelley, *Fortunes of History*, 226.

44. Gooch, *History and Historians in the Nineteenth Century*, 12; Donald Kelley, *Fortunes of History*, 28–29; den Boer, *History as a Profession*, 118–19.

45. On the involvement of French historians in politics, see Iggers, *Historiography in the Twentieth Century*, 27. Specifically on Thierry, Guizot, and Michelet, see Donald Kelley, *Fortunes of History*, 145–72; Thompson, *History of Historical Writing* 2:227–42, 257–63; and Gooch, *History and Historians in the Nineteenth Century*, 162–84.

46. On the influence of French historians on early nineteenth-century American historical writing, see Callcott, *History in the United States*, 10–11. For reviews of Guizot, see, for example, Arnold, "Cromwell and the Revolution"; Edward Everett, "Guizot's Washington"; Lunt, "Review of Carlyle's Edition"; C. C. Smith, "Guizot on the English Revolution"; "Cromwell and His Times"; "General History of Civilization in Europe," *Princeton Review*; "Guizot's Essay on Washington"; "Guizot's Washington"; "History of the English Revolution of 1640"; and "General History of Civilization in Europe," *Southern Quarterly Review*. For reviews of Michelet, see, for example, Brownson, "Remarks on Universal History"; "Michelet's Works"; and "Reformation the Source of American Liberty." For references by American historical writers to Thierry, see William Prescott to Augustin Thierry, 29 June 1840, in Wolcott, *Correspondence of William Hickling Prescott*, 139–40, and Simms, "Prescott's Conquest of Peru," 138. For translations of works by these historians published in the United States, see Jules Michelet, *Modern History* (New York: Harper and Brothers, 1855); Michelet, *Life of Martin Luther*, trans. G. H. Smith (New York: D. Appleton and Co., 1846); Michelet, *Women of the French Revolution*, trans. Meta Roberts Pennington (Philadelphia: H. C. Baird, 1855); Augustin Thierry, *Historical Essays* (Philadelphia: Carey and Hart, 1845); François Guizot, *History of the English Revolution of 1640* (New York: D. Appleton and Co., 1846); Guizot, *History of Oliver Cromwell and the*

English Commonwealth (Philadelphia: Blanchard and Lea, 1854); Guizot, *General History of Civilization in Europe*, 2nd ed. (New York: D. Appleton and Co., 1840); and Guizot, *Essay on the Character and Influence of Washington in the Revolution of the United States of America*, trans. George Stillman Hillard (Boston: J. Munroe and Co., 1840).

47. On Hallam's and Lingard's background and purposes, see Donald Kelley, *Fortunes of History*, 95–96, 99–102; Kenyon, *History Men*, 70–71, 89–100; Gooch, *History and Historians in the Nineteenth Century*, 265–76; Thompson, *History of Historical Writing* 2:184–87, 569–71; and Lang, *Victorians and the Stuart Heritage: Interpretations of a Discordant Past*, 26–29. See Edward Brooks, "Constitutional History," for a review of both Hallam and Lingard. For other reviews of Hallam, see "Hallam's Constitutional History"; "Constitutional History of England"; "Italy in the Middle Ages"; and "Review of Hallam's View of the State of Europe during the Middle Ages." For a review of Lingard, see "Lingard's History of England." For editions of Lingard's and Hallam's histories published in the United States, see John Lingard, *Abridgement of the History of England* (Baltimore: J. Murphy and Co., 1855); Henry Hallam, *View of the State of Europe during the Middle Ages* (Philadelphia: T. Dobson, 1821); and Hallam, *The Constitutional History of England* (Boston: Wells and Lilly, 1829). On Carlyle as a historian, see Gooch, *History and Historians in the Nineteenth Century*, 301–9; Thompson, *History of Historical Writing* 2:301–3; and Kenyon, *History Men*, 100–111. Reviews of Carlyle's works include "Carlyle's Cromwell"; Lunt, "Review of Carlyle's Edition"; Arnold, "Cromwell and the Revolution"; Ralph Waldo Emerson, "French Revolution"; W. B. O. Peabody, "Carlyle's Letters of Cromwell"; "Carlyle's French Revolution"; "Cromwell and His Times"; "Oliver Cromwell"; "Cromwell's Letters and Speeches."

48. On the reception for Macaulay's history in America, see Clark, "Vogue of Macaulay in America." On Macaulay's conception of history and its relationship to his political activities, see Donald Kelley, *Fortunes of History*, 106–11, and Hamburger, *Macaulay and the Whig Tradition*, esp. 73–113. For further discussion of Macaulay as a historian, see Kenyon, *History Men*, 73–87, and Gooch, *History and Historians in the Nineteenth Century*, 276–85.

49. George Bancroft to William Prescott, 11 Jan. 1849, in Mark Anthony de Wolfe Howe, *Life and Letters of George Bancroft*, 2:43–44.

50. On the emergence of historical societies in this period, see Callcott, *History in the United States*, 36–43, and Van Tassel, *Recording America's Past*, 95–102.

51. Van Tassel, *Recording America's Past*, 103–7.

52. On the membership of these societies and the nonprofessional character of history in this period, see Callcott, *History in the United States*, 37, 68–71. On the development of historical societies in the South and the limits to that development, see Michael O'Brien, *Conjectures of Order*, 623–33.

53. Callcott, *History in the United States*, 57–59.

54. Donald Kelley, *Fortunes of History*, 285; Stevens, "Jared Sparks," 308; and Herbert Baxter Adams, *Life and Writings of Jared Sparks*, 2:369.

55. On the status of history as a discipline at the college level in the United States, see

Callcott, *History in the United States*, 59–61, and Kraus and Joyce, *Writing of American History*, 141–43. On the status of history in southern colleges and the continued associa-tion of history with other disciplines, see Michael O'Brien, *Conjectures of Order*, 622–23.

56. Daniel Walker Howe, *Unitarian Conscience*, 14, 309.

57. Stevens, "Jared Sparks," 308.

58. On this point, I differ from Donald Kelley, *Fortunes of History* (289), who points to how the friendship among these historians made them unwilling to criticize one another.

59. On Sparks's centrality to the writing of historical biography in particular, see Casper, *Constructing American Lives*, 152; and on his leading role in the establishment of history as an autonomous discipline, see Conn, *History's Shadow*, 200.

60. William Prescott to Jared Sparks, 1 Feb. 1841, in Wolcott, *Correspondence of Wil-liam Hickling Prescott*, 203–4.

61. Alexander Everett to Jared Sparks, 2 Sept. 1828, Alexander Hill Everett Letters, Massachusetts Historical Society, Boston, microfilm reel 2, vol. 11. See Donald Kelley, *For-tunes of History*, 289, on how this circle of historians endorsed one another's histories.

62. H. C. Van Schaack to Jared Sparks, 18 May 1842, Sparks Papers, MS Sparks 153. By permission of the Houghton Library, Harvard University.

63. Specifically on southern resentment at New England dominance in the domain of historical interpretation, see Bonner, "Americans Apart," 203–4. See Casper, *Con-structing American Lives*, 137, 178–92, on how southern biographers both adapted and departed from the standards of New England biography in their efforts to resist north-ern cultural imperialism. On the South's anxieties about both its cultural inferiority and northern cultural imperialism in general, see Faust, *Sacred Circle*, 7–11, and McCardell, *Idea of a Southern Nation*, 141–65.

64. William Henry Trescot to George Bancroft, 19 Oct. 1852; William B. Reed to George Bancroft, 20 Mar. 1848; Reed to Bancroft, 18 Mar. 1850, all in Bancroft Papers.

65. William Gilmore Simms to Nathaniel Beverly Tucker, 13 May 1849, in Simms, *Letters*, 2:526; William Gilmore Simms to John Pendleton Kennedy, 5 Apr. 1852, in ibid., 3:174–75. On Simms's criticism of Bancroft's bias, see Wakelyn, *Politics of a Literary Man*, 118. On Simms's centrality to southern historical writing and his relationship to other historians of his time, see Busick, *Sober Desire for History*, xi, 16–28. On the develop-ment of a sense of scholarly community among southern historians and the conflicts within that community, and, in general, on both the sectional orientation of southern intellectual life and the limited efforts that southern intellectuals made to reach out to their northern counterparts in his analysis of the regional origins of contributors to southern periodicals, see Michael O'Brien, *Conjectures of Order*, 545–47, 635–36.

66. William Gilmore Simms to George Bancroft, 26 Jan. 1858, in Simms, *Letters*, 4:15; William Gilmore Simms to George Bancroft, 19 Aug. 1858, in Simms, *Letters*, 4:92–93.

67. William Prescott to George Bancroft, 16 Dec. 1837, Bancroft Papers.

68. On the sectional bias of the *North American Review*, as well as of New England historical writing in general, see Sheidley, *Sectional Nationalism*, 99–147. And, as Mi-chael O'Brien, *Conjectures of Order* (547), notes, only about 1 percent of the contributors

to the *North American Review* were southern, revealing even more clearly its section-ally exclusive character. For these reviews, see Perkins, "Border War of the Revolution," 277–317; Upham, "History of Virginia and Georgia"; Upham, "Reed's Life of President Reed"; and Felton, "Simms's Stories and Reviews," 357–81.

69. Bancroft to Campbell, 16 July 1846, Bancroft Papers. Sparks to Campbell, 12 Sept. 1843, Sparks Papers, MS Sparks 147h. By permission of the Houghton Library, Harvard University. Jared Sparks to William Stevens, 28 Sept. 1841, Sparks Papers, MS Sparks 147g. By permission of the Houghton Library, Harvard University. For background on Stevens, see W. Todd Groce, "William Stevens," *The New Georgia Encyclopedia*, http://www.georgiaencyclopedia.org/nge/Article.jsp?id=h-2896 (29 Aug. 2007).

70. On how such claims for the primacy of the Union could be at once sectional and national, see Sheidley's discussion of Sparks's contemporary Daniel Webster in Sheidley, *Sectional Nationalism*, 148–68.

71. Jared Sparks to Edward Everett, 3 Jan. 1853, Sparks Papers, MS Sparks 147j. By permission of the Houghton Library, Harvard University.

72. Jared Sparks to William Trescot, 1 Sept. 1852, Sparks Papers, MS Sparks 147j. By permission of the Houghton Library, Harvard University.

73. Jared Sparks to William Trescot, 31 Mar. 1852, Sparks Papers, MS Sparks 147j. By permission of the Houghton Library, Harvard University.

74. Francis Bowen to Lorenzo Sabine, 25 Oct. 1844, Sabine Papers.

75. Bowen to Sabine, 25 Oct. 1844, Sabine Papers.

76. On how New England Federalists responded to these changes, see Foletta, *Coming to Terms with Democracy*, 1–75. See Sheidley, *Sectional Nationalism*, 17–19, on the impact of the War of 1812 and the Hartford Convention on the Massachusetts elite.

77. On the Whig appeal to history, see Daniel Walker Howe, *Political Culture of the American Whigs*, 69–95, and Matthews, "Whig History."

78. See Foletta, *Coming to Terms with Democracy*, 4–7, 70, on the Federalist commitment to deferential politics and classical republican ideals of virtue, and Sheidley, *Sectional Nationalism*, ix–xii, 47–51, on the efforts of the Massachusetts elite to maintain these ideals against the challenges posed by the market revolution and the rise of democracy.

79. On the Whigs' political ideology and their efforts to combine the old and the new, see Daniel Walker Howe, *Political Culture of the American Whigs*, esp. 8–9, 11–68, 96–122. See Sheidley, *Sectional Nationalism*, 9–16, on how the Massachusetts elite sought to reconcile republican ideals with their own participation in the market revolution.

80. Jared Sparks to Lafayette, 25 Mar. 1834, Sparks Papers, MS Sparks 147f. By permission of the Houghton Library, Harvard University. On how Sparks and other New England Federalists of his generation sought to adapt their deferential vision of politics to democracy, see Foletta, *Coming to Terms with Democracy*, esp. 2–16, 45–75.

81. On Bancroft's political career, see Wood, "George Bancroft," 16–17, and Nye, *George Bancroft: Brahmin Rebel*, 85–183. On how Bancroft reconciled his political with his historical activities, see Handlin, *George Bancroft*, 115–45.

82. Charles C. Hazewell to Lorenzo Sabine, 19 Dec. 1852, Sabine Papers.

83. William Prescott to Edward Everett, 28 Sept. 1840, in Wolcott, *Correspondence of William Hickling Prescott*, 162.

84. William Prescott to George Bancroft, 29 May 1838, Bancroft Papers; Prescott to Bancroft, 12 Jan. 1838, Bancroft Papers.

85. Francis Bowen to Lorenzo Sabine, April 1844, Sabine Papers. On how Prescott's choice of a historical career represented an effort to adapt his Federalist background and principles to democracy, see Foletta, *Coming to Terms with Democracy*, 214–15.

86. On Prescott's ambivalence about the relationship between his literary activities and his sense of public duty, see Foletta, *Coming to Terms with Democracy*, 213–15.

87. On this controversy, see Daniel Walker Howe, *Unitarian Conscience*, 309–10.

88. Edward Everett to Lord Mahon, 9 Dec. 1845, Edward Everett Papers, Massachusetts Historical Society, Boston (hereafter cited as Edward Everett Papers), microfilm reel 27, vol. 77. On how Everett at once reconciled his literary and political aspirations and revealed the tensions between them, see Foletta, *Coming to Terms with Democracy*, 216–19.

89. On the tensions between Whig ideology and party politics, see Daniel Walker Howe, *Political Culture of the American Whigs*, 43–48. See also Sheidley, *Sectional Nationalism*, 64–85, on the tensions between the Massachusetts elite's commitment to a deferential politics of virtue and the demands of party politics.

90. Jared Sparks to John Bowring, 1 Jan. 1838, Sparks Papers, MS Sparks 147g. By permission of the Houghton Library, Harvard University.

91. See Sheidley, *Sectional Nationalism*, 86–91, on the Massachusetts elite's view of culture as a political vehicle. On the moral purposes that these New England intellectuals assigned to literature, and the importance of literature as a way to express and promote virtue, see Foletta, *Coming to Terms with Democracy*, 88–100; Daniel Walker Howe, *Unitarian Conscience*, 174–204; and Field, "Birth of Secular High Culture," 578–95. On how the Brahmin elites substituted culture for politics as a source of social authority, see Field, *Crisis of the Standing Order*, 85–110.

92. Alexander Everett to Jared Sparks, 18 Nov. 1826, Alexander Hill Everett Letters, Massachusetts Historical Society, Boston, microfilm reel 2. On the importance of the *North American Review* to the cultural purposes of these New England intellectuals, see Sheidley, *Sectional Nationalism*, 97–116, and Foletta, *Coming to Terms with Democracy*, 73–80.

93. William Gilmore Simms to Nathaniel Beverly Tucker, 15 Mar. 1849, in Simms, *Letters*, 2:496. On Simms's moral conception of politics and his belief in the importance of periodicals as instruments for moral improvement, see Faust, *Sacred Circle*, 87–111. On the mixture of democracy and elitism that characterized southern periodicals, see Michael O'Brien, *Conjectures of Order*, 550–53.

94. Mott, *History of American Magazines*, 722, 231–32. On the importance of periodicals to southern intellectual life, see Michael O'Brien, *Conjectures of Order*, 529–53.

95. On the changing character of the market for literature in this period, see Gilmore, *American Romanticism and the Marketplace*, 1–5; Mary Kelley, *Private Woman, Public*

Stage, 7–12; Charvat, *Literary Publishing in America*, 17–60; and Tebbel, *History of Book Publishing in the United States*, 203–62. On the expansion and centralization of the market for books in this period, see Casper, *Constructing American Lives*, 78–81.

96. William Prescott to George Bancroft, 20 Dec. 1837, Bancroft Papers. On Prescott's concern with the marketing and appearance of his books, see C. Harvey Gardiner, *Prescott and His Publishers*, 135–201.

97. Kraus, and Joyce, *Writing of American History*, 104. On the popular appeal of history in this period, see also Charvat, *Literary Publishing in America*, 74–75.

98. For these numbers, see Stevens, "Jared Sparks," 307, and Wish, *American Historian*, 50.

99. Callcott, *History in the United States*, 32–33; Mott, *Golden Multitudes*, 307, 317, 318; Pearce, *Savagism and Civilization*, 118.

100. On how the Massachusetts elite used these celebrations to disseminate their views on history, see Sheidley, *Sectional Nationalism*, 134–41. On the historical character of Fourth of July orations, see Somkin, *Unquiet Eagle*, 177, and Welter, *Mind of America*, 396. On the importance of Fourth of July and other nationalist celebrations to the political culture of the early republic, see Waldstreicher, *In the Midst of Perpetual Fetes*, and Travers, *Celebrating the Fourth*.

101. George Edward Ellis, "Oliver's Puritan Commonwealth," 427. On the role of these commemorative orations as instruments for inculcating and defining national and sectional identity, see Sheidley, *Sectional Nationalism*, 134–47; Curti, *Roots of American Loyalty*, 137–41; and Welter, *Mind of America*, 396. On the tendency of such commemorative works to be more "overblown" and heroic in their language than formal historical writing in the early republic, see Purcell, *Sealed with Blood*, 5. On the filiopietistic character of these orations and their role in glorifying the Puritans, see Buell, *New England Literary Culture*, 197–200, 224.

102. William Prescott to Washington Irving, 10 May 1842, in Wolcott, *Correspondence of William Hickling Prescott*, 303.

103. George Edward Ellis, "Oliver's Puritan Commonwealth," 427. For other writers who implicated these orations in the idealization of the Puritans, see "Politics of the Puritans," 50, and "Puritanism," 372. While Peter Oliver's main target of attack was Bancroft, he also attributed the idealization of the Puritans to "fourth of July hyperboles" in his "Charter of the Massachusetts Bay Company," 527.

104. On other ways in which the elite used these celebrations to maintain their superiority to ordinary people, see Sheidley, *Sectional Nationalism*, 140–43. See Foletta, *Coming to Terms with Democracy*, on the ambivalence of New England Federalist intellectuals about democracy in general. On the ambivalence of New England intellectuals about the filiopietism expressed in these orations, see Buell, *New England Literary Culture*, 201–6.

105. Edward Everett to H. H. Milman, 21 May 1849, Edward Everett Papers, microfilm reel 29, vol. 89. On popular history in this period, see Van Tassel, *Recording America's Past*, 87–94.

106. On Headley's popular success, see Owen Connelly and Jesse Scott, "Joel T. Headley," in *American Historians, 1607–1865*, vol. 30 of *Dictionary of Literary Biography*, 107–10, and Mott, *Golden Multitudes*, 96, 307.

107. Joel Tyler Headley to Jared Sparks, 30 Dec. 1846, Sparks Papers, MS Sparks 153. By permission of the Houghton Library, Harvard University.

108. Jared Sparks to Joel Tyler Headley, 14 July 1847, Sparks Papers, MS Sparks 147h. By permission of the Houghton Library, Harvard University.

109. "Headley's Histories," 85, 88–89, 102. For other reviews of Headley, see "Life of Oliver Cromwell," *Princeton Review*; "Life of Oliver Cromwell," *Graham's American Monthly Magazine*; "Life of Cromwell," *American Literary Magazine*; "Martial Men and Martial Books"; "Washington and the Generals of the American Revolution"; "Headley's Writings"; "Washington and His Generals"; "Mr. Headley's New Book"; Simms, "Headley's Life of Cromwell"; and Minor, "Washington and His Generals."

110. Baym, *American Women Writers and the Work of History*. On the exclusion of women from the *North American Review*, see Foletta, *Coming to Terms with Democracy*, 103–9. See also Douglas, *Feminization of American Culture*, 169–99, on the opposition between the masculine character of Brahmin scholarly history and the local, "antiquarian," or social forms of history produced by women and clergymen in this period.

111. Jared Sparks to Elizabeth Ellet, 13 Dec. 1850, Sparks Papers, MS Sparks 147i. By permission of the Houghton Library, Harvard University. On Ellet's ambivalent relationship with Sparks and his scholarly circle, see Casper, *Constructing American Lives*, 158–78.

112. Elizabeth Ellet to Jared Sparks, 6 May 1850, Sparks Papers, MS Sparks 153. By permission of the Houghton Library, Harvard University.

113. On the feminine associations of the novel, see Davidson, *Revolution and the Word*, 110–50; Kerber, *Women of the Republic*, 235–64; and Joseph Ellis, *After the Revolution*, 95–97.

114. On the treatment of novels by the *North American Review*, see Foletta, *Coming to Terms with Democracy*, 103–12. For examples of such reviews, see William Howard Gardiner, "Cooper's Novels"; William Howard Gardiner, Review of *The Spy*; Greenwood, Review of *Hope Leslie*; Hillard, Review of *Clarence*; Gray, Review of *The Rebels*; Willard Phillips, Review of *The Pilot*.

115. Jared Sparks to Catharine Sedgwick, 28 Oct. 1833, Sparks Papers, MS Sparks 147f. By permission of the Houghton Library, Harvard University. Foletta, *Coming to Terms with Democracy*, 105–8.

116. For a discussion of how Hawthorne challenged patriotic mythology about American history, see Bell, *Hawthorne and the Historical Romance of New England*, and Colacurcio, *The Province of Piety*. While Philip Gould recognizes the complex relationship between historical novels and histories in the early republic and the way they influenced each other, he also differentiates between historical novels and histories and identifies "revisionist" history with novels in his argument that novels "provided greater flexibility" than histories "as a medium for dissent" (13). See Gould, *Covenant and Repub-*

lic, esp. 9–13, and Gould, "Catharine Sedgwick's 'Recital' of the Pequot War." Likewise, Colacurcio emphasizes how Hawthorne departed from contemporary historiography in his critical perspective on American history, but as David Levin argues, in depicting this perspective as unique to Hawthorne, Colacurcio oversimplifies or neglects the views of other historical writers—both novelists and historians—who had already begun to question patriotic mythology about American history (283–84). See David Levin, "The Province of Historical Criticism: Historical Fact in Hawthorne and Colacurcio," in *Forms of Uncertainty*, 279–88. Buell, *New England Literary Culture* (214–38), in contrast, recognizes the complexity of early national historiography about the Puritans and shows how novels of the period reflected that complexity.

TWO. "Histories in Novels," "Novels in Histories"

1. "Thacher's History of Plymouth," 443–44.

2. On the implications of an expressive theory of art for British historical writing in this period, see Phillips, "Macaulay, Scott, and the Literary Challenge to Historiography."

3. On how the Revolutionary historians brought together these two conceptions of the historian's role, see Cohen, *Revolutionary Histories*, 163–67.

4. John Adams to Thomas McKean, 31 Aug. 1813, in Charles Francis Adams, *Works of John Adams*, 10:62. For further background on the rise of the novel in the early American republic and the opposition this development provoked, see Davidson, *Revolution and the Word*; Cowie, *Rise of the American Novel*, 1–37; Herbert Ross Brown, *Sentimental Novel in America*; Petter, *Early American Novel*; and Orians, "Censure of Fiction in American Romances and Magazines." On the concern of the Revolutionary historians to distinguish their works from novels and romances, see Cohen, *Revolutionary Histories*, 217–19.

5. Modern scholars have differed over how to define the novel, in particular over the relationship between the novel and the romance. Because my concern is with how early national historians defined history in relation to the novel, my analysis focuses on the characteristics that these historians associated with the novel, rather than trying to answer the question of what really distinguished the novel from other fictional genres. And because early national historians themselves did not clearly differentiate between the "novel" and "romance," I use the term *novel* broadly to include books that are often categorized as romances, such as the works of Sir Walter Scott and James Fenimore Cooper. On the emergence of the novel and the way in which Fielding and Richardson sought to differentiate their works from romances, see Watt, *Rise of the Novel*. On the opposition between the novel and the romance and the blurring of that opposition, see Dekker, *American Historical Romance*, 14–28. For the different meanings of the term *romance*, see *Oxford English Dictionary Online*. On the complex meanings of this term in late seventeenth-century and early eighteenth-century England and the generic instability signified by those meanings, see McKeon, *Origins of the English Novel*, esp. 25–64.

For differing views of the relationship between the novel and the romance, see Lennard Davis, *Factual Fictions*, 25–41, and Frye, *Anatomy of Criticism*, 303–14. See Martin, *Instructed Vision*, 58–59, on how early national American critics of fiction blurred the distinction between novel and romance. See also Chase, *American Novel and Its Tradition*, 1–28, and Perry Miller, "The Romance and the Novel," 241–78, on the relationship between the novel and the romance in American literature.

6. Samuel Miller, *Brief Retrospect of the Eighteenth Century*, 2:176. On the suspicion of novels as works of the imagination, see Joseph Ellis, *After the Revolution*, 95. See Martin, *Instructed Vision*, 54–103, 153, and Charvat, *Origins of American Critical Thought*, esp. 135–59, on the importance of common sense philosophy to early hostility to the novel. On the more general influence of common sense philosophy in this period, see Wills, *Inventing America*, and May, *Enlightenment in America*, 337–57. See also Daniel Walker Howe, *Unitarian Conscience*, 27–44, on the assumptions and influence of common sense philosophy in the early nineteenth century. For a different perspective on the rise of this opposition between history and fiction, see Hayden White, "The Fictions of Factual Representation," in *Tropics of Discourse*, 122–25. On the development of an increasing sense of distinction between history and fiction in early modern England, see Shapiro, *Culture of Fact*, 59, 40–42.

7. For background on Belknap and his historical views, see Louis Tucker, *Clio's Consort*; Kirsch, "Jeremy Belknap"; and Frank Meers, "Jeremy Belknap," in *American Historians, 1607–1865*, 30–33.

8. Hayden White, "The Irrational and the Problem of Historical Knowledge in the Enlightenment," in *Tropics of Discourse*, 142.

9. Belknap, *History of New Hampshire*, viii.

10. Ibid. See Kamrath, "Charles Brockden Brown and the 'art of the historian,'" 237–38, on the limits to the Revolutionary historians' willingness to acknowledge a role for fiction in history, though he attributes this tendency to a lack of interest in epistemological questions about the nature of truth, whereas I attribute to the Revolutionary historians both a more conscious desire to differentiate history from fiction and a greater ambivalence about this relationship. On Belknap's view of history as literary art and his use of anecdotes to make the past come to life for the reader, see Kaplan, "*History of New Hampshire*."

11. Burk, *History of Virginia*, 1:188. For background on Burk, see *Dictionary of American Biography*, 1929 ed., s.v. "Burk, John Daly." For further discussion of the tendency among the Revolutionary historians to distinguish history from romance, see Cohen, *Revolutionary Histories*, 212–19, 275–77.

12. See Phillips, *Society and Sentiment*, 21–32, and Phillips, "Macaulay, Scott, and the Literary Challenge to Historiography," 120. On these tensions, see also Shapiro, *Culture of Fact*, 59. For further discussion of this exemplary theory of history, see Nadel, "Philosophy of History before Historicism." On the importance of the exemplary theory to the Revolutionary historians, see Cohen, *Revolutionary Histories*, 188–211, and Cohen, "Explaining the Revolution." On Enlightenment historical writing in general, see Trevor-Roper, "Historical Philosophy of the Enlightenment."

13. Burk, *History of Virginia*, 1:iii.

14. On how the Revolutionary historians reconciled their belief in the moral function of history with their commitment to impartial truth, see Cohen, *Revolutionary Histories*, 161–67, 181–88, 212–19. On how Enlightenment historians at once emphasized the importance of factual accuracy and believed that history involved more than just the collection of facts, see Stromberg, "History in the Eighteenth Century." On how history came to be viewed as a branch of natural philosophy during the eighteenth century, and on how historians in this period sought to reconcile their belief in the moral function of history with their view of history as a science, see Nadel, "Philosophy of History before Historicism," 311–15, though Nadel ultimately emphasizes the difficulties involved in this endeavor. See Shapin, *Scientific Revolution*, 5–6, on the use of the term *natural philosophy* to denote science.

15. Burk, *History of Virginia*, 2:178. On how the assumption of a universal human nature and the desire to use history to improve society limited the historical consciousness of Enlightenment historians, see Stromberg, "History in the Eighteenth Century," 301–4.

16. For further discussion of the assumptions and purposes of the Scottish conjectural historians, see Poovey, *History of the Modern Fact*, 214–49, and Phillips, *Society and Sentiment*, 171–89.

17. On the moral concerns of the Scottish conjectural historians, see Poovey, *History of the Modern Fact*, 218–26, and Phillips, *Society and Sentiment*, 171–73. Specifically on Smith's desire to promote morality and virtue, see Phillipson, "Adam Smith as Civic Moralist," 179–202.

18. Mercy Otis Warren to Mary Warren, November 1791, Mercy Otis Warren Letterbook, Mercy Otis Warren Papers, Massachusetts Historical Society, Boston, microfilm reel 1, p. 486.

19. On Warren's view of history as an alternative to fiction, see Kerber, *Women of the Republic*, 246–47. On the opposition between history and the novel as reading matter for women, see Baym, *American Women Writers and the Work of History*, 14–23. See Watt, *Rise of the Novel*, 174–207, on the private character of the novel. On how the association of the novel with both women and the private sphere contributed to the belief that novels were frivolous and immoral, see Michael Gilmore, "Literature of the Revolutionary and Early National Periods," in Bercovitch, *Cambridge History of American Literature*, 1:621–22.

20. On the roots of this ambivalence about the relationship between embellishment and the historian's responsibility to provide a faithful record of fact in early modern English historical writing, see Shapiro, *Culture of Fact*, 58–59.

21. On the complex relationship between gender and the novel and the tendency to associate novels with women, see Davidson, *Revolution and the Word*, 110–50; Kerber, *Women of the Republic*, 235–64; and Joseph Ellis, *After the Revolution*, 95–97.

22. See Woolf, "Feminine Past?" for a discussion of the close relationship between the definition of history as a genre and the development of modern gender ideology in early modern England. On the close association between reason, historical truth, and

men in British historical writing of this period and the way in which the opposition between history and novel symbolized the differences between men and women, see Phillips, *Society and Sentiment*, 103–4, 114. For an important and provocative analysis of the way in which the ideal of historical truth has been defined in terms of gender, see Bonnie Smith, *Gender of History*. On the exclusion of women as actors in the public realm of history by provincial American and loyalist historians, see Messer, "Writing Women into History," 341–47.

23. Warren, *History of the Rise, Progress, and Termination of the American Revolution*, 1:xli–xlii. See Baym, "Mercy Otis Warren's Gendered Melodrama of Revolution," 531–54, and Baym, *American Women Writers and the Work of History*, 31, for a discussion that emphasizes the way in which Warren upheld traditional ideas about women.

24. Warren, *History of the Rise, Progress, and Termination of the American Revolution*, 1:xliii.

25. Ibid., 1:xlii. See Burstein, "Political Character of Sympathy," 606–9, on the importance of sympathy to Warren. On how Warren justified her work as a historian by defining citizenship in terms of feminine traits and appealing to sympathy as a basis for women's claims to virtue and republican citizenship, see Messer, "Writing Women into History," 351–56, and Messer, *Stories of Independence*, 133–35. On the feminine associations of sympathy in general, and the way in which British historical writers of this period used these associations to include women as readers of history, see Phillips, *Society and Sentiment*, 103–28.

26. Warren, *History of the Rise, Progress, and Termination of the American Revolution*, 1:324.

27. See Davidson, *Revolution and the Word*, 50–51, for a discussion of how novelists in this period sought to counter criticism of the novel by emphasizing their moral purposes.

28. David Ramsay to John Coakley Lettsom, 29 Oct. 1808, in Brunhouse, "David Ramsay," 163. For a discussion of how this statement revealed both Ramsay's commitment to objective truth and his recognition of the artistic element to history, see Cohen, *Revolutionary Histories*, 217–18.

29. See Davidson, *Revolution and the Word*, 38–40, 50–53; Kerber, *Women of the Republic*, 248–64; and Kamrath, "Charles Brockden Brown and the 'art of the historian,'" 236–38, on how novelists legitimized their works by emphasizing their basis in truth. On the concern with realism as a distinguishing trait of the novel, see Watt, *Rise of the Novel*, 9–34. On the similarities between history and the novel in this period and the complex relationship between these similarities and efforts to differentiate between the two genres, see Braudy, *Narrative Form in History and Fiction*, esp. 3–13.

30. Philip Gould, *Covenant and Republic* (7–13), discusses the complex relationship between history and fiction in this period, as historians and novelists alike simultaneously equated and distinguished these two genres. On the American reaction to Scott in this period, see Orians, "Romance Ferment after *Waverly*." On the influence of Scott in the development of the American historical novel, see Dekker, *American Historical*

Romance, 29–72. Specifically on how Scott influenced American historical writing in this period, see Callcott, *History in the United States*, 11–13; Levin, *History as Romantic Art*, 9–13, 236; and Kraus, *Writing of American History*, 139, 145.

31. On how Scott's use of history contributed to the growing acceptance of the novel, see Phillips, "Macaulay, Scott, and the Literary Challenge to Historiography," 127–28, and Orians, "Romance Ferment after *Waverly*," 409.

32. See Baym, *Novels, Readers, and Reviewers*, 26–43, on the accommodation that critics of this period reached with fiction and the growing acceptance of novels in the antebellum period.

33. Francis Bowen to John Gorham Palfrey, 20 Nov. 1857, Palfrey Family Papers, Houghton Library, Harvard University, bMS 1704. By permission of the Houghton Library, Harvard University. On this Romantic conception of history as art, see in particular Levin, *History as Romantic Art*, esp. 3–23, and Callcott, *History in the United States*, 139–50.

34. On the distinction between expressive and mimetic theories of art and the complex implications of an expressive theory of art for ideas about truth, see Abrams, *The Mirror and the Lamp*, 8–14, 21–26, 30–69, 47–69, 298–326. On the implications of an expressive art for history, see Phillips, "Macaulay, Scott, and the Literary Challenge to Historiography," 122–24.

35. For background on Prescott, see C. Harvey Gardiner, *William Hickling Prescott: A Biography*. On Prescott as a historian, see Darnell, *William Hickling Prescott*, and especially Levin, *History as Romantic Art*, 163–85.

36. Phillips, "Macaulay, Scott, and the Literary Challenge to Historiography," 131.

37. Prescott, *History of the Conquest of Mexico*, 444. On how Prescott sought to describe scenes from the Spanish point of view, see Levin, *History as Romantic Art*, 170–71.

38. On the importance of Scott to the Romantic historians, see Callcott, *History in the United States*, 11–13, and Levin, *History as Romantic Art*, 9–13, 236. On how the novel contributed to this concern with inner experience, and on Scott's role in this development, see Phillips, "Macaulay, Scott, and the Literary Challenge to Historiography," 124–33.

39. William Hickling Prescott to Richard Bentley, 31 Dec. 1842, in Wolcott, *Correspondence of William Hickling Prescott*, 328. On how Romantic historians simultaneously likened their works to novels and emphasized the factual basis for their works in general, see Levin, *History as Romantic Art*, 11. For comparisons to how biographers, starting in the 1850s, imitated the novel in drawing on the imagination, while at the same time maintaining a firm commitment to truth, see Casper, *Constructing American Lives*, 212–13.

40. Prescott, *History of the Conquest of Mexico*, 4.

41. William Howard Gardiner to William Hickling Prescott, 27 Dec. 1843, in C. Harvey Gardiner, *Papers of William Hickling Prescott*, 213.

42. Hillard, "Prescott's History of the Conquest of Mexico," 161.

43. Whipple, "Prescott's Works," 13.

44. Ibid., 7.

45. Whipple, "Prescott's Conquest of Peru," 271

46. Whipple, "Prescott's Works," 12. On the importance of feeling and emotion to historians in this period in general, and on how they reconciled this emphasis on feeling with their belief in objective truth, see Callcott, *History in the United States*, 149–50.

47. Whipple, "Prescott's Conquest of Peru," 272.

48. C. Harvey Gardiner, *Literary Memoranda of William Hickling Prescott*, 1:139. For further discussion of how Prescott and other Romantic historians reconciled their belief in the moral function of history with their artistic purposes, see Levin, *History as Romantic Art*, 24–45.

49. Prescott, *History of the Conquest of Mexico*, 277–78.

50. Ibid., 278. On how historians in this period combined a belief in the moral function of history with a recognition of the need to judge historical actors according to the standards of their own time, see Callcott, *History in the United States*, 156–60. On how the Romantic historians reconciled their belief in the moral function of history with their commitment to impartiality, see Levin, *History as Romantic Art*, 25–27.

51. Prescott, *History of the Conquest of Mexico*, 6.

52. "Prescott's Conquest of Mexico," 190.

53. Ibid., 196.

54. Ibid., 190.

55. Parker, "Character of Mr. Prescott as an Historian," 219–20. Levin, *History as Romantic Art* (24–25), briefly discusses Parker's criticism of Prescott. On the political purposes that Parker sought to further in this review, see Teed, "Politics of Sectional Memory," 312–13.

56. Parker, "Character of Mr. Prescott as an Historian," 247.

57. Ibid., 220.

58. Ibid., 235.

59. Ibid., 220. On how some Romantic poets reconciled an expressive theory of art with their claims to truth by associating truth with a higher eternal reality, see Abrams, *The Mirror and the Lamp*, 312–13.

60. Parker, "Character of Mr. Prescott as an Historian," 223, 219.

61. For further background on Parker's social activism, see Henry Warner Bowden, "Parker, Theodore," *American National Biography Online*, February 2000, http://www.anb.org/articles/08/08-01925.html (27 July 2007).

62. On the earlier roots of this expansion in the definition of fact, see Shapiro, *Culture of Fact*, 39–40, 61–62. For further background on the changing and contested meanings of the very concept of fact in early modern and eighteenth-century England, see also Poovey, *History of the Modern Fact*.

63. On how Ellet brought together these two conceptions of truth, see Casper, "Uneasy Marriage of Sentiment and Scholarship," 10–28.

64. On the Enlightenment interest in social and cultural history, see Phillips, *Society and Sentiment*, 4–6, 15–19, 131–70, and Peter Burke, "Ranke the Reactionary," in Iggers

and Powell, *Leopold von Ranke*, 38–41. On the early origins of the interest in cultural history in general, see Peter Burke, "Reflections on the Origins of Cultural History," in Wear and Pittock, *Interpretation and Cultural History*, 5–24. On the eighteenth-century interest in social and cultural history and its connection to concerns about fiction, see Haywood, *Making of History*, 11–72. See Messer, *Stories of Independence*, 105–38, on the redefinition of virtue by the Revolutionary historians.

65. Phillipson, "Scottish Enlightenment." On changing ideas about virtue in this period, see Bloch, "Gendered Meanings of Virtue in Revolutionary America." On the importance of Scottish Enlightenment thought to understanding the Revolutionary historians' redefinition of virtue, see Messer, *Stories of Independence*, 141–43.

66. On the influence of the Romantic concern with the *Volksgeist* and Scott's influence on American historical writing of this period, see Callcott, *History in the United States*, 6–13. See Dekker, *American Historical Romance*, 30–32, 46, on Scott's contribution to the interest in the history of everyday life. On the growing American interest in folklore during this period, see Perry, *Boats against the Current*, 58–61.

67. Cooper, *Early Critical Essays*, 370. On this quotation, see Davidson, *Revolution and the Word*, 200.

68. On Macaulay as a historian and on his interest in social history, see especially George Levine, *Boundaries of Fiction*, 83–163, and Hamburger, *Macaulay and the Whig Tradition*, 21–113. On the reception for Macaulay's history in America, see Clark, "Vogue of Macaulay in America."

69. John Reuben Thompson, "History of England," 125. See Callcott, *History in the United States*, 104–7, for a general discussion of the trend in favor of social history.

70. Thomas Macaulay, "History," in Stern, *Varieties of History*, 86. See Levine, *History as Romantic Art*, 110–25, on the direct connection between Macaulay's attitude toward fiction and his interest in social history. On the importance of the novel to Macaulay's understanding of the historian's role, see Phillips, "Macaulay, Scott, and the Literary Challenge to Historiography," 117–23, 131–33. For another perspective on Macaulay's attitude toward fiction, see Jann, *Art and Science of Victorian History*, 66–103.

71. "Macaulay's History of England," 430.

72. On Hewes, and on Thatcher's portrayal of him, see Young, "George Robert Twelves Hewes," and Young, *The Shoemaker and the Tea Party*, 173–77. For additional background on Thatcher, see *Dictionary of American Biography*, 1935 ed., s.v. "Thatcher, Benjamin Bussey."

73. Thatcher, "History of Plymouth," 68.

74. Ibid., 66.

75. Leopold von Ranke, *Histories of the Latin and Germanic Nations from 1494–1514*, in Stern, *Varieties of History*, 57; Thatcher, "History of Plymouth," 68.

76. "Thacher's History of Plymouth," 462.

77. Ibid., 444.

78. On the trend in favor of local history, see Russo, *Keepers of Our Past*, 1–39. On the early development of local history, see Van Tassel, *Recording America's Past*, 46–58.

79. Burke, "Ranke the Reactionary," 41–43.

80. Iggers, *New Directions in European Historiography*, 17–25.

81. Ellet, *Domestic History*, v. For background on Ellet as a historian, see also Conrad, *Perish the Thought*, 116–22.

82. On Ellet as a historian and on her effort to integrate social and political history, see Kerber, "'History Can Do It No Justice,'" 3–42.

83. Ellet, *Domestic History*, vi.

84. Ibid., 66.

85. Ibid., vii.

86. Ellet, *Women of the American Revolution*, 1:xi.

87. Ellet, *Domestic History*, vi–vii.

88. Ellet, *Women of the American Revolution*, 1:ix. On Ellet's concern with establishing the truthfulness of her account and on her efforts to differentiate between "tradition" and "fact," see Casper, *Constructing American Lives*, 159, 162–63, 169.

89. On Ellet's use of the recollections of her subjects' descendants to access this realm of feeling, see Casper, *Constructing American Lives*, 163–65, 169–72.

90. Ellet, *Domestic History*, v–vi.

91. See especially Cott, *Bonds of Womanhood*, on the dual implications of domesticity.

92. On how Ellet upheld the assumptions of domesticity in her depictions of Revolutionary women, see Casper, *Constructing American Lives*, 165–69. See Douglas, *Feminization of American Culture*, 212–39, on how both women and ministers challenged the masculine emphasis of scholarly history in this period by focusing on domestic and social history. On the different ways that women historical writers in this period sought to insert women into the historical record, and on how Ellet differed from these writers in her concern with social history, see Baym, *American Women Writers and the Work of History*, 214–39. See also Baym, "Between Enlightenment and Victorian," on how antebellum women historical writers appealed to the belief in women's difference to assert a role for women in history.

93. On how Ellet sought to integrate the female world of domesticity with the male world of historical scholarship and the limits to her challenge to conventional definitions of history, see Casper, *Constructing American Lives*, 158–59, 173–78. For a discussion of how this scientific ideal of truth was defined in male terms by the late nineteenth century, and of how the dismissal of nineteenth-century women historical writers itself reflected and furthered this male definition of historical truth, see Bonnie Smith, *Gender of History*, 37–156.

94. On this hierarchy of genres and the concept of the dignity of history, see Phillips, *Society and Sentiment*, 24–26, 131–46.

95. On the hierarchical implications of the belief in the dignity of history, see ibid., 24–26. See, for example, Kerber, *Women of the Republic*, on how republican ideology at once excluded women from the political sphere and allowed them a limited political role. While Gordon Wood's *The Radicalism of the American Revolution* (95–109)

emphasizes the radical character of republican ideology, he acknowledges its "patrician bias" (106).

96. Samuel Johnson, *The Rambler*, in *The Works of Samuel Johnson: LL.D. A New Edition in Twelve Volumes. With an Essay on His Life by Arthur Murray* (London: F. C. and J. Rivington, 1823), 2:384, 382. On the belief that the private orientation of biography would make it more accessible to ordinary people, see Phillips, *Society and Sentiment*, 134–39. For a discussion of Johnson's influence over early national American biographical criticism, see Casper, *Constructing American Lives*, 33–34.

97. Weems, *Life of George Washington*, 9. On Weems's concern with Washington's private character, see Casper, *Constructing American Lives*, 68–76. On Weems's interest in the private side of Washington's character and the more general fascination with the private and the domestic in this period, see also Forgie, *Patricide in the House Divided*, 36–49, 161–90.

98. On how the novel contributed to the growing recognition of the importance of popular taste, and the way in which elites sought to accommodate this recognition, see Baym, *Novels, Readers, and Reviewers*, 27–35, 44–48. On the tensions that resulted from the effort to appeal to the people and at the same time assert superiority over them, see Sheidley, "Sectional Nationalism," 189–98.

99. "Biographical Mania," *New York Mirror, and Ladies' Literary Gazette*, 15 May 1830, 359. On the widespread interest in biography in general, see Callcott, *History in the United States*, 97–101; Casper, *Constructing American Lives*, 77–87; and Van Tassel, *Recording America's Past*, 66–76.

100. "American Biography," 4–5.

101. Oliver William B. Peabody, "Sparks's Life of Gouverneur Morris," 465.

102. Ibid. On how American biographical criticism in this period embraced the Johnsonian conception of biography as the record of private life, see Casper, *Constructing American Lives*, 35–38.

103. On the reasons for the disparity between the theory and practice of biography in this period, and the influence of classical republicanism on American biographers' concern with the public sphere, see Casper, *Constructing American Lives*, 38–46. On how antebellum New England Federalist intellectuals revealed a tension between their view of literature as an agent of public morality and a more privatized conception of the artist's function derived from Romanticism, see Foletta, *Coming to Terms with Democracy*, 114–23.

104. For background on Sparks, see Herbert Baxter Adams, *Life and Writings of Jared Sparks*, and Michael Stevens, "Jared Sparks," in *American Historians, 1607–1865*, 298–309.

105. Jared Sparks, advertisement, in Sparks, *Library of American Biography*, 1:iv.

106. Jared Sparks, "Historical Notes and Memoranda—Notes for a Course of Lectures, 1839–41," Sparks Papers, 5–6, MS Sparks 132. By permission of the Houghton Library, Harvard University.

107. Thomas Carlyle, "On History," in Stern, *Varieties of History*, 93.

108. On Sparks's editorial practices and their methodological context, see Herbert Baxter Adams, *Life and Writings of Jared Sparks*, 2:265–78, 479–506; Stevens, "Jared Sparks," 306–8; Cappon, "American Historical Editors before Jared Sparks"; Cappon, "Jared Sparks"; Bassett, *Middle Group of American Historians*, 100–113; and Wish, *American Historian*, 48–55.

109. Quoted in Lord Mahon, *History of England from the Peace of Utrecht to the Peace of Versailles, 1713–1783* (Boston: Little, Brown, 1853), 6: appendix, vi. On the controversy over Sparks's editorial practices, see Casper, *Constructing American Lives*, 193–201.

110. Sparks, "Mr. Wirt's Life of Patrick Henry," 294. On how this conception of truth contributed to Sparks's focus on the public sphere, see Casper, *Constructing American Lives*, 139–41.

111. Sparks, *Writings of George Washington*, 1:xiii.

112. Sparks, advertisement in *Library of American Biography*, 1:iv.

113. Sparks, "Historical Notes and Memoranda—Notes for a Course of Lectures, 1839–41," 7, Sparks Papers, MS Sparks 132. By permission of the Houghton Library, Harvard University. On the didactic understanding of biography in this period, see Casper, *Constructing American Lives*, 30–33.

114. Jared Sparks to George Bancroft, 22 Nov. 1832, Bancroft Papers. On Sparks's concern with popularity, see Casper, *Constructing American Lives*, 142.

115. Jared Sparks to Alexander Slidell Mackenzie, 28 Oct. 1839, Sparks Papers, MS Sparks 147g. By permission of the Houghton Library, Harvard University.

116. Sparks to Mackenzie, 28 Oct. 1839, Sparks Papers, MS Sparks 147g. By permission of the Houghton Library, Harvard University.

117. Jared Sparks to John Armstrong, 3 Mar. 1834, Sparks Papers, MS Sparks 147f. By permission of the Houghton Library, Harvard University.

118. On Simms's importance as a historian, see Busick, *Sober Desire for History*. For further background on Simms, see Wakelyn, *Politics of a Literary Man*, and Faust, *Sacred Circle*.

119. Simms, "Ellet's Women of the Revolution," 319–20, 325, 333. On Simms's review of Ellet and his interest in social history, see Busick, *Sober Desire for History*, 18–19, 22–24, 26.

120. Simms, "Prescott's Conquest of Peru," 136–38. On Simms's view of Prescott and the similarities between them, see Busick, *Sober Desire for History*, 6–7, 25–26.

121. Simms, "Prescott's Conquest of Peru," 138. On Simms's belief in how the artistic element to history could further its moral purpose, see Busick, *Sober Desire for History*, 7. For further discussion of Simms's views on the purpose of history, especially his belief in its didactic function, see Wakelyn, *Politics of a Literary Man*, 116–22.

122. Simms, *The Yemassee*, xxix–xxx. On Simms's distinction between the novel and romance, see Dekker, *American Historical Romance*, 58. And because Simms used the term "romance" to refer to works that other historians of his time considered novels, I use his discussion of the relationship between history and romance to illuminate ideas about the relationship between history and the novel in this period. For further dis-

cussion of this distinction, see Michael O'Brien, *Conjectures of Order*, 746–47. On how Simms differed from Prescott in his greater willingness to blur the line between history and romance, see Busick, *Sober Desire for History*, 7.

123. William Gilmore Simms, "History for the Purposes of Art," in *Views and Reviews in American Literature, History and Fiction*, 1:25. On Simms's belief in the historian's use of the imagination to dramatize and give coherence to history, see Busick, *Sober Desire for History*, 6, 18.

124. Simms, "History for the Purposes of Art," 1:34. On how southern historical novelists blurred the line between fact and fiction, see Michael O'Brien, *Conjectures of Order*, 763.

125. Simms, "History for the Purposes of Art," 1:57–58. For striking parallels to modern discussions of the relationship between history and fiction, see especially Hayden White, "The Historical Text as Literary Artifact," in *Tropics of Discourse*, 81–100. On the threat that White's challenge to the distinction between history and fiction posed to the belief in objective truth, see Novick, *That Noble Dream*, 599–603. For other parallels to modern conceptions of history as art, see Busick, *Sober Desire for History*, 5–6.

126. Simms, "History for the Purposes of Art," 1:27. On Simms's didactic understanding of history and his permissive attitude toward conjecture, see Faust, *Sacred Circle*, 74–79. On Simms's moral absolutism and the precedence he gave to the greater moral truths of history over specific facts and details, see Busick, *Sober Desire for History*, 6–9, 18–21.

127. Felton, "Simms's Stories and Reviews," 379, 381.

128. George Atkinson Ward, "Curwen's Journal," 51.

129. Sherman, "Views and Reviews in American History, Literature and Fiction," 250–51.

130. William Gilmore Simms to James Lawson, 26 Jan. 1847, in Simms, *Letters*, 2:262.

131. Simms, "History for the Purposes of Art," 1:42. On Simms's commitment to factual accuracy and the restrictions he placed on the use of the imagination, see Busick, *Sober Desire for History*, 6–7, 18–22, 26–28, 37, 50, though I differ from Busick in my emphasis on Simms's ambiguity and ambivalence on these points.

132. On Simms's preoccupation with the factual accuracy of his historical novels, see Wakelyn, *Politics of a Literary Man*, 117, and Jerome King Brown, "William Gilmore Simms and the American Historical Romance," 241–47. On the research that Simms did for his novels and his belief that fiction could provide readers with greater access to historical truth than conventional histories, Busick, *Sober Desire for History*, 2, 10, 27, 63–71.

133. Simms, *Mellichampe*, 2–3. On Simms's belief that historical fact was based on a critical analysis of both oral tradition and primary documents, see Busick, *Sober Desire for History*, 24–25, 32–33, 39–40. See Casper, *Constructing American Lives*, 137, 178–83, on Simms's similarity to Ellet in bringing together a belief in the importance of sentiment with a documentary approach to truth. On the use of tradition and oral history by southern historians, see Michael O'Brien, *Conjectures of Order*, 633–34.

134. Simms, *Katharine Walton*, 3–4. On Simms's use of fiction to illuminate social history, see Jerome King Brown, "William Gilmore Simms and the American Historical Romance," 251–55.

135. Simms, *The Partisan*, ix. On Simms's belief that historical novels were truer than conventional histories in their concern with social history, see Busick, *Sober Desire for History*, 64.

136. Quoted in Gilmore, "Literature of the Revolutionary and Early National Periods," 1:620. On the close relationship between the rise of the novel and the growing concern with newness and originality, see Watt, *Rise of the Novel*, 12–14.

THREE. "To express old things in a new way"

1. Jared Sparks to Stephen W. Williams, 21 Mar. 1836, Sparks Papers, MS Sparks 147f. By permission of the Houghton Library, Harvard University. For the title quotation, see "Thoughts on Plagiarism," 406. Here, I apply M. H. Abrams's distinction between expressive and mimetic theories of art to views on the historian's role. On this distinction, see Abrams, *The Mirror and the Lamp*, esp. 8–14, 21–26, 30-69. On the implications of an expressive art for history, see Phillips, "Macaulay, Scott, and the Literary Challenge to Historiography," 122–24.

2. On how Sparks's own editorial practices embodied the undeveloped state of historical methodology in this time, see Herbert Baxter Adams, *Life and Writings of Jared Sparks*, 2:265–78, 479–506; Michael Stevens, "Jared Sparks," in *American Historians, 1607–1865*, 306–8; Cappon, "American Historical Editors before Jared Sparks"; Cappon, "Jared Sparks"; Bassett, *Middle Group of American Historians*, 100–13; and Wish, *American Historian*, 48–55. For an influential and early discussion of the prevalence of plagiarism among Sparks's Revolutionary predecessors, see Libby, "Some Pseudo Histories of the American Revolution," and Fisher, "Legendary and Myth-Making Process," 56. Later works that have perpetuated this view include Newmyer, "Charles Stedman's History of the American War"; Newmyer, "John Andrews's 'History of the War with America'"; and Kraus, *Writing of American History*, 72–73, 78, 86, 108-13. While recognizing the complex meaning of such practices in George Bancroft's case, Vitzthum perpetuates this general characterization of early national historiography by emphasizing Bancroft's uniqueness in *American Compromise*, 8, 45–48. Callcott, *History in the United States* (128–38), does recognize that early nineteenth-century historians were more rigorous in their scholarly practices than modern scholars have assumed, but even he, in the end, points to the limitations on their methodology. For an important exception to this tendency, see Newmyer, "Nineteenth-Century View." The lack of attention given to early national historical methodology by scholars since the 1970s points to the low regard in which that methodology continues to be held. Indeed, the brief section that Hoffer's recent study of plagiarism and standards of scholarly integrity in American historical writing, *Past Imperfect* (17–28), allots to this period reveals the persisting view of early national historians as slipshod and untrustworthy in their treatment of sources.

Two recent works that do recognize early nineteenth-century historians' commitment to documentary research are Conn, *History's Shadow*, 21–24, and Casper, *Constructing American Lives*, 135–201. However, neither of these works really delves into the issue of citation and plagiarism, and while Casper focuses on how the interest in documentary research related to definitions of biography as a genre, Conn discusses this development primarily to show how it contributed to the exclusion of Native Americans from American historical consciousness.

3. On the modern function of the footnote in demonstrating the historian's originality, see Grafton, *The Footnote*, 4–5.

4. While John Higham, *History* (94), briefly notes the adherence of the Romantic historians to "the critical outlook associated with scientific inquiry," he in the end still emphasizes the opposition between Romantic and scientific history.

5. For a useful overview of the history of plagiarism that subscribes to the belief in the autonomous author, see Mallon, *Stolen Words*, esp. 1–12, 239–50. The starting point for challenges to this conception of the author is Foucault, "What Is an Author?" Important works that analyze the implications of this challenge to conventional assumptions about authorship for ideas about plagiarism and textual appropriation include Woodmansee and Jaszi, *Construction of Authorship*, especially Martha Woodmansee, "On the Author Effect: Recovering Collectivity," 1–14, and Peter Jaszi, "On the Author Effect: Contemporary Copyright and Collective Creativity," 29–56, and Rosenthal, *Playwrights and Plagiarists*, 1–57. On the derivation of the word *plagiarism*, see the *Oxford English Dictionary*. For an example of modern views and definitions of plagiarism in the historical profession, see Hoffer, "Reflections on Plagiarism—Part 1," and Hoffer, "Reflections on Plagiarism—Part 2."

6. Gordon, *History of the Rise, Progress and Establishment*, 1:vii. On the prevalence of this practice among the Revolutionary historians, see Callcott, *History in the United States*, 134–38; Newmyer, "Charles Stedman's History of the American War"; Newmyer, "John Andrews's 'History of the War with America'"; Fisher, "Legendary and Myth-Making Process," 57–63; and Libby, "Some Pseudo Histories of the American Revolution." Specifically on plagiarism in Gordon's history, see Libby, "Critical Examination of William Gordon's History."

7. Ramsay, *History of the American Revolution*, 2:540; Gordon, *History of the Rise, Progress and Establishment*, 4:18. On the similarity between these two passages, and on Ramsay's plagiarism in general, see Johnson, "David Ramsay." See also Johnson, "Alexander Hewat," 57–58, and Libby, "Ramsay as a Plagiarist."

8. On the long-standing practice of writing history according to a "scissors-and-paste" approach, and its classical roots, see Collingwood, *Idea of History*, 33–40, 257–61. On the prevalence of this practice among eighteenth- and early nineteenth-century American historians, see Vitzthum, *American Compromise*, 7–10, 45–59. See Fliegelman, *Declaring Independence*, 170–75, for a discussion of this editorial conception of authorship. See Abrams, *The Mirror and the Lamp*, 8–14, 30–46, on this mimetic theory of art. See also Woodmansee, *Author, Art, and the Market*, 13–18, 36–37, on neoclassical con-

ceptions of art and authorship. On the relationship between neoclassicism and American attitudes toward originality in this period, see Spencer, *Quest for Nationality*, 34–36.

9. Lendrum, *Concise and Impartial History of the American Revolution*, 1:i–ii. On Warren's treatment of footnotes, see Lester Cohen, editor's note, in Warren, *History of the Rise, Progress and Termination of the American Revolution*, 1:xxxv. See Louis Tucker, *Clio's Consort* 37–46, generally on Belknap's commitment to accuracy and modern standards of scholarship.

10. For an important discussion of the origins and lineage of the footnote, see Grafton, "Footnote from De Thou to Ranke," 55–76, and Grafton, *The Footnote*, esp. 94–222. On the emerging preoccupation with plagiarism in this period, see Fliegelman, *Declaring Independence*, 164–70, and Mallon, *Stolen Words*, 8–26. On the conflicts over Jefferson's authorship of the Declaration and the role that changing conceptions of authorship played in these conflicts, see McDonald, "Thomas Jefferson's Changing Reputation."

11. See Fliegelman, *Declaring Independence*, 169–74, on the role of changing conceptions of originality in this process and its implications for ideas about authorship. On the changing meanings of the terms *original* and *originality*, see especially Williams, *Keywords*, 192–93. On Young's role in this transformation, see Rosenthal, *Playwrights and Plagiarists*, 14–21, and McFarland, *Originality and Imagination*, 5–6. For the quotation from Young, see Edward Young, *Conjectures on original composition. In a letter to the author of Sir Charles Grandison* (London: A. Millar; and R. and J. Dodsley, 1759), 12, Gale Group, http://galenet.galegroup.com/servlet/ECCO, 18 Sept. 2007. On this quotation, see Abrams, *The Mirror and the Lamp*, 199. On the transition to this modern conception of authorship, see also Woodmansee, *Author, Art, and the Market*, 35–55, and Mark Rose, "The Author in Court: *Pope v. Curll* (1741)," in Woodmansee and Jaszi, *Construction of Authorship*, 211–29. On the complex sources of the growing concern with originality in American literature, see Spencer, *Quest for Nationality*, 26–39.

12. Marshall, *Life of George Washington*, 1:xix. On Marshall's reputation as a historian, see Marcus Cunliffe, introduction to Marshall, *Life of George Washington* (1804; New York: Chelsea House, 1983).

13. Marshall, *Life of George Washington*, 1:xvii–xviii. On the limits to early national historians' recognition of the interpretive element to history, see Kamrath, "Charles Brockden Brown and the 'art of the historian,'" 237–38, though I differ from Kamrath in attributing to Marshall a greater concern with fact and truth than he suggests was the case for historians in this period.

14. See Foran, "John Marshall as a Historian," on the incidence of plagiarism throughout his history.

15. On the deeply rooted view of history as a mirror, see Bonnie Smith, *Gender of History*, 1–13. On the development of the belief that style was supposed to reflect the personality of the author, see Abrams, *The Mirror and the Lamp*, 226–35. On the role of citation in giving authority and legitimacy to the historian's claims, see Grafton, *The Footnote*, 7–8. On how a view of truth as the accumulation of fact could sanction plagiarism, Hoffer, *Past Imperfect*, 20.

16. Hannah Adams, "Answer to the Rev. Dr. Morse's Appeal, in the Last Centinel," in Morse, *Appeal to the Public*, 8n.

17. Elijah Parish to Hannah Adams, 10 Nov. 1804, in Morse, *Appeal to the Public*, 21–22. For further discussion of the Adams-Morse dispute, see Buell, *New England Literary Culture*, 224, and Wright, "Controversial Career of Jedidiah Morse," 76–85.

18. Hannah Adams, *Summary History of New England*, i.

19. For a different view of how Adams sought to legitimize her work as a historian through the content of her history, see Messer, *Stories of Independence*, 131–37. On how women in this period were able to write history despite their exclusion from the public sphere, see Baym, *American Women Writers and the Work of History*.

20. Hannah Adams, *Summary History of New England*, i. For an important and provocative analysis of the complex relationship between gender and ideas about historical truth, see Bonnie Smith, *Gender of History*.

21. Adams, *Summary History of New England*, i. For another example of a historian who used the idea of compilation to legitimize his claims to truth, see Grafton's discussion of Pierre Bayle in *The Footnote*, 198–99. On how the ideal of the autonomous author could be used to erase the role of women in the writing of history and how that ideal was defined in opposition to women, see Bonnie Smith, *Gender of History*, 70–102. For different views of the relationship between gender and originality, see Rosenthal, *Playwrights and Plagiarists*, and Battersby, *Gender and Genius*. Whereas Battersby emphasizes the ways in which the Romantic ideal of originality was defined in male terms, Rosenthal demonstrates how women writers in early modern England used this ideal to establish their authority as writers.

22. "Compendious History of New England," 542–44.

23. For an opposing view, which emphasizes the lack of concern with originality displayed by early nineteenth-century historians, see Callcott, *History in the United States*, 136–38.

24. On annals as a historical genre, see Shapiro, *Culture of Fact*, 39–40.

25. For background on Holmes, see *Dictionary of American Biography*, 1932 ed., s.v. "Holmes, Abiel."

26. Holmes, "Ramsay's History of the United States," 336.

27. Holmes, *Annals of America*, 1:572n. Holmes's use of footnotes in this way was admittedly not new to the nineteenth century, as demonstrated by the running commentary found throughout Edward Gibbon's notes. For comparisons to Gibbon's use of footnotes, see John Clive, "The Most Disgusting of Pronouns," in *Not by Fact Alone*, 26–27.

28. Holmes, *Annals of America*, 1:iv. For a different view that emphasizes the limits to Holmes's concern with impartiality and the obstacles to this ideal, see Kamrath, "Charles Brockden Brown and the 'art of the historian,'" 237–38.

29. On the notion of footnotes and text as constituting a "double narrative," see Grafton, "Footnote from De Thou to Ranke," 74, and Grafton, *The Footnote*, 23–24, 200.

30. On how footnotes functioned in this way for Pierre Bayle, see Grafton, *The Footnote*, 200.

31. Holmes, *Annals of America*, 1:iv.

32. For the argument that historical skepticism and a faith in the possibility of sound historical knowledge were not necessarily mutually exclusive, see Momigliano, "Ancient History and the Antiquarian," 10–11. See Grafton, *The Footnote*, 23, on the role of the footnote in revealing the historian's limitations to the reader. Also see Grafton, "Footnote from De Thou to Ranke," 72–76, and Grafton, *The Footnote*, 195–212, on how Bayle helped establish a more secure basis for historical knowledge, even as he expressed skepticism about the possibility of accurate history. For a discussion of the importance of footnotes in modern scholarship as a means of making the historian accountable to the reader, and of protecting against distortion, see Himmelfarb, "Where Have All the Footnotes Gone?"

33. Bozman, *History of Maryland*, 1:22n. For background on Bozman, see *Dictionary of American Biography*, 1927 ed., s.v. "Bozman, John Leeds," and Shaffer, *Politics of History*, 55–56.

34. Bozman, *History of Maryland*, 1: ix–x. For another perspective on how the cult of originality undermined a belief in absolute and transcendent truths during the Renaissance, see Quint, *Origin and Originality in Renaissance Literature*, ix–xi, 1–31, 207–20.

35. Bozman, *History of Maryland*, 1:ix–x. For parallels to Ranke's recognition of the multifaceted character of truth, see Krieger, *Ranke*, 12.

36. On Prescott's concern with citation, see Callcott, *History in the United States*, 126.

37. William Hickling Prescott to George Bancroft, 30 Dec. 1837, Bancroft Papers. For background on Prescott, see C. Harvey Gardiner, *William Hickling Prescott: A Biography*. On Prescott as a historian, see Darnell, *William Hickling Prescott*, and especially Levin, *History as Romantic Art*, 163–85.

38. C. Harvey Gardiner, *Literary Memoranda of William Hickling Prescott*, 2:70.

39. C. Harvey Gardiner, *Literary Memoranda of William Hickling Prescott*, 2:37.

40. On the development of the belief that literature was supposed to express the personality of the author and that style offered one measure of the author's distinguishing traits, see Abrams, *The Mirror and the Lamp*, 226–35.

41. C. Harvey Gardiner, *Literary Memoranda of William Hickling Prescott*, 2:39. On Prescott's Romantic conception of history as a literary art, see Levin, *History as Romantic Art*, 9–23, 163–85. On this expressive theory of art and the concept of natural genius, see Abrams, *The Mirror and the Lamp*, 21–26, 47–69, 184–201.

42. On the development of this view of literature and authorship in eighteenth-century English debates about copyright, see Mark Rose, "Author as Proprietor," 54, 69–70, 75.

43. On the close relationship between the Romantic conception of authorship as the expression of original genius and the professionalization of literature in Germany, see Woodmansee, "The Genius and the Copyright," and Woodmansee, *Author, Art, and the Market*, 35–55. On the relationship between these developments in eighteenth-century English debates about copyright, see Mark Rose, "Author as Proprietor," 51–85.

44. Woodmansee, *Author, Art, and the Market*, 51–53.

45. On Prescott's view of his literary work as his property, see C. Harvey Gardiner, *Prescott and His Publishers*, 101.

46. On the commercialization of literature and the professionalization of authorship in this period, see Michael Davitt Bell, "Conditions of Literary Vocation," in Bercovitch, *Cambridge History of American Literature*, 2:11–17, and Charvat, *Literary Publishing in America*, 38–60. On the relationship between this development and Romantic aesthetic ideals, see Gilmore, *American Romanticism and the Marketplace*, 1–17, and Michael T. Gilmore, "Literature of the Revolutionary and Early National Periods," in Bercovitch, *Cambridge History of American Literature*, 1:550–56. On the relationship between hostility to plagiarism and the professionalization of authorship, and the connection between debates about copyright and attitudes toward plagiarism, see Mallon, *Stolen Words*, 3–4, 38–40. See Barnes, *Authors, Publishers and Politicians*, on the campaign for an Anglo-American copyright agreement, and Tebbel, *History of Book Publishing in the United States*, 558–61, on the movement for an international copyright law.

47. McGill, *American Literature and the Culture of Reprinting*, 93.

48. On the resistance to international copyright and the limits to individual authorship it implied, see ibid., 80–108.

49. On the increasingly commercial and market orientation of literature in this period and the lack of copyright as an obstacle to the professionalization of authorship, see Bell, "Conditions of Literary Vocation," 2:11–17, and Gilmore, *American Romanticism and the Marketplace*, 1–5. On how the commercialization of literature contributed to the movement for international copyright in America, see Spencer, *Quest for Nationality*, 143–46. For a different view that emphasizes the complex relationship between the demand for copyright and market culture, see McGill, *American Literature and the Culture of Reprinting*, 10–14, 42–43, 45–49, 63–75, 87–92, 102–4. On the professionalization of authorship and its relationship to the movement for international copyright, see also Anne C. Rose, *Voices of the Marketplace*, 92–93.

50. William Prescott to Francis Lieber, 10 Feb. 1840, in C. Harvey Gardiner, *Papers of William Hickling Prescott*, 154–55. On Prescott's concern with protecting his property rights in his writing and both the extent of and limits to his support for international copyright, see C. Harvey Gardiner, *Prescott and His Publishers*, 101–34. On this provision of English copyright law, see Tebbel, *History of Book Publishing in the United States*, 209.

51. On Prescott's concern with the financial success of his work, see Peck, *William Hickling Prescott*, 95. See C. Harvey Gardiner, *Prescott and His Publishers*, 46–100, 167–245, for the role that Prescott played in marketing his books and for further details about his publishing arrangements, though Gardiner takes a different view that emphasizes the limits to Prescott's desire for profit.

52. On these changes, see Bell, "Conditions of Literary Vocation," 2:11–17; Gilmore, *American Romanticism and the Marketplace*, 1–4; Charvat, *Literary Publishing in America*, 17–60; and Tebbel, *History of Book Publishing in the United States*, 203–62.

53. William Hickling Prescott to George Bancroft, 30 July 1847, in Wolcott, *Correspondence of William Hickling Prescott*, 663. For a different view that emphasizes the ten-

sions between Romantic aesthetics and the social concerns of Prescott and other New England intellectuals of his generation, see Foletta, *Coming to Terms with Democracy*, 114–34.

54. William Hickling Prescott to George Bancroft, 20 Dec. 1837, Bancroft Papers.

55. Prescott, "Bancroft's History of the United States," 95.

56. Prescott, *History of the Conquest of Mexico*, 34n.

57. Ibid., 35n.

58. On the dual role of footnotes in supporting the historian's claims and demonstrating the historian's limitations to the reader, see Grafton, *The Footnote*, 23–32.

59. Prescott, "Bancroft's History of the United States," 103.

60. Ibid.

61. "Howison's History of Virginia," 235.

62. Stevens, *History of Georgia*, 1:xxxii.

63. "Introduction to the History of the Colony and Ancient Dominion of Virginia," 311.

64. On the concern with accuracy that took hold in this period, and on the importance of footnotes as a sign of accuracy, see Callcott, *History in the United States*, 121–24, 126–28. For parallels to Leopold von Ranke's methodology and use of footnotes, see Grafton, *The Footnote*, 44–48.

65. Howison, *History of Virginia*, 1:ix.

66. See also Grafton, *The Footnote*, esp. 73–77, 83–93, 123–89, on the early predecessors to Ranke in developing critical methods of historical scholarship, as well as Donald Kelley, *Foundations of Modern Historical Scholarship*, and Huppert, *Idea of Perfect History*, on the contribution of French Renaissance scholars to such methods. On extent to which English Renaissance scholars incorporated the techniques of philology and legal scholarship into the writing of history and contributed to the development of critical scholarship in historical writing, see Woolf, "Erudition and the Idea of History in Renaissance England," and Joseph Levine, "The Antiquarian Enterprise, 1500–1800," in *Humanism and History*, 9–16, 73–99. On the Göttingen school, see Butterfield, *Man on His Past*, 32–61. On the development of this scientific ideal in general, see Iggers, "The Crisis of the Conventional Conception of Scientific History," in *New Directions in European Historiography*, 3–26. For a summary of the Rankean ideal, see Krieger, *Ranke*, 2–7.

67. Markoe, "Documentary History of the American Revolution," 82–89. On how Markoe anticipated modern critical scholarship in his views on citation and historical accuracy, see Newmyer, "Nineteenth-Century View." For a different reading of this review, see Hoffer, *Past Imperfect*, 20.

68. Markoe, "Documentary History of the American Revolution," 82–83. On Ranke's famous statement of this ideal, see Krieger, *Ranke*, 107.

69. Markoe, "Documentary History of the American Revolution," 83. On how Markoe combined nationalist purposes with a Rankean ideal, see Newmyer, "Nineteenth-Century View," 166. On how Chalmers contributed to the widely held belief in America's uniquely intelligible origins, see Craven, *Legend of the Founding Fathers*, 53–54. On

American anxieties about the nation's lack of romantic associations and how American writers responded to these anxieties, see Spencer, *Quest for Nationality*, 68–70, 95–101, and Orians, "Romance Ferment after *Waverly*."

70. On the use of original sources as a defining quality of critical scholarship, see Krieger, *Ranke*, 2–3. See Grafton, *The Footnote*, 48–60, on Ranke's concern with primary documents. As Ranke himself demonstrated, scientific and Romantic ideals were not mutually exclusive, for he also recognized the literary and artistic dimension to history. See Rudolf Vierhaus, "Historiography between Science and Art," in Iggers and Powell, *Leopold von Ranke*, 61–69. On Ranke's view of history as an art and his desire to re-create the past, rather than just objectively report on it, see Krieger, *Ranke*, 7, 20. On how the Göttingen school likewise at once embraced critical methods of scholarship and recognized the subjective element to historical understanding, see Iggers, *New Directions in European Historiography*, 15–17. On the earlier roots of the belief that primary documents were necessary to validate the historian's truth claims, see Shapiro, *Culture of Fact*, 49–51.

71. Brigham, "Chronicles of the Pilgrim Fathers," 116, 124. On the emerging interest in documentary sources in this period, see Van Tassel, *Recording America's Past*, 103–10; Callcott, *History in the United States*, 124–26; Bassett, *Middle Group of American Historians*, 88; and Kraus and Joyce, *Writing of American History*, 79–84. See Casper, *Constructing American Lives*, 135–92, on the importance of documentary research to biographers in this period, and Douglas, *Feminization of American Culture*, 174–75, on the Romantic historians' concern with archival and documentary research.

72. Brigham, "Chronicles of the Pilgrim Fathers," 116. On the notion of documents as an antidote to the historian's bias in early modern English historical writing, see Shapiro, *Culture of Fact*, 57–58.

73. Brigham, "Chronicles of the Pilgrim Fathers," 124. See the *Oxford English Dictionary* on the different uses of the term *compiler*.

74. Daniel, "History of Virginia," 10.

75. Ibid., 10–11.

76. Upham, "Reed's Life of President Reed," 447–48.

77. Charles Upham to Jared Sparks, December 1834, Sparks Papers, MS Sparks 153, Upham folder. By permission of the Houghton Library, Harvard University.

78. Charles Upham to Jared Sparks, 15 Dec. 1834, Sparks Papers, MS Sparks 153, Upham folder. By permission of the Houghton Library, Harvard University. On this Romantic conception of history, see Levin, *History as Romantic Art*, esp. 3–23.

79. Upham to Sparks, December 1834, Sparks Papers. On this artistic conception of biography and its implications for the biographer's authorial role, see Casper, *Constructing American Lives* (206–13), who demonstrates how this understanding of biography could also discourage a documentary approach.

80. Upham to Sparks, 15 Dec. 1834, Sparks Papers.

81. Upham, *Life of George Washington*, 6. On how southern writers blurred the line between biography and autobiography, see Michael O'Brien, *Conjectures of Order*, 673–75.

82. On the importance of feeling to truth in this period, see Callcott, *History in the United States*, 147–50.

83. Charles Francis Adams, *Letters of Mrs. Adams*, xxii. On Adams's contributions as a historian and literary figure, see Harbert, "Charles Francis Adams." On how the concern with re-creating inward experience and feeling contributed to the interest in documentary sources in eighteenth-century British historiography, see Phillips, *Society and Sentiment*, 98–102. As Casper, *Constructing American Lives* (162–76), demonstrates, while Elizabeth Ellet shared this concern with recovering sentiment and feeling, she reconciled this concern with her interest in documentary sources in a different way.

84. Charles Francis Adams, *Letters of Mrs. Adams*, xxii. On the development of the doctrine of privacy in American biographical criticism from 1830 to 1860, see Casper, *Constructing American Lives*, 204–11. On Adams's belief that private documents would contribute to historical truth, see Harbert, "Charles Francis Adams," 261–64.

85. On the conflict between these different conceptions of virtue in early nineteenth-century American theory and practice of biography, see Casper, *Constructing American Lives*, 19–67.

86. On the fascination with deception and its cultural implications, see Wood, "Conspiracy and the Paranoid Style."

87. Charles Francis Adams, *Letters of Mrs. Adams*, xxii. On the fear of hypocrisy and deception in a "world of strangers," see Halttunen, *Confidence Men and Painted Women*, 33–51.

88. On the nineteenth-century cult of sincerity, see Halttunen, *Confidence Men and Painted Women*, 51–57.

89. Charles Francis Adams, *Letters of Mrs. Adams*, xxii–xxiii. On the identification of the private sphere with the exercise of sincerity, see Halttunen, *Confidence Men and Painted Women*, 56–59.

90. Charles Francis Adams, *Letters of Mrs. Adams*, xxiv–xxv. On the assumption that women were by nature more sincere than men, see Halttunen, *Confidence Men and Painted Women*, 55–59. For comparisons to how Helena Maria Williams's status as a female letter writer made her an ideal historical observer, see Phillips, *Society and Sentiment*, 94.

91. For comparisons to how Elizabeth Ellet at once recognized and limited women's role in the Revolution, see Casper, *Constructing American Lives*, 177. For parallels to the contemporary response to Hannah Adams's work as a historian, see Messer, *Stories of Independence*, 136. On nineteenth-century domestic ideology, see especially Cott, *Bonds of Womanhood*.

92. On how Bancroft brought together Romantic ideals with German critical methods, see Appleby, Hunt, and Jacob, *Telling the Truth about History*, 112–13, though in contrast to my analysis, Appleby, Hunt, and Jacob emphasize the way these impulses were at odds with each other.

93. On Bancroft and his history, see Handlin, *George Bancroft*, esp. 115–33; Nye, *George Bancroft: Brahmin Rebel*, esp. 94–105; Canary, *George Bancroft*; Wish, *Ameri-*

can Historian, 71–86; Ross, "Historical Consciousness in Nineteenth-Century America," 915–19; and Kraus and Joyce, *Writing of American History*, 97–108. See Vitzthum, *American Compromise*, esp. 48–51, 73–74, for Bancroft's treatment of quotations and footnotes, and Hoffer, *Past Imperfect*, 22. For his problematic treatment of quotations, see also Watt Stewart, "George Bancroft," in Hutchinson, *Marcus W. Jernegan Essays*, 20–22. Interestingly, Bancroft became less conscientious about citation in his later volumes; volumes 7 and 8 contained no footnotes, and he provided only sporadic citations in volumes 9 and 10.

94. Henry Brown, *History of Illinois*, 126, 136, 137, 138, 139, 141, 209, vi.

95. George Bancroft to Henry Brown, 12 Aug. 1845, Bancroft Papers.

96. On the development of this notion of authorship and literary property in eighteenth-century discussions of copyright, see Mark Rose, *Authors and Owners*, 5–6. On the convergence between Romantic and liberal capitalist understandings of authorship, see Mark Rose, "Author as Proprietor," 56, 75–76, and Gilmore, "Literature of the Revolutionary and Early National Periods," 1:555. On the relationship between originality and concerns about literary property, see Rosenthal, *Playwrights and Plagiarists*, 23–31.

97. See McGill, *American Literature and the Culture of Reprinting*, 3–5, on her use of this term.

98. Prescott, "Bancroft's History of the United States," 94–95.

99. George Bancroft to Buckingham, 4 Dec. 1844, Bancroft Papers.

100. Chalmers, *Political Annals of the Present United Colonies*, 1:535–36. On Bancroft's use of Chalmers, see Vitzthum, *American Compromise*, 51–53, 62–65.

101. Bancroft, *History of the United States*, 2:159. On the similarities between Bancroft's and Chalmers's account of this revolt and Bancroft's reinterpretation of Chalmers, see Vitzthum, *American Compromise*, 62–65.

102. Bancroft, *History of the United States*, 2:160n1, 161n2, 162n6. On Bancroft's use of Williamson and Williamson's debt to Chalmers, see Vitzthum, *American Compromise*, 62–63.

103. Vitzthum, *American Compromise* (42–65), points to the complex nature of Bancroft's plagiarism as he demonstrates how Bancroft used the language of his sources for his own purposes and so departed from his predecessors in adopting an active interpretive approach to his sources. In this way, Vitzthum suggests, Bancroft found a way to reconcile traditional scissors-and-paste methods of historical writing with his desire for originality (8–10).

104. McGill, *American Literature and the Culture of Reprinting*, 20–23, 45–49, 93–108.

105. Bancroft, *History of the United States*, 1:v. On how Ranke also used a critical analysis of primary sources to demonstrate his originality, see Grafton, *The Footnote*, 56–57.

106. George Bancroft to Edward Everett, 23 Oct. 1833, Bancroft Papers. On Bancroft's relationship to German philosophy and thought, and on his admiration for Heeren in

particular, see Handlin, *George Bancroft*, 65–66, 100–101; Nye, *George Bancroft: Brahmin Rebel*, 32–58; Wish, *American Historian*, 71–75; and Rathbun, "George Bancroft on Man and History," 51–56, 62–66. On the role of the Göttingen school as precursors to Ranke, see Butterfield, *Man on His Past*, 40–61. Specifically on Heeren's contribution to the Göttingen school, see James Westfall Thompson, *History of Historical Writing*, 2:120–31.

107. Bancroft, *History of the United States*, 1:300n.

108. Ibid., 355n. On Bancroft's sources, see Vitzthum, *American Compromise*, 45, 65.

109. Bancroft, *History of the United States*, 1:59n.

110. Bancroft to Everett, 23 Oct. 1833, Bancroft Papers.

111. Bancroft, *History of the United States*, 8:118. On Bancroft's genuine belief in his own impartiality, see Handlin, *George Bancroft*, 126–27, 341–42. For a different view of Bancroft's attitude toward impartiality, see Rathbun, "George Bancroft on Man and History," 66. On how Bancroft reconciled his claims to impartiality with his belief in the historian's moral function, and on how he viewed Ranke's approach to history, see Handlin, *George Bancroft*, 295–96. In this understanding of impartiality, Bancroft was not as different from Ranke as has been conventionally assumed, for there was a moral component to Ranke's view of history as well. On Ranke's view of the relationship between impartiality and morality, see Iggers, *New Directions in European Historiography*, 23, and Krieger, *Ranke*, 155–56. On the idealist element to Ranke's conception of history, see Novick, *That Noble Dream*, 26–29.

112. See Woodmansee, *Author, Art, and the Market*, 11–33, 40–55, on how this conception of art developed in conjunction with the commercialization of literature.

FOUR. Puritanism, Slavery, and the American Revolution

1. Francis Bowen to John Gorham Palfrey, 30 Jan. 1858, Palfrey Family Papers, Houghton Library, Harvard University, bMS 1704. By permission of the Houghton Library, Harvard University. Works that emphasize the uncritical and celebratory character of American historical writing in this period include Grant, *North over South*, 24–26; Sheidley, *Sectional Nationalism*, 118–34; Jameson, *History of Historical Writing in America*, 104–8; and Bassett, *Middle Group of American Historians*, 184–87.

2. On the mixture of confidence and anxiety that characterized American nationalism in this period, see Grant, *North over South*, 26–28; Somkin, *Unquiet Eagle*; and Nagel, *This Sacred Trust*.

3. See Greene, *Intellectual Construction of America*, esp. 1–7, 200–209.

4. Morse and Parish, *Compendious History of New England*, 113. On the relationship between Protestant millennialism and exceptionalist ideology, see Ross, "Historical Consciousness in Nineteenth-Century America," 909, 912–13, and Tuveson, *Redeemer Nation*, esp. 52–175. On the Puritan roots of this sense of providential mission, see Perry G. Miller, *Errand into the Wilderness*, esp. 1–15. On this sense of destiny and its nationalist function, see Shaffer, *Politics of History*, 49–50, 59–66. On providential thought as

an ingredient in this sense of destiny and its role as a unifying force in the new nation, see Berens, *Providence and Patriotism in Early America*, 6–7, and Greene, *Intellectual Construction of America*, 195–96.

5. Burk, *History of Virginia*, 1:160. On the sectional character of this nationalism and Burk's effort to claim priority for his own state in the development of liberty, see Craven, *Legend of the Founding Fathers*, 66–73, and Shaffer, *Politics of History*, 54–59.

6. On this teleological, or to use Herbert Butterfield's term, "Whig" interpretation of colonial history, see Cohen, *Revolutionary Histories*, 97–101. On the Revolutionary historians' efforts to locate the roots of Revolutionary principles in the colonial past, see Shaffer, *Politics of History*, 50–59, 117. For further discussion of the Revolutionary historians' linear account of how republican ideals had developed in America, see Messer, *Stories of Independence*, 107–13.

7. Lendrum, *Concise and Impartial History of the American Revolution*, 1:257. For further discussion of how the Revolutionary historians emphasized the revolutionaries' attachment to liberty and republican ideals as a cause of the Revolution, see Shaffer, *Politics of History*, 103–18. On Revolutionary conceptions of historical causation and their explanations for the Revolution in general, see Cohen, "American Revolution and Natural Law Theory"; Cohen, "Explaining the Revolution"; and Cohen, *Revolutionary Histories*, 107–211. See also Messer, *Stories of Independence*, 145–50, 152–58, on the Revolutionary historians' explanations for the development of Revolutionary resistance to British policies.

8. Hannah Adams, *Summary History of New England*, 243.

9. Ramsay, *History of the American Revolution*, 1:147. On the Revolutionary historians' firm belief in contingency and human agency and their use of providential language as a descriptive metaphor rather than a meaningful explanatory concept, see Cohen, *Revolutionary Histories*, 57–113. On the different forms that providence took in the Revolutionary histories and how these historians reconciled a providential interpretation with their secular explanations for the Revolution, see Shaffer, *Politics of History*, 59–63. See also Messer, *Stories of Independence*, 110, 114–17, on the role of providence in the Revolutionary historians' interpretations of American history and their firm belief in human agency.

10. Ramsay, *History of the American Revolution*, 1:26–27. On Ramsay's interpretation of the Revolution, see Cohen, foreword to Ramsay's *History of the American Revolution*, 1:xviii–xxi. For further discussion of Ramsay as a historian, see Karen O'Brien, "David Ramsay"; Kornfeld, "From Republicanism to Liberalism"; Shaffer, *To Be an American*, 88–189; Messer, "From a Revolutionary History to a History of Revolution"; and Messer, *Stories of Independence*, 107–8, 115–18, 122–23, 130–31, 170–82.

11. Ramsay, *History of the American Revolution*, 1:28.

12. Ibid., 25.

13. Ibid., 40. On how the Revolutionary historians reconciled their belief in contingency and human agency with their teleological view of American history, see Cohen, *Revolutionary Histories*, 97–101.

14. On Ramsay's and the Revolutionary historians' view of their work as a form of Revolutionary activism and their concern with combating corruption in their own time, see Cohen, *Revolutionary Histories*, 113–21, 198–211, and Cohen, foreword to Ramsay's *History of the American Revolution*, 1:xxiii–xxiv. For a different view of how the Revolutionary historians used their histories to promote virtue, see Messer, *Stories of Independence*, 105–38. See also Messer, "From a Revolutionary History to a History of Revolution," 209–20, on Ramsay's view of the writing of history as a continuation of his Revolutionary activism.

15. On Bancroft's influence as an exponent of exceptionalist ideology and his ability to mythologize American history by combining the sacred with the secular, see Bercovitch, *Rites of Assent*, 173–89; Ross, "Historical Consciousness in Nineteenth-Century America," 915–20; and Noble, *Historians against History*, 18–36. For further background on Bancroft's history, see Vitzthum, *American Compromise*, 12–14; Wish, *American Historian*, 70–87; Nye, *George Bancroft*, 136–93; Nye, *George Bancroft: Brahmin Rebel*, 86–132; Kirk Wood, "George Bancroft," in *American Historians, 1607–1865*, 6–21; Bassett, *Middle Group of American Historians*, 152–210; and Handlin, *George Bancroft*, 115–36. Handlin (126–29) briefly discusses Bancroft's conviction that his history represented an unprejudiced account of historical truth, and she attributes his success to his ability to combine a recognition of the problems and failures that early Americans suffered with a larger optimistic framework, but she does not go into depth about the relationship between his commitment to impartiality and his social purposes. For a different view that emphasizes the disparity between Bancroft's commitment to a Rankean ideal of critical scholarship and the celebratory patriotism of his history, see Appleby, Hunt, and Jacob, *Telling the Truth about History*, 112–14. Wish, *American Historian* (77–85), likewise emphasizes the tensions between Bancroft's epic view of American history and his claims to objectivity.

16. Bancroft, *History of the United States*, 7:23, 295. On Bancroft's providential perspective, see Ross, "Historical Consciousness in Nineteenth-Century America," 915–19; Noble, *Historians against History*, 18–36; and Bercovitch, *Rites of Assent*, 174–79. On exceptionalist ideology, see Ross, *Origins of American Social Science*, 22–50. For further discussion of the assumptions of American exceptionalism, see Tuveson, *Redeemer Nation*, 91–186; and Merk, *Manifest Destiny*.

17. Bancroft, *History of the United States*, 7:301–2, 2:454. On liberty as a central theme in Bancroft's history, see also Vitzthum, *American Compromise*, 15–20, and Rathbun, "George Bancroft on Man and History," 68–73. See also Noble, *Historians against History*, 22–31, on Bancroft's analysis of the progress of liberty in American history.

18. Quoted in Nye, *George Bancroft: Brahmin Rebel*, 106.

19. On how Bancroft's history reflected his Jacksonian sympathies and how he used history to demonstrate the conservative character of Jacksonian democracy, see Noble, *Historians against History*, 22–24.

20. Bancroft, *History of the United States*, 9:257–58. On Bancroft's conservative interpretation of the Revolution, and on Bancroft's essentially "middle-class" vision of social

order, see Bercovitch, *Rites of Assent*, 169–82. On Bancroft's conservatism, see Handlin, *George Bancroft*, 146–53, and Vitzthum, *American Compromise*, 32–33. In general, on how the Massachusetts elite in this period sought to further conservative social purposes by emphasizing the Puritan origins of American liberty, and the orderly character of the Revolution, see Sheidley, *Sectional Nationalism*, 122–32, and Matthews, "Whig History," 201–8.

21. Bancroft, *History of the United States*, 9:283.

22. On Bancroft's faith in progress, see Noble, *Historians against History*, 20–27, 31–34, and Nye, *George Bancroft: Brahmin Rebel*, 99–103. See Bercovitch, *Rites of Assent*, 175–84, on how Bancroft reconciled his belief in progress and continual revolution with his conservative desire for unity and social order. On how Bancroft shared with other Romantic historians a belief in the inevitability of progress, see Levin, *History as Romantic Art*, 27–36.

23. On how nature would enable the United States to escape from historical complexity in Bancroft's exceptionalist vision, see Noble, *Historians against History*, 30–34. On how Bancroft expressed the more general exceptionalist assumption that the United States was exempt from the normal processes of historical change, see Ross, "Historical Consciousness in Nineteenth-Century America," 912–13, 917–19. On Bancroft's vision of America as a society in which humanity could remain in a state of perpetual innocence, free of the corruption of the Old World, see Merrill Lewis, "Organic Metaphor and Edenic Myth."

24. Ross, "Historical Consciousness in Nineteenth-Century America," 919.

25. Quoted in George Bancroft to J. C. Bancroft Davis, 27 Dec. 1867, in Mark Anthony DeWolfe Howe, *Life and Letters of George Bancroft*, 2:183. While noting that Bancroft's response to this exchange revealed that he shared Ranke's commitment to objectivity, Handlin, *George Bancroft* (295–96), in the end differentiates between Ranke and Bancroft by pointing to Bancroft's criticism of Ranke for his unwillingness to make judgments about historical events and actors. See also Wish, *American Historian*, 75, 84, on the contrast between Ranke and Bancroft. On Bancroft's studies with Ranke, see Nye, *George Bancroft: Brahmin Rebel*, 98, and Iggers, "Image of Ranke," 19.

26. Ranke, quoted in Krieger, *Ranke*, 361. On this quotation and the misunderstanding of Ranke by American historians, see Novick, *That Noble Dream*, 26–31; Iggers, "Image of Ranke," 17–40; and Iggers, *German Conception of History*, 63–89.

27. On the ambiguous meaning of this term, see Georg Iggers, introduction to Ranke, *Theory and Practice of History*, xix–xx, and Novick, *That Noble Dream*, 28.

28. Ranke, quoted in Leopold von Ranke, *The Secret of World History: Selected Writings on the Art and Science of History*, ed. Roger Wines (New York: Fordham University Press, 1981), 21. On this quotation, see Novick, *That Noble Dream*, 28.

29. On Ranke's belief in a higher spiritual reality underlying the "actual" reality of historical events, see Iggers, *German Conception of History*, 76–80.

30. See Vitzthum, *American Compromise*, 33–36, on Bancroft's belief that an impartial analysis of empirical reality would reveal providential design. On Bancroft's assump-

tion that the progress of democracy represented objective truth, see Handlin, *George Bancroft*, 295.

31. Bancroft, "Documentary History of the Revolution," 480.

32. Bancroft, *History of the United States*, 8: 116–17. On how Bancroft was influenced by the view of history as philosophy and how he combined what Nye terms a "Rationalistic" scientific approach with a Romantic conception of history, see Nye, *George Bancroft: Brahmin Rebel*, 94–100. See also Rathbun, "George Bancroft on Man and History," 67–68, and Vitzthum, *American Compromise*, 33–36, on how Bancroft reconciled his view of history as an empirical science with his view of history as philosophy. On how Bancroft shared with other Romantic historians the belief that the historian was supposed to be a judge whose purpose was to measure historical actors according to universal moral laws, see Levin, *History as Romantic Art*, 24–27.

33. Bancroft, *History of the United States*, 1:502. On Bancroft's treatment of Puritan intolerance, see Handlin, *George Bancroft*, 136.

34. Bancroft, *History of the United States*, 1:500, 508. See Dawson, *Unusable Past*, 27–31, on Bancroft's role in establishing the identification between Puritanism and democracy.

35. In general, on how historians from the Massachusetts elite sought to define the nation in terms of New England by glorifying the Puritans, see Sheidley, *Sectional Nationalism*, 122–27.

36. On the theme of union in Bancroft's history, see Vitzthum, *American Compromise*, 15–17. See Bercovitch, *Rites of Assent*, 181–84, on Bancroft's desire to promote unity and consensus.

37. Lord Mahon to George Bancroft, 14 Nov. 1852, Bancroft Papers. For a discussion of how Bancroft's history was both praised for its impartiality and criticized for its bias by Bancroft's contemporaries, see Nye, *George Bancroft: Brahmin Rebel*, 102–4, 112–13. See also Handlin, *George Bancroft*, 126, on the critical response to Bancroft's history.

38. Bancroft, "Documentary History of the Revolution," 483. For parallels to Ranke's belief that impartiality involved a recognition of universal connections in history, see Krieger, *Ranke*, 270–72.

39. On Bancroft's insight into the international context for American developments, and on the attention he gave to English and European events, see Kraus, *History of American History*, 224–30, and Nye, *George Bancroft*, 154–60. For parallels to William Robertson's understanding of impartiality to mean a comprehensive view and the religious roots of this understanding, see Smitten, "Impartiality in Robertson's *History of America*," 58–72.

40. Bancroft, *History of the United States*, 8: 120–21.

41. John Kenrick to George Bancroft, 4 June 1852, Bancroft Papers.

42. Bancroft, *History of the United States*, 3:2. For a brief discussion of Bancroft's attitude toward the English civil wars and the Glorious Revolution, see Noble, *Historians against History*, 25–26.

43. Bancroft, *History of the United States*, 4:243–44.

44. Ibid., 6:56.

45. Ibid., 3:1–2.

46. Bancroft, "Early Colonial History," 434. Here, I depart from Ross, "Historical Consciousness in Nineteenth-Century America" (915–19), who emphasizes the limits on Bancroft's historical understanding and attributes these limitations to his providential perspective. See Allan, *Virtue, Learning and the Scottish Enlightenment*, 109–19, 207–18, on the Calvinist understanding of causality in Scottish historical writing and on the close relationship between the Scottish theory of unintended consequences and providential theories of causation.

47. For a discussion of the Romantic historians' insight into the historical role played by the "involuntary agents of progress," see Levin, *History as Romantic Art*, 30–31. See Wood, "Conspiracy and the Paranoid Style," 429–39, on the emergence of a theory of unintended consequences in history and its relationship to liberal capitalism and Protestant conceptions of Providence.

48. Kant, "Idea for a Universal History," 11–12. On how Bancroft's "idealistic interpretation of history" contributed to his disregard for economic forces in his history, and on the influence of Kant and other German idealist philosophers on this perspective, see Wish, *American Historian*, 70–87. For the influence of German idealism and Kant in particular on Bancroft's theory of history and his recognition of the human capacity for both good and evil, see Rathbun, "George Bancroft on Man and History," 54–56, 62–64. See also Nye, *George Bancroft: Brahmin Rebel*, 98–101, and Nye, *George Bancroft*, 110–27, on how German idealism influenced Bancroft. While pointing to the conflict between Bancroft's "cloudy idealism" and his more realistic side, Vitzthum, *American Compromise* (17–41), is insightful in recognizing how Bancroft's philosophical perspective may have contributed to his "intelligent and perceptive" understanding of American history.

49. For a discussion of how Hawthorne and other historical novelists in this period challenged patriotic mythology about the Puritans, see Bell, *Hawthorne and the Historical Romance of New England*; Colacurcio, *Province of Piety*; and Gould, *Covenant and Republic*.

50. On the development of a more critical view of the Puritans by historians in this period, and on the conflicts in historical treatments of the Puritans, see Buell, *New England Literary Culture*, 211–38, and Craven, *Legend of the Founding Fathers*, 112–17. On the tensions in early nineteenth-century interpretations of the Puritans, see Bell, *Hawthorne and the Historical Romance of New England*, 5–50. See Dawson, *Unusable Past*, esp. 25–38, for further discussion of perceptions of the Puritans in this period. For the sake of convenience, in this chapter and the following chapter, I use the term *revisionist* to refer to those historians who challenged patriotic myths by offering a more critical view of colonial and Revolutionary American history. Though this was not a term that they or their contemporaries would have used, and though, as I will demonstrate, there were important differences between individuals within this group, they could be classified as part of a revisionist school, for they were similar in self-consciously distinguishing themselves from what they believed was the orthodox patriotic interpretation of American history.

51. "Bancroft's History of the United States," 178–79.

52. Ibid., 173. On the image of the southern Cavalier, see Ritchie Devon Watson Jr., *Cavalier in Virginia Fiction*, and Taylor, *Cavalier and Yankee: The Old South and American National Character*. See also Dawson, *Unusable Past*, 61–68, on how antebellum southerners used the image of the Cavalier to critique the New England Puritans. On the popular image of the Cavalier and the resistance of southern historians to this image, see Craven, *Legend of the Founding Fathers*, 109–113. On how sectional concerns contributed to the Southern rejection of the Puritan myth and how southerners sought to develop their own alternative to this account of the nation's origins, see Bonner, "Americans Apart," 203–16.

53. Oliver, *Puritan Commonwealth*, 73.

54. Ibid., 151. For further discussion of Oliver's interpretation of the Puritans, see Buell, *New England Literary Culture*, 229–30.

55. George Edward Ellis, "Oliver's Puritan Commonwealth," 426–27. On how interpretations of the Puritan history reflected sectarian disputes between orthodox Congregationalists and Unitarians, and on the ambivalence that Unitarian historians displayed toward their Puritan ancestors, see Buell, *New England Literary Culture*, 215–38. On how liberal Unitarian ambivalence about the Puritans corresponded to their desire to establish a middle position between evangelical Calvinists and conservative Unitarians, see Dawson, *Unusable Past*, 31–38.

56. Motley, "Polity of the Puritans," 476. On this essay and Motley's attitude toward the Puritans, see Sargent, "Conservative Covenant," 248–49. For a more general discussion of Motley as a historian, see Levin, *History as Romantic Art*, esp. 186–209, and Owen Dudley Edwards, "John Lothrop Motley," in *American Historians, 1607–1865*, 175–91.

57. Motley, "Polity of the Puritans," 477, 472.

58. Ibid., 478–79.

59. Ibid., 480.

60. Ibid., 486.

61. Ibid., 471. On how Motley shared the assumptions of those he challenged in his depiction of the Pilgrims, see Sargent, "Conservative Covenant," 248–49. See also Buell, *New England Literary Culture*, 200–201, on how Bancroft shared with Whig orators the belief in America's special destiny.

62. Motley, "Polity of the Puritans," 497. On Motley's Whig affiliation and his distrust of democracy, see Edwards, "John Lothrop Motley," 179, 181–82. On Whig political ideology and its regard for tradition and experience, see Daniel Walker Howe, *Political Culture of the American Whigs*, esp. 33–35, 69–75, 227–37, and Matthews, "Whig History," 193–208. On how these assumptions contributed to Whig skepticism about the French Revolution of 1848, see Rohrs, "American Critics of the French Revolution of 1848," 367–69.

63. Motley, "Polity of the Puritans," 492. On the Whig response to the revolutions of 1848, see Daniel Walker Howe, *Political Culture of the American Whigs*, 34. On the American reaction to the European revolutions of 1848, Morrison, "American Reaction to European Revolutions," 111–122; Roberts, "'Revolutions Have Become the Bloody Toy

of the Multitude'"; Curtis, "American Opinion of the French Nineteenth-Century Revolutions," 254–63; Curti, "Impact of the Revolutions of 1848 on American Thought"; and Rohrs, "American Critics of the French Revolution of 1848," 359–77.

64. Motley, "Polity of the Puritans," 497.

65. On how the New England elite used Puritan history to further their conservative social purposes in general, see Matthews, "Whig History," 200–202, and Sheidley, *Sectional Nationalism*, 122–32. Both Matthews and Sheidley, however, emphasize the way in which those purposes contributed to a heroic view of the Puritans. On how Motley's fellow members of the New England intellectual elite expressed their ambivalence about democracy through their faith in progress and their view of America's special role as an agent of progress, see Foletta, *Coming to Terms with Democracy*, 182–97. On the importance of the belief in America's distinctive social conditions to exceptionalist ideology, see Greene, *Intellectual Construction of America*, 142–47, 175–82.

66. Melish, *Disowning Slavery*, 1–6, 210–37. See Seelye, *Memory's Nation*, 222–49, 259–77, for a discussion of how abolitionists used the memory of the Pilgrims to legitimize their own activism against slavery. On how nineteenth-century New Englanders used the Puritans to legitimize the politicization of moral issues such as abolition, see Dawson, *Unusable Past*, 39–44. In general, on how antebellum northerners defined their nationalism in opposition to the South, see Grant, *North over South*.

67. Motley, "Polity of the Puritans," 479. On the erasure of slavery by New England historians from their own region, see also Teed, "Politics of Sectional Memory," 324.

68. Oliver, *Puritan Commonwealth*, 346; see, for example, 120–21, 131, 147.

69. Bancroft, *History of the United States*, 4:150.

70. Ibid., 3:408.

71. Ibid., 8:466, 3:402. On Bancroft's portrayal of slavery as a southern and un-American institution imposed by the British, see Noble, *Historians against History*, 35–36. In general, on how Bancroft expressed his hostility to slavery in his history, see Nye, *George Bancroft: Brahmin Rebel*, 105–6. On the limited character of that opposition, see Handlin, *George Bancroft*, 172–73, 186–87.

72. Palfrey, *History of New England*, 1:xv. For background on Palfrey, see Gatell, *John Gorham Palfrey*.

73. Palfrey, *History of New England*, 1:xiii. On the biases of Palfrey's history and his effort to provide a critical analysis of his sources, see Gatell, *John Gorham Palfrey*, 271–76. On Palfrey's filiopiety and his merits as a historian, see also Alexander Moore, "John Gorham Palfrey," in *American Historians, 1607–1865*, 198–201; and Craven, *Legend of the Founding Fathers*, 115–16. See also Buell, *New England Literary Culture*, 227–28, on the relationship between Palfrey's documentary approach and his bias in favor of the Puritans.

74. Palfrey, *History of New England*, 1:xv.

75. Ibid., xvi.

76. Ibid., viii. On Palfrey's racial prejudices, see Gatell, *John Gorham Palfrey*, 155–56, 228. See also Moore, "John Gorham Palfrey," 198–99, on how he expressed his concern

with racial homogeneity in his history. On how the marginalization of slavery from New England's past functioned to define the nation as white, see Melish, *Disowning Slavery*, 210–22, 236–37.

77. Palfrey, *History of New England*, 1:30n. On how both colonizationists and abolitionists alike softened New England's complicity in slavery by emphasizing its mild and limited character, see Melish, *Disowning Slavery*, 210–12, 221–22.

78. Palfrey, *History of New England*, 3:334–35n.

79. Sabine, *American Loyalists*, 1–2. For background on Sabine, see *Dictionary of American Biography*, 1935 ed., s.v. "Sabine, Lorenzo."

80. Sabine, *American Loyalists*, 40, 45.

81. Ibid., 50–57.

82. Ibid., 49.

83. On the development and influence of free labor ideology, see Foner, *Free Soil, Free Labor, Free Men*, esp. 11–72. On how northerners portrayed the South's commitment to slavery as a threat to the nation, see Grant, *North over South*, 47–53.

84. Sabine, *American Loyalists*, 32.

85. Ibid., 36. On how the erasure of slavery from New England's past went hand in hand with efforts to define New England—and national identity—in terms of free labor and in opposition to the South, see Melish, *Disowning Slavery*, 3, 217–23. On the sectional character of New England nationalism, see Grant, *North over South*, and Sheidley, *Sectional Nationalism*.

86. On the complex relationship between northern nationalism and slavery, and on northern attacks on the South as a threat to a nation based on commerce and industry, see Grant, *North over South*, 42–57.

87. Amicus, *Slavery among the Puritans*, 20.

88. Ibid., 31.

89. Ibid., 5.

90. Ibid., 39.

91. Ibid., 7.

92. Ibid., 10.

93. Ibid., 3.

94. Ibid., 27. See Melish, *Disowning Slavery*, for an influential challenge to the image of colonial New England as a free society.

95. On how, in general, antebellum southern historical interpreters at once embraced a "shared national frame of reference" (154) and sought to articulate a distinctive sectional identity based partly on the incorporation of slavery into their region's history, see Bonner, "Americans Apart," 150–216.

96. Cartwright, "Canaan Identified with the Ethiopian," 322. On Cartwright's influence as a pro-slavery theorist and his appeal to scientific authority in his medical writing on slavery, see Guillory, "Pro-Slavery Arguments of Dr. Samuel A. Cartwright." For background on Cartwright, see also Kenneth H. Williams, "Cartwright, Samuel Adolphus," *American National Biography Online*, Feb. 2000, http://www.anb.org/articles/12/12-01227.html (20 Mar. 2007).

97. Cartwright, "Canaan Identified with the Ethiopian," 348. On how antebellum American religious thinkers reconciled a Baconian ideal of scientific inquiry based on induction from empirical evidence with their religious beliefs, see Bozeman, *Protestants in an Age of Science.*

98. Cartwright, "Canaan Identified with the Ethiopian," 360, 359. On how Cartwright appealed to history in his defense of slavery, see Guillory, "Pro-Slavery Arguments of Dr. Samuel A. Cartwright," 216–18.

99. Cartwright, "Canaan Identified with the Ethiopian," 359.

100. Ibid., 357, 359.

101. For similarities to Simms's concern with avoiding the appearance of partisanship in his defense of slavery, and on his belief that such a defense was supposed to both express "transcendent values" and be based on objective empirical analysis, see Faust, *Sacred Circle,* 117–27.

102. Cartwright, "Canaan Identified with the Ethiopian," 355.

103. Ibid., 360–61. On Cartwright's belief that northern abolitionist agitation was the product of British intrigues and his desire to combat the divisive effects of such intrigues, see Guillory, "Pro-Slavery Arguments of Dr. Samuel A. Cartwright," 211–12, 217–18, though Guillory emphasizes to a greater extent Cartwright's effort to target northern antislavery activists and the limits to his concern with national unity.

104. Cartwright, "Canaan Identified with the Ethiopian," 380, 382, 363, 344–45. See Guillory, "Pro-Slavery Arguments of Dr. Samuel A. Cartwright," 216, 222, 224, on the religious basis for Cartwright's claims that Africans were innately suited for slavery and his use of the Revolution to demonstrate their natural attachment to slavery. On the southern commitment to its own version of manifest destiny, see McCardell, *Idea of a Southern Nation,* 227–76.

105. Cartwright, "Canaan Identified with the Ethiopian," 367.

106. Donald E. Emerson, *Richard Hildreth,* offers the most complete biographical discussion of Hildreth. See also John Braeman, "Richard Hildreth," in *American Historians, 1607–1865,* 116–33.

107. For the view of Hildreth as anomalous in his concern with objective truth, see, for example, Alfred H. Kelly, "Richard Hildreth," in Hutchinson, *Marcus W. Jernegan Essays,* 27–41; Van Tassel, *Recording America's Past,* 139–40; Wish, *American Historian,* 58–69; and Kraus, *Writing of American History,* 129–31. For further discussion of the complex relationship between Hildreth's historical and political thought, see Schlesinger, "Problem of Richard Hildreth," who, however, still perpetuates the view of Hildreth's history as concerned with objectivity for its own sake. For exceptions to this tendency, see Loewenberg, *American History in American Thought,* 260–84, who demonstrates how Hildreth used his history to further his philosophical and social purposes, and Buell, *New England Literary Culture,* 230–32, who recognizes that Hildreth's critical perspective on American history was not as anomalous as other scholars have assumed.

108. Hildreth, *History of the United States of America, from the Discovery of the Continent,* 1:iii.

109. Schlesinger, "Problem of Richard Hildreth," 226–29. See also Loewenberg,

American History in American Thought, 261–63, for a challenge to the view of Hildreth as the antithesis of Bancroft.

110. On Hildreth's definition of truth and how his style reflected his assumptions about truth, see Loewenberg, *American History in American Thought*, 284; Kelly, "Richard Hildreth," 29–32; Schlesinger, "Problem of Richard Hildreth," 231–33; and Donald E. Emerson, "Hildreth, Draper, and 'Scientific History,'" 152.

111. On how Hildreth embodied the tendency to define objective truth in opposition to feminine qualities, see Bonnie Smith, *Gender of History*, 139.

112. On Hildreth's critical view of the Puritans, see Braeman, "Richard Hildreth," 125, and Wish, *American Historian*, 62.

113. Hildreth, *History of the United States of America, from the Discovery of the Continent*, 1:403–4.

114. Braeman, "Richard Hildreth," 126–27, summarizes Hildreth's account of this process.

115. Hildreth, *History of the United States of America, from the Discovery of the Continent*, 2:143–44.

116. Ibid., 3:391, 1:508. On Hildreth's portrayal of slavery as a southern institution, see Teed, "Politics of Sectional Memory," 324.

117. Hildreth, *History of the United States of America, from the Discovery of the Continent*, 1:508.

118. Ibid., 3:97.

119. Ibid., 1:508. On Hildreth's belief that slavery was wrong because it violated the individual's right to free labor, see Emerson, *Richard Hildreth*, 77. On Hildreth's commitment to free labor ideology, see Foner, *Free Soil, Free Labor, Free Men*, 51.

120. Hildreth, *History of the United States of America, from the Discovery of the Continent*, 2:197, 430. On Hildreth's economic interpretation of history, see Braeman, "Richard Hildreth," 125–26, and Schlesinger, "Problem of Richard Hildreth," 239–41.

121. Hildreth, *History of the United States of America, from the Discovery of the Continent*, 3:390.

122. Ibid., 390–91. Braeman, "Richard Hildreth" (120, 126), discusses Hildreth's reservations about the consequences of the Revolution and his belief that the nation's fate depended on its ability to resolve the problem of slavery.

123. On the belief in the success of the Revolution and the importance of this belief to exceptionalist ideology, see Ross, *Origins of American Social Science*, 22–23; Greene, *Intellectual Construction of America*, 162–74, 194–97; and Craven, *Legend of the Founding Fathers*, 59–63.

124. Hildreth, *History of the United States of America, from the Discovery of the Continent*, 3:400–401.

125. Wish, *American Historian* (58–69); Braeman, "Richard Hildreth" (125–26); Donald E. Emerson, "Hildreth, Draper, and 'Scientific History'"; Schlesinger, "Problem of Richard Hildreth" (237–41); and Loewenberg, *American History in American Thought* (260, 270, 272, 282), discuss Hildreth's positivist outlook and the influence of utilitarian philosophy on his *History*.

126. On the cosmic framework for exceptionalist ideology and Hildreth's rejection of this millennial framework, see Ross, *Origins of American Social Science*, 24–26, and Ross, "Historical Consciousness in Nineteenth-Century America " 909–17, 919.

127. See Schlesinger, "Problem of Richard Hildreth," 234, on the centrality of democracy to Hildreth's social thought.

128. Hildreth, *Theory of Politics*, v. On the close relationship between the ideas discussed in these two works, see Braeman, "Richard Hildreth," 130. See Loewenberg, *American History in American Thought*, 272–77, on how Hildreth used his history to express his philosophical views. See Buell, *New England Literary Culture*, 231–32, on the philosophical outlook embedded in Hildreth's history.

129. Hildreth, *Theory of Politics*, 264–65. On Hildreth's hostility to religion, see Schlesinger, "Problem of Richard Hildreth," 234–35. On how Hildreth's history reflected his hostility to religion and mystical ideas, see Loewenberg, *American History in American Thought*, 271, 277, and Wish, *American Historian*, 62.

130. Hildreth, *Theory of Politics*, 265.

131. Ibid., 262.

132. Ibid., 261–62. See Braeman, "Richard Hildreth," 130, for Hildreth's views on the advantages of democracy. On Hildreth's general faith in progress, see Braeman, "Richard Hildreth," 126, and Pingel, *American Utilitarian*, 9, and on how Hildreth sought to further progress through his historical and philosophical works, see Loewenberg, *American History in American Thought*, 272–84. On Hildreth's commitment to a Scottish view of progress, see Ross, "Historical Consciousness in Nineteenth-Century America," 919. On Hildreth's commitment to the assumptions of classical liberalism and his "middle-class" vision of American society, see Braeman, "Richard Hildreth," 131.

133. These figures come from Emerson, *Richard Hildreth* (142–43), who takes them from Hildreth's "Literary Memoranda" and from *Trübner's Bibliographical Guide to American Literature* (London: Trübner and Co., 1859), lxxxvi, respectively. On the critical and popular reception for Hildreth's *History*, see Emerson, *Richard Hildreth*, 131–34. On the mixed and contradictory critical response to Hildreth's history, see Buell, *New England Literary Culture*, 230–32.

134. Curry, "Hildreth's History of the United States," 418–19.

135. Ibid., 425.

136. On Parker and the relationship between history and his reform concerns, see Teed, "Politics of Sectional Memory."

137. Parker, "Hildreth's History of the United States," 425, 423.

138. Ibid., 397.

139. Ibid., 398.

140. Ibid., 396, 407. On the limits to Parker's critical view of the Puritans, see Teed, "Politics of Sectional Memory," 323–24.

141. On the relationship between Parker's desire to formulate what he considered an objective antislavery stance and his portrayal of the Puritans, see Teed, "Politics of Sectional Memory," 302, 307–9, 322–27.

142. Parker, "Hildreth's History of the United States," 391, 386. On the exceptionalist

belief in the United States as a political model for the rest of humanity, see Greene, *Intellectual Construction of America*, 207–8.

143. Parker, "Hildreth's History of the United States," 389.

144. Ibid., 391.

145. Ibid., 391, 423–24.

146. Ibid., 423, 391.

147. "Recent American Histories," 201.

148. Ibid., 198.

149. Ibid., 201.

150. For background on Bowen, see *Dictionary of American Biography*, 1927 ed., s.v. "Bowen, Francis"; and William Rossi, "Francis Bowen," *The American Renaissance in New England, Third Series*, vol. 235 of *Dictionary of Literary Biography*, ed. Wesley T. Mott (Detroit: Gale Group, 2001), 33–37. On the importance of impartiality as a principle in Bowen's literary criticism, see Monica Green, "Francis Bowen," *American Literary Critics and Scholars, 1800–1850*, vol. 59 of *Dictionary of Literary Biography*, ed. John Rathbun and Monica Green (Detroit: Gale Group, 1987), 20–25, in *Literature Resource Center*, http://galenet.galegroup.com/servlet/LitRC?vrsn=3&OP=contains&locID=nypl &srchtp=athr&ca=1&c=2&stab=128&ste=9&tab=4&tbst=arp&ai=U13687928&n=10& docNum=H1200004970&ST=francis+bowen&bConts=8365#WritingsSection (28 June 2007).

151. Bowen, "Hildreth's History of the United States," 414–15.

152. Ibid., 413.

153. Ibid., 412–13.

154. Ibid., 412.

155. Ibid., 444.

156. Ibid., 427.

157. Ibid., 411–12.

158. Ibid., 426. On the dangerous social connotations of "zealotry" for historical writers in this period, see Gould, *Covenant and Republic*, 172–209, and his "New England Witch-Hunting," 62–68.

159. Francis Bowen to Lorenzo Sabine, April 1844, Sabine Papers.

160. Bowen, "Recent Contest in Rhode Island," 404. On the Whig response to the Dorr Rebellion, see Daniel Walker Howe, *Political Culture of the American Whigs*, 85–86, and Matthews, "Whig History," 204–5.

161. Bowen, "Revolutions in Europe," 197.

162. Bowen, "Hildreth's History," 446.

163. Ibid., 444–46.

164. Ibid., 446.

165. And in this understanding of impartiality, they differed from the scientific historians of the late nineteenth century, who, as Novick, *That Noble Dream* (37), discusses, believed that "objectivity" required the historian to eschew such questions.

FIVE. The "Losers" of the Revolution

1. George Atkinson Ward, *Journal and Letters of the Late Samuel Curwen*, 3d ed., 618.

2. Important essays on loyalist historiography include Wallace Brown, "View at Two Hundred Years"; Bernard Bailyn, "The Losers: Notes on the Historiography of Loyalism," in *Ordeal of Thomas Hutchinson*, 383–408; George A. Billias, "The First Un-Americans: The Loyalists in American Historiography," in Billias and Vaughan, *Perspectives on Early American History*, 282–324; and most recently, Patton, "The Beat of a Different Drummer." Both Brown and Patton recognize to a limited extent that complaints about loyalist neglect have been exaggerated, particularly with respect to the nineteenth century, but even they ultimately emphasize the general antagonism toward the loyalists. Works that emphasize the uncritical patriotism of historians in this period, and their filiopietistic view of history, include Bassett, *Middle Group of American Historians*, 184–87, and Jameson, *History of Historical Writing in America*, 104–8.

3. For a useful discussion and critique of the tendency to define American nationalism in terms of ideals, see Waldstreicher, *In the Midst of Perpetual Fetes*, 1–14. See also Rogers Smith, *Civic Ideals*, 14–15, for a challenge to the deeply rooted assumption that the idealistic character of American nationalism made it universalistic and inclusive. For another recent challenge to the belief that American identity was based on ideals, see Purcell, *Sealed with Blood*.

4. See Shaffer, *The Politics of History*, 120–23, on how the desire to promote unity contributed to the neglect and vilification of the loyalists by the Revolutionary historians. For the way in which American nationalist mythology contributed to the repudiation of the loyalists as un-American, see especially Billias, "First Un-Americans," 282–324. See also Fisher, "Legendary and Myth-Making Process," 54–56, on how nationalist imperatives contributed to the neglect and vilification of the loyalists. On the problems that the loyalists caused for efforts to create a national identity based on memories of the Revolutionary War during this period, see Purcell, *Sealed with Blood*, 66–70.

5. See Lendrum, *Concise and Impartial History of the American Revolution*, and Burk, *History of Virginia*.

6. For further discussion of the vilification of Hutchinson during the Revolution, see Bailyn, *Ordeal of Thomas Hutchinson*.

7. Warren, *History of the Rise, Progress, and Termination of the American Revolution*, 1:45–46. Billias, "First Un-Americans" (284–85), takes Warren's hostile portrayal of Hutchinson as representative of how the Revolutionary historians viewed the loyalists. For further discussion of Warren's history, see Cohen, "Explaining the Revolution."

8. Warren, *History of the Rise, Progress, and Termination of the American Revolution*, 1:70.

9. On Warren's perception of corruption and degeneration in her own time, see Cohen, foreword to ibid., 1:xviii–xxii, and Cohen, "Explaining the Revolution," 200–203, 212–13. For the similarities to Ramsay's conception of American nationality, see Shaffer,

To Be an American, 124–25, and Shaffer, *Politics of History*, 43–48. On the efforts that the Revolutionary generation made to establish American nationality on this basis, see Royster, "Founding a Nation in Blood," 27–29. For background on the difficulties that the loyalists created for Revolutionary conceptions of national allegiance, and on their role in the development of the idea of volitional allegiance, see Kettner, *Development of American Citizenship*, 183–209.

10. For background on Ramsay, see Shaffer, *To Be an American*.

11. Ramsay, *History of the American Revolution*, app. 3, 2:603.

12. Ibid., app. 4, 2:629.

13. On Ramsay's complex view of patriot and loyalist motivation and his exclusion of the loyalists from any claims to American nationality, see Shaffer, *Politics of History*, 120–22, and Shaffer, *To Be an American*, 123–25. The ambiguous character of Ramsay's analysis is evident in the varying assessments of his attitude toward the loyalists. Compare Brown, "View at Two Hundred Years," 26, with Billias, "First Un-Americans," 285. On Ramsay's changing view of the loyalists, see Kornfeld, "From Republicanism to Liberalism," 293, 297. On both the extent of and limits to Ramsay's appreciation for dissent in general, see Messer, *Stories of Independence*, 148–49.

14. On the development of American nationalism immediately following the War of 1812, see Dangerfield, *Awakening of American Nationalism*. On how a growing sense of national confidence affected American literature, see Spencer, *Quest for Nationality*, 102–55. On the differences between the Revolutionary historians and their successors, see Shaffer, *Politics of History*, 174–80. See Billias, "First Un-Americans," 291–92, on how this strident nationalism intensified hostility to the loyalists. I depart from Billias, however, in arguing that this tendency represented only one strand in antebellum portrayals of the loyalists. While recognizing that Americans in this period felt undercurrents of anxiety, Rush Welter emphasizes their sense of national complacency and confidence in his *The Mind of America*, 3–44. See Hoffer, *Liberty or Order*, 152–68, on how American historians reacted to this sense of uncertainty by advancing an uncritical form of nationalism that emphasized unity and order.

15. Bancroft, *History of the United States*, 6:462–63. For works that portray Bancroft as a leading exponent of American nationalist mythology, see Ross, "Historical Consciousness in Nineteenth-Century America," and Bercovitch, *Rites of Assent*, 168–93. On Bancroft's hostility to the loyalists and the influence of his interpretation over his contemporaries, see Billias, "First Un-Americans," 291–92; Brown, "View at Two Hundred Years," 32; and Fisher, "Legendary and Myth-Making Process," 68–69.

16. Bancroft, *History of the United States*, 8:250. For the similarities to Ramsay's conception of American nationality, see Shaffer, *To Be an American*, 124–25, and Shaffer, *Politics of History*, 43–48. See Curti, *Roots of American Loyalty*, 146–47, on American hostility to the doctrine of perpetual allegiance and the way in which a voluntary conception of national loyalty served both American ideals and interests. On the development of this voluntary notion of allegiance, see Kettner, *Development of American Citizenship*.

17. Bancroft, *History of the United States*, 8:598–99.

18. For further background on this circle, see Sheidley, *Sectional Nationalism*; Foletta, *Coming to Terms with Democracy*; Simpson, *Federalist Literary Mind*; Daniel Walker Howe, *Unitarian Conscience*; and Field, "Birth of Secular High Culture."

19. William Smith, *History of the Province of New-York*; Carroll, *Historical Collections of South Carolina*; Chalmers, *Introduction to the History of the Revolt of the Colonies*; George Atkinson Ward, *Journal and Letters of the Late Samuel Curwen*; Van Schaack, *Life of Peter Van Schaack*; Simcoe, *Simcoe's Military Journal*; Sabine, *American Loyalists*. For one of the few studies that recognizes the emergence of this critical perspective, see Weddington, "Image of the American Revolution in the United States," 170–99. For examples of such reviews, see George Edward Ellis, "Sabine's Sketches of the Loyalists"; "Curwen's Journal and Letters," *Democratic Review*; Ware, "Curwen's Journal and Letters"; [W. Smith], "American Loyalists"; Peale, "American Loyalists"; Minor, "Impartiality of History"; "Simcoe's Military Journal."

20. Minor, "Impartiality of History," 448.

21. Ibid.

22. Jared Sparks to George Atkinson Ward, 20 May 1845, Sparks Papers, MS Sparks 147h. By permission of the Houghton Library, Harvard University. For background on Sparks, see Herbert Baxter Adams, *Life and Writings of Jared Sparks*, and Michael Stevens, "Jared Sparks," in *American Historians, 1607–1865*, 298–309.

23. Sparks to Ward, 20 May 1845, Sparks Papers.

24. Jared Sparks, preface to Chalmers's *Introduction to the History of the Revolt of the Colonies*, viii. On the origins of this understanding of impartiality in the legal discourse of early modern England, see Shapiro, *Culture of Fact*, 29–30.

25. On how the Revolutionary historians reconciled their commitment to impartiality with their moral theory of history, see Cohen, *Revolutionary Histories*, 161–92. On the importance of judgment to historical analysis in early modern English conceptions of history, see Shapiro, *Culture of Fact*, 43–44.

26. Sabine, "Chalmers's History of the American Colonies," 369.

27. On how the growing importance of public opinion in this period challenged the belief in absolute truth, see Wood, *Radicalism of the American Revolution*, 362–46.

28. On Adams's notions of social hierarchy, see David Donald and Aida Donald, introduction to Charles Francis Adams, *Diary*, ed. Donald and Donald, 1:ix–xxi. For further background on Adams, see Duberman, *Charles Francis Adams*, and Kinley Brauer, "Adams, Charles Francis," *American National Biography Online*, February 2000, http://www.anb.org/articles/04/04-00004.html (24 June 2007). For a more general discussion of the democratic tendencies that caused Adams and his cohorts such anxiety, see Wood, *Radicalism of the American Revolution*, and Sheidley, *Sectional Nationalism*, 20–21. On the ambivalence of Adams's fellow Brahmins toward both democracy and their Federalist heritage, see Foletta, *Coming to Terms with Democracy*, esp. 11–13, 45–75.

29. Charles Francis Adams, 19 Sept. 1833, in Charles Francis Adams, *Diary*, ed. Friedlaender and Butterfield, 5:173–74.

30. On Adams's desire to live up to his family heritage and the anxieties this heritage caused him, see Donald and Donald, introduction to Charles Francis Adams, *Diary*, ed. Donald and Donald, 1:xxiii–xxxi. Specifically on his efforts to follow his family's tradition of political independence, see Marc Friedlaender and L. H. Butterfield, introduction to Charles Francis Adams, *Diary*, ed. Friedlaender and Butterfield, 5:xxiv–xxvi, and Marc Friedlaender and others, introduction to Charles Francis Adams, *Diary*, ed. Friedlaender and others, 7:xvi–xxii. On Adams's decision to join the Antimasons and his distrust of democracy, see Duberman, *Charles Francis Adams*, 43–55, 75.

31. Charles Francis Adams, "Hutchinson's Third Volume," 136. Adams's argument here anticipates in an interesting way Bernard Bailyn's interpretation of Hutchinson. See Bailyn, *Ordeal of Thomas Hutchinson*, esp. 2, 375–80, on John Adams's hatred for Hutchinson.

32. On the importance of the Revolution to the ideology of American exceptionalism, see Baym, *American Women Writers and the Work of History*, 56, and Greene, *Intellectual Construction of America*, 162–74, 207–8.

33. Charles Francis Adams, "Hutchinson's Third Volume," 154–55.

34. Charles Francis Adams, "Life of Peter Van Schaack," 99.

35. Charles Francis Adams, "Ward's Memoir of Samuel Curwen," 97.

36. For a discussion of the evolution of Adams's views on slavery and his role in the antislavery movement, see Duberman, *Charles Francis Adams*, 61–66, 80–138.

37. Charles Francis Adams, "Ward's Memoir of Samuel Curwen," 97.

38. See Kettner, *Development of American Citizenship*, 13–61, 173–247, 287–333, for a discussion of the historical roots of this notion of natural and perpetual allegiance and, in general, on the ambiguities and inconsistencies in American conceptions of citizenship and allegiance. On how both Jacksonians and Whigs appealed to ascriptive doctrines of nationality during the Jacksonian era, see Rogers Smith, *Civic Ideals*, 197–242.

39. George Atkinson Ward, "Curwen's Journal," 51. For Ward's interpretation of the loyalists, see especially George Atkinson Ward, *Journal and Letters of the Late Samuel Curwen*, 3rd ed., 648, and George Atkinson Ward, "Notice of a Review of 'Curwen's Journal,'" 424. For a strikingly similar modern interpretation, see Becker, "John Jay and Peter Van Schaack," 297–98.

40. Ward, quoted in Charles Francis Adams, "Ward's Memoir of Samuel Curwen," 93.

41. Charles Francis Adams, "Ward's Memoir of Samuel Curwen," 93.

42. In general on the difficulties that the loyalists created for the belief in American exceptionalism, see Billias, "First Un-Americans," 284. On the relationship between the Revolution and the belief in American distinctiveness, see Bercovitch, *Rites of Assent*, 168–93; Greene, *Intellectual Construction of America*, 162–74, 207–8; and Baym, *American Women Writers and the Work of History*, 56. For a discussion of the antebellum belief that the nation represented a demonstration of inherently valid principles, see Welter, *Mind of America*, 23–25.

43. Charles Francis Adams, "Ward's Memoir of Samuel Curwen," 92–93.

44. Ibid., 93.

45. Lorenzo Sabine to Jared Sparks, 31 Dec. 1845, Sparks Papers, MS Sparks 153. By permission of the Houghton Library, Harvard University. For background on Sabine, see *Dictionary of American Biography*, 1935 ed., s.v. "Sabine, Lorenzo," and Welch, "Lorenzo Sabine in Maine."

46. Sabine, "Simcoe's Military Journal," 263.

47. Sabine, *American Loyalists*, 34.

48. Ibid., 113.

49. On changing ideas about political parties in this period, see Hofstadter, *Idea of a Party System*, and Formisano, *Transformation of Political Culture*.

50. Lorenzo Sabine to Charles Hazewell, 11 Dec. 1852, Sabine Papers.

51. Sabine, *American Loyalists*, 66.

52. Sabine, "British Colonial Politics," 15.

53. Sabine, *American Loyalists*, 113–14.

54. On the rise of Anglo-Saxon racialism in this period and its exclusionary implications, see Horsman, *Race and Manifest Destiny*. On the Whig appeal to the idea of America's Anglo-Saxon racial destiny, see Rogers Smith, *Civic Ideals*, 206–12. Bailyn, Billias, and Brown point to the close relationship between Anglo-Saxon racialism and loyalist revisionism, but they focus on the role of Anglo-Saxon racialism among late nineteenth- and early twentieth-century historians. See Bailyn, "The Losers," 394–404; Billias, "First Un-Americans," 296–97; and Brown, "View at Two Hundred Years," 28–30.

55. Sabine, "Simcoe's Military Journal," 300. On the growing importance of race to conceptions of American nationality in this period, see Curti, *Roots of American Loyalty*, 75–91, and Rogers Smith, *Civic Ideals*, 197–242.

56. Sabine, "Simcoe's Military Journal," 301, 277. On the duality in American views of England and the relationship of these views to Anglo-Saxon racialism, see Horsman, *Race and Manifest Destiny*, 95–96, 220–27, 292–96. For further discussion of American ambivalence toward England, see Brock, "Image of England and American Nationalism"; Strout, *American Image of the Old World*; and Kohn, *American Nationalism*, 47–56. On the importance of the belief in America's special destiny to the ideology of American exceptionalism, see Welter, *Mind of America*, 45–74; Tuveson, *Redeemer Nation*, 91–186; Merk, *Manifest Destiny*, 3–60, 261–66; Bercovitch, *Rites of Assent*, 147–67; and Ross, *Origins of American Social Science*, 23–26.

57. On the mixture of confidence and anxiety that characterized American nationalism, see Somkin, *Unquiet Eagle*, and Nagel, *Sacred Trust*.

58. Sabine, "Past and Present of the American People," 443–44.

59. William Gilmore Simms to Lorenzo Sabine, 8 Sept. 1856, Sabine Papers. For more on the sectional reverberations of Sabine's book and its role in the Sumner-Brooks incident, see Van Tassel, *Recording America's Past*, 136; Welch, "Lorenzo Sabine and the Assault on Sumner"; Franklin, "The North, the South, and the American Revolution"; and Weddington, "Image of the American Revolution in the United States," 199–234. On

how New England efforts to use history to promote national unity actually contributed to sectional tensions, see Sheidley, *Sectional Nationalism*, 120–22.

60. See Wakelyn, *Politics of a Literary Man*, and Faust, *Sacred Circle*, for background on Simms.

61. Simms, "South Carolina in the Revolution," 38, 40.

62. On Simms's fascination with the loyalists, see Holman, "William Gilmore Simms' Picture of the Revolution," and Busick, *Sober Desire for History*, 47–49, 56–58, 69–70, 72–74, 76, 79–82, 84–85, 92.

63. Simms to Sabine, 8 Sept. 1856, Sabine Papers.

64. Simms, "South Carolina in the Revolution," 51, 53.

65. Sabine, *American Loyalists*, 35–36. Here I offer a more complex view of Sabine's portrayal of the South than do other accounts of this controversy, which take Simms's accusations at face value. See, for example, Van Tassel, *Recording America's Past*, 135–36, and Franklin, "The North, the South, and the American Revolution," 8–18. Likewise, even while recognizing that Simms shared Sabine's interest in the loyalists, Busick, *Sober Desire for History* (79–85), uncritically accepts Simms's characterization of the sectional bias to Sabine's interpretation. On Simms's claims for the disinterested character of South Carolina's support for Revolutionary resistance to Britain, see Busick, *Sober Desire for History*, 54–56.

66. For a discussion of this tendency among the Revolutionary historians, see Shaffer, *Politics of History*, 16–19, 54. On New England efforts to establish cultural dominance over the rest of the nation, see Sheidley, *Sectional Nationalism*, 86–147. On southern concerns about northern cultural imperialism, see McCardell, *Idea of a Southern Nation*, 141–65. For a discussion of southern resentment at New England dominance in the domain of historical interpretation, see Bonner, "Americans Apart," 203–4. On southern anxieties about its cultural inferiority, see Faust, *Sacred Circle*, 7–11. For the dependence of southern writers on northern publishers, see Michael O'Brien, *Conjectures of Order*, 571–80. On how Simms sought to combat New England claims to cultural hegemony through his response to Sabine, see Busick, *Sober Desire for History*, 79–82.

67. Simms, "South Carolina in the Revolution," 44–45. See Wakelyn, *Politics of a Literary Man*, 127–29, on how Simms used the history of the Revolution to defend southern sectional interests against northern attacks. See Franklin, "The North, the South, and the American Revolution," 6–16, on how southerners viewed Sabine's book as part of a broader attack on their region.

68. Simms to Sabine, 8 Sept. 1856, Sabine Papers.

69. See Waldstreicher, *In the Midst of Perpetual Fetes*, 251–62, on how New Englanders and southerners of the early republic used this strategy to reconcile their national and regional loyalties.

70. Simms, "South Carolina in the Revolution," 61.

71. For a different view of the relationship between Simms's national and sectional loyalties, see Higham, "Changing Loyalties of William Gilmore Simms." For another challenge to Higham's interpretation and a discussion of the national framework em-

ployed by South Carolinians as they debated the meaning of the Revolution and sought to articulate a distinctive sectional identity based partly on the incorporation of slavery into their region's history, see Bonner, "Americans Apart," 150–216. See McCardell, *Idea of a Southern Nation*, 143–54, on how Simms reconciled his sectional and national loyalties up through the 1840s. On how Simms brought together these loyalties in his historical writing and on the way he used his recognition of the loyalists to magnify South Carolina's contribution to the Revolution, see Busick, *Sober Desire for History*, 10–13, 50, 81–86. For further discussion of the complex relationship between regional and national loyalties and the way in which these loyalties could converge and reinforce each other, see Curti, *Roots of American Loyalty*, 47–48; Potter, "Historian's Use of Nationalism," 60–83; Sheidley, *Sectional Nationalism*, 119–20; and Waldstreicher, *In the Midst of Perpetual Fetes*, 246–93.

72. Simms, "South Carolina in the Revolution," 46. On Simms's elitism and his distrust of the masses, see Wakelyn, *Politics of a Literary Man*, 51, and Faust, *Sacred Circle*, 105–11.

73. Simms, "Civil Warfare in the Carolinas and Georgia," 260, 264. On Simms's effort to provide a sympathetic and balanced view of the loyalists, see Busick, *Sober Desire for History*, 47, 49, 56–58.

74. Simms, "Civil Warfare in the Carolinas and Georgia," 264. On Simms's belief that citizenship required a willingness to act against external threats, see Busick, *Sober Desire for History*, 60.

75. On the parallels that Simms drew between the revolutionaries and present-day southerners, and on his efforts to use Revolutionary history to incite southerners to action in defense of their own interests and identity, see Faust, *Sacred Circle*, 75, and Wakelyn, *Politics of a Literary Man*, 126. For a different view of the relationship between southern sectional concerns and the belief in American destiny, one that emphasizes the growing tensions between these imperatives, see McCardell, *Idea of a Southern Nation*, 227–76.

76. Simms, *History of South Carolina*, 252–53. On Simms's portrayal of the Revolution as a civil conflict and his complex attitude toward the loyalists in his fictional works, see Busick, *Sober Desire for History*, 47–48, 69–70, 72–74; Holman, "William Gilmore Simms' Picture of the Revolution," 441–62; and Kammen, *Season of Youth*, 177. For a discussion of the influence of contemporary sectional tensions on Simms's interpretation of the Revolution as a civil war, see Wakelyn, *Politics of a Literary Man*, 56.

77. Simms, *History of South Carolina*, 236–37.

78. For another perspective on the political significance of Simms's warning, see Bonner, "Americans Apart," 159–60, 166–69. On how Simms used his account of the Revolution in South Carolina to demonstrate the need for unity within the state, see Busick, *Sober Desire for History*, 51. See also Wakelyn, *Politics of a Literary Man*, 128–29, on how Simms used history to promote southern unity.

79. Simms, *History of South Carolina*, 136–37. On the persistence of Simms's hopes for national unity, even as he became increasingly alienated from the North, and on the

complex relationship between Simms's national and sectional loyalties in general, see Bonner, "Americans Apart," 170.

80. On the role of bloodshed in American conceptions of national identity, see Royster, "Founding a Nation in Blood," 25–48. On how Simms in his novels at once dwelled on the bitter passions engendered by the partisan war within South Carolina and offered hope that such passions could be overcome, see Bonner, "Americans Apart," 166.

81. On the dual image of the American Indian and the myth of the noble savage, see Berkhofer, *White Man's Indian*, 1–28, 72–80, 86–96; Slotkin, *Regeneration through Violence*, 194–205; Pearce, *Savagism and Civilization*, 76, 135–50; Jones, *O Strange New World*, 1–61; and Horsman, *Race and Manifest Destiny*, 103–17. On American outrage at British–Native American collaboration during the Revolution and the myth of the noble savage in the Jeffersonian era, see Sheehan, *Seeds of Extinction*, 89–116, 207–10. See Messer, *Stories of Independence*, 124–29, on the Revolutionary historians' portrayal of Native Americans.

82. See Conn, *History's Shadow*, 156–66, on the relationship between Heckewelder's and Cooper's portrayal of Native Americans and on how the emergence of ethnography contributed to the exclusion of Native Americans from American historical consciousness. On Morgan's role as a founder of the discipline of ethnography in the United States and his portrayal of Native Americans, see Berkhofer, *White Man's Indian*, 51–55. See Pearce, *Savagism and Civilization*, 128–34, 196–212, on Morgan's role in the development of a more "scientific" view of Native Americans by the 1850s and on Cooper's image of Native Americans. See also Slotkin, *Regeneration through Violence*, 356–58, on how the dispossession and removal of Native Americans contributed to the growing fascination with Indian culture in this period.

83. For background on Brant, see Kelsay, *Joseph Brant*. On Stone, see *Dictionary of American Biography*, 1935 ed., s.v. "Stone, William Leete." For a discussion of the conventional emphasis on the brutality of the revolutionaries' Native American opponents and the view of the Wyoming massacre as the epitome of Indian savagery, see Robert Shepard Schwartz, "Image of the American Revolution," 152–59.

84. William L. Stone, *Life of Joseph Brant*, 2:490–91.

85. On the persisting hostility to Indians in historical writing of this period, see Baym, *American Women Writers and the Work of History*, 59–61. For reviewers sympathetic to Brant and his followers, see Thatcher, "Life of Joseph Brant," 137–62; "Stone's Life of Brant"; Perkins, "Border War of the Revolution"; Alexander, "Life of Joseph Brant Thayendanegea"; and "Indian Biography," *Democratic Review*. For a more critical assessment, see "Thayendanega." On Stone's contribution to changing interpretations of Brant, see Kelsay, *Joseph Brant*, 655–56.

86. Alexander, "Life of Joseph Brant Thayendanegea," 2–3.

87. Stone, *Life of Joseph Brant*, 1:xiv–xv. On Stone's condemnation of white American cruelty to Native Americans, see Casper, *Constructing American Lives*, 154.

88. Stone, *Life of Joseph Brant*, 1:xiv, 2:461–62. On the emergence of a willingness to understand Native Americans on their own terms beginning in the mid-nineteenth

century, see Pearce, *Savagism and Civilization*, 128–34. On how the rise of cultural relativism in the twentieth century challenged traditional views of Native Americans, see
Berkhofer, *White Man's Indian*, 62–69.

89. Stone, *Life of Joseph Brant*, 1:xiii–xiv.

90. See Gould, "Catharine Sedgwick's 'Recital' of the Pequot War," 653–56, for parallels to the way in which Catharine Sedgwick's revisionist interpretation of the Pequot
Indians questioned the possibility of achieving objective historical truth.

91. Stone, *Life of Joseph Brant*, 1:xxv.

92. Ibid., xvi.

93. Ibid., xxvi. On Stone's belief in the importance of documentary research as an
antidote to the biases of American writers and records, see Casper, *Constructing American Lives*, 155.

94. See Conn, *History's Shadow*, 6–12, 20–24, 33–34, 56, 198–226, on how the exclusion of Native Americans contributed to the definition of history as a formal discipline.
On the view of documents as a way to counteract the problem of bias and demonstrate
the historian's impartiality in early modern English historical writing, see Shapiro, *Culture of Fact*, 57–58.

95. Stone, *Life of Joseph Brant*, 1:xxvi–xxvii.

96. Ibid., 188. On the deeply rooted tendency to measure Native Americans against
white cultural standards and the inability to understand them on their own terms, see
Berkhofer, *White Man's Indian*, 25–27, and Sheehan, *Seeds of Extinction*, 101–2. See
Pearce, *Savagism and Civilization*, 103–4, 206, for a discussion of how relativism and
absolutism could coexist in portrayals of Native Americans.

97. Stone, *Life of Joseph Brant*, 2:430–31.

98. See Pearce, *Savagism and Civilization*, 66–73, 82–100, for a discussion of the
influence of Scottish conjectural history on American perceptions of Native Americans
and the belief that, as a "hunter" society, they were less civilized than white farmers.
On the influence of this theory in America in general during this period, see Dekker,
American Historical Romance, 73–98.

99. Stone, *Life of Joseph Brant*, 2:25.

100. Ibid., 1:36.

101. Ibid., xiii. While, as Conn, *History's Shadow* (61–62, 157–61), notes, George Cat-
lin and John Heckewelder likewise used their injunctions for the need to record the
history of Native Americans to highlight their imminent extinction, Conn's emphasis
differs from mine in focusing on how the exceptionalist vision of American progress
contributed to the exclusion of Native Americans from American historical consciousness (24–34), whereas, as I further discuss in the next section, I seek to demonstrate how
that vision could actually fuel historical interest in Native Americans.

102. Stone, *Life of Joseph Brant*, 1:xxvii. On the widespread assumption that the Indians, however noble, were doomed to give way to white civilization, see Berkhofer, *White
Man's Indian*, 86–96, and Pearce, *Savagism and Civilization*, 53–75, 160–68, 212–16. On
how the displacement of Native Americans by white settlers enabled Americans of this

period to reaffirm their belief in progress, see Slotkin, *Regeneration through Violence*, 357. See Horsman, *Race and Manifest Destiny*, 189–207, for a discussion of how the belief in America's destiny as an Anglo-Saxon nation increased popular hostility to Native Americans in this period. On the portrayal of the Indians as a doomed race in Romantic historical writing, see Levin, *History as Romantic Art*, 126–41.

103. On the conventional view that Indian violence was a sign of savagery, see Sheehan, *Seeds of Extinction*, 185–212. For background on Thatcher, see *Dictionary of American Biography*, 1935 ed., s.v. "Thatcher, Benjamin Bussey."

104. Snelling, "Thatcher's Indian Biography," 387–88. For examples of other favorable reviews of Thatcher, see "Indian Biography," *New England Magazine*; "Indian Biography," *Knickerbocker*; and Oliver William B. Peabody, "Thatcher's Indian Biography." For background on Snelling, see *Dictionary of American Biography*, 1935 ed., s.v. "Snelling, William."

105. On how a growing sympathy for and fascination with the Indian developed as the threat of real Indians receded from the East, see Berkhofer, *White Man's Indian*, 88–95, and Slotkin, *Regeneration through Violence*, 354–58. On Snelling's view of Indians, see Pearce, *Savagism and Civilization*, 220–22.

106. Snelling, "Thatcher's Indian Biography," 394. For a discussion of sectional variations in portrayals of the Indian, see Slotkin, *Regeneration through Violence*, 394–440.

107. On the debate over Cherokee removal, see Pearce, *Savagism and Civilization*, 63–64; Sheehan, *Seeds of Extinction*, 256–75; Berkhofer, *White Man's Indian*, 157–65; and Horsman, *Race and Manifest Destiny*, 189–207. Specifically on Whig opposition to Cherokee removal, see Daniel Walker Howe, *Political Culture of the American Whigs*, 40–42. On the connection between Indian removal and the development of a more sympathetic view of Native Americans in this period, see Lepore, *Name of War*, 191–212.

108. Snelling, "Thatcher's Indian Biography," 394.

109. Thatcher, *Indian Biography*, 1:175–76. See Gould, *Covenant and Republic*, 162–70, on reassessments of Philip as the embodiment of republican virtue in early national histories and novels. On the changing and conflicting portrayals of Philip in this period, see Lepore, *Name of War*, 173–226.

110. Thatcher, *Indian Biography*, 2:80–81.

111. Ibid., 1:264. For a discussion of Thatcher's portrayal of Philip and the more general tendency in this period to associate Native Americans with the virtues that defined America, see Slotkin, *Regeneration through Violence*, 358–68. On how Americans in this period used this identification with Philip to define their own identity, see Lepore, *Name of War*, 192–226.

112. Thatcher, *Indian Biography*, 1:265. On how Americans of this period could at once celebrate Philip as a hero and believe in the rightfulness of white settlement without seeing any conflict between these assumptions, see Lepore, *Name of War*, 206.

113. Thatcher, "Life of Joseph Brant," 154.

114. Ibid., 141.

115. Ibid., 140. Thus, contrary to Conn, *History's Shadow* (79–94), I demonstrate how Thatcher could at once disparage Indian oratory and acknowledge Native Americans as both national entities and as part of history.

116. Thatcher, "Life of Joseph Brant," 143–44.

117. On the development of the myth of the frontier hero, see Slotkin, *Regeneration through Violence*, esp. 268–354, 369–465.

118. Thatcher, "Life of Joseph Brant," 144–45.

119. Thatcher, "History of Plymouth," 65–66.

120. Ibid., 72–73. Here, then, I differ from Conn's analysis of how both the Romantic narrative of American progress and the ideal of scientific objectivity contributed to the exclusion of Indians from American historical consciousness. See Conn, *History's Shadow*, esp. 198–219.

121. Thatcher, "Life of Joseph Brant," 147–48.

122. On how the duty to preserve the Revolutionary legacy created anxieties about fame for post-heroic Americans, see Forgie, *Patricide in the House Divided*, 55–87. On the importance of fame to the founders, see Adair, "Fame and the Founding Fathers." See Welter, *Mind of America*, 36, for another way in which Americans of this period sought to avoid the static view of history implied by exceptionalist ideology.

123. Thatcher, "Life of Joseph Brant," 148. On the belief that the availability of land would enable Americans to escape time and on the importance of this belief to exceptionalist ideology, see Ross, "Historical Consciousness in Nineteenth-Century America," 912; Ross, *Origins of American Social Science*, 23–26; Henry Nash Smith, *Virgin Land*, esp. 123–32; and Noble, *Historians against History*, esp. 18–36. On this belief and on Jeffersonian anxieties about what would happen when Americans ran out of land, see McCoy, *Elusive Republic*, 48–85, 185–208, 253–59.

Conclusion

1. And, in turn, as Ian Tyrrell has demonstrated, American historians throughout the twentieth century have continued to show a "remarkable amnesia" regarding the historical roots of contemporary concerns about the relationship between professional historians and the public by oversimplifying their predecessors' understanding of that relationship. On this point, see Tyrrell, *Historians in Public*, 21.

2. On the exaggerated nature of recent complaints about the declining popularity and relevance of history to general audiences, see ibid., 1–40.

3. Quoted in Honan, "Footnotes Offering Fewer Insights."

4. Himmelfarb, "Where Have All the Footnotes Gone?" 1–2.

5. For further discussion of the controversy over these two cases, see Hoffer, *Past Imperfect*, 172–207.

6. "Introduction to the History of the Colony and Ancient Dominion of Virginia," 311.

7. Jared Sparks to Charles Upham, 27 Nov. 1832, Sparks Papers, MS Sparks 147f. By

permission of the Houghton Library, Harvard University. On how American historians throughout the twentieth century sought to balance their commitment to scholarship with their desire for popular appeal, see Tyrrell, *Historians in Public*.

8. Hayden White, "The Historical Text as Literary Artifact," in *Tropics of Discourse*, 82; William Gilmore Simms, "History for the Purposes of Art," in *Views and Reviews in American Literature, History and Fiction*, 1:25. On the postmodern challenge to the ideal of objectivity and White's role in this challenge, see Appleby, Hunt, and Jacob, *Telling the Truth about History*, 199–237; Evans, *In Defense of History*, 80–87; and Novick, *That Noble Dream*, 522–72, 599–607. On how postmodern theory has blurred the distinction between history and fiction by emphasizing the literary character of history, see Iggers, *Historiography in the Twentieth Century*, 9–13, 118–22.

9. On the revival of narrative, see Stone, "Revival of Narrative."

10. On the importance of the distinction between history and fiction to professional historians' definition of their discipline, see Novick, *That Noble Dream*, 600.

11. Schama, *Dead Certainties*. For other recent examples of the "new" narrative history, see John Demos, *The Unredeemed Captive* (New York: Knopf, 1994); Linda Gordon, *The Great Arizona Orphan Abduction* (Cambridge: Harvard University Press, 2001); and Thomas Slaughter, *The Natures of John and William Bartram* (New York: Vintage Books, 1996). On the dangerous implications of this trend for the belief in objective truth, see Novick, *That Noble Dream*, 622–25.

12. Wood, "Novel History," 15; Felton, "Simms's Stories and Reviews," 381.

13. Wood, "Novel History," 15–16.

14. Schama, *Dead Certainties*, 322; William Gilmore Simms to James Lawson, 26 Jan. 1847, in Simms, *Letters*, 2:262.

15. White, *Metahistory*, xii. On White's desire to return to a "pre-professional" state when history was a "moral science," see Novick, *That Noble Dream*, 599.

16. Gaddis, *Landscape of History*, 122.

17. Charles Francis Adams, "Hutchinson's Third Volume," 136; Bailyn, *Ordeal of Thomas Hutchinson*, 378.

18. Jared Sparks to George Atkinson Ward, 20 May 1845, Sparks Papers, MS Sparks 147h. By permission of the Houghton Library, Harvard University. Bailyn, *Ordeal of Thomas Hutchinson*, ix.

19. Parker, "Character of Mr. Prescott as an Historian," 230; Lemisch, "American Revolution Seen from the Bottom Up," 3–29. On the earlier roots of the "new" social history in late nineteenth- and early twentieth-century American historical writing, see Fitzpatrick, *History's Memory*.

20. On how the New Left historians of the 1960s and the social history they helped pioneer at once adhered to the ideal of objectivity and unintentionally undermined it, see Novick, *That Noble Dream*, 422–45. On the more self-conscious challenge to objectivity posed by the "particularistic sensibilities" of many practitioners of women's history and African American history and the limits to that challenge, see ibid., 469–510. For further discussion of the impact of the new social history, see Appleby, Hunt, and

Jacob, *Telling the Truth about History*, 146–59; and Evans, *In Defense of History*, 139–63. On how postmodernism has also contributed to the politicization of history and on the dangerous implications of such politicization for truth, see Evans, *In Defense of History*, 165–92.

21. Lemisch, "American Revolution Seen from the Bottom Up," 5–6; Thatcher, "History of Plymouth," 68.

22. See, for example, Gertrude Himmelfarb, "History with the Politics Left Out," in *The New History and the Old*, 22.

23. William L. Stone, *Life of Joseph Brant*, 1:xiv. On how American historians of the 1920s and 1930s expressed and furthered their commitment to social history through Native American history, see Fitzpatrick, *History's Memory*, 98–140.

24. On debates over this issue, see Appleby, Hunt, and Jacob, *Telling the Truth about History*, 158–59.

25. Haskell, "Objectivity Is Not Neutrality."

26. On the value of the postmodern challenge to truth in stimulating historians to think more critically and deeply about the basis for their discipline, see Evans, *In Defense of History*, 10, 216. For the argument that historical skepticism and a faith in the possibility of sound historical knowledge were not necessarily mutually exclusive, see Momigliano, "Ancient History and the Antiquarian," 10–11. Specifically on how Pierre Bayle helped establish a more secure basis for historical knowledge, even as he expressed skepticism about the possibility of accurate history, see Grafton, "Footnote from De Thou to Ranke," 72–76, and his *The Footnote*, 195–212.

27. Appleby, Hunt, and Jacob, *Telling the Truth About History*; Kloppenberg, "Objectivity and Historicism," 1011–1030; Haskell, "Objectivity Is Not Neutrality." See also Evans, *In Defense of History*, and Gaddis, *Landscape of History*, for two other recent efforts to establish a basis for historical knowledge in response to the challenge of postmodernism. On the value of recognizing both the continuities and the changes in the history of the historical discipline, see Tyrrell, *Historians in Public*, 252–55.

BIBLIOGRAPHY

Primary Sources

Manuscript Collections

Bancroft, George. Papers. Masschusetts Historical Society, Boston.

Everett, Alexander Hill. Letters. Massachusetts Historical Society, Boston.

Everett, Edward. Papers. Massachusetts Historical Society, Boston. Microfilm.

Palfrey Family Papers. Houghton Library, Harvard University.

Prescott, William Hickling. Papers. Massachusetts Historical Society, Boston.

Sabine, Lorenzo. Papers. New Hampshire Historical Society, Concord.

Sparks, Jared. Papers. Houghton Library, Harvard University.

Warren, Mercy Otis. Papers. Massachusetts Historical Society, Boston. Microfilm.

Books and Articles

Adams, Charles Francis. *Diary of Charles Francis Adams*. Edited by David Donald and Aida Donald. Vols. 1–2. Cambridge: Harvard University Press, 1964.

———. *Diary of Charles Francis Adams*. Edited by Marc Friedlaender and L. H. Butterfield. Vols. 5–6. Cambridge: Harvard University Press, 1974.

———. *Diary of Charles Francis Adams*. Edited by Marc Friedlaender and others. Vols. 7–8. Cambridge: Harvard University Press, 1986.

———. "Grahame's History of the United States." *North American Review* 32 (January 1831): 174–96.

———. "Hutchinson's Third Volume." *North American Review* 38 (January 1834): 134–58.

———, ed. *Letters of Mrs. Adams*. Boston: Charles C. Little and James Brown, 1840.

———. "Life of Peter Van Schaack." *North American Review* 55 (July 1842): 97–114.

———. "Politics of the Puritans." *North American Review* 50 (April 1840): 432–61.

———. "Politics of the Puritans." *North American Review* 51 (July 1840): 252–74.

———. "Ward's Memoir of Samuel Curwen." *North American Review* 56 (January 1843): 89–109.

———, ed. *The Works of John Adams*. Boston: Little, Brown, 1856.

Adams, Hannah. *An Abridgement of the History of New England*. Boston: B. and J. Homans, and John West, 1805.

———. *A Summary History of New England*. Dedham, Mass.: H. Mann and J. H. Adams, 1799.

Adams, John. *Letters of John Adams, Addressed to His Wife*. Edited by Charles Francis Adams. 2 vols. Boston: Charles C. Little and James Brown, 1841.

Alexander, James Waddel. "Life of Joseph Brant Thayendanegea." *Princeton Review*, n.s., 11 (January 1839): 1–31.

"American Biography." *American Quarterly Review* 1 (March 1827): 1–38.

"American History." *Democratic Review* 24 (February 1849): 151–62.

Amicus. *Slavery among the Puritans: A Letter to the Rev. Moses Stuart*. Boston: Charles C. Little and James Brown, 1850.

"Ante-Roman Races of Italy." *Southern Quarterly Review* 7 (April 1845): 261–300.

Arnold, S. G. "Cromwell and the Revolution." *Methodist Quarterly Review* 30 (January 1848): 51–84.

Austin, James T. *The Life of Elbridge Gerry, with Contemporary Letters, to the Close of the American Revolution*. 2 vols. Boston: Wells and Lilly, 1828.

Bancroft, George. "Documentary History of the Revolution." *North American Review* 46 (April 1838): 475–87.

———. "Early Colonial History." *American Quarterly Review* 12 (December 1832): 426–41.

———. *History of the United States from the Discovery of the American Continent to the Present Time*. 10 vols. Boston: Charles Bowen, 1834–74.

———. *Literary and Historical Miscellanies*. New York: Harper and Brothers, 1855.

"Bancroft's History of the United States." *DeBow's Review* 15 (August 1853): 160–86.

Bassett, John Spencer, ed. "The Correspondence of George Bancroft and Jared Sparks." *Smith College Studies in History* 2 (January 1917): 67–143.

Belknap, Jeremy. *American Biography*. 2 vols. Boston: Isaiah Thomas and Ebenezer T. Andrews, 1794–98.

———. *The Foresters: An American Tale*. 1792. Reprint, Gainesville, Fla.: Scholars' Facsimiles and Reprints, 1969.

———. *The History of New Hampshire*. Edited by John Farmer. 1784–91. Rev. ed., Dover, N.H.: S. C. Stevens and Ela and Wadleigh, 1831.

———. *The history of New-Hampshire. Containing a geographical description of the state; with sketches of its natural history, productions, improvements, and present state of society and manners, laws and government*. Vol. 3. Boston, for the author, by Belknap and Young, 1792.

"Belknap Papers." *Collections of the Massachusetts Historical Society*. 5th ser., vols. 2, 3; 6th ser., vol. 4. Boston: Massachusetts Historical Society, 1877–91.

Bowen, Francis. "Continuation of Bancroft's History." *North American Review* 74 (April 1852): 507–15.

———. "Frothingham's Siege of Boston." *North American Review* 70 (April 1850): 405–24.

———. "Hildreth's History of the United States." *North American Review* 73 (October 1851): 411–48.

———. "Life of James Otis." In *Library of American Biography*, edited by Jared Sparks, 2nd ser., vol. 2. Boston: Charles C. Little and James Brown, 1844.

———. "The Recent Contest in Rhode Island." *North American Review* 58 (April 1844): 371–436.

———. "The Revolutions in Europe." *North American Review* 67 (July 1848): 194–240.

———. "Trumbull's Public Records of Connecticut." *North American Review* 71 (July 1850): 34–51.

Bozman, John Leeds. *The History of Maryland, from Its First Settlement, in 1633, to the Restoration in 1660*. Baltimore: James Lucas and E. K. Drawer, 1837.

Brigham, William. "Chronicles of the Pilgrim Fathers." *Christian Examiner* 31 (September 1841): 116–227.

Brooks, Edward. "Constitutional History." *North American Review* 29 (July 1829): 265–82.

Brown, Henry. *History of Illinois*. New York: J. Winchester, New World Press, 1844.

Brownson, Orestes. "Bancroft's History." *Brownson's Quarterly Review* 4 (October 1841): 512–18.

———. "Remarks on Universal History." *Democratic Review* 12 (May 1843): 457–74.

———. *Works of Orestes Brownson*. Edited by Henry F. Brownson. Vol. 19. New York: AMS Press, 1966.

Brunhouse, Robert L., ed. "David Ramsay, 1749–1815: Selections from His Writings." *American Philosophical Society Transactions*, n.s., 55, no. 4 (1965).

Burk, John Daly. *The History of Virginia*. 4 vols. Petersburg, Va.: Dickson and Pescud, 1804–16.

"Carlyle's Cromwell." *New Englander* 4 (April 1846): 211–29.

"Carlyle's French Revolution." *Democratic Review* 2 (July 1838): 323–37.

"Carolina Political Annals." *Southern Quarterly Review* 7 (April 1845): 479–526.

Carroll, B. R., comp. *Historical Collections of South Carolina*. New York: Harper and Brothers, 1836.

Cartwright, Samuel. "Canaan Identified with the Ethiopian." *Southern Quarterly Review* 2 (October 1842): 321–83.

Chalmers, George. *An Introduction to the History of the Revolt of the Colonies; Being a Comprehensive View of Its Origin, Derived from the State Papers Contained in the Public Offices of Great Britain*. Edited by Jared Sparks. Boston: J. Munroe, 1845.

———. *Political Annals of the Present United Colonies*. 1780. New York: B. Franklin, 1968.

"Chalmers' Revolt of the American Colonies." *Southern and Western Monthly Magazine and Review* 1 (April 1845): 285–86.

"Compendious History of New England." *Monthly Anthology* 2 (October 1805): 541–49.

"Constitutional History of England." *American Whig Review* 6 (July 1847): 110.

Cooper, James Fenimore. *Early Critical Essays*. Edited by James Beard Jr. Gainesville, Fla.: Scholars' Facsimiles and Reprints, 1955.

"Cromwell and His Times." *Democratic Review* 18 (May 1846): 336–44.

"Cromwell's Letters and Speeches." *Methodist Quarterly Review* 28 (October 1846): 573–97.

Curry, Daniel. "Hildreth's History of the United States." *Methodist Quarterly Review* 32 (July 1850): 411–31.

"Curwen's Journal and Letters." *Democratic Review* 11 (December 1842): 663–64.

Daniel, John Moncure. "The History of Virginia." *Southern Literary Messenger* 13 (January 1847): 1–14.

Davezac, A. "The Literature of Fiction." *Democratic Review* 16 (March 1845): 268–82.

Ellet, Elizabeth F. *Domestic History of the American Revolution.* New York: Baker and Scribner, 1850.

———. *The Women of the American Revolution.* 3 vols. New York: Baker and Scribner, 1848–50.

Ellis, George Edward. "The Fathers of New England." *North American Review* 68 (January 1849): 82–99.

———. "Oliver's Puritan Commonwealth." *North American Review* 84 (April 1857): 426–69.

———. "Sabine's Sketches of the Loyalists." *North American Review* 65 (July 1847): 138–59.

———. "Young's Chronicles of Massachusetts." *North American Review* 63 (July 1846): 237–60.

Emerson, Ralph Waldo. "The French Revolution: A History." *Christian Examiner* 23 (January 1838): 386.

———. *Selected Essays.* Edited by Larzer Ziff. New York: Penguin Books, 1982.

Everett, Alexander H. "Life of Joseph Warren." In *Library of American Biography*, edited by Jared Sparks. Vol. 10. Boston: Charles C. Little and James Brown, 1838.

Everett, Edward. "Bancroft's History of the United States." *North American Review* 40 (January 1835): 99–122.

———. "Guizot's Washington." *North American Review* 51 (July 1840): 69–92.

———. "Niebuhr's Roman History." *North American Review* 39 (April 1823): 425–45.

Felton, Cornelius Conway. "Simms's Stories and Reviews." *North American Review* 63 (October 1846): 357–81.

Frothingham, Richard. *History of the Siege of Boston, and of the Battles of Lexington, Concord, and Bunker Hill.* 4th ed. 1849. Boston: Little, Brown, 1873.

Gardiner, C. Harvey, ed. *The Literary Memoranda of William Hickling Prescott.* Norman: University of Oklahoma Press, 1961.

———. *The Papers of William Hickling Prescott.* Urbana: University of Illinois Press, 1964.

Gardiner, William Howard. "Cooper's Novels." *North American Review* 23 (July 1826): 150–97.

———. "Prescott's Ferdinand and Isabella." *North American Review* 46 (January 1838): 203–92.

———. Review of *The Spy. North American Review* 15 (July 1822): 250–83.

"General History of Civilization in Europe." *Princeton Review*, n.s., 11 (January 1839): 114–42.

"General History of Civilization in Europe." *Southern Quarterly Review* 3 (January 1843): 1–17.

Gordon, William. *The History of the Rise, Progress and Establishment of the Independence of the United States of America.* 4 vols. London: Charles Dilly, 1788.

———. "The Letters of William Gordon, Historian of the American Revolution." *Massachusetts Historical Society Proceedings* 62 (October 1929–June 1930): 303–613.

Gray, John Chipman. Review of *The Rebels. North American Review* 22 (April 1826): 400–409.

Greenwood, Francis. Review of *Hope Leslie. North American Review* 26 (April 1828): 403–21.

"Guizot's Essay on Washington." *Democratic Review* 8 (July 1840): 3–13.

"Guizot's Washington." *Brownson's Quarterly Review* 4 (January 1841): 136.

"Haliburton and Hildreth, and the *North American Review." Church Review* 4 (January 1852): 523–47.

"Hallam's Constitutional History." *American Quarterly Review* 3 (March 1828): 26–61.

Headley, Joel Tyler. *Washington and His Generals.* New York: Baker and Scribner, 1847.

"Headley's Histories." *Methodist Quarterly Review* 30 (January 1848): 84–103.

"Headley's Writings." *New Englander* 5 (July 1847): 402–15.

Hildreth, Richard. *Despotism in America.* Boston: Whipple and Damrell, 1840.

———. *The History of the United States of America from the Adoption of the Federal Constitution to the End of the Sixteenth Congress, 1788–1821.* 3 vols. New York: Harper, 1851–52.

———. *The History of the United States of America, from the Discovery of the Continent to the Organization of Government under the Federal Constitution.* 3 vols. New York: Harper, 1849.

———. *Theory of Morals: An Inquiry Concerning the Law of Moral Distinctions and the Variations and Contradictions of Ethical Codes.* Boston: Charles C. Little and James Brown, 1844.

———. *Theory of Politics: An Inquiry into the Foundations of Governments and the Causes and Progress of Political Revolutions.* 1853. Reprint, New York: Augustus M. Kelley, 1969.

"Hildreth's History of the United States of America." *Church Review* 4 (April 1851): 136.

"Hildreth's History of the United States of America." *Church Review* 4 (October 1851): 468–69.

"Hildreth's History of the United States of America." *Church Review* 5 (October 1852): 451–52.

"Hildreth's United States." *Southern Quarterly Review* 16 (October 1849): 258.

Hillard, George Stillman. "Prescott's History of the Conquest of Mexico." *North American Review* 58 (January 1844): 157–211.

———. Review of *Clarence. North American Review* 32 (January 1831): 73–95.

"History of the English Revolution of 1640." *American Review* 3 (March 1846): 334.

"History of the United States of America." *Democratic Review* 25 (July 1849): 92–93.

Holmes, Abiel. *Annals of America, from the Discovery by Columbus in the Year 1492, to the Year 1826.* 2 vols. 1805. 2nd ed. Cambridge, Mass.: Hilliard and Brown, 1829.

———. "Ramsay's History of the United States." *North American Review* 6 (March 1818): 331–44.

Howe, Mark Anthony de Wolfe. *The Life and Letters of George Bancroft.* 2 vols. New York: Scribner's, 1908.

Howes, H. "History of Rome." *North American Review* 42 (October 1836): 388–422.

Howison, Robert R. *The History of Virginia.* 2 vols. Philadelphia: Carey and Hart, 1846–47.

"Howison's History of Virginia." *Princeton Review,* n.s., 19 (April 1847): 224–36.

"Hutchinson's History of Massachusetts." *Atheneum,* 2d ser., 9 (August 1828): 358–61.

"Indian Biography." *Democratic Review* 12 (April 1843): 401–8.

"Indian Biography." *Knickerbocker* 2 (August 1833): 139–40.

"Indian Biography." *New England Magazine* 3 (December 1832): 510.

"Introduction to the History of the Colony and Ancient Dominion of Virginia." *Princeton Review,* n.s., 20 (April 1848): 310–11.

"Italy in the Middle Ages." *North American Review* 50 (January 1840): 43–75.

Lendrum, John. *A Concise and Impartial History of the American Revolution.* 2 vols. Boston: Thomas and Andrews, 1795.

"Life of Cromwell." *American Literary Magazine* 3 (July 1848): 33–43.

"Life of Oliver Cromwell." *Graham's American Monthly Magazine* 33 (August 1848): 118–19.

"Life of Oliver Cromwell." *Princeton Review,* n.s., 20 (July 1848): 499–500.

"Life of Peter Van Schaack." *Southern Literary Messenger* 8 (May 1842): 361.

"Lingard's History of England." *North American Review* 80 (April 1855): 538–39.

Lunt, W. P. "Review of Carlyle's Edition of Cromwell's Letters and Speeches and F. Guizot's History of the English Revolution." *Christian Examiner* 40 (May 1846): 440–59.

"Macaulay's History of England." *American Literary Magazine* 4 (January 1849): 421–42.

Markoe, Francis, Jr. "Documentary History of the American Revolution." *American Quarterly Review* 18 (September 1835): 82–112.

Marshall, John. *The Life of George Washington.* 5 vols. London: Richard Phillips, 1804–7.

"Martial Men and Martial Books." *New Englander* 6 (October 1848): 482–99.

McCall, Hugh. *The History of Georgia.* 2 vols. Savannah: Seymour and Williams, 1811–16.

"Memoirs of Aaron Burr." *American Quarterly Review* 21 (March 1837): 74–111.

"Michelet's Works." *Democratic Review* 25 (August 1849): 129–37.

Miller, Samuel. *A Brief Retrospect of the Eighteenth Century.* New York: T. and J. Swords, 1803.

Minor, Benjamin Blake. "The Impartiality of History." *Southern Literary Messenger* 13 (July 1847): 448.

———. "Washington and His Generals." *Southern Literary Messenger* 13 (May 1847): 316–19.

Morse, Jedidiah. *Annals of the American Revolution*. Hartford, Conn.: Oliver D. Cooke and Sons, 1824.

———. *An Appeal to the Public*. Charlestown: printed for the author, 1814.

Morse, Jedidiah, and Elijah Parish. *A Compendious History of New England*. Charlestown, Mass.: Samuel Etheridge, 1804.

Motley, John Lothrop. "Polity of the Puritans." *North American Review* 69 (October 1849): 470–98.

———. *Rise of the Dutch Republic*. New York: Harper and Brothers, 1856.

"Mr. Headley's New Book." *New Englander* 4 (July 1846): 364–68.

"Niebuhr's Lectures on Roman History." *North American Review* 73 (July 1851): 267–70.

"Niebuhr's Roman History." *American Quarterly Review* 4 (December 1828): 367–95.

Oliver, Peter. "Charter of the Massachusetts Bay Company." *Church Review* 2 (January 1850): 524–58.

———. *The Puritan Commonwealth*. Boston: Little, Brown, 1856.

"Oliver Cromwell." *American Review* 3 (April 1846): 396–414.

Palfrey, John Gorham. *History of New England during the Stuart Dynasty*. Vols. 1–3. 1858–64. Boston: Little, Brown, 1859–65.

———. "Massachusetts Common Schools." *North American Review* 44 (April 1837): 503–37.

———. "The New England Character." *North American Review* 44 (January 1837): 237–60.

Parker, Theodore. "Character of Mr. Prescott as an Historian." *Massachusetts Quarterly Review* 2 (March 1849): 215–48.

———. "Character of Mr. Prescott as an Historian." *Massachusetts Quarterly Review* 2 (September 1849): 437–70.

———. "Hildreth's History of the United States." *Massachusetts Quarterly Review* 3 (June 1850): 386–425.

Peabody, Oliver William B. "Sparks's Life of Gouverneur Morris." *North American Review* 34 (April 1832): 465–94.

———. "Thatcher's Indian Biography." *North American Review* 36 (April 1833): 472–88.

Peabody, W. B. O. "Carlyle's Letters of Cromwell." *North American Review* 62 (April 1846): 380–429.

Peale, Jonathan. "The American Loyalists." *Christian Examiner* 43 (July 1847): 118–37.

Perkins, James Handasyd. "Border War of the Revolution." *North American Review* 49 (October 1839): 277–317.

———. "Gregory the Seventh and His Age." *North American Review* 61 (July 1845): 20–54.

Phillips, Willard. Review of *The Pilot*. *North American Review* 18 (April 1824): 314–29.

"Politics of the Puritans." *New York Review* 6 (January 1840): 48–73.

Prescott, William Hickling. "Bancroft's History of the United States." *North American Review* 52 (January 1841): 75–103.

———. *History of the Conquest of Mexico*. 1843. New York: Modern Library, 1931.

———. *History of the Reign of Philip the Second*. Boston: Phillips, Sampson, 1855.

"Prescott's Conquest of Mexico." *Democratic Review* 14 (February 1844): 189–96.

"Puritanism." *Church Review* 2 (October 1849): 370–90.

Ramsay, David. *The History of the American Revolution.* Edited by Lester Cohen. 2 vols. 1789. Indianapolis: Liberty Classics, 1990.

Randolph, Edmund. *History of Virginia.* Edited by Arthur H. Shaffer. Charlottesville: University Press of Virginia, 1970.

"Reading of History." *Princeton Review* 19 (April 1847): 211–23.

"Recent American Histories." *Christian Review* 15 (April 1850): 182–202.

Reed, William Bradford. "Life and Character of John Adams." *New York Review* 10 (January 1842): 1–67.

———. *Life and Correspondence of Joseph Reed.* 2 vols. Philadelphia: Lindsay and Blakiston, 1847.

———. "Pennsylvanian Biography." *North American Review* 33 (July 1831): 105–22.

"Reformation the Source of American Liberty." *Methodist Quarterly Review* 28 (January 1846): 5–24.

"Review of Hallam's View of the State of Europe during the Middle Ages." *Southern Literary Messenger* 4 (February 1838): 111–13.

Review of *Princes and Nations of the South of Europe in the Sixteenth and Seventeenth Centuries* by Leopold von Ranke. *North American Review* 31 (October 1830): 291–309.

Sabine, Lorenzo. *The American Loyalists, or Biographical Sketches of Adherents to the British Crown in the War of the Revolution.* Boston: Charles C. Little and James Brown, 1847.

———. "British Colonial Politics." *North American Review* 67 (July 1848): 1–26.

———. "Chalmers's History of the American Colonies." *North American Review* 60 (April 1845): 368–93.

———. "The Past and Present of the American People." *North American Review* 66 (April 1848): 426–46.

———. "Simcoe's Military Journal." *North American Review* 59 (October 1844): 261–302.

Sedgwick, Catharine. *The Linwoods; or, Sixty Years Since in America.* 2 vols. New York: Harper and Brothers, 1835.

Sherman, William T. "Views and Reviews in American History, Literature and Fiction." *Southern Literary Messenger* 13 (April 1847): 250–51.

Simcoe, John Grewes. *Simcoe's Military Journal.* New York: Bartlett and Welford, 1844.

"Simcoe's Military Journal." *Democratic Review* 14 (February 1844): 213–14.

Simms, William Gilmore. "Biographical Sketch of the Career of Major William Cunningham." *Southern Literary Messenger* 12 (September 1846): 513–24.

———. "The Civil Warfare in the Carolinas and Georgia, during the Revolution." *Southern Literary Messenger* 12 (May 1846): 257–65.

———. "Ellet's Women of the Revolution." *Southern Quarterly Review*, n.s., 1 (July 1850): 314–54.

———. "Headley's Life of Cromwell." *Southern Quarterly Review* 14 (October 1848): 506–38.

———. *The History of South Carolina, from Its First European Discovery to Its Erection into a Republic.* 1840. Charleston, S.C.: S. Babcock, 1842.

———. *Katharine Walton, or the Rebel of Dorchester.* 1851. Rev. ed., New York: Redfield, 1856.

———. "Kennedy's Life of Wirt." *Southern Quarterly Review,* n.s., 1 (April 1850): 192–236.

———. *The Letters of William Gilmore Simms.* Edited by Mary Simms Oliphant, Alfred Taylor Odell, and T. C. Duncan Eaves. 6 vols. Columbia: University of South Carolina Press, 1952–82.

———. *The Life of Francis Marion.* New York: Henry G. Langley, 1844.

———. *The Life of Nathanael Greene.* New York: Derby and Jackson, 1856.

———. *Mellichampe: A Legend of the Santee.* 1836. Rev. ed., New York: Redfield, 1854.

———. *The Partisan: A Romance of the Revolution.* 1835. Rev. ed., New York: Redfield, 1854.

———. "Prescott's Conquest of Peru." *Southern Quarterly Review* 13 (January 1848): 136–87.

———. "The Siege of Charleston in the American Revolution." *Southern Quarterly Review* 14 (October 1848): 261–337.

———. "South Carolina in the Revolution." *Southern Quarterly Review* 14 (July 1848): 37–77.

———. "Topics in the History of South-Carolina." *Southern Quarterly Review,* n.s., 2 (September 1850): 66–84.

———. *Views and Reviews in American Literature, History and Fiction.* Vol. 1. New York: Wiley and Putnam, 1845.

———. *The Yemassee: A Romance of Carolina.* Edited by John Caldwell Guilds. 1835. Fayetteville: University of Arkansas Press, 1994.

Smith, C. C. "Guizot on the English Revolution." *Christian Examiner* 49 (September 1850): 287–89.

[Smith, W]. "American Loyalists." *Southern Quarterly Review* 4 (July 1843): 97–156.

Smith, William. *History of the Province of New-York.* In *Collections of the New York Historical Society* 4 (1829).

Snelling, William Joseph. "Thatcher's Indian Biography." *Christian Examiner* 13 (January 1833): 386–94.

Sparks, Jared. "Holmes's American Annals." *North American Review* 29 (October 1829): 428–41.

———. *Letter to Lord Mahon, Being an Answer to His Letter Addressed to the Editor of Washington's Writings.* Boston: Little, Brown, 1852.

———, ed. *The Library of American Biography.* Vol. 1. 1834. New York: Harper and Brothers, 1839.

———. *The Life of Gouverneur Morris.* 3 vols. Boston: Gray and Bowen, 1832.

———. "Materials for American History." *North American Review* 23 (October 1826): 275–95.

———. "Mr. Wirt's Life of Patrick Henry." *North American Review* 6 (March 1818): 293–324.

———. "Pitkin's History of the United States." *North American Review* 30 (January 1830): 1–26.

———. *The Writings of George Washington; Being His Correspondence, Addresses, Messages, and Other Papers, Official and Private, Selected and Published from the Original Manuscripts; with a Life of the Author, Notes and Illustrations.* 12 vols. Boston: American Stationers' Co., 1834–37.

Stevens, William Bacon. *A History of Georgia.* 2 vols. 1847. Savannah: Beehive Press, 1972.

Stone, William L. *Life of Joseph Brant—Thayendanegea, Including the Indian Wars of the American Revolution.* 2 vols. New York: George Dearborn, 1838.

"Stone's Life and Times of Red Jacket." *Southern Quarterly Review* 1 (January 1842): 270–73.

"Stone's Life of Brant." *New York Review* 3 (July 1838): 195–224.

Thacher, James. *History of the Town of Plymouth.* 1832. Boston: Marsh, Capen, and Lyon, 1835.

———. *A Military Journal during the American Revolutionary War, from 1775 to 1783.* 2nd ed. 1823. Boston: Coltons and Barnard, 1827.

"Thacher's History of Plymouth." *American Quarterly Review* 19 (June 1836): 443–66.

Thatcher, Benjamin Bussey. *Indian Biography.* 2 vols. 1840. New York: Harper, 1832.

———. "Life of Joseph Brant." *Christian Examiner* 26 (May 1839): 137–62.

———. "Thacher's History of Plymouth." *Christian Examiner* 21 (September 1836): 65–73.

———. *Traits of the Tea Party; Being a Memoir of George R. T. Hewes, One of the Last of Its Survivors; with a History of That Transaction; Reminiscences of the Massacre, and the Siege, and Other Stories of Old Times.* New York: Harper and Brothers, 1835.

"Thayendanega." *Democratic Review* 3 (October 1838): 113–29.

Thompson, John Reuben. "History of England." *Southern Literary Messenger* 15 (February 1849): 125–26.

Thomson, Charles W. "Notice of the Life and Character of Robert Proud, Author of 'The History of Pennsylvania.'" *Memoirs of the Historical Society of Pennsylvania* 1 (1826): 494–506.

"Thoughts on Plagiarism." *Monthly Anthology* 2 (August 1805): 405–6.

Trumbull, Benjamin. *A Complete History of Connecticut.* 2 vols. 1797. New London: H. D. Utley, 1898. New Haven: Maltby, Goldsmith, 1818.

[Tucker, Beverly]. "A History of the United States." *Southern Literary Messenger* 1 (June 1835): 587–91.

Tudor, William. *The Life of James Otis of Massachusetts: Containing Also, Notices of Some Contemporary Characters and Events from the Year 1760 to 1775.* Boston: Wells and Lilly, 1823.

Upham, Charles. "History of Virginia and Georgia." *North American Review* 67 (October 1848): 291–322.

———, ed. *Life of George Washington*. London: Office of the National Illustrated Library, 1852.

———. "Life of Sir Henry Vane. In *Library of American Biography*, edited by Jared Sparks. 2d ser., vol. 4. Boston: Hilliard, Gray, and Co., 1844.

———. "Reed's Life of President Reed." *North American Review* 65 (October 1847): 441–61.

Van Schaack, Henry C. *The Life of Peter Van Schaack*. New York: D. Appleton, 1842.

Ward, George Atkinson. "Curwen's Journal." *Southern Literary Messenger* 13 (January 1847): 48–51.

———, ed. *Journal and Letters of the Late Samuel Curwen*. New York and Boston: C. S. Francis and Co. and J. H. Francis, 1842.

———, ed. *Journal and Letters of the Late Samuel Curwen*. 3rd ed. New York and Boston: C. S. Francis and Co. and J. H. Francis, 1845.

———. "Notice of a Review of 'Curwen's Journal.'" *Southern Literary Messenger* 13 (July 1847): 422–28.

Ware, William. "Curwen's Journal and Letters." *Christian Examiner* 33 (January 1843): 259–381.

Warren, Mercy Otis. *The History of the Rise, Progress, and Termination of the American Revolution*. Edited by Lester Cohen. 2 vols. 1805. Indianapolis: Liberty Classics, 1988.

"Washington and His Generals." *American Review* 5 (May 1847): 517–34.

"Washington and the Generals of the American Revolution." *Democratic Review* 22 (January 1848): 92–93.

Watson, John F. *Annals of Philadelphia*. Philadelphia and New York: E. L. Carey and A. Hart/G. & C. & H. Carvill, 1830.

Weems, Mason Locke. *The Life of George Washington*. Edited by Peter Onuf. 1800. Rev. ed., Armonk, N.Y.: M. E. Sharpe, 1996.

Whipple, E. P. "Prescott's Conquest of Peru." *Methodist Quarterly Review* 30 (April 1848): 268–82.

———. "Prescott's Works." *Methodist Quarterly Review* 30 (January 1848): 5–28.

Williamson, Hugh. *The History of North Carolina*. 2 vols. 1812. Reprint, Spartanburg, S.C.: Reprint Co., 1973.

Wolcott, Roger, ed. *The Correspondence of William Hickling Prescott, 1833–1847*. Boston: Houghton Mifflin, 1925.

Secondary Sources

Abrams, M. H. *The Mirror and the Lamp: Romantic Theory and the Critical Tradition*. New York: Oxford University Press, 1953.

Adair, Douglass. "Fame and the Founding Fathers." In *Fame and the Founding Fathers*, edited by Trevor Colbourn, 3–26. New York: W. W. Norton, 1974.

Adams, Herbert Baxter. *The Life and Writings of Jared Sparks*. 2 vols. Boston: Houghton Mifflin, 1893.

Albanese, Catherine L. *Sons of the Fathers: The Civil Religion of the American Revolution.* Philadelphia: Temple University Press, 1976.

Allan, David. *Virtue, Learning and the Scottish Enlightenment: Ideas of Scholarship in Early Modern History.* Edinburgh: Edinburgh University Press, 1993.

American Historians, 1607–1865. Vol. 30 of *Dictionary of Literary Biography.* Detroit: Gale Research Co., 1984.

Anderson, Benedict. *Imagined Communities: Reflections on the Origin and Spread of Nationalism.* London: Verso, 1983.

Appleby, Joyce. *Capitalism and a New Social Order.* New York: New York University Press, 1984.

———. *Liberalism and Republicanism in the Historical Imagination.* Cambridge: Harvard University Press, 1992.

Appleby, Joyce, Lynn Hunt, and Margaret Jacob. *Telling the Truth about History.* New York: W. W. Norton, 1994.

Arch, Stephen Carl. *Authorizing the Past: The Rhetoric of History in Seventeenth-Century New England.* DeKalb: Northern Illinois University Press, 1994.

Arieli, Yehoshua. *Individualism and Nationalism in American Ideology.* Cambridge: Harvard University Press, 1964.

Bailyn, Bernard. *The Ideological Origins of the American Revolution.* Cambridge: Harvard University Press, 1967.

———. *The Ordeal of Thomas Hutchinson.* Cambridge: Harvard University Press, 1974.

Barnes, James. *Authors, Publishers and Politicians: The Quest for an Anglo-American Copyright Agreement, 1815–1854.* Columbus: Ohio State University Press, 1974.

Bassett, John Spencer. *The Middle Group of American Historians.* New York: Macmillan, 1917.

Battersby, Christine. *Gender and Genius: Toward a Feminist Aesthetics.* Bloomington: Indiana University Press, 1989.

Baym, Nina. *American Women Writers and the Work of History.* New Brunswick, N.J.: Rutgers University Press, 1995.

———. "Between Enlightenment and Victorian: Toward a Narrative of American Women Writers Writing History." *Critical Inquiry* 18 (Fall 1991): 22–41.

———. "Mercy Otis Warren's Gendered Melodrama of Revolution." *South Atlantic Quarterly* 90 (Summer 1991): 531–54.

———. *Novels, Readers, and Reviewers: Responses to Fiction in Antebellum America.* Ithaca, N.Y.: Cornell University Press, 1984.

———. "Onward Christian Women: Sarah J. Hale's History of the World." *New England Quarterly* 68 (1990): 249–70.

Becker, Carl. "John Jay and Peter Van Schaack." In *Everyman His Own Historian: Essays on History and Politics.* New York: F. S. Crofts and Co., 1935.

Bell, Michael Davitt. *Hawthorne and the Historical Romance of New England.* Princeton, N.J.: Princeton University Press, 1971.

Bercovitch, Sacvan, ed. *Cambridge History of American Literature.* Vols. 1 and 2. Cambridge: Cambridge University Press, 1994–96.

———. *The Rites of Assent*. New York: Routledge, 1993.

Berens, John F. *Providence and Patriotism in Early America, 1640–1815*. Charlottesville: University Press of Virginia, 1978.

Berkhofer, Robert F. *The White Man's Indian: Images of the American Indian from Columbus to the Present*. New York: Vintage Books, 1978.

Billias, George A., and Alden T. Vaughan, eds. *Perspectives on Early American History: Essays in Honor of Richard B. Morris*. New York: Harper and Row, 1973.

Black, J. B. *The Art of History*. London: F. S. Crofts, 1926.

Bloch, Ruth H. "The Gendered Meanings of Virtue in Revolutionary America." *Signs: Journal of Women in Culture and Society* 13 (1987): 37–58.

———. *Visionary Republic: Millennial Themes in American Thought, 1756–1800*. Cambridge: Cambridge University Press, 1985.

Bode, Carl. *The Anatomy of American Popular Culture, 1840–1861*. Berkeley: University of California Press, 1959.

Bodnar, John, ed. *Bonds of Affection: Americans Define Their Patriotism*. Princeton, N.J.: Princeton University Press, 1996.

Bonner, Robert E. "Americans Apart: Nationality in the Slaveholding South." PhD diss., Yale University, 1997.

Boorstin, Daniel. *The Genius of American Politics*. Chicago: University of Chicago Press, 1953.

Bowerstock, G. W. "The Art of the Footnote." *American Scholar* 53 (1984): 54–62.

Bozeman, Theodore Dwight. *Protestants in an Age of Science: The Baconian Ideal and Antebellum American Religious Thought*. Chapel Hill: University of North Carolina Press, 1977.

Braudy, Leo. *Narrative Form in History and Fiction*. Princeton, N.J.: Princeton University Press, 1970.

Brock, William. "The Image of England and American Nationalism." *Journal of American Studies* 5 (December 1971): 225–45.

Brooks, Van Wyck. *The Flowering of New England, 1815–65*. 1936. Rev. ed., New York: Dutton, 1937.

Brown, Herbert Ross. *The Sentimental Novel in America, 1789–1860*. Durham, N.C.: Duke University Press, 1940.

Brown, Jerome King. "William Gilmore Simms and the American Historical Romance." PhD diss., University of Kansas, 1978.

Brown, Roger. *Republic in Peril*. New York: Columbia University Press, 1964.

Brown, Wallace. "The View at Two Hundred Years: The Loyalists of the American Revolution." *American Antiquarian Society Proceedings* 80 (1970): 25–47.

Bryan, William Alfred. *George Washington in American Literature, 1775–1865*. New York: Columbia University Press, 1952.

Buell, Lawrence. *New England Literary Culture: From Revolution through Renaissance*. Cambridge: Cambridge University Press, 1986.

Burrow, J. W. *A Liberal Descent: Victorian Historians and the English Past*. Cambridge: Cambridge University Press, 1981.

Burstein, Andrew. "The Political Character of Sympathy." *Journal of the Early Republic* 21 (Winter 2001): 601–32.

Busick, Sean. *A Sober Desire for History: William Gilmore Simms as Historian.* Columbia: University of South Carolina Press, 2005.

Butterfield, Herbert. *Man on His Past: The Study of the History of Historical Scholarship.* Boston: Beacon Press, 1955.

———. *The Whig Interpretation of History.* New York: W. W. Norton, 1965.

Callcott, George. *History in the United States, 1800–1860: Its Practice and Purpose.* Baltimore: Johns Hopkins Press, 1970.

Canary, Robert. *George Bancroft.* New York: Twayne, 1974.

Cañizares-Esguerra, Jorge. *How to Write the History of the New World: Histories, Epistemologies, and Identities in the Eighteenth-Century Atlantic World.* Stanford, Calif.: Stanford University Press, 2001.

Cappon, Lester J. "American Historical Editors before Jared Sparks." *William and Mary Quarterly* 30 (1973): 375–400.

———. "Jared Sparks: The Preparation of an Editor." *Massachusetts Historical Society Proceedings* 90 (1978): 3–20.

Casper, Scott Evan. *Constructing American Lives: Biography and Culture in Nineteenth-Century America.* Chapel Hill: University of North Carolina Press, 1999.

———. "An Uneasy Marriage of Sentiment and Scholarship: Elizabeth F. Ellet and the Domestic Origins of American Women's History." *Journal of Women's History* 4 (Fall 1992): 10–35.

Charvat, William. *Literary Publishing in America, 1790–1850.* Philadelphia: University of Pennsylvania Press, 1959.

———. *The Origins of American Critical Thought, 1810–1835.* 1936. New York: A. S. Barnes, 1961.

Chase, Richard. *The American Novel and Its Tradition.* Garden City, N.Y.: Doubleday, 1957.

Clark, Harry Hayden. "Vogue of Macaulay in America." *Transactions of the Wisconsin Academy of Sciences, Arts and Letters* 34 (1942): 237–89.

Clive, John. *Not by Fact Alone: Essays on the Writing and Reading of History.* Boston: Houghton Mifflin, 1989.

Cohen, Lester. "The American Revolution and Natural Law Theory." *Journal of the History of Ideas* 39 (1976): 491–502.

———. "Explaining the Revolution: Ideology and Ethics in Mercy Otis Warren's Historical Theory." *William and Mary Quarterly* 37 (1980): 200–218.

———. "Narrating the Revolution: Ideology, Language, and Form." *Studies in Eighteenth Century Culture* 9 (1979): 455–76.

———. *The Revolutionary Histories: Contemporary Narratives of the American Revolution.* Ithaca, N.Y.: Cornell University Press, 1980.

Colacurcio, Michael. *The Province of Piety: Moral History in Hawthorne's Early Tales.* Cambridge: Harvard University Press, 1984.

Colbourn, H. Trevor. *The Lamp of Experience: Whig History and the Intellectual Origins of the American Revolution*. Chapel Hill: University of North Carolina Press, 1965.

Cole, Charles W. "Jeremy Belknap: Pioneer Nationalist." *New England Quarterly* 10 (1937): 743–51.

Colley, Linda. "Whose Nation? Class and National Consciousness in Britain, 1750–1830." *Past and Present* 113 (November 1986): 97–117.

Collingwood, R. G. *The Idea of History*. 1946. Rev. ed., Oxford: Clarendon Press, 1994.

Commager, Henry Steele. "The Past as an Extension of the Present." In *Jefferson, Nationalism and the Enlightenment*, 143–56. New York: George Brailler, 1975.

Conn, Steven. *History's Shadow: Native Americans and Historical Consciousness in the Nineteenth Century*. Chicago: University of Chicago Press, 2004.

———. "Who You Callin' an Intellectual?" *Reviews in American History* 33 (March 2005): 64–70.

Conrad, Susan. *Perish the Thought: Intellectual Women in Romantic America, 1830–1860*. New York: Oxford University Press, 1976.

Copeland, Thomas W. "Burke and Dodsley's Annual Register." *PLMA* 54 (March 1939): 223–45.

Cott, Nancy. *The Bonds of Womanhood: "Woman's Sphere" in New England, 1780–1835*. New Haven, Conn.: Yale University Press, 1977.

Cowie, Alexander. *The Rise of the American Novel*. New York: American Book Co., 1948.

Craven, Wesley Frank. *The Legend of the Founding Fathers*. New York: New York University Press, 1956.

Curti, Merle. "The Impact of the Revolutions of 1848 on American Thought." *Proceedings of the American Philosophical Society* 93 (June 1949): 209–15.

———. *The Roots of American Loyalty*. New York: Columbia University Press, 1946.

Curtis, Eugene N. "American Opinion of the French Nineteenth-Century Revolutions." *American Historical Review* 29 (1924): 249–70.

Dangerfield, George. *The Awakening of American Nationalism, 1815–1828*. New York: Harper Torchbooks, 1965.

Danzer, Gerald A. "America's Roots in the Past: Historical Publication in America to 1860." PhD diss., Northwestern University, 1967.

Darnell, Donald G. *William Hickling Prescott*. Boston: Twayne, 1975.

Daston, Lorraine. "Baconian Facts, Academic Civility, and the Prehistory of Objectivity." In *Rethinking Objectivity*, edited by Allan Megill, 37–63. Durham, N.C.: Duke University Press, 1994.

———. "Objectivity and the Escape from Perspective." *Social Studies of Science* 22 (1992): 597–618.

Daston, Lorraine, and Peter Galison. "The Image of Objectivity." *Representations* 40 (Fall 1992): 81–128.

Davidson, Cathy. *Revolution and the Word: The Rise of the Novel in America*. New York: Oxford University Press, 1986.

Davis, David Brion. *Revolutions: Reflections on American Equality and Foreign Liberations*. Cambridge: Harvard University Press, 1990.

Davis, H. "The Augustan Conception of History." In *Reason and the Imagination: Studies in the History of Ideas, 1600–1800*, edited by J. A. Mazzeo, 214–27. New York: Columbia University Press, 1962.

Davis, Lennard. *Factual Fictions: The Origins of the English Novel*. New York: Columbia University Press, 1983.

Dawson, Jan C. *The Unusable Past: America's Puritan Tradition, 1830 to 1930*. Chico, Calif.: Scholars Press, 1984.

Dekker, George. *The American Historical Romance*. Cambridge: Cambridge University Press, 1987.

den Boer, Pim. *History as a Profession: The Study of History in France, 1818–1914*. Princeton, N.J.: Princeton University Press, 1998.

DesJardins, Julie. *Women and the Historical Enterprise in America: Gender, Race, and the Politics of Memory, 1880–1945*. Chapel Hill: University of North Carolina Press, 2003.

Douglas, Ann. *The Feminization of American Culture*. New York: Avon Books, 1977.

Duberman, Martin. *Charles Francis Adams, 1807–86*. Boston: Houghton Mifflin, 1961.

Dunlap, Leslie W. *American Historical Societies, 1790–1860*. Madison, Wis.: privately printed, 1944.

Ekirch, Arthur K. *The Idea of Progress in America, 1815–1860*. 1944. New York: AMS Press, 1969.

Elkins, Stanley, and Eric McKitrick. *The Age of Federalism: The Early American Republic, 1788–1800*. New York: Oxford University Press, 1993.

Ellis, Joseph J. *After the Revolution: Profiles of Early American Culture*. New York: W. W. Norton, 1979.

Emerson, Donald E. "Hildreth, Draper, and 'Scientific History.'" In *Historiography and Urbanization: Essays in American History in Honor of W. Stull Holt*, edited by Eric F. Goldman, 139–52. Baltimore: Johns Hopkins University Press, 1941.

———. *Richard Hildreth*. Baltimore: Johns Hopkins University Press, 1946.

Evans, Richard. *In Defense of History*. New York: W. W. Norton, 1999.

Faust, Drew. *A Sacred Circle: The Dilemma of the Intellectual in the Old South, 1840–1860*. Baltimore: Johns Hopkins University Press, 1977.

Field, Peter S. "The Birth of Secular High Culture: *The Monthly Anthology and Boston Review* and Its Critics." *Journal of the Early Republic* 17 (Winter 1997): 575–609.

———. *The Crisis of the Standing Order: Clerical Intellectuals and Cultural Authority in Massachusetts, 1780–1833*. Amherst: University of Massachusetts Press, 1998.

Firda, Richard. "German Philosophy of History and Literature in the North American Review: 1815–60." *Journal of the History of Ideas* 32 (1971): 133–42.

Fisher, Sydney G. "The Legendary and Myth-Making Process in Histories of the American Revolution." *Proceedings of the American Philosophical Society* 51 (April–June 1912): 53–75.

Fitzpatrick, Ellen. *History's Memory: Writing America's Past, 1880–1980*. Cambridge: Harvard University Press, 2002.

Fliegelman, Jay. *Declaring Independence: Jefferson, Natural Language, and the Culture of Performance*. Stanford, Calif.: Stanford University Press, 1993.

Foletta, Marshall. *Coming to Terms with Democracy*. Charlottesville: University of Virginia Press, 2001.

Foner, Eric. *Free Soil, Free Labor, Free Men: The Ideology of the Republican Party before the Civil War*. New York: Oxford University Press, 1970.

Foran, William. "John Marshall as a Historian." *American Historical Review* 43 (1937): 51–64.

Forgie, George B. *Patricide in the House Divided: A Psychological Interpretation of Lincoln and His Age*. New York: W. W. Norton, 1979.

Formisano, Ronald. *The Transformation of Political Culture: Massachusetts Parties, 1790s–1840s*. New York: Oxford University Press, 1983.

Foucault, Michel. "What Is an Author?" In *Textual Strategies: Perspectives in Post-Structuralist Criticism*, edited by Josue Harari, 141–60. Ithaca, N.Y.: Cornell University Press, 1979.

Franklin, John Hope. "The North, the South, and the American Revolution." *Journal of American History* 62 (1975): 5–23.

Friedland, Louis S. "Richard Hildreth's Minor Works." *Papers of the Bibliographical Society of America* 40, no. 2 (1946): 127–50.

Frye, Northrop. *Anatomy of Criticism: Four Essays*. Princeton, N.J.: Princeton University Press, 1971.

Fussner, F. Smith. *The Historical Revolution: English Historical Writing and Thought, 1580–1640*. New York: Columbia University Press, 1962.

Gaddis, John Lewis. *The Landscape of History: How Historians Map the Past*. New York: Oxford University Press, 2002.

Gardiner, C. Harvey. *Prescott and His Publishers*. Carbondale: Southern Illinois University Press, 1959.

———. *William Hickling Prescott*. Boston: Twayne, 1975.

———. *William Hickling Prescott: A Biography*. Austin: University of Texas Press, 1969.

Gatell, Frank O. *John Gorham Palfrey and the New England Conscience*. Cambridge: Harvard University Press, 1963.

Gay, Peter. *A Loss of Mastery: The Puritan Historians in Colonial America*. Berkeley: University of California Press, 1966.

Gilmore, Michael T. *American Romanticism and the Marketplace*. Chicago: University of Chicago Press, 1985.

Gooch, George Peabody. *History and Historians in the Nineteenth Century*. New York: P. Smith, 1959.

Gould, Philip. "Catharine Sedgwick's 'Recital' of the Pequot War." *American Literature* 66 (December 1994): 641–62.

———. *Covenant and Republic: Historical Romance and the Politics of Puritanism*. Cambridge: Cambridge University Press, 1996.

———. "New England Witch-Hunting and the Politics of Reason in the Early Republic." *New England Quarterly* 68 (1995): 58–82.

———. "Reinventing Benjamin Church: Virtue, Citizenship and the History of King Philip's War in Early National America." *Journal of the Early Republic* 16 (Winter 1996): 645–57.

Grafton, Anthony. *The Footnote: A Curious History.* Cambridge: Harvard University Press, 1997.

———. "The Footnote from De Thou to Ranke." *History and Theory* 33 (1994): 53–76.

Grant, Susan-Mary. *North over South: Northern Nationalism and American Identity in the Antebellum Era.* Lawrence: University Press of Kansas, 2000.

Greene, Jack. *The Intellectual Construction of America: Exceptionalism and Identity from 1492 to 1800.* Chapel Hill: University of North Carolina Press, 1993.

Gribbin, William. "A Mirror to New England: The *Compendious History* of Jedidiah Morse and Elijah Parish." *New England Quarterly* 45 (1972): 340–54.

Guillory, James Denny. "The Pro-Slavery Arguments of Dr. Samuel A. Cartwright." *Louisiana History* 9, no. 3 (1968): 209–27.

Halttunen, Karen. *Confidence Men and Painted Women: A Study of Middle-Class Culture in America, 1830–1870.* New Haven, Conn.: Yale University Press, 1982.

Hamburger, Joseph. *Macaulay and the Whig Tradition.* Chicago: University of Chicago Press, 1976.

Handlin, Lilian. *George Bancroft: The Intellectual as Democrat.* New York: Harper and Row, 1984.

Harbert, Earl N. "Charles Francis Adams: A Forgotten Family Man of Letters." *Journal of American Studies* 6 (December 1972): 249–65.

Haskell, Thomas. "Objectivity Is Not Neutrality: Rhetoric and Practice in Peter Novick's *That Noble Dream.*" *History and Theory* 29 (1990): 129–57.

Hatch, Nathan. *The Sacred Cause of Liberty: Republican Thought and the Millennium in Revolutionary New England.* New Haven, Conn.: Yale University Press, 1977.

Hay, Robert P. "Providence and the American Past." *Indiana Magazine of History* 65 (June 1969): 79–101.

Haywood, Ian. *The Making of History: A Study of the Literary Forgeries of James Macpherson and Thomas Chatterton in Relation to Eighteenth-Century Ideas of History and Fiction.* Rutherford, N.J.: Fairleigh Dickinson University Press, 1986.

Hicks, Philip. *Neoclassical History and English Culture: From Clarendon to Hume.* New York: St. Martin's Press, 1996.

Higham, John. "The Changing Loyalties of William Gilmore Simms." *Journal of Southern History* 9 (1943): 210–23.

———. *History: Professional Scholarship in America.* 1965. New York: Harper Torchbooks, 1973.

Himmelfarb, Gertrude. *The New History and the Old.* Cambridge: Harvard University Press, 1987.

———. "Where Have All the Footnotes Gone?" *New York Times Book Review,* 16 June 1991, 1–2.

Hoffer, Peter C. *Liberty or Order: Two Views of American History from the Revolutionary*

Crisis to the Early Works of George Bancroft and Wendell Phillips. 1970. New York: Garland Publishing, 1988.

———. *Past Imperfect: Facts, Fictions, Fraud—American History from Bancroft and Parkman to Ambrose, Bellesiles, Ellis, and Goodwin.* New York: Public Affairs, 2004.

———. "Reflections on Plagiarism—Part 1: 'A Guide for the Perplexed.'" *American Historical Association Perspectives* 42 (February 2004): 17–23.

———. "Reflections on Plagiarism—Part 2: 'The Object of Trials.'" *American Historical Association Perspectives* 42 (March 2004): 21–25.

———. *Revolution and Regeneration: Life Cycle and the Historical Vision of the Generation of 1776.* Athens: University of Georgia Press, 1983.

Hofstadter, Richard. *The Idea of a Party System: The Rise of Legitimate Opposition in the United States, 1780–1840.* Berkeley: University of California Press, 1969.

Hollinger, David. "Postmodernist Theory and Wissenschaftliche Practice." *American Historical Review* 96 (1991): 688–92.

Hollis, C. Carroll. "Brownson on George Bancroft." *South Atlantic Quarterly* 49 (January 1950): 42–52.

Holman, C. Hugh. "William Gilmore Simms' Picture of the Revolution as a Civil Conflict." *Journal of Southern History* 15 (1949): 441–62.

Honan, William. "Footnotes Offering Fewer Insights." *New York Times,* 14 August 1996.

Honour, Hugh. *Romanticism.* New York: Harper and Row, 1979.

Hook, Andrew. "Macaulay and America." *Journal of American Studies* 9 (December 1975): 335–46.

Horsman, Reginald. *Race and Manifest Destiny: The Origins of American Racial Anglo-Saxonism.* Cambridge: Harvard University Press, 1981.

Howe, Daniel Walker. *Making the American Self: Jonathan Edwards to Abraham Lincoln.* Cambridge: Harvard University Press, 1997.

———. *The Political Culture of the American Whigs.* Chicago: University of Chicago Press, 1979.

———. "The Political Psychology of The Federalist." *William and Mary Quarterly* 44 (1987): 485–509.

———. *The Unitarian Conscience: Harvard Moral Philosophy, 1805–61.* 1970. Middletown, Conn.: Wesleyan University Press, 1988.

Huppert, George. *The Idea of Perfect History: Historical Erudition and Historical Philosophy in Renaissance France.* Urbana: University of Illinois Press, 1970.

Hutchinson, William T., ed. *Marcus W. Jernegan Essays in American Historiography.* Chicago: University of Chicago Press, 1937.

Iggers, Georg G. *The German Conception of History: The National Tradition of Historical Thought from Herder to the Present.* 1968. Rev. ed., Middletown, Conn.: Wesleyan University Press, 1983.

———. *Historiography in the Twentieth Century: From Scientific Objectivity to the Postmodern Challenge.* Middletown, Conn.: Wesleyan University Press, 1997.

———. "The Image of Ranke in American and German Historical Thought." *History and Theory* 2 (1962): 17–40.

———. *New Directions in European Historiography.* 1975. Rev. ed., Middletown, Conn.: Wesleyan University Press, 1984.

Iggers, Georg, and James M. Powell, eds. *Leopold von Ranke and the Shaping of the Historical Discipline.* Syracuse, N.Y.: Syracuse University Press, 1990.

Jameson, John Franklin. *The History of Historical Writing in America.* 1891. Reprint, Dubuque, Iowa: William C. Brown, 1972.

Jann, Rosemary. *The Art and Science of Victorian History.* Columbus: Ohio State University Press, 1985.

Johnson, Elmer. "Alexander Hewat: South Carolina's First Historian." *Journal of Southern History* 20 (1954): 50–62.

———. "David Ramsay: Historian or Plagiarist?" *South Carolina Historical Magazine* 57 (October 1956): 189–98.

Jones, Howard Mumford. *O Strange New World: American Culture: The Formative Years.* New York: Viking Press, 1964.

Kammen, Michael. *Mystic Chords of Memory: The Transformation of Tradition in American Culture.* New York: Vintage Books, 1991.

———. "The Problem of American Exceptionalism: A Reconsideration." *American Quarterly* 45 (March 1993): 1–43.

———. *A Season of Youth: The American Revolution and the Historical Imagination.* New York: Alfred A. Knopf, 1978.

Kamrath, Mark. "Charles Brockden Brown and the 'art of the historian': An Essay Concerning (Post)modern Historical Understanding." *Journal of the Early Republic* 21 (Summer 2001): 231–60.

Kant, Immanuel. "Idea for a Universal History from a Cosmopolitan Point of View." In *On History,* edited by Lewis White Beck. New York: Macmillan, 1963.

Kaplan, Sidney. "*The History of New Hampshire*: Jeremy Belknap as Literary Craftsman." *William and Mary Quarterly* 21 (1964): 18–39.

Kelley, Donald. *Fortunes of History: Historical Inquiry from Herder to Huizinga.* New Haven, Conn.: Yale University Press, 2003.

———. *Foundations of Modern Historical Scholarship: Language, Law, and History in the French Renaissance.* New York: Columbia University Press, 1970.

Kelley, Mary. *Private Woman, Public Stage: Literary Domesticity in Nineteenth-Century America.* New York: Oxford University Press, 1984.

Kelsay, Isabel Thompson. *Joseph Brant, 1743–1807: Man of Two Worlds.* Syracuse, N.Y.: Syracuse University Press, 1984.

Kenyon, John. *The History Men: The Historical Profession in England since the Renaissance.* 1983. Rev. ed., London: Weidenfeld and Nicolson, 1993.

Kerber, Linda. *Federalists in Dissent: Imagery and Ideology in Jeffersonian America.* Ithaca, N.Y.: Cornell University Press, 1970.

———. "'History Can Do It No Justice': Women and the Reinterpretation of the American Revolution." In *Women in the Age of the American Revolution*, edited by Ronald Hoffman and Peter Albert, 3–42. Charlottesville: University Press of Virginia, 1989.

———. *Women of the Republic: Intellect and Ideology in Revolutionary America*. New York: W. W. Norton, 1986.

Kettner, James. *The Development of American Citizenship, 1608–1870*. Chapel Hill: University of North Carolina Press, 1979.

Kibler, James E., Jr. *Pseudonymous Publications of William Gilmore Simms*. Athens: University of Georgia Press, 1976.

Kirsch, George. "Jeremy Belknap: A Biography." PhD diss., Columbia University, 1972.

Klein, Kerwin Lee. *Frontiers of Historical Imagination: Narrating the European Conquest of Native America, 1890–1990*. Berkeley: University of California Press, 1997.

Kloppenberg, James. "Objectivity and Historicism: A Century of American Historical Writing." *American Historical Review* 94 (1989): 1011–30.

Kohl, Lawrence Frederick. *The Politics of Individualism: Parties and the American Character in the Jacksonian Era*. New York: Oxford University Press, 1989.

Kohn, Hans. *American Nationalism: An Interpretative Essay*. New York: Macmillan, 1957.

Kornfeld, Eve. "From Republicanism to Liberalism: The Intellectual Journey of David Ramsay." *Journal of the Early Republic* 9 (Fall 1989): 289–313.

Kraus, Michael. *A History of American History*. New York: Farrar and Rinehart, 1937.

———. *The Writing of American History*. Norman: University of Oklahoma Press, 1953.

Kraus, Michael, and David Joyce. *The Writing of American History*. 1953. Rev. ed., Norman: University of Oklahoma Press, 1985.

Krieger, Leonard. *Ranke: The Meaning of History*. Chicago: University of Chicago Press, 1977.

Lader, Lawrence. *The Bold Brahmins: New England's War against Slavery*. New York: Dutton, 1961.

Lang, Timothy. *The Victorians and the Stuart Heritage: Interpretations of a Discordant Past*. Cambridge: Cambridge University Press, 1995.

Lemisch, Jesse. "The American Revolution Seen from the Bottom Up." In *Towards a New Past: Dissenting Essays in American History*, edited by Barton Bernstein, 3–29. New York: Pantheon Books, 1968.

Lepore, Jill. *The Name of War: King Philip's War and the Origins of American Identity*. New York: Vintage Books, 1998.

Levin, David. *Forms of Uncertainty: Essays in Historical Criticism*. Charlottesville: University of Virginia Press, 1992.

———. *History as Romantic Art: Bancroft, Prescott, Motley, and Parkman*. Stanford, Calif.: Stanford University Press, 1959.

Levine, George. *The Boundaries of Fiction: Carlyle, Macaulay, Newman*. Princeton, N.J.: Princeton University Press, 1968.

Levine, Joseph. *The Autonomy of History: Truth and Method from Erasmus to Gibbon*. Chicago: University of Chicago Press, 1999.

———. *Humanism and History: Origins of Modern English Historiography* (Ithaca, N.Y.: Cornell University Press, 1987.

Lewis, Merrill. "Organic Metaphor and Edenic Myth in George Bancroft's History of the United States." *Journal of the History of Ideas* 26 (1965): 587–92.

Lewis, R. W. B. *The American Adam: Innocence, Tragedy, and Tradition in the Nineteenth Century.* Chicago: University of Chicago Press, 1955.

Libby, Orin G. "A Critical Examination of William Gordon's History of the American Revolution." *Annual Report of the American Historical Association* (1899): 367–88.

———. "Ramsay as a Plagiarist." *American Historical Review* 7 (1902): 697–703.

———. "Some Pseudo Histories of the American Revolution." *Transactions of the Wisconsin Academy of Sciences, Arts, and Letters* 13 (1900): 419–25.

———. "William Gordon's *History of the American Revolution.*" *Annual Report of the American Historical Association* (1899): 367–77.

Lipking, Lawrence. "The Marginal Gloss." *Critical Inquiry* 3 (June 1977): 609–51.

Loewenberg, Bert James. *American History in American Thought: Christopher Columbus to Henry Adams.* New York: Simon and Schuster, 1972.

Mallon, Thomas. *Stolen Words.* 1989. San Diego: Harcourt, 1991.

Martin, Terence. *The Instructed Vision: Scottish Common Sense Philosophy and the Origins of American Fiction.* 1961. Bloomington: Indiana University Press, 1971.

Matthews, Jean V. "Whig History: The New England Whigs and a Usable Past." *New England Quarterly* 51 (1978): 193–208.

May, Henry. *The Enlightenment in America.* New York: Oxford University Press, 1976.

Mayo, Lawrence S. "Jeremy Belknap and Ebenezer Hazard, 1782–1784." *New England Quarterly* 2 (1929): 183–98.

McCardell, John. *The Idea of a Southern Nation: Southern Nationalists and Southern Nationalism, 1830–1860.* New York: W. W. Norton, 1979.

McCoy, Drew. *The Elusive Republic: Political Economy in Jeffersonian America.* Chapel Hill: University of North Carolina Press, 1980.

McDonald, Robert. "Thomas Jefferson's Changing Reputation as Author of the *Declaration of Independence*: The First Fifty Years." *Journal of the Early Republic* 19 (Summer 1999): 169–96.

McFarland, Thomas. *Originality and Imagination.* Baltimore: Johns Hopkins University Press, 1985.

McGill, Meredith. *American Literature and the Culture of Reprinting, 1834–1853.* Philadelphia: University of Pennsylvania Press, 2003.

McKeon, Michael. *The Origins of the English Novel, 1600–1740.* Baltimore: Johns Hopkins University Press, 1987.

Megill, Allan. "Fragmentation and the Future of Historiography." *American Historical Review* 96 (1991): 693–98.

———, ed. *Rethinking Objectivity.* Durham, N.C.: Duke University Press, 1994.

Melish, Joanne Pope. *Disowning Slavery: Gradual Emancipation and "Race" in New England, 1780–1860.* Ithaca, N.Y.: Cornell University Press, 1998.

Merk, Frederick. *Manifest Destiny and Mission in American History*. 1963. Cambridge: Harvard University Press, 1995.

Messer, Peter. "From a Revolutionary History to a History of Revolution: David Ramsay and the American Revolution." *Journal of the Early Republic* 22 (July 2002): 205–33.

———. *Stories of Independence: Identity, Ideology, and Independence in Eighteenth-Century America*. DeKalb: Northern Illinois University Press, 2005.

———. "Writing Women into History: Defining Gender and Citizenship in Post-Revolutionary America." *Studies in Eighteenth-Century Culture* 28 (1999): 341–60.

Meyer, Donald. *The Instructed Conscience: The Shaping of the American National Ethic*. Philadelphia: University of Pennsylvania Press, 1972.

Meyers, Marvin. *The Jacksonian Persuasion: Politics and Belief*. Stanford, Calif.: Stanford University Press, 1957.

Middleton, Richard. "British Historians and the American Revolution." *Journal of American Studies* 5 (April 1971): 43–58.

Miller, Perry G. *Errand into the Wilderness*. Cambridge: Harvard University Press, 1956.

———. "The Romance and the Novel." In *Nature's Nation*, 241–78. Cambridge: Harvard University Press, 1967.

Momigliano, A. D. "Ancient History and the Antiquarian." In *Studies in Historiography*, 1–39. New York: Harper and Row, 1966.

———. "Gibbon's Contribution to Historical Method." In *Studies in Historiography*, 40–55. New York: Harper and Row, 1966.

Morrison, Michael A. "American Reaction to European Revolutions, 1848–1852: Sectionalism, Memory, and the Revolutionary Heritage." *Civil War History* 49, no. 2 (2003): 111–32.

Mott, Frank. *Golden Multitudes: The Story of Best Sellers in the United States*. New York: Macmillan, 1947.

———. *A History of American Magazines*. Cambridge: Harvard University Press, 1938.

Nadel, G. H. "Philosophy of History before Historicism." *History and Theory* 3 (1964): 291–315.

Nagel, Paul C. *This Sacred Trust: American Nationality, 1798–1898*. New York: Oxford University Press, 1971.

Newmyer, R. Kent. "Charles Stedman's History of the American War." *American Historical Review* 63 (1958): 924–34.

———. "John Andrews's 'History of the War with America': A Further Note on Eighteenth-Century Plagiarism." *Papers of the Bibliographical Society of America* 55, 4th quarter (1961): 385–92.

———. "A Nineteenth-Century View of the Historiography of the American Revolution: A Footnote on Plagiarism." *Papers of the Bibliographical Society of America* 58, no. 2 (1964): 164–69.

Noble, David. *Historians against History: The Frontier Thesis and the National Covenant in American Historical Writing since 1830*. Minneapolis: University of Minnesota Press, 1965.

Novick, Peter. "My Correct Views on Everything." *American Historical Review* 96 (1991): 699–703.

———. *That Noble Dream: The "Objectivity Question" and the American Historical Profession.* Cambridge: Cambridge University Press, 1988.

Nye, Russel Blaine. *The Cultural Life of the New Nation, 1776–1830.* New York: Harper and Row, 1960.

———. *George Bancroft.* New York: Twayne, 1964.

———. *George Bancroft: Brahmin Rebel.* New York: Alfred A. Knopf, 1944.

O'Brien, Karen. "David Ramsay and the Delayed Americanization of American History." *Early American Literature* 29 (1994): 1–18.

———. *Narratives of Enlightenment: Cosmopolitan History from Voltaire to Gibbon.* New York: Cambridge University Press, 1997.

O'Brien, Michael. *Conjectures of Order: Intellectual Life and the American South, 1810–1860.* Chapel Hill: University of North Carolina Press, 2004.

O'Leary, Cecilia. *To Die For: The Paradox of American Patriotism.* Princeton, N.J.: Princeton University Press, 1999.

Orians, G. Harrison. "Censure of Fiction in American Romances and Magazines, 1789–1810." *PMLA* 52 (1937): 195–214.

———. "The Romance Ferment after *Waverley*." *American Literature* 3 (January 1932): 408–31.

Palmer, Gregory. *Biographical Sketches of Loyalists of the American Revolution.* Westport, Conn.: Meckler, 1984.

Patton, Jack Thomas. "The Beat of a Different Drummer: The Loyalists in American Historiography." MA thesis, California State University, Fresno, 1993.

Pearce, Roy Harvey. *Savagism and Civilization: A Study of the Indian and the American Mind.* 1953. Rev. ed., Berkeley: University of California Press, 1988.

Peardon, Thomas. *The Transition in English Historical Writing, 1760–1830.* New York: Columbia University Press, 1933.

Peck, Harry Thurston. *William Hickling Prescott.* New York: Macmillan, 1905.

Perry, Lewis. *Boats against the Current: American Culture between Revolution and Modernity, 1820–1860.* New York: Oxford University Press, 1993.

Persons, Stow. "The Cyclical Theory of History in Eighteenth-Century America." *American Quarterly* 6 (Summer 1954): 147–63.

Petter, Henri. *The Early American Novel.* Columbus: Ohio State University Press, 1971.

Phillips, Mark Salber. "Macaulay, Scott, and the Literary Challenge to Historiography." *Journal of the History of Ideas* 50 (1989): 117–33.

———. "Reconsiderations on History and Antiquarianism: Arnaldo Momigliano and the Historiography of Eighteenth-Century Britain." *Journal of the History of Ideas* 57 (1996): 297–316.

———. *Society and Sentiment: Genres of Historical Writing in Britain, 1740–1820.* Princeton, N.J.: Princeton University Press, 2000.

Phillipson, Nicholas. "Adam Smith as Civic Moralist." In *Wealth and Virtue: The Shaping of Political Economy in the Scottish Enlightenment*, edited by Istvan Hont and Michael Ignatieff, 179–202. New York: Cambridge University Press, 1986.

———. "The Scottish Enlightenment." In *The Enlightenment in National Context*, edited by Roy Porter and Mikulas Teich, 19–40. New York: Cambridge University Press, 1981.

Pingel, Martha M. *An American Utilitarian: Richard Hildreth as a Philosopher*. New York: Columbia University Press, 1948.

Pocock, J. G. A. *The Ancient Constitution and the Feudal Law: A Study of English Historical Thought in the Seventeenth Century*. 1957. New York: W. W. Norton, 1967.

———. *The Machiavellian Moment: Florentine Political Thought and the Atlantic Republican Tradition*. Princeton, N.J.: Princeton University Press, 1975.

Poovey, Mary. *A History of the Modern Fact: Problems of Knowledge in the Sciences of Wealth and Society*. Chicago: University of Chicago Press, 1998.

Potter, David. "The Historian's Use of Nationalism and Vice Versa." In *The South and Sectional Conflict*, 34–83. Baton Rouge: Louisiana State University Press, 1968.

Purcell, Sarah. *Sealed with Blood: War, Sacrifice, and Memory in Revolutionary America*. Philadelphia: University of Pennsylvania Press, 2002.

Quint, David. *Origin and Originality in Renaissance Literature: Versions of the Source*. New Haven, Conn.: Yale University Press, 1983.

Ranke, Leopold von. *The Theory and Practice of History*. Edited by Georg Iggers and Konrad von Moltke. Indianapolis: Bobbs-Merrill Co., 1973.

Rathbun, John W. "George Bancroft on Man and History." *Transactions of the Wisconsin Academy of Sciences, Arts and Letters* 43 (1954): 51–73.

———. "The Historical Sense in American Associationist Literary Criticism." *Philological Quarterly* 44 (October 1961): 553–68.

Roberts, Timothy M. "'Revolutions Have Become the Bloody Toy of the Multitude': European Revolutions, the South, and the Crisis of 1850." *Journal of the Early Republic* 25 (Summer 2005): 259–83.

Rodgers, Daniel. "Republicanism: The Career of a Concept." *Journal of American History* 79 (1992): 11–39.

Rohrs, Richard C. "American Critics of the French Revolution of 1848." *Journal of the Early Republic* 14 (Fall 1994): 359–377.

Rose, Anne C. *Voices of the Marketplace: American Thought and Culture, 1830–1860*. New York: Twayne Publishers, 1995.

Rose, Mark. "The Author as Proprietor: Donaldson v. Becket and the Genealogy of Modern Authorship." *Representations* 23 (1988): 51–85.

———. "The Author in Court: Pope v. Curll (1741)." *Cultural Critique* 21 (1992): 197–217.

———. *Authors and Owners: The Invention of Copyright*. Cambridge: Harvard University Press, 1993.

Rosenthal, Laura. *Playwrights and Plagiarists in Early Modern England: Gender, Authorship, Literary Property*. Ithaca, N.Y.: Cornell University Press, 1996.

Ross, Dorothy. "Historical Consciousness in Nineteenth-Century America." *American Historical Review* 89 (1984): 909–28.

————. *The Origins of American Social Science*. Cambridge: Cambridge University Press, 1991.

Royster, Charles. "Founding a Nation in Blood: Military Conflict and American Nationality." In *Arms and Independence: The Military Character of the American Revolution*, edited by Ronald Hoffman and Peter J. Albert, 25–48. Charlottesville: University Press of Virginia, 1984.

Russo, David J. *Keepers of Our Past: Local Historical Writing in the United States, 1820s–1930s*. New York: Greenwood Press, 1988.

Sargent, Mark L. "The Conservative Covenant: The Rise of the Mayflower Compact in American Myth." *New England Quarterly* 61 (1988): 233–51.

Schama, Simon. *Dead Certainties*. New York: Knopf, 1991.

Schlesinger, Arthur. "The Problem of Richard Hildreth." *New England Quarterly* 13 (1940): 223–45.

Schwartz, Barry. *George Washington: The Making of an American Symbol*. New York: Free Press, 1987.

Schwartz, Robert Shepard. "The Image of the American Revolution, 1783–1826." PhD diss., University of Chicago, 1975.

Seelye, John. *Memory's Nation: The Place of Plymouth Rock*. Chapel Hill: University of North Carolina Press, 1998.

Sellers, Charles. *The Market Revolution: Jacksonian America, 1815–1846*. New York: Oxford University Press, 1991.

Shaffer, Arthur H. *The Politics of History: Writing the History of the American Revolution, 1783–1815*. Chicago: Precedent Publishing, 1975.

————. *To Be an American: David Ramsay and the Making of the American Consciousness*. Columbia: University of South Carolina Press, 1991.

Shalhope, Robert. "Toward a Republican Synthesis: The Emergence of an Understanding of Republicanism in American Historiography." *William and Mary Quarterly* 29 (1972): 49–80.

Shapin, Steven. *The Scientific Revolution*. Chicago: University of Chicago Press, 1996.

————. *A Social History of Truth: Civility and Science in Seventeenth-Century England*. Chicago: University of Chicago Press, 1994.

Shapiro, Barbara. *A Culture of Fact: England, 1550–1720*. Ithaca, N.Y.: Cornell University Press, 2000.

Sheehan, Bernard W. *Seeds of Extinction: Jeffersonian Philanthropy and the American Indian*. Chapel Hill: University of North Carolina Press, 1973.

Sheidley, Harlow. "Sectional Nationalism: The Culture and Politics of the Massachusetts Conservative Elite, 1815–36." PhD diss., University of Connecticut, 1990.

————. *Sectional Nationalism: Massachusetts Conservative Leaders and the Transformation of America, 1815–1836*. Boston: Northeastern University Press, 1998.

————. "The Webster-Hayne Debate: Recasting New England's Sectionalism." *New England Quarterly* 67 (1994): 5–29.

Shelley, Fred. "Ebenezer Hazard: America's First Historical Editor." *William and Mary Quarterly* 12 (1955): 44–73.

Simpson, Lewis. *The Federalist Literary Mind*. Baton Rouge: Louisiana State University Press, 1962.

———. *The Man of Letters in New England and the South: Essays on the History of the Literary Vocation in America*. Baton Rouge: Louisiana State University Press, 1973.

Slotkin, Richard. *Regeneration through Violence: The Mythology of the American Frontier, 1600–1860*. Middletown, Conn.: Wesleyan University Press, 1973.

Smith, Bonnie. *The Gender of History: Men, Women, and Historical Practice*. Cambridge: Harvard University Press, 1998.

Smith, Henry Nash. *Virgin Land*. Cambridge: Harvard University Press, 1950.

Smith, Page. "David Ramsay and the Causes of the American Revolution." *William and Mary Quarterly* 17 (1960): 51–77.

Smith, Rogers. *Civic Ideals: Conflicting Visions of Citizenship in U.S. History*. New Haven, Conn.: Yale University Press, 1997.

Smith, William Raymond. *History as Argument: Three Patriot Historians of the American Revolution*. The Hague: Mouton, 1966.

Smitten, Jeffrey. "Impartiality in Robertson's *History of America*." *Eighteenth-Century Studies* 19, no. 1 (1985): 56–77.

Somkin, Fred. *Unquiet Eagle: Memory and Desire in the Idea of American Freedom, 1815–1860*. Ithaca, N.Y.: Cornell University Press, 1967.

Spencer, Benjamin T. *The Quest for Nationality: An American Literary Campaign*. Syracuse, N.Y.: Syracuse University Press, 1957.

Stern, Fritz, ed. *The Varieties of History: From Voltaire to the Present*. 1956. New York: Vintage Books, 1972.

Stone, Lawrence. "The Revival of Narrative: Reflections on a New Old History." *Past and Present* 85 (November 1979): 3–24.

Story, Ronald. *The Forging of an Aristocracy: Harvard and the Boston Upper Class, 1800–70*. Middletown, Conn.: Wesleyan University Press, 1980.

Streeter, Ronald. "Association Psychology and Literary Nationalism in the *North American Review*, 1815–25." *American Literature* 17 (January 1946): 243–54.

Stromberg, R. N. "History in the Eighteenth Century." *Journal of the History of Ideas* 12 (1951): 295–304.

Strout, Cushing. *The American Image of the Old World*. New York: Harper and Row, 1963.

Taylor, William. *Cavalier and Yankee: The Old South and American National Character*. 1957. New York: Oxford University Press, 1993.

Tebbel, John. *A History of Book Publishing in the United States: The Creation of an Industry, 1640–1865*. New York: R. R. Bowker, 1972.

Teed, Paul. "The Politics of Sectional Memory: Theodore Parker and the *Massachusetts Quarterly Review*, 1847–1850." *Journal of the Early Republic* 21 (Summer 2001): 301–29.

Thompson, James Westfall. *A History of Historical Writing*. 2 vols. New York: Macmillan, 1942.

Tocqueville, Alexis de. *Democracy in America*. Abridged by Thomas Bender. New York: Modern Library, 1981.

Travers, Len. *Celebrating the Fourth: Independence Day and the Rites of Nationalism in the Early Republic*. Amherst: University of Massachusetts Press, 1997.

Trent, William. *William Gilmore Simms*. Boston: Houghton Mifflin, 1892.

Trevor-Roper, H. R. "The Historical Philosophy of the Enlightenment." *Studies on Voltaire and the Eighteenth Century* 27 (1963): 1667–87.

Tucker, Louis. *Clio's Consort: Jeremy Belknap and the Founding of the Massachusetts Historical Society*. Boston: Massachusetts Historical Society, 1990.

Tuveson, Ernest Lee. *The Redeemer Nation: The Idea of America's Millennial Role*. Chicago: University of Chicago Press, 1968.

Tyack, David B. *George Ticknor and the Boston Brahmins*. Cambridge: Harvard University Press, 1967.

Tyrrell, Ian. *Historians in Public: The Practice of American History, 1890–1970*. Chicago: University of Chicago Press, 2005.

Van Tassel, David D. *Recording America's Past: An Interpretation of the Development of Historical Studies in America, 1607–1884*. Chicago: University of Chicago Press, 1960.

Vella, Michael W. "Theology, Genre, and Gender: The Precarious Place of Hannah Adams in American Literary History." *Early American Literature* 28 (1993): 21–41.

Vitzthum, Richard C. *The American Compromise: Theme and Method in the Histories of Bancroft, Parkman, and Adams*. Norman: University of Oklahoma Press, 1974.

———. "Theme and Method in Bancroft's History of the United States." *New England Quarterly* 41 (1968): 362–80.

Wakelyn, Jon. *The Politics of a Literary Man: William Gilmore Simms*. Westport, Conn.: Greenwood Press, 1973.

Waldstreicher, David L. *In the Midst of Perpetual Fetes: The Making of American Nationalism, 1776–1820*. Chapel Hill: University of North Carolina Press, 1997.

Ward, John William. *Andrew Jackson: Symbol for an Age*. New York: Oxford University Press, 1953.

Warner, Michael. *The Letters of the Republic: Publication and the Public Sphere in Eighteenth Century America*. Cambridge: Harvard University Press, 1990.

Watson, Ritchie Devon, Jr.. *The Cavalier in Virginia Fiction*. Baton Rouge: Louisiana State University Press, 1985.

Watt, Ian. *The Rise of the Novel: Studies in Defoe, Richardson and Fielding*. Berkeley: University of California Press, 1957.

Wear, Joan H., and A. Pittock, eds. *Interpretation and Cultural History*. New York: St. Martin's Press, 1991.

Weddington, Carolyn Sue. "Image of the American Revolution in the United States, 1815–60." PhD diss., Louisiana State University, 1972.

Welch, William L. "Lorenzo Sabine and the Assault on Sumner." *New England Quarterly* 65 (1992): 298–302.

———. "Lorenzo Sabine in Maine." *New England Quarterly* 70 (1997): 642–49.

Welter, Rush. *The Mind of America, 1820–1865*. New York: Columbia University Press, 1975.

White, Hayden. *Metahistory: The Historical Imagination in Nineteenth Century Europe.* Baltimore: Johns Hopkins University Press, 1973.

———. *Tropics of Discourse: Essays in Cultural Criticism.* Baltimore: Johns Hopkins University Press, 1978.

Williams, Raymond. *Keywords: A Vocabulary of Culture and Society.* 1976. New York: Oxford University Press, 1985.

Wills, Garry. *Inventing America: Jefferson's Declaration of Independence.* New York: Random House, 1978.

Wilson, Major. *Space, Time, and Freedom: The Quest for Nationalism and the Irrepressible Conflict, 1815–1861.* Westport, Conn.: Greenwood Press, 1974.

Wish, Harvey. *The American Historian: A Socio-Intellectual History of the Writing of the American Past.* New York: Oxford University Press, 1960.

Wood, Gordon. "Conspiracy and the Paranoid Style: Causality and Deceit in the Eighteenth Century." *William and Mary Quarterly* 39 (1982): 401–41.

———. *The Creation of the American Republic, 1776–1787.* 1969. New York: W. W. Norton, 1972.

———. "Novel History." *New York Review of Books,* 27 June 1991, 12–16.

———. *The Radicalism of the American Revolution.* New York: Alfred A. Knopf, 1992.

———. "Rhetoric and Reality in the American Revolution." *William and Mary Quarterly* 23 (1966): 3–32.

Woodmansee, Martha. *The Author, Art, and the Market: Rereading the History of Aesthetics.* New York: Columbia University Press, 1994.

———. "The Genius and the Copyright: Economic and Legal Conditions of the Emergence of the 'Author.'" *Eighteenth-Century Studies* 17 (Summer 1984): 425–48.

Woodmansee, Martha, and Peter Jaszi, ed. *The Construction of Authorship: Textual Appropriation in Law and Literature.* Durham, N.C.: Duke University Press, 1994.

Woolf, D. R. "Disciplinary History and Historical Discourse. A Critique of the History of History: The Case of Early Modern England," *Cromohs* 2 (1997): 1–25, http://www.unifi.it/riviste/cromohs/2_97/woolf.html.

———. "Erudition and the Idea of History in Renaissance England." *Renaissance Quarterly* 40 (Spring 1987): 11–48.

———. "A Feminine Past? Gender, Genre, and Historical Knowledge in England, 1500–1800." *American Historical Review* 102 (1997): 645–79.

Wright, Conrad. "The Controversial Career of Jedidiah Morse." *Harvard Library Bulletin* 31 (1983): 64–87.

Young, Alfred. "George Robert Twelves Hewes: A Boston Shoemaker and the Memory of the American Revolution." *William and Mary Quarterly* 38 (1981): 561–623.

———. *The Shoemaker and the Tea Party.* Boston: Beacon Press, 1999.

Zagarri, Rosemarie. *A Woman's Dilemma: Mercy Otis Warren and the American Revolution.* Wheeling, Ill.: Harlan Davidson, 1995.

Index